The Heroic Ideal

The Heroic Ideal

Western Archetypes from the Greeks to the Present

M. GREGORY KENDRICK

McFarland & Company, Inc., Publishers
Jefferson, North Carolina, and London

"Mrs. Robinson" lyric copyright ©1968 Paul Simon.
Used by permission of the Publisher: Paul Simon Music

LIBRARY OF CONGRESS CATALOGUING-IN-PUBLICATION DATA

Kendrick, M. Gregory, 1953–
The heroic ideal : Western archetypes from the
Greeks to the present / by M. Gregory Kendrick.
p.   cm.
Includes bibliographical references and index.

ISBN 978-0-7864-3786-3
softcover : 50# alkaline paper ∞

1. Heroes — History.   I. Title.
BJ1533.H47K46   2010   202'.13 — dc22   2010016513

British Library cataloguing data are available

Cover image: Jacques-Louis David. *The Death of Socrates.*
Oil on canvas. 51⅛" × 77⅛". 1787.

Manufactured in the United States of America

McFarland & Company, Inc., Publishers
Box 611, Jefferson, North Carolina 28640
www.mcfarlandpub.com

Ackowledgments

This book would never have seen the light of day without the indulgence, encouragement, and assistance of students, colleagues, and friends. I am particularly grateful to all of the freshmen at UCLA who have taken my first year seminar on the heroic ideal in the West and afforded me the opportunity to develop and explore the ideas and themes at the heart of this work. Special thanks are also in order to the following individuals who read and edited various drafts of this book's chapters, and provided me with thoughtful advice and criticism — Richard Hoffman, Jon Friedman, David Mattingly, Dennis Claxton, Joseph Nagy, and Joe Menosky. And last but certainly not least, I wish to express my gratitude to the many people — you know who you are — whose love and encouragement have sustained me through the six years of this project.

Table of Contents

Introduction

Heroism and the Human Condition

There is a brief scene in *Return of the Jedi*, the third installment of George Lucas' original *Star Wars* space opera, in which Luke Skywalker's "droid" companion, C3PO, relates to an audience of Ewok villagers some of the particulars of his human master's struggle against the evil Empire's Darth Vader. The recounting of this tale takes place in a large fire–lit arboreal hall and is accompanied by some dazzling special effects, courtesy of the advanced digital circuitry of its android narrator. While C3PO describes space battles, breathtaking escapes, and light saber duels, the camera moves in on his attentive listeners, treating the film viewer to tight close-ups of wide-eyed children and their thoughtful, appreciative elders. As the scene draws to a close, it is evident to the movie audience that they are witnessing the birth of a heroic saga that will entertain and enlighten generations of this alien tribe — as well as their counterparts in galaxies far, far away — for centuries to come.

Mention is made of this particular scene because it underscores both the venerable nature and the enduring popularity of the heroic ideal in human culture. One does not have to be steeped in film theory and practice, for example, to realize that Lucas has inserted this episode in his movie for the purpose of alerting his audience to the fact that they are participating in a tradition that stretches back to pre-literate times. Just as bards and poets once recounted the deeds of extraordinary hunters and warriors to human bands huddled around nighttime fires, this scene reminds us that filmmakers now use the lexicon and technology of the cinema to recreate similar tales of heroism for a modern public huddled together in darkened movie houses around the arc lights of film projectors. Indeed, one of the most striking aspects of the heroic ideal is that some four hundred thousand years after the first appearance of "thinking man" on this planet, heroes and the tales of their adventures remain a constant of the human condition.

Lucas' scene also highlights some of the reasons why our societies continue to embrace these extraordinary figures. The obvious enjoyment of the Ewoks, for example, underscores the fact that stories about heroes are usually ripping good yarns that allow their listeners to escape from the doldrums of their daily lives and vicariously enjoy unfamiliar experiences and emotions. It is also important to note, however, that in this scene the narrator, C3PO, is doing something more than merely recounting entertaining tales of Luke Skywalker's derring-do. He is also telling his audience a story about the perils of untrammeled power, the

1

necessity of defending republican democracy, and the importance of loyalty, self-sacrifice, and public service. In doing so, Lucas' android surrogate is reminding us that the tale of the hero is not merely a vehicle of escape but also a powerful heuristic in the search for answers to questions about lawful authority, right conduct and essential goodness. Indeed, from Homer to the present, individuals, tribes, movements, and nation states have all used the heroic ideal to propagate and perpetuate codes of moral conduct, religious beliefs and practices, and systems of economic, social and political control.

Thinking About Heroism

Given its persistence and utility as a source of education and acculturation, one would think that the historical development of the heroic ideal, as well as the ways in which human societies have exploited it, would be a subject of considerable interest among thinkers. With the notable exception of Thomas Carlyle and Friedrich Nietzsche, however, heroism is an idea that has been given surprisingly short shrift in the annals of modern intellectual history. To be sure, a number of folklorists, linguists, and cultural anthropologists have considered the hero in larger studies of myth, religion, and narratology, but by and large most scholars have avoided the subject, considering it to be grist better suited to the mills of poets, novelists, and filmmakers.

Such scholarly neglect was not always the case. Throughout most of Western history, intellectuals and the educated lay public tended to attribute all progress in human affairs to the ideas and deeds of a handful of extraordinary individuals with exceptional abilities. If someone were interested in understanding any given historical moment and its accomplishments in art, science, and statecraft, it was commonplace to identify and assiduously study the actions of that period's heroic figures. Indeed, there is a whole tradition in Western history of dividing the past into a succession of "ages," each one dominated by an archetypal hero, such as Caesar, Louis XIV, or Napoleon Bonaparte, whose ambitions and intelligence were believed to have dominated their time period. Concurrently, if one were doing a study aimed at explaining some kind of social phenomena, the tendency was to look at the patterns of behavior on the part of certain key players in the history of religion, politics, commerce, and war. Niccolò Machiavelli, for example, framed his discourses on the acquisition and uses of power around the lives and actions of such "great" men as Alexander of Macedon, Augustus Caesar, and Lorenzo de Medici. Even revolutionaries bent on affecting a complete break with tradition still found it expedient to study and emulate the deeds of heroic rebels and reformers from the past. A case in point was the American constitutional convention where many of the founding fathers carried about copies of Plutarch's *Lives of the Noble Greeks and Romans* and are reputed to have derived considerable comfort and inspiration from the biography of the great Athenian lawgiver Solon.

The twentieth century saw a marked decline in this kind of hero worship. In part, this development can be attributed to the swath of bloodshed and terror that followed in the wake of a slough of self-styled heroes — Mussolini, Hitler, Stalin, and others of their ilk — who established fascist and communist dictatorships throughout much of the West during the first half of the century. It was not lost on people, both at that time and later, that these figures and their followers justified all manner of murder and mayhem on the basis of their claim to be latter-day knights-errant, chosen by providence or the laws of historical materialism to defend, purify, and ultimately transform their societies into either racial or classless paradises. The hot and cold wars that resulted from the actions of these dictatorships further contributed to a widespread feeling among intellectuals that heroes and ideals of heroism were ultimately elitist, undemocratic, and dangerous atavisms.

In tandem with these political developments, the twentieth century also witnessed a shift in disciplinary perspectives that essentially consigned the heroic tradition to the status of an antiquarian pastime for students of folklore, myth, and literature. Whereas scholars once accorded considerable importance to the role of individual agency in the shaping of human affairs, the growth of such disciplines as social history, macro-economics, game theory, psychobiology, evolutionary physiology, and genomics fostered a set of paradigms that favored more impersonal explanations for the development of states, industries, religions, and social hierarchies. More to the point, over the last fifty years, these new disciplines have done an impressive job of demonstrating the obvious impact of geography, commerce, class relations, guns, germs, and steel on the "fate of human societies."[1] While attention is still given in historical studies to the lives and actions of certain key statesmen, artists, and scientists, the notion that any of these individuals might be the principal engine of human development is now viewed as little more than an anachronistic idea from a less enlightened time.

These twentieth century political and intellectual developments aside, it should also be noted that any serious attempt by modern thinkers to examine the ideal of heroism in Western culture and society must contend with the protean nature of heroes and the actions that define them as exceptional. Starting out some three millennia ago as a Greek expression for any "free man" or "noble," the term hero has since been applied to demigods, bandit warriors, martyrs, knights, artists, hedonists, rogues, misfits, and comic-book characters. Moreover, to be "heroic" has gone from a description of simply not being ordinary to an all purpose rubric for any kind of extra-ordinary action outside, above, or even in disregard of social norms. Suffice it to say that tracing these changes in the etymology of heroism, and attempting to explain why they occurred, constitutes a daunting challenge.

Further complicating matters is the fact that these changes in the lexicon of heroism are also inextricably bound up with shifts in Western thinking about religion, social relations, political authority, and, perhaps most importantly, notions of how people should behave. The heroic warriors of Homer's epics, for example, were essentially a self-interested group of well-born freebooters who viewed their neighbors and social inferiors as little more than raw material to be exploited as they saw fit. Latter-day military heroes, on the other hand, follow the orders of popularly elected civilians and adhere to strict codes of conduct based on internationally approved customs and usages of war. Making sense of this kind of caesura requires one to examine not just changes in the definition of heroism, but also how this shift in the vocabulary of the heroic ideal is connected to what some scholars have referred to as the history of the "civilizing process" in the West, i.e., that complex of technology, manners, knowledge, self-perception, and worldview that distinguishes Western society from other societies.[2] Undertaking such a project ultimately involves nothing less than an examination of the linkages between the idea of the hero and the progress of Western civilization over the last three millennia. Given the complexity of such a task, it is hardly surprising that the history of the Western heroic ideal remains a subject in search of an author.

A History of the Heroic Ideal

This account is the first step in an effort aimed at filling this lacuna in the historical record. Towards that end, it examines the development of the heroic ideal in the West over the last three millennia, as well as the ways in which changes in the vocabulary of that ideal have both reflected and influenced shifts in the ethical, social, and political thinking of Western society and culture. To achieve this ambitious undertaking, I have taken a leaf from the methodology of Max Weber and concentrated on a number of heroic "types"— warrior, martyr, athlete, knight, saint, explorer, artist, anti-hero. The following pages study these heroic typologies from within the context of the historical eras that produced them, i.e., the ancient, medieval, and modern periods of the Western world, with an eye aimed at addressing the following questions:

- What were the characteristics that distinguished these different heroic types from one another?
- What do the attitudes, manners, and actions of these heroic figures tell us about the civilizations of the time periods with which they are associated?
- How do the heroic ideals that are associated with these different hero types actually influence and even shape the ethical, social, and political behavior of their civilizations?
- What historical factors give rise to new conceptions of the heroic, and how do older notions of the hero continue to inform and shape these shifts in the vocabulary of heroism?

To find answers to these questions, I have made use of a wide variety of primary and secondary texts that I believe shed considerable light on the development of the heroic tradition in the West. These include poems, plays, books of chivalry, works of philosophy, novels, histories, and films that are focused in one way or another on the lives and actions of figures that have been and continue to be regarded as heroes. What follows is a deeply syncretistic study that attempts to deepen our understanding of the connections between the changing conceptions of the heroic ideal and the process by which the West has defined its moral, social, and political values.

PART ONE

Myrmidons, Martyrs, and Muscle Men: Heroism in the Ancient World

Honor is the value of a person in his own eyes, but also in the eyes of his society. It is his esti-mation of his own worth, his claim to pride, but it is also the acknowledgement of that claim, *his excellence recognized by society, his* right *to pride.*

— Julian Pitt-Rivers

O Zeus and the other gods grant that this my son shall become as I am, most distinguished among the Trojans, as strong and valiant, and that he rule by might in Ilion. And then may men say "He is far braver than his father!" as he returns from war, and may he bring back spoils stained with the blood of men he has slain, making his mother's heart rejoice.

— Homer: *Iliad* VI 476–481

At the beginning of the 21st century, hero and heroism are ubiquitous words applied to all kinds of people and every manner of action. Heroes are Congressional Medal of Honor recipients, Hollywood celebrities, unconventional schlumps, and fictitious comic book char-acters; and heroism encompasses everything from selfless acts of courage to the assuaging of public boredom. To paraphrase David Bowie, in the mass society of the modern era, all of us "can be heroes, just for one day."

As the following section on heroism in the ancient world demonstrates, the Greeks who gave us these words were far less liberal in their usage of them. Their notions of heroes and heroic action were rooted in ideas about personal honor, or considerations of individ-ual value and worth, which were enmeshed within a social, political, economic, and cul-tural framework that was family-centered, unequal, hierarchical, male-dominated, largely poor, and frequently violent. In this world, hero was an honorific of the highest order that was applied only to a very select group of individuals who enjoyed pride of place in both life and death because their deeds and accomplishments surpassed normal expectations and singled them out as first and best among their peers.

Not surprisingly, in a world where most people lived a hardscrabble existence, women were expected to tend the hearth and life was a "nasty, brutish and short" affair, these ancient heroes were usually male, nobly born, well-to-do, exceptionally strong, terribly proud, and very good-looking. Indeed, the word hero was first used by the Greeks to identify either a legendary semi-divine race of strongmen, law givers and city founders, or flesh and blood aristocratic warriors with superlative combat skills and a proven track record of bringing home the booty and beating off the enemies of their communities. These individuals were adjudged heroic because their breeding, resources, and actions singled them out as potent, dangerous "godlike" men who could defend and enrich their compatriots while alive, and continue to exercise a benign influence over their affairs when dead. In return for the protection they could offer in life and beyond the grave, these heroized demigods and myrmidons expected and were accorded such honors as statues, paeans of praise, exemption from taxes, free meals, special seats at performances, high office, and posthumous hero cults.

Over time, the inhabitants of the Greco-Roman world expanded their use of the word "hero" to encompass a wider range of individuals and actions. While dynasts and noble warriors would remain favored candidates for inclusion in antiquity's heroic pantheon, intellectual inquiry, religious devotion, and the quest for personal excellence also laid the groundwork for new ideas about what it meant to be an extraordinary, godlike individual. The execution of Socrates, and Plato's memorable treatment of that event, made it heroic to be an intellectual dissident willing to die in defense of one's convictions. The advent of Judaism and Christianity established the notion that a hero was anyone — man or woman, commoner or aristocrat, shepherd or warrior — who heeded the call of his god and showed himself willing to follow that summons even if it took him to death's door. And the establishment of competitive sports and the Greek crown games paved the way for the heroization of champion athletes and, by extension, anyone seeking and attaining a level of unparalleled professional achievement.

These shifting notions in the ancient understanding of what it meant to be a hero also played an important role in the development of the West. Inspired by Homer's epics, Alexander the Great set out to surpass the deeds of Achilles and Odysseus by conquering the Persian Empire and carving out a Hellenic imperium in the east. In turn, Alexander's life and achievements fired the imaginations of succeeding generations of Roman generals who sought to follow in his footsteps by creating an even greater empire encompassing vast stretches of western Europe, northern Africa, and the Near East.

Out of this Greco-Roman "heroic imperialism" emerged new ways of waging war, a more disciplined, if not more humane, code of military conduct, and a common civilization in the lands bordering the Mediterranean. From a series of sporadic clashes between rival freebooters and city states, Alexander and his ilk transformed ancient warfare into a continent-spanning activity that required the mobilization and deployment of large well-trained and organized armies. The personnel of these new killing machines were increasingly professional men-at-arms whose actions were governed by an ethic rooted, not in the quest for personal glory, but in expectations of steady remuneration and traditions of service and loyalty to commander and *patria*. And in the wake of these warrior adepts and the latter day Homeric heroes that led them followed commerce, urbanization, Greek and Latin literature, philosophy, science, the Hebrew testament, and the gospels of the early Christian church; in short, the stuff that would guide, shape, and define the Western civilizing process.

The elevation of iconoclasts and martyrs into the ranks of the ancient heroic pantheon also fostered new thinking in the West about individual liberty, heterodoxy, and monotheism. Plato's recounting of Socrates' spirited defense of his right to question convention, challenge authority, and live life in a manner of his own choosing became a cornerstone of Western intellectual and political history. Countless generations of ancients and moderns alike read or listened to this account and embraced its central idea that every individual — no matter how noxious — has an inalienable right to engage in self-exploration and enlightenment without interference from community or state. This assertion of personal freedom received further validation when steadfast Jews and Christians also offered up their lives rather than comply with the demands of conquerors and countrymen to conform to Greco-Roman religious and social norms. Indeed, the example of these ancient Hebrew and Christian martyrs inspired rebellions, polemics, intellectual exchanges, and conversions that both undermined paganism in the West and laid the foundations of modern Judaism and Christianity.

Finally, the modern Western love affair with competitive sports and their star players is deeply rooted in the athletic culture of the Greco-Roman world. For over a thousand years, the inhabitants of the lands adjoining the Mediterranean flocked to the local, regional, and international sports festivals that were sponsored by the Greek city states, enticed by the prospect of witnessing extraordinary feats of strength and skill in running, discus and javelin-throwing, racing, wrestling, and boxing. These contests were immortalized in ancient mythology, poetry, drama, literature, painting and sculpture, and their victors were idolized and showered with honors. Economic downturns, barbarian invasions, Christian bans, and the collapse of the Roman Empire could not efface the memory of these events, and their example inspired the rebirth of the Olympic games, the development of competitive team sports in the West, and the cult of celebrity that has surrounded every modern athletic champion from Babe Ruth to David Beckham.

The following section examines the development of the idea of the hero in antiquity from its beginnings as a Greek rubric for semi-divine men and aristocratic warriors to its later application as an honorific for stalwart martyrs and champion athletes. Each chapter addresses a particular type of person — the *hemitheoi*, or half-god, the warrior, the martyr, and the athlete — as well as certain actions associated with these figures — assisting humanity, making war, dying for a cause, and winning in athletic competitions — that the inhabitants of the Greco-Roman world embraced as heroic. Particular attention is paid in these chapters to the historical factors that made these individuals and their activities the stuff of heroism in antiquity, as well as to the ways in which a longing to emulate these heroic types contributed to the development of that complex of political, social, and cultural ideas, values, and pastimes that we associate with Western civilization.

This examination of the idea of the hero in antiquity does not encompass all of the different heroic traditions that were to be found in the lands bordering the Mediterranean. It does not treat Gilgamesh and the heroes of early Mesopotamia, Egypt's god-kings, or the legends of Cuchulainn and his Celtic kin. With the exception of a brief examination of Hebrew biblical heroes, this treatment of heroism is very much centered on the Greco-Roman world that gave the West its word for "hero," as well as the myths, epics, odes, rhetorical treatises, hagiographies, and art works that have defined the meaning of that term for Europe and its colonial offshoots for over three millennia.

Within the context of Greco-Roman heroism, this section does not limit its use of the term "hero" to only those individuals who received heroic cult status after death. While it is true that the official heroization of an individual in Archaic and Classical Greece always involved the institution of a posthumous cult, there is also evidence that *heros* was used during these periods as a rubric to connote both aristocratic warriors and persons who were regarded as larger than life, extraordinary, or godlike. Certainly by the Hellenic period, if not before, most Greeks are using hero in this latter fashion, i.e., as an honorific for individuals living and dead who had achieved some measure of *arête* (excellence) and *kleos* (renown) in their lifetime. This more expansive, post-classical usage of hero is the one subscribed to in the pages that follow.

Finally, this treatment of Greco-Roman heroism does not pretend to be an exhaustive one. Such a history would require an examination of not only demi-gods, warriors, martyrs, and athletes, but also that "strange world of anonymous daimonic beings, epichoric figures of strictly local importance (when 'local' means at the neighborhood level),"[1] heroine cults, the war dead, poets, and artists that comprised the heroic pantheon of every Greek and Greco-Roman community. Doing full justice to this ancient heroic realm would require a book unto itself, and it is the fervent hope of this author that others will step forward and enrich our knowledge of heroism in the ancient world.

1

Neither Human nor Divine
The Hemitheoi *and Their Cults*

Zeus, the son of Cronos made ... a god-like race of hero-men who are demi-gods, the race before our own, throughout the boundless earth. Grim war and dread battle destroyed a part of them ... to the others Zeus gave a living and an abode apart from men, and made them dwell at the ends of earth ... far from the deathless gods.

—Hesiod: *Works and Days*

Do you not know that the heroes are half gods? ... All to be sure were born when a God loved a mortal woman or a goddess loved a mortal man.

—Plato: *Cratylus*

There is evidence that *heros*, the Greek word from which our modern term "hero" is derived, was a title for a "lord" who served under a *wanax*, or "king," during the Mycenaean Age (ca. 1600–1100 BCE). These heroes were probably chariot-owning noblemen who were responsible for military operations in both the internecine and foreign wars waged by the Mycenaean kings; one of which was probably against the city of Troy around 1250 BCE. Evidence also indicates that the Mycenaean Greeks used *heros* as a religious expression to designate a subset of divine beings that, while stronger than mortal men, were inferior to the Olympian gods. Some scholars conjecture that these sacred and secular Mycenaean usages for *heros* continued into the Archaic and Classical periods and were used by the poets, dramatists and philosophers of those times to designate both the Bronze Age "heroes" of the Trojan War, as well as human beings who had attained godlike or semi-divine status.[1]

Another school of thought has conjectured that the term "hero" was originally derived from an ancient Greek expression for a pre-historic earth goddess who exercised dominion over the dead. For reasons that are not completely clear, in the centuries before Homer this deity's name began to be applied to some of the individuals that were entrusted to her care after their deaths. One explanation for this etymological development is that the ancient Greeks were searching for an appropriate way to signify a class of deceased men and women whose deeds in life had marked them out as not only different from their fellow mortals, but as actually being on a par with the gods. A word such as "hero," which was associated with both the underworld and its immortal guardian, may have appeared an apt honorific for such individuals because it served to single them out as mortals who had won the right in life to share in the name and power of the god who governed them after death. While it is impossible to determine if such philological considerations were actually in play prior to the 8th century BCE, existing evidence does suggest that when pre–Homeric Greeks spoke of "heroes" they were referring not only to aristocratic warriors and a subset of the gods, but to the "powerful dead," a group of beings neither human nor divine, but something in between.[2]

Whatever the origins of the word hero, by 700 BCE Archaic Greek writers such as Hesiod were using the term to describe the *hemitheoi,* or "half gods," sprung from the union of a god or goddess and a mortal man or woman. This group, which included such semi-divine progeny as Heracles, Dionysus, Asclepius, Perseus, Theseus, and Achilles was also blessed with a wide range of extraordinary abilities such as superhuman strength and courage, great craftiness, irresistible sex appeal, the ability to heal wounds and cure ailments, and exceptional horticultural skills. Over the course of their lives, these heroic demigods — often unintentionally — used their exceptional gifts in ways that ultimately benefited humanity. This included slaying assorted monsters and villains, founding various dynasties and cities, liberating the oppressed, curing pestilence, and introducing the joys of wine and song into human life.

Despite their divine DNA, however, this first race of heroes was also mortal and doomed to die. As the classical scholar C. Kerényi notes, in all of the legends surrounding the classical Greek hero, "death belongs to his shape" and the smell of the grave hangs about him.[3] Nevertheless, despite the bane of mortality, death does not efface these beings. Certain among their number — Heracles, Dionysus, and Asclepius, for example — ascend to full-fledged godhood after their demise. Others, such as Perseus and his beloved Andromeda, are placed among the deathless stars. Even those consigned to the underworld are accorded either a place of honor and comfort in the Elysian Fields or a position of power and influence in the house of Hades.[4]

Whatever the final destination of these heroic figures, the ancient Greeks continued to regard their shades as potent entities capable of exercising influence over the affairs of the living. Consequently, beginning in the 8th century BCE cults dedicated to the honor and appeasement of the heroic dead became increasingly common throughout the Greek world. Unlike the cults that surrounded the worship of the Olympians, however, this hero worship tended to be a modest affair.[5] Sanctuaries dedicated to the cult of a hero were usually smaller and less impressive than those of the celestial deities, and, in keeping with the fact that these were cults of the dead, the sacrifices performed within their precincts were likely to be carried out at night on a low altar using dark animals that were completely burned.[6]

If these hero cults did not command the lavish temple complexes and rituals accorded to Zeus and his relatives, they were still a central and important part of Greek civic life well into the Common Era. While much of this hero worship was rooted in a fear that the spirits of these individuals were easily angered and potentially malign, there was also a considerable measure of genuine admiration, respect and even love for the beings that were honored by these cults. During the Archaic period of their history, Greeks looked to these figures as models of an idealized past that was worthy of emulation, and their counterparts in the Classical and Hellenistic periods were no less adulatory.[7] Urban folk regarded these *hemitheoi* as the founders and defenders of their cities. Athletes, artisans, physicians, and rhetoricians revered them as the inaugurators and patrons of their professions. People in all walks of life appealed to them for assistance in times of illness or personal danger. And the young found in these hero cults models of right conduct and the promise that even a mortal doomed to die might achieve, if not immortality, then undying renown (*kleos*).

The rise of the *polis*, or independent city-state, towards the end of the Archaic period witnessed both a proliferation of these hero cults and a shift in their focus. Increasingly, these cults were established by cities throughout Greece to heroize recently deceased individuals whose actions in life had benefited their communities, i.e., city founders, lawgivers, artists, champions of the various Pan-Hellenic games, and the war dead. Aside from neutralizing any potential harm that the shades of these individuals might do to their homelands after death, the heroization of these individuals also allowed the Greek *poleis* to honor important and powerful families, celebrate civic virtues, and signal their commitment to specific domestic or foreign policies.[8]

For reasons that are not completely clear, these heroic cults entered a period of decline during the Hellenistic period (323–31 BCE). In part, this may have been due to the military reversals suffered by the Greek city states from the 4th through the 2nd centuries. The objects of these cults were honored, in part, out of a belief that they would protect their communities from any troubles that might befall them. When these cities lost their independence to first Philip and Alexander of Macedon, and later the Roman Republic, their populations may have begun to question the efficacy of worshiping individuals that had proven themselves inadequate to the task of defending them from foreign invasion and conquest.

Economic factors may also have played a role in the decline of these cults. As already mentioned, during both the classical and post-classical periods, Greek city states increasingly heroized citizens who had achieved some measure of *arête* (excellence) and *kleos* (renown) in their lifetime. While this liberality in awarding heroic status may have spurred many politicians, philanthropists, athletes, and artists to achieve great things on behalf of their communities, it also no doubt added to the financial burdens of the cities maintaining the cults of these individuals. In the centuries of Macedonian and Roman rule, these communities were subject to repeated and onerous economic exactions, which likely compelled them to seriously curtail, if not eliminate, the cult celebrations and offerings of their many heroes.

Finally, during the Hellenistic period, the term hero also appears to have become an almost ubiquitous honorific applied to historical figures, characters in Greek drama and even the ordinary dead. It is likely that this "democratization" of the word was another result of the tendency of the Greek cities at this time to heroize citizens who had rendered honorable service to their communities. The increasing acceptance of the idea that meritorious individuals were worthy of heroic status very likely played some role in the undermining of a cult tradition that was rooted in a more restricted and elitist notion of the hero as a semi-divine being.[9]

Whatever the reasons for the decline of the Greek hero cults, the objects of their devotion provided the West with models of heroic behavior that have shaped our thinking about heroism to the present day. Indeed, from Homer to George Lucas, our heroes have tended to be individuals who shared the following characteristics of the heroic demi-gods of classical Greek mythology:

- A pedigree that includes, if not divine, than nobly born ancestors;
- Exceptional talents and abilities;
- Fame won for prowess in war, on the playing field, or at the helm of a ship;
- Deeds that benefit humanity;
- A terrible, albeit glorious, death; and
- The enduring honor and reverence of the living.

Over the course of time, shifts in thinking about right conduct, religious belief, lawful authority, and social standing will make possible heroes who do not fit these criteria. As we will see in later chapters, the Western civilizing process will ultimately produce a heroic pantheon that not only includes commoners, but individuals who shun wars, athletic contests, foreign adventures, and unpleasant deaths as well. This said, however, for almost two millennia, heroes in the West, like their mythic Greek counterparts a long time ago, have tended to be well born people with extraordinary abilities, a penchant for travel, and terribly short life spans.

2

"Of arms and the man I sing"
The Hero as Myrmidon

My mother, Thetis of the silvery feet, tells me of two possible destinies carrying me toward death: if on the one hand I remain to fight around Troy town, I lose all hope of home but gain unfading glory; on the other, if I sail back to my own land my glory fails—but a long life lies ahead for me.

—Homer: *Iliad* IX 599–506

There is for all, a short, irreparable time of life; the task of courage: to prolong one's fame by acts.

—Virgil: *Aeneid* X 648–650

The World of Homer and Hesiod

If we are to understand why the ancient hero is so often associated with the figure of a nobly born champion, well-schooled in soldiering, sailing, and sportsmanship and marked for an early grave, then we need to understand the nature of the world that shaped Homer, Hesiod and the other bards who composed our first accounts of heroism. The historical era in which these individuals lived and worked has been labeled the Archaic Age in ancient Greek history. This period stretched from 800–600 BCE and it witnessed the flowering of epic poetry, the extensive colonization of lands adjoining the Greek mainland, and the emergence of the *polis*, or independent city state. It was also an age characterized by widespread warfare, scarce foodstuffs, and rudimentary health care. By all accounts, this was a time in which life was short, men were considered foolish, strangers dangerous, nature angry and implacable, and the gods capricious and hard.[1]

At the center of this world was the *oikos* or family household, a largely self-sufficient enterprise that was dependent on subsistence farming, pasturage, and a primitive barter economy. The social strata of each Greek community was determined by the size of these households, i.e. the total amount of a family's cultivated land and herded livestock, the number of retainers and slaves that they supported, and the amount of metallic goods (cauldrons, braziers, tripods, and armor) that they owned. Large landowners with sizable households and surpluses of food and metal comprised the aristocracy of these communities. They were followed in turn by smaller freeholders, who were often retainers of the principal landown-

13

ing families, and a small, often mobile, middling group of craftsmen and bards who were paid for their services with food, raw materials, or other goods. At the bottom of this *oikos* centered society were landless unskilled laborers, or *thetes*, who wandered from community to community in search of seasonal work and whatever handouts they could beg. These *thetes* also figured prominently among the banditry that infested the local countryside and made travel a risky proposition.[2]

Politics in this period was largely a matter of personal power with most communities governed by kings who could lay claim to authority by dint of a large family, sufficient resources for gift-giving, a sizable clientele of *xenoi*, or "guest-friends," and a proven proficiency at arms. Even with these resources at their command, a king in Archaic Greece remained essentially a *primus inter pares*, or "first among equals," whose power was held in check by the ambitions of other notable families, the feckless loyalty of smaller freeholders, and the ever shifting political fortunes of foreign allies. During their tenure as rulers, these kings largely concerned themselves with staving off challenges to their authority at home and protecting their kingdoms from internal strife and external aggression. Meeting these challenges required considerable military and diplomatic skills. In times of conflict, a king needed to be a proficient swordsman capable of meeting any challenger in personal combat, as well as a commander with the experience and resources necessary to raise, equip, and lead an army of loyal retainers. During times of peace, a ruler needed to be an impresario, benefactor, and matchmaker, for it was only through lavish entertaining, generous gifts of grain, livestock and metals, and advantageous marriages that a king could secure the support of the domestic and foreign notables so central to the defense of his position and his kingdom.[3]

Suffice it to say that everything about these Archaic Greek communities — their subsistence economies, family households, stratified societies, and warrior kings — contributed to a constant state of intermittent conflict. Chronic shortages of food and metals insured these kingdoms would be raided by their neighbors and that they would respond in kind. An *oikos* centered society made kinship loyalties paramount and encouraged family rivalries and feuds. Social inequalities between large and small landholders, mobile and settled craftsmen, and landless laborers and their employers also generated tensions and resentments that often led to internecine conflicts. And to be a king in such a world was essentially to resign oneself to a life of warfare fighting off rivals, acquiring booty, and protecting one's subjects and foreign allies.

In such a world, moral behavior was governed by a simple set of concrete precepts considered essential to survival. First and foremost, a person was expected to uphold and defend the family household that provided sustenance, protection from the elements, and social standing in one's community. Secondly, honor was due the gods who were selfish, easily angered, and quick to punish any mortal that displeased them. Finally, hospitality was offered to both neighbors and strangers alike because such generosity facilitated economic exchanges, friendships, and political alliances.

Outside of these basic strictures in favor of family, piety, and hospitable behavior, moral standards at this time were both ambiguous and haphazardly enforced. To be sure, then, as now, acts of murder, rape, and theft were regarded as crimes. However, both the apprehension and punishment of those responsible for such deeds was considered a private matter for the injured party to pursue. Further, if such crimes were committed within the context of a raid or a war, they were more likely to be met with praise than moral opprobrium. Indeed, as the Homeric epics make abundantly clear, it was standard behavior at this time for a warrior seeking glory and riches to practice deceit, engage in piracy, and pillage foreign communities — with all the murder, rape, and theft attendant on such an act. As Odysseus boasts to his admiring, and unprotesting, Phaiakian hosts in *The Odyssey*:

> From Ilion the wind took me and drove me ashore at Ismaros by the Kikonians. I sacked their city and killed their people, and out of their city taking their wives and many possessions we share them out, so none might go cheated of his proper portion.[4]

Greek religious thinking at this time certainly contributed to the period's rather laissez-faire attitude towards capital crimes. Aside from a concern for hospitality, which was motivated by a desire to be properly entertained when paying unexpected visits, and an extreme sensitivity to the protocols and prerogatives of their cults, the Greek gods were largely unconcerned about the depredations that human beings visited on one another. As M.I. Finley notes in his *World of Odysseus*:

> Homer's gods ... were essentially devoid of any ethical quality whatsoever. The ethics of the world of Odysseus were man-made and man-sanctioned. Man turned to the gods for help in his manifold activities, for the gifts it was in their power to offer or to withhold. He could not turn to them for moral guidance; that was not in their power. The Olympian gods had not created the world, and they were therefore not responsible for it.[5]

Prevailing concepts of the afterlife also did little to deter wrongdoing among the living. While later generations would embrace a notion of Hades replete with resorts for the blessed and places of torment for the wicked, during the pre-classical period of Greek history, the underworld was conceived of as a sunless, perpetually dusty place where all of the dead — good and bad alike — were consigned to a state of eternal wandering as mindless shades. So dismal an affair was this afterlife that Achilles complained to Odysseus in Book XI of *The Odyssey* that it is "better ... to break sod as a farm hand for some poor country man, on iron rations, than lord it over all the exhausted dead."[6] Given such a prospect, it is hardly surprising that the living would take whatever steps they thought were necessary to ensure both a long life and, where possible, an eventful one.

Heroism in a Dark Age

In this morally ambiguous world, the inhabitants of Archaic Greece embraced an idea of heroism that was a celebration of the bravery and valor of hard-living warriors intent on securing a measure of deathless glory. Given what we know about this period, it is obvious that this conflation of heroism with the actions of men-at-arms was a response to the existing security concerns that discolored every aspect of Greek life. As already noted, Greek communities were threatened by clan conflicts at home, banditry in the surrounding countryside, and raids from abroad. In such an environment, only warriors possessed the skills, equipment, and time necessary to maintain local order, repel foreign invasions, and carry out expeditions against neighboring cities for additional food, slaves, and scarce metals. The martial success of these fighting men often meant the difference between life and death for a population largely comprised of farmers and herders struggling to eke out a living in a subsistence economy. Given this reality, it is not surprising that the people of this time viewed their warriors as the logical successors of those legendary heroes who had also used their strength at arms to defend their dependents from the depredations of others.

Prowess in the art of combat, however, was not the only reason warriors might enjoy the status of heroes at this time. Equally important was the fact that a great many of these armed men were also the protégés of the landholding gentry that dominated the affairs of their local communities. Confronted by the need to protect their property, and keenly aware of the benefits attendant on seizing the belongings of others, noble families during this time used their resources to train and equip their relatives and retainers in the profession of arms. Such patronage not only allowed the nobility to strengthen their control over local affairs through the threat and use of force, but it also served to ennoble and enrich the warriors that they patronized. This enhancement of the warrior's social prestige and economic clout, in tandem with their military skills, lent additional credence to the idea that a man of arms was an uncommon and exceptional figure fully worthy of heroic status.

Finally, this period's cultural producers also played a not insubstantial role in promoting the idea that the stuff of heroes was best found in the person of the well-born warrior. The Archaic Age was an illiterate oral culture and the poems, songs, and stories of Homer and his peers were regarded by their listeners as both sources of entertainment and historical information. Young, old, rich, and poor all heard these tales in market places, over meals, and around their hearths, and much of their understanding about the shape and order of their world — its cosmogony, politics, social relations, and ethics — was derived from these narratives. This was particularly true with regard to the subject of heroism. Indeed, for centuries, bards and storytellers regaled their audiences with tales about heroic protagonists, skilled in arms and favored by princely patrons, mortal and divine, who struggled mightily to defend their honor, protect their families, and win a measure of deathless glory. Add to these story lines the fact that they were set in a world not that far removed from the one in which their listeners lived and worked, and it is easy to understand why the people of this time conflated hero and warrior into synonymous terms.[7]

The Ethos of the Warrior Hero

Prowess and pedigree may have singled out the warrior as a prime candidate for heroic status during the Archaic period, but those qualities alone could not ensure that he would be regarded as a hero by his contemporaries. To attain that stature, a warrior needed to differentiate himself, not only from the common folk, but also from those among his peers for whom the profession of arms was primarily a pecuniary pastime. What was entailed in the achievement of such a distinction was a willingness on the part of an aspiring martial hero to adopt an ethos, a way of life, which was focused not on the acquisition of wealth, but on the attainment of *kleos*, or "deathless glory."

The allure of such undying renown was rooted in a warrior's sense that life was a "short, irreparable time" followed by oblivion. As Glaukos reminds Diomedes in the *Iliad*:

Very like leaves upon this earth are the generations of men — old leaves, cast on the ground by wind, young leaves the greening forest bears when spring comes in. So mortals pass; one generation flowers even as another dies away.[8]

Rather than acquiesce to this existential reality, or try to put off his inevitable demise by staying out of harm's way, a warrior seeking the status of a hero embraced a life that was an ongoing contest with death. To be sure, the profession of the fighting man played some role in this response to the human condition. Dealing death was, after all, the métier of a man-at-arms, and such a vocation could not help but bring him into repeated contact with situations that might result in his demise. This professional consideration to the side, however, a warrior who wanted to be counted a hero actively sought out the dark ferryman on the battlefield, at the prow of a ship, and in personal combat, and he approached these encounters with a grim joy.

Why this was so lay in the fact that this kind of martial derring-do was a sure way of "bringing-glory-to-men."[9] Indeed, extraordinary deeds in war, on the high seas, and at athletic competitions were the essential stuff, the heroic resume if you will, that singled out a warrior as something more than a mere mercenary. While most fighting men engaged in combat and sporting events to enrich themselves, a warrior seeking *kleos* undertook these activities out of a desire to acquire, not just personal wealth, but a reputation as an unconquered champion. For in the end, it was this reputation that earned the man of arms the sobriquet of "hero," and with that honorific the renown that would move poets, like Homer, to celebrate his exploits in songs that would never die.

Winning laurels in sporting contests and battles was only one of the reputation enhancing exercises expected of a warrior seeking a place in the heroic lays of Archaic poets. A fighting man's renown was also augmented when he used his prowess, and the wealth won by its exercise, to defend his family, honor the gods, and show hospitality to neighbors and strangers alike. Behaving in this manner not only singled a warrior out as a champion of traditional Greek moral values, but it also served to further differentiate him from those among his peers who viewed their profession as a license for murder and mayhem.

These moral considerations to the side, however, the Archaic martial hero also championed family, piety, and hospitality because these customs and practices were the underpinnings of his honor and fame. This was particularly the case with a hero's family, which protected his material wealth in life and served as the caretaker of his heroic cult after death. Consequently, any dishonor or injury visited on a warrior's kin also constituted a direct assault on his right to enjoy the honors due to him in this world and the next.

This interplay between a fighting man's familial obligations and his personal honor is best illustrated in those primers of archaic heroism, the Homeric epics. The war at the heart of the *Iliad*, for example, is launched by Agamemnon not for fair Helen's sake, but because the theft of his brother's wife and "her Spartan gold" was an affront to the Mycenaean king's personal honor and a threat to the political standing and economic well being of his house.[10] In the same epic, one sees this nexus of personal and familial honor at work again when Achilles puts aside his quarrel with Agamemnon and re-enters the war against Troy. Achilles takes this action because the slaying of his dependent Patroclus by Hector is an injury to his family that can only be redressed by the killing and despoliation of the Trojan champion. And in the *Iliad's* sister epic, the *Odyssey*, Odysseus feels compelled to slay the suitors of his wife because their actions against his household have endangered his family line and besmirched his honor by calling into question his ability to defend his dependents.

Homer's works also demonstrate how considerations of self-interest even informed a martial hero's relations with his gods. While all the heroes of the Homeric epics pay homage to Zeus, the lord of Olympus and the *primus inter pares* of the immortals, they are considerably less pious in their relationships with the cloud gatherer's extended family. Instead, they direct their praise, sacrifices, and gift-giving to those deities who were their patrons, while treating the others with either perfunctory respect or, in some cases, open disdain. Perhaps no heroic figure demonstrates this discriminating piety better than Odysseus, who honors Zeus, wars with Poseidon, and slavishly obeys Athena. As M.I. Finley notes, among the Dark Age heroes:

> There was no reverential fear of the gods. "Homer's princes bestride their world boldly, they fear the gods only as they fear their human overlords." No word for "god-fearing" is ever used in the Iliad. Nor, it scarcely need be added, was there a word for "love of god." ... For moral support the men of the Iliad relied not on the gods but on their fellow-men, on the institutions and the customs by which they lived.[11]

Ironically, even something as selfless as the rule of hospitality was ultimately upheld by these heroic warriors because the gift giving, which lay at the heart of this custom, was also central to a hero's personal fortunes, status, and renown. The gifts that are given and received in the *Iliad* and the *Odyssey*, for example, provided the families of the heroes involved in these exchanges with the scarce and valuable goods that were the literal stuff of economic, social, and political power in pre-classical Greece. With these materials, lands and flocks could be purchased, foreign and domestic alliances cemented, and advantageous marriages arranged.

More important, however, than the economic and political advantages that accrued to those engaged in these gift exchanges, was the *status* that the giving and receiving transmitted to both their donors and recipients. As the Homeric epics demonstrate, nothing proffered greater evidence of a martial hero's honor and renown than the number and quality of the gifts he could lavish on, and receive from, his peers. Achilles' fame as a warrior was underscored in the *Iliad* by the rich prizes he was able to bestow on the contestants who participated in the funeral games he held in honor of his fallen comrade Patroclus. And in the *Odyssey*, the critical importance of these presents to a hero's reputation is driven home by Odysseus when he consents to the Phaiakian king's request that he stay an additional day so the proper gifts can be assembled for him:

> Alcinous, king and admiration of men, even a year's delay, if you should urge it, in loading gifts and furnishing for sea — I too could wish it; better far that I return with some largesse of wealth about me — I shall be thought more worthy of love and courtesy by every man who greets me home in Ithaca.[12]

Whatever the self-interested motives behind the custom of gift-giving, it should be evident from the foregoing discussion that the heroic ethos of an archaic Greek warrior had little in common with the Judeo-Christian moral principles that would later inform the actions of martial heroes in both the medieval and modern world. Indeed, the strictures of the Decalogue and the humility and social consciousness of the gospels would have been completely alien to a warrior intent on following in the footsteps of the epic heroes celebrated in the songs of Homer and his peers. The code of conduct that these men followed was one that required them to be first and best in all of their endeavors, to kill and humiliate their enemies, to acquire wealth and honor through piracy, war, and gift exchange, and to vie with the gods for control of their destiny.

If notions of "thou shalt not" and "the first shall be last" were absent from the ethos of these ancient warrior heroes, so too was any sense of social responsibility. With the exception of their families, these fighting men felt "no obligation to anyone or anything" outside of their "own drive to victory and power."[13] Their *raison d'être* was the achievement of a deathless fame, and, as Homer demonstrates, the attainment of that goal was a distinctly individualistic, even anarchic, enterprise. In the end, the purpose of society for these men was to provide — either voluntarily or at the point of a sword — the resources necessary to sustain them in the wars, athletic contests, and expeditions that were essential to their acquisition of *kleos*.

The Warrior Hero and the Civilizing Process of the Ancient World

Long after the passing of the Archaic period, this violent, selfish, and asocial warrior ethos, celebrated and immortalized in the works of Homer and his compatriots, continued to exercise a hold on the ancient imagination. Even though the growth of law-governed city states, the creation of citizen and mercenary armies, and the expansion of Roman hegemony throughout the Mediterranean world all served to check the pursuit of fame and glory by individual warriors, generations of Greeks and Romans continued to long for the chance to follow in the footsteps of Achilles and Odysseus. This was particularly so among the aristocracy of Greece and Rome, and more than one king, consul, and general aspired to a glory commensurate with that of the Homeric heroes. Indeed, the actions that these individuals took to achieve such renown often exercised a profound impact on the civilization of antiquity.

This was certainly the case with Alexander the Great whose desire to emulate and even surpass Homer's legendary heroes took him to the ends of the earth and made him master of the known world. The son of a brilliant general, Philip II of Macedon, and his fourth wife, Olympias, a princess of Epirus whose family claimed Achilles as an ancestor, Alexander was raised in an atmosphere where the Homeric epics and the usages of warfare permeated every aspect of his life. Given this environment, it is not terribly surprising that at an early age he demonstrated both a fondness for war and an aptitude in the waging of it. At the tender age of sixteen, he conquered a tribe on Macedon's eastern border and founded on its territory the first of the many cities that would bear his name, Alexandropolis. At eighteen, he led his father's cavalry to victory against a Greek coalition at the Battle of Chaeronea, a triumph which cemented Macedonian hegemony over Greece. By the age of twenty, when he was named king in the aftermath of his father's assassination, Alexander had not only proven himself a worthy descendant of Achilles, but had also acquired the wherewithal — the battle skills, reputation, and devoted army — that would make possible the conquests which would transform him into one of the greatest military heroes of all time.

In 334 BCE, when he crossed into Asia Minor to invade the Persian Empire, the twenty-two year old Alexander carried with him as part of his household equipment a special casket that contained the Homeric epics. Plutarch tells us that he was so attached to the *Iliad* that he laid it "with his dagger under his pillow, declaring that he esteemed it a perfect portable treasure of all military virtue and knowledge."[14] Indeed, as the first Greek since Agamemnon to lead an army across the Hellespont, Alexander went to great lengths at this time to identify himself as the reborn Achilles, and his war as a continuation of that first epic struggle between Greece and Asia. Arriving at the reputed site of Troy, he and his companion of many years, Hephaestion, laid wreaths at the tombs of Achilles and Patroclus, and afterwards Alexander entered the shrine of the great hero, took his shield, and left his own in its place.[15]

Within three years of invading Asia, Alexander had far surpassed the deeds of his distant ancestor. He decisively defeated the Persian king Darius III in three battles, acquired his treasuries in Babylon, Susa, and Persepolis, and carved out an empire that stretched from the Danube River in the north, to the Nile valley in the south, and to the Indus in the east. Rather than rest on his laurels and consolidate his conquests, Alexander continued his relentless march to the east, subduing large areas in what are now Afghanistan, Uzbekhistan, and Tajikistan. When he attempted to push still further into India, mutinies among his troops and a grave lung wound received during a battle with an Indian tribe finally compelled him to return to Babylon. Not long afterwards, Alexander's companion in arms, Hephaestion, died of typhus and was honored by his friend with funeral games modeled on those given for Patroclus by Achilles in the last book of the *Iliad*. A year later, Alexander too was dead, of a fever, at thirty-two.[16]

What Alexander's motives were in destroying the Persian Empire and expanding his realm to the limits of the known world have been debated by historians for centuries. Some have argued that he acted out of a desire to decisively end Persian meddling in the affairs of Greece. Others conjecture that exposure to older, wealthier, and, in some respects, more sophisticated cultures inspired Alexander to dream of a new society that would fuse Greeks, Macedonians, Phoenicians, Egyptians, Persians and the other peoples he had conquered into one hybrid culture ruled by his descendants and infused with Hellenic values. Given what we know about Alexander's obsession with the Homeric heroes, it seems more likely that

> Like Achilles, he wanted fame through battle and conquest. But like Odysseus, he was constantly on the move, impelled by an urge to see and do more than any Macedonian or Greek ever had before.... In his short life of thirty-three years, Alexander constantly posed, fulfilled, and then went far beyond a series of new roles and new challenges until he himself was the only standard by which he could be measured. At the head of his army, his eyes forever on the horizon, he stood self-sufficient but never self-satisfied.[17]

In the end, Alexander's *pothos*, or "yearning," for the deathless glory of his legendary predecessors resulted in a process of Hellenization in the east that would have a major impact on the development of Western culture. By resettling his troops in the territories he conquered, founding twenty cities (eighteen named after himself, one after his horse, and another for his dog) and encouraging the spread of Greek language, literature, philosophy, and science, Alexander laid the groundwork for a common civilization throughout the lands bordering the Mediterranean. This Hellenized culture in turn eased the way for Rome's expansion in the centuries following Alexander's death, and provided the early Christian church with a common lingua franca with which to communicate its gospels to all the peoples of the Greco-Roman world.

During the heyday of the Roman Republic, Alexander's military career also became a source of inspiration to more than one politician aspiring to be the first and best man in Rome. Indeed, in the Roman political culture of this period, where a nobleman's chances of distinction, wealth, and electoral advancement were dependent on his success in war, the life of Alexander often served as a model of how a nobly born warrior and leader of men should conduct himself. Certainly, Alexander had no dearth of admirers among the Roman dynasts of the republic's last two centuries. Among these men were such figures as Publius Cornelius Scipio Africanus, the conqueror of Hannibal in the Second Punic War; Pompey the Great, who secured many of Alexander's eastern territories for Rome in the Mithradatic wars of the 70s BCE; Julius Caesar, conqueror of Gaul and victor in the Republican civil war of 49–45 BCE; and Caesar's nephew Octavian, the first emperor of Rome who sported Alexander's portrait on his signet ring and visited his tomb following the final defeat of Antony and Cleopatra in Egypt.

The consolidation of the Roman Empire at the end of the first century BCE worked against the kind of untrammeled military heroics celebrated in Homer and realized in the life of Alexander and his Roman imitators. A century of internecine conflicts between Rome's military strongmen had left countless thousands dead and the survivors hungry for peace. Coupled with this wide-spread war weariness were a number of social and economic developments — the growth of large population centers, increased opportunities for trade, and more expansive agricultural, mining, and manufacturing enterprises — that called for a more stable and orderly set of political arrangements than those that had made possible either Homer's heroes or the lives of the noble Greeks and Romans who had followed in their footsteps.

Indeed, the political settlement of Augustus Caesar, which established the Roman Empire and ushered in a *Pax Romana* that would endure for two centuries, was very much informed by a desire on the part of its creator to severely restrict the ability of would-be Alexanders — and Caesars for that matter — from acquiring the authority and resources necessary to realize their dreams of conquest and heroic glory. To achieve this end, Augustus consolidated military and political power in the hands of himself and his successors, established a permanent, professional, and salaried army commanded by officers appointed by and loyal to the imperial government, curtailed the autonomy of provincial governors, and ended some four centuries of incessant military expansion by stabilizing the empire's frontiers. For the next 200 years, these arrangements largely succeeded in curtailing the kinds of military adventurism that had helped to destabilize the Roman Republic. And in later centuries, other rulers and governments would implement similar measures in order to keep their own aspiring Alexanders in check.[18]

If the political and military policies of Augustus Caesar limited the opportunities for mayhem available to aspiring *milites gloriosi*, the literary efforts of his favorite poet, P. Vergilius Maro — more commonly known as Virgil — offered the inhabitants of his empire a far more civilized model of martial heroism than the one celebrated in Homer. Having lived through two civil wars, in which he witnessed savage proscriptions, famine, and the devastation of Italy, Virgil was all too aware of the dire consequences that often followed in the wake of glory seeking military strongmen. Consequently, when he set himself the task of penning a Latin equivalent to the works of Homer, he selected as the protagonist of his epic *Aeneid* a warrior hero quite different from the *kleos* hungry freebooters of the *Iliad* and the *Odyssey*.

The warrior celebrated in Virgil's work was the Trojan hero Aeneas, son of Aphrodite and Anchises, legendary founder of Rome's parent city, Lavinium, and sire of the Julii, the ancestral clan of the Caesars. The *Aeneid* recounts the adventures of this fighting man as he leads his family and a band of survivors out of burning Troy to a new home in Italy. As in the *Odyssey*, Virgil's hero is persecuted by a vengeful deity (in this case Juno) who insures that his journey has its share of shipwrecks, love affairs, and gratuitous violence. And like the warriors in the *Iliad*, Aeneas is also an accomplished, fearsome man-at-arms with few equals on the field of battle. These parallels to the side, however, Virgil's hero is neither an Achilles nor an Odysseus. He is instead a new kind of heroic warrior who acts not out of a desire for glory, self-aggrandizement, and adventure, but in response to a highly developed sense of piety, civic duty, and responsibility for his people and their descendants.

Virgil underscores the difference between his hero and those of Homer by the epithet that he uses to identify him. Whereas the different warriors of the *Iliad* and the *Odyssey* are singled out by such martial sounding monikers as "raider of cities," "the great tactician," and "the breaker of wild horses," Virgil names his hero *pius Aeneas*, the pious Aeneas, in order to highlight his loyal and selfless attention to the needs of his family, his countrymen, and his gods. Virgil also demonstrates the aptness of this epithet by lacing his tale with countless examples of his champion's dutiful nature. Early in the story, when Aeneas describes the fall of Troy to a Carthaginian audience, it is clear that he would rather have made a last stand in defense of his city and gone down fighting in a blaze of deathless glory. Instead, he attends to his familial duties and carries his aged and infirm father, his son, and his household gods out of the burning city to safety. In the aftermath of Troy's destruction, when he is confronted by "a crowd of sorrow,"[19] Aeneas takes it upon himself to lead his homeless countrymen in search of a new land where they can live in peace and security. And when he falls in love with Dido, the queen of Carthage, he shows himself obedient to the will of heaven by abandoning his newfound wife when commanded to do so by his mother, the goddess Aphrodite.

Virgil also differentiates his hero from his Dark Age counterparts by having Aeneas treat the foreign peoples that he comes into contact with in a manner quite different from the standard tack of an Achilles or Odysseus. Instead of sacking their cities and raping their women, Virgil's hero strives to make the Carthaginian and Italian communities that he encounters on his journey friends and allies of his countrymen. As he explains to the Carthaginian queen, Dido, at their first encounter:

> We do not come to devastate your homes and with the sword to loot the household gods of Libya or to drive down stolen booty toward the beaches. That violence is not within our minds; such arrogance is not for the defeated.[20]

In fact, the waging of war is not something Aeneas seeks at all, and when Juno forces him into one with the people of Italy at the end of the *Aeneid*, he derives no joy from the ensuing carnage. Indeed, in a stunning reversal of the heroic pattern found in Homer, Virgil has his hero pledge before the final battle against his Italian foes:

> If the war is settled in our favor ... then I shall not subject Italians to Teucrians, ask kingdoms for myself: both nations, undefeated, shall accept the equal laws of an eternal compact: their sacred rites, their gods, shall be intact.[21]

These words, so unlike anything found in the *Iliad* and the *Odyssey*, point to a profound shift in the thinking of the ancients on the subject of martial heroism. Whatever the reasons behind Virgil's decision to pen the *Aeneid*—whether as Augustan propaganda, or as a personal expression of his aversion to military heroics and the horrors of civil war — this epic gave voice to the idea that a hero could be something more than a selfish freebooter intent only on the acquisition of personal fame. In Virgil's Aeneas, we have a heroic warrior whose prowess at arms and hunger for glory is tempered by a new kind of responsibility for his city, people, and descendants. Indeed, the *kleos* of Aeneas rests not so much on his military skills or his capacity to give and receive great gifts — though these are considerable — but on the ways in which he uses his ability and wealth to preserve the *mos maiorum* ("ways of the ancestors") as well as protect and advance the general welfare of the body politic.

This idea of martial heroism as a form of service to god, tradition, and country exercised a powerful hold on the imagination of the Roman world. Augustus, for one, appears to have found in Virgil's stoic dutiful hero a model for his own leadership, and his supporters filled Rome with images of Aeneas in his various guises as pious son, loving father, magnanimous conqueror, and beneficent leader. Even after Rome's fall, Virgil's Aeneas continued to exemplify the qualities essential to a good leader, and, as we shall see, this Virgilian notion of the warrior hero as a loyal and selfless servant to his people is one that will resonate through the centuries to come.[22]

3

"Here I stand.
I cannot do otherwise"
The Hero as Martyr

More: And what would you do with a water spaniel that was afraid of water? You'd hang it!
Well, as a spaniel is to water, so is a man to his own self. I will not give in because I oppose
it—I do—not my pride, not my spleen, nor any other of my appetites but I do—I!

— Robert Bolt: *A Man for All Seasons*

The battle for us is that we are called forth to the tribunals so that there at the risk of death
we may fight for the truth.... The victory hold both the fame of pleasing God and the prize
of living for eternity.

— Tertullian: *Apologeticus* 50.2

This thing of being a hero, about the main thing to it is to know when to die.

— Will Rogers

One suspects Will Rogers was thinking about martyrs when he made the quip that
being a hero is largely a question of knowing when to die. While the warriors, athletes,
explorers, rebels, and rogues that Westerners have lauded as heroes through the centuries
have often put themselves in harm's way, their heroic status ultimately rested on something
more than the manner and timing of their demise. Indeed, these heroic figures more often
than not sought to defy death. Martyrs, on the other hand, owe their place in the heroic
pantheon of the West precisely because of their willingness — sometimes even eagerness —
to die at an appointed hour and place, and in a fashion that is often painful and grisly.

This is not to say, of course, that martyrdom is simply an act of voluntary death, or
that all martyrs qualify as heroes. If this were the case, suicides would have to be included
in the ranks of the martyred, and anyone who had ever surrendered their life for a cause —
no matter how noxious — would be counted a hero.[1] Rather, we single out as heroic those
individuals who embrace martyrdom, not out of despair with life, but as a way of affirming their allegiance to an idea that eventually acquires widespread acceptance and legitimacy.

It should also be noted that martyr heroes are further distinguished by the circumstances surrounding their journey to the gibbet. Whatever their frame of mind or the nature
of their cause, the passage of these heroic martyrs from life to death is a highly ritualized,

well-choreographed *Totentanz* that commences with a simple choice — renounce the ideas and behavior separating you from your neighbors or die. In the passion play that follows this ultimatum, martyr heroes hold fast to their beliefs, resolutely defend their heterodoxy in public, and accept — sometimes even welcome — the sentence of death that invariably follows their obstinate refusal to recant. This drama of martyrdom ends when the condemned fearlessly confront the instrument of their doom — be it an axe, gallows, stake, or cross — and die, usually in an exceptional fashion.

At the beginning of the 21st century, it is still commonplace to regard the individuals who subject themselves to this ritual of martyrdom as heroes of the first rank. Indeed, Western culture abounds in religious hagiographies, reliquaries, monuments, paintings, sculptures, plays, films, television programs, and even comic books that relate, often in graphic detail, the trials, tribulations, tortures, and final death throes of those persons who bore witness to their beliefs by willingly submitting to death. Such adulation, however, was not always the case.

In the Greco-Roman world, self-destruction was seldom viewed as an act of zeal or courage. Rather, if a person embraced voluntary death for any reason — save to obtain respite from a terminal illness or to avoid some personal dishonor such as falling into the hands of one's foes — it was seen as divine retribution for hubris, impiety, or some unnatural crime such as incest. Further, in a culture where one of the marks of heroism was a surfeit of honor and an absence of shame, there could be no greater dishonor, no less heroic act, than surrendering oneself to an enemy for the purpose of being publicly humiliated, tormented, and executed like a common criminal. Indeed, individuals who voluntarily surrendered their lives — for whatever reason — were more likely to arouse among the ancients feelings of pity and horror rather than admiration and reverence.

Despite its revulsion for willful self-destruction, the world of antiquity did give birth to both the cult of the hero martyr and the criteria governing which individuals are allowed into its pantheon. The story of this development spans some six centuries, three Mediterranean civilizations — Greek, Roman and Jewish — and two of the West's principal monotheistic religions. And the genesis of this heroic ideal is to be found in the trial and execution in 399 BCE of an obscure and impoverished Athenian pedagogue who fancied himself the wisest man in the world.

"I to die and you to live": Socrates and the Advent of Heroic Martyrdom

WHO WAS SOCRATES?

Though the scholarly literature on Socrates is voluminous, the direct evidence about his life is surprisingly meager.[2] While he was alive, Socrates penned neither an autobiography nor a corpus of teachings. The contemporary accounts of his life include Plato's dialogues, especially the *Euthyphro, Apology, Crito,* and *Phaedo* that deal with his trial and execution; Xenophon's *Apology, Memorabilia, Symposium,* and *Oeconomicus*; and Aristophanes' comedic satires, the *Clouds,* the *Birds,* the *Frogs,* and the *Wasps.* None of these primary sources provide us with a complete biography of Socrates, all of them are biased, and Plato and Xenophon's accounts often conflict with one another on a number of key points relating to the philosopher's life and death. Evidence for his life can also be found in the texts of a number of ancient authors who wrote about Socrates — or at least referenced him in some way — after his death, but these works are scattered over several centuries and are of varying quality. The most important of these secondary texts are Aristotle's works on politics, metaphysics, and ethics written two generations after Socrates' death; Plutarch's second-century CE *Life of Alcibiades*; a biography of Socrates written by Diogenes Laertius in the third-century of the Common Era; and a little known *Apology of Socrates* that was penned in the fourth-century CE by the pagan statesman and orator, Libanius. These materials, as well as some scattered fragmentary remarks found in Greek and Latin literature down to and including the early Church Fathers, constitute the whole of the ancient record on the father of Western philosophy and history's first recorded martyr.[3]

On the basis of these texts, we know that Socrates was born in Athens sometime around 469 BCE, the son of Sophroniscus, a stonecutter, and Phainarete, a midwife. Though not of the city's aristocracy, Socrates' family appears to have been quite prosperous. This is attested to by the fact that they were able to provide their son with an education in gymnastics and music, as well as with the weapons and armor of a *hoplite*, or fully-armed infantryman, in times of war. There is also credible evidence to suggest that at his father's death Socrates inherited both a house and an inheritance of seventy *minae*.[4] This paternal endowment, in tandem with an extremely abstemious lifestyle that included walking barefoot and wearing the same simple garment throughout the year, appear to have afforded Socrates the wherewithal to support both a family (a wife and three children) and a leisurely life of the mind up until his execution at age 70.[5]

With regard to his physical appearance, our sources all agree that Socrates was not the most attractive of men. Xenophon describes him as a short stout fellow with a paunch, protruding eyes, thick lips, and a snub-nose with wide nostrils. Plato confirms this description in his *Symposium* where he has Alcibiades describe Socrates as looking like the satyr Silenus. Other accounts indicate that he was bald, walked funny, and constantly rolled his eyes during conversations. While some of these descriptions may be exaggerated, it is probably safe to say that Socrates would not have been singled out by his peers as an example of a comely well-made man.[6]

While our sources provide us with some information regarding Socrates' family, finances, lifestyle, and physical appearance, they are almost completely silent with regard to how he spent the first half of his life. One tradition holds that he practiced the trade of his father in his younger years, but none of the contemporary accounts of Socrates' life make any mention of such work. What appears to be more likely is that up until the age of 40 Socrates spent most of his time in the marketplace and gymnasia of Athens studying logic and natural philosophy, practicing his "rough" method of cross-examining individuals about their beliefs, and developing his trademark ideas about the soul, universal truths, and the necessity of dedicating one's life to the pursuit of wisdom. This being the case, it is also probable this was the period in Socrates' life when he acquired his reputation for brilliant, albeit eccentric free-thinking, gathered together a circle of devoted and socially well-connected students, and received from the oracle at Delphi the pronouncement that he was the wisest of men.[7]

Unlike the early years of his life, the latter half of Socrates' career is much better documented. We know, for example, that he was actively involved in the Peloponnesian War between Athens and Sparta (431–404 BCE), and that he displayed considerable courage and physical endurance during that conflict.[8] Our sources also tell us that during this time Socrates experienced a number of "rapts" or trances, which, in tandem with the oracular judgment of Apollo's priestess, convinced him he had a divinely ordained mission to expose the ignorance of his fellow Athenians and help them find goodness through the pursuit of knowledge.[9] In an effort to carry out this charge, Socrates became a self-described "gadfly" intent on stinging his fellow Athenians into awareness through a series of public dialogues in which he disparaged Athenian democracy, cast aspersions on Athens' most prominent statesmen, and ridiculed the intelligence of his city's leading politicians, tradesmen, artisans, and poets.[10] Not surprisingly, this "missionary" activity aroused considerable enmity against Socrates and earned him a reputation as a pedantic and seditious crank.

In a time of peace, it is unlikely such a reputation would have posed much of a problem for Socrates. Athens was, after all, a city state that was proud of its democratic form of government, political freedoms, and reputation as a center of intellectual inquiry and learning. However, in the midst of a world war that was going very badly for the Athenians, Socrates unrelenting criticism of his fellow citizens increasingly came to be seen as an act of disloyalty that was undermining public morale and lending comfort to the enemy. This sentiment was reinforced during the last seven years of the Peloponnesian War by a series of political crises in which Socrates and a number of young men who were counted among his students engaged in activity viewed as anti-democratic and tyrannical.

The first of these was the short-lived effort in 411 BCE by Socrates' former student Alcibiades to overthrow the Athenian government and replace it with a pro–Spartan oligarchy of aristocrats known as the Four Hundred. During the four months this group governed Athens, organized squads of assassins murdered prominent members of the democratic party and terrorized the city. Five years later (406 BCE), while serving as a member of the committee charged with presiding over the business of the popular assembly, Socrates tried, unsuccessfully, to block a demand by that body for a collective trial of a number of Athenian admirals who had failed to pick up survivors in the aftermath of the naval battle of Arginusae. While his opposition was motivated by constitutional considerations — Athenian law required individual prosecutions — it was viewed by the populace-at-large as yet another example of Socrates' contempt for majority rule.

This prejudice gained further credibility two years later (404 BCE) when two more of Socrates' former students — Critias and Charmides — collaborated with the victorious Spartans to establish yet another aristocratic dictatorship — this time known as the Thirty — that abolished democratic rule and launched a reign of terror in which thousands died or were driven into exile. While Socrates refused to cooperate with this group in the arrest and prosecution of a prominent democratic leader, his decision to remain in Athens during their eight month rule, coupled with his silence in the face of their crimes, cemented the popular perception that he was an enemy of Athenian democracy whose teachings had informed and inspired the actions of a vicious, tyrannical, and pro–Spartan cabal.[11]

This widespread popular resentment, in tandem with a fear that another aristocratic coup d'état was in the works, probably lay behind the decision by a group of democratic politicians in late 400 or early 399 to charge Socrates with impiety ("not recognizing the gods which the city recognizes, and introducing new divinities") and corrupting the young.[12] Given the fact that this indictment called for a penalty of death, it is likely that its authors hoped to frighten Socrates into exile. Whatever the intentions of Socrates' persecutors, however, he opted to stay in Athens and his case came to trial before a jury of 500 citizens in the early spring of 399.

With regard to what transpired at this trial, we have no record of the case made by the prosecution and only Xenophon and Plato's differing recollections — both penned long after the event — of what Socrates purportedly said in his defense. Of these two apologies, Xenophon's speech is a rather short bland rebuttal in which Socrates presents himself as a pious conventional man whose dedication to the education of Athens' youth should be counted a benefit rather than a crime. Further, in Xenophon's account, Socrates welcomes the prospect of a conviction because:

> If my years are prolonged, I know that the frailties of old age will inevitably be realized, — that my vision must be less perfect and my hearing less keen, that I shall be slower to learn and more forgetful of what I have learned.... Perhaps," he added "God in his kindness is taking my part and securing me the opportunity of ending my life not only in season but also in the way that is easiest.[13]

By contrast, Plato's apology is a long rhetorical masterpiece in which Socrates vigorously defends himself and, in so doing, exposes the case against him as a politically motivated show trial that was instigated for the purpose of ending his divinely ordained mission to seek out truth, expose ignorance, and help his fellow countrymen attain wisdom. In marked contrast to Xenophon's account, Plato's Socrates accepts the prospect of death not out of any desire to escape the infirmities of old age, but because:

> The truth of the matter is this, gentlemen. Where a man has once taken up his stand, either because it seems best to him or in obedience to orders, there I believe he is bound to remain and face the danger, taking no account of death, or anything else before dishonor.[14]

While it is impossible to know which of these two accounts is the most authentic, on one thing they both agree, Socrates' defense failed to sway his jury, which voted 280 to 220 to condemn him. Following this verdict, both parties in the case were given the opportunity to argue for a penalty. The prosecution pressed for a sentence of death while Socrates rather flippantly suggested that he be designated a public hero and treated to free meals for life. When pressed by his adherents to take the proceedings more seriously, Socrates retracted his initial proposal and recommended instead that the jury levy a considerable fine against him. In the end, Socrates' peers voted for his death, with eighty more jurors voting for this sentence than had agreed to convict him in the first place.

The execution of Socrates did not take place for a full month after his trial because of a religious festival that made it unlawful to carry out such sentences. During this time, his friends, probably with the assistance of the Athenian authorities, made arrangements for Socrates to escape and live out the remainder of his life in exile. Whether out of a genuine desire to end his life without suffering the further infirmities of old age (Xenophon), or because he felt it his duty to obey the laws of the state in which he had spent his whole life (Plato), Socrates peacefully accepted the cup of hemlock that was given to him on the day of his execution and passed into history as the West's first recorded martyr.

THE REACTION TO SOCRATES' DEATH

Aside from Plato and Xenophon's apologies, the only other mention we have of Socrates' trial and execution in the half century following his death is in a speech, *Against Timarchus*, by the Athenian orator Aeschines. Delivered in a trial in 345 BCE against a protégé of Aeschines' rival Demosthenes, this speech cites the execution of Socrates as a precedent justifying a similar verdict of death against Timarchus. Given the fact Aeschines won this case, we can only assume that 54 years after Socrates' death a majority of Athenians continued to believe his prosecution and execution had been justified. This is further substantiated by the fact that one finds no mention of Socrates' trial in any of the dramas written after his death, nor does one see any effort by his countrymen in the centuries following his demise to accord him the divine honors, posthumous votes of thanks, or statues normally awarded to those individuals the Greeks regarded as figures worthy of praise and remembrance. Indeed, with the exception of Plato, the adherents of his Academy, and a handful of other philosophers, no one appears to have regarded Socrates as either a martyr or a hero until rather late in Antiquity.[15]

Given fifth century Greek notions of what it meant to be a hero, this widespread indifference to the persecution of Socrates in the centuries following his death is not unexpected. While the Greeks were increasingly willing at this time to confer heroic status on professional athletes, lawgivers, statesmen, generous philanthropists, and even the occasional artist (e.g., Aeschylus, Sophocles, or Euripides), they still tended to think of a hero in Homeric terms, i.e., as a well-born, divinely favored, physically attractive aristocrat who had distinguished himself in war and on the playing field. Further, whether a hero was a Homeric-like princely warrior or a public benefactor of the Greek *polis*, fifth-century Greeks expected their heroic figures to meet a certain set of criteria. These included: (1) the right to be counted the first and best among one's peers; (2) actions that surpassed ordinary expectations; (3) achievements that were not the result of chance; and (4) a claim to honor, privilege, and precedence that was recognized by the public-at-large, and acknowledged through

> Sacrifices [made to the hero after death], memorial inscriptions in verse or prose, receipt of special awards, grants of land, front seats at festivals, burial at public expense, statues, free food in the state dining room, among barbarians such things as proskynesis and rights of precedence, and gifts that are held in honor in each society.[16]

On all of these counts, Socrates would have been found wanting. Unlike the Homeric heroes of old, he was neither well born nor attractive, and while he demonstrated uncommon valor in war, he neither regarded himself as a warrior, nor did he seek glory for himself or his city on the field of battle. Further, as an ascetic apolitical sophist of modest means, Socrates lacked the wherewithal, inclination, and aesthetic sensibility that was necessary to win a place among Athens' revered benefactors. He possessed no wealth with which to shower his fellow countrymen with gifts and public buildings; he was indifferent, even hostile, to their political order; and his muse was deaf to the poetry, music, and drama so deeply loved by his fellow Athenians. He also did not meet — at least at first glance — any of the aforementioned criteria that identified a Greek of his time as a hero. Among his fellow philosophers, Socrates does not appear to have enjoyed any kind of primacy. He could boast of no solid achievements such as a corpus of philosophical work or an academy. His claim to be the wisest of men rested on a Delphic pronouncement that was not readily recognized either by himself or his peers. And his compatriots regarded his efforts to enlighten them as worthy of little more than a cup of hemlock.

FROM SEDITIOUS CRANK TO SECULAR SAINT: THE APOTHEOSIS OF SOCRATES

It was Plato who ultimately insured that Socrates would be remembered in history as a heroic martyr, rather than as a despised pedant and convicted criminal. Opting to serve as his late mentor's public relations agent, Plato devoted his life in the years following Socrates' death to the task of preserving his teacher's intellectual legacy and rehabilitating his tarnished reputation. Plato achieved these ends by applying his considerable philosophical, rhetorical and poetic talents to the creation of a series of dialogues in which he presented Socrates to posterity as a wrongfully executed man of extraordinary wisdom, piety, honor, and courage.

Of these Platonic dialogues, the ones that were most influential in winning public opinion over to the side of Socrates were the *Euthyphro, Apology, Crito,* and *Phaedo.* Purportedly an accounting of Socrates' final days, these four works are at once an apology, a tragic drama, and a posthumous panegyric in which Plato lays out the case for the innocence, heroic nature, and noble death of his beloved mentor. As a formal apologia, these texts provide an eloquent defense against the charges of impiety and corrupting the young that were leveled against Socrates by his enemies. In them, Plato demonstrates both Socrates' profound piety towards the gods and the laws of his community, as well as the absurdity of blaming him for the corruption of Athens' youth. Plato also uses these works to blacken the legal proceedings against his teacher by presenting them as a political show trial, which was motivated out of enmity against Socrates for his teaching and his association with the aristocrats who had twice tried to overthrow Athens' democracy. Indeed, as a work of apologetic literature, Plato's retelling of Socrates' trial and execution is a masterful *tour de force* that leaves the reader convinced of the calumny of the prosecution and the innocence of the accused.

Plato also used his account of Socrates' final days to establish his teacher's heroic credentials. Aware of the fact that his audience expected its heroes to be divinely favored, possessed of outstanding abilities, competitive, boastful, obsessed with honor, and unafraid of death, Plato crafted the defense speech that Socrates delivers in his *Apology* to highlight the ways in which his mentor's life satisfied these different heroic criteria. In that speech, Socrates presents himself as a man of exceptional wisdom who has been charged by the gods to seek out truth, expose ignorance and help his fellow countrymen attain self-awareness. He also proudly relates — in a manner not unlike that of a Homeric hero boasting of his deeds — how he accepted this divine mission, dedicated his life to learning, challenged and overthrew the intellectual pretensions of his peers, and proved himself worthy of the Delphic pronouncement that he was the wisest man in the world. At the end of this declamation, Socrates confirms both his love of honor and his fearlessness by calmly accepting — even welcoming — a penalty of death rather than abandoning his principles or behaving in an ignoble fashion.

Plato further underscores Socrates' heroic nature by infusing his account with many of the elements of a Greek tragedy. As with Homer's Achilles or Sophocles' Antigone, Plato's Socrates is confronted with a choice between remaining true to the ideas and values that define him as a person, and, in so doing, sealing his doom, or foregoing his principles and dying comfortably of old age. In a manner befitting a tragic hero, Socrates refuses to compromise himself, rejects the entreaties of family and friends to flee, and calmly accepts the draught of poison that ends his life. As I.F. Stone notes in his own account of Socrates' trial:

> The four dialogues that describe the trial and death of Socrates — the Euthyphro, Apology, Crito, and Phaedo — live as tragic drama. It is hard to read Socrates' serene farewell to his disciples in the Phaedo without a tear, nor can one fail to be moved in the Apology — no matter how many times one has read it — by Socrates' last words to his judges. The Platonic account is theater at its highest level. Socrates is as much a tragic hero as Oedipus or Hamlet.[17]

Whether or not Plato's portrayal of his teacher as a tragic hero is factual, or, as seems more likely, a fanciful reworking of the facts aimed at casting him in the best possible light for posterity, it becomes the master narrative of Socrates' trial and death. In part, Plato's work achieves this status because it is by far the better written and certainly the more entertaining of the two accounts of Socrates' last days. As already mentioned, Xenophon's Socrates is, at best, a well meaning, eccentric educator who essentially commits suicide. While such a narrative might actually be a more accurate portrayal of Socrates' life and death, it is hardly the kind of account that would move future generations to tears.

Stylistic considerations to the side, however, Plato's posthumous panegyric to Socrates ultimately wins pride of place in the ancient (and modern) world because of the reputation of its author. From the Hellenistic period to late antiquity, a certain familiarity with Plato's works was expected of any individual aspiring to be counted among the learned. This was particularly the case from the first century BCE through the third century of the Common Era, when a majority of the Greco-Roman intelligentsia — pagan and Christian alike — subscribed to Platonic ideas of divine transcendence, free will, the immortality of the soul, and the necessity of living a virtuous life.[18] In light of this widespread respect for his work, as well as the fact that he credited his mentor with many of the ideas central to his philosophical outlook, Plato's heroic portrayal of Socrates could not help but find favor among the educated classes of the Greek and Roman world.[19]

Plato's case for Socrates' heroic status was further strengthened by a number of historical events that reshaped the ancient world in the centuries after his death. The subjugation of Greece by Macedon and Rome ushered in the rule of aristocratic oligarchies in Athens and her sister cities, and these new rulers were not only more sympathetic to Socrates' anti-democratic attitudes, but more inclined to regard him as a heroic figure. The fact that Socrates had defied both mob rule (the prosecution of the Athenian admirals) and the tyranny of the Thirty (his refusal to arrest Leon of Salamis), also played well with a Roman elite weary of the dictatorships, mob violence, and civil wars of the Republic's last century.[20] And for many educated Christians of the early and late Roman Empire, Socrates' life and death offered a prefiguration of their own persecution at the hands of their pagan neighbors. As the second century Christian martyr, Justin Martyr, would note in his Second Apology:

> He [Socrates] was accused on the same charges as we are. They said that he introduced new
> divinities and did not acknowledge the gods the State honored. He in fact expelled the evil
> spirits from the community, those whom the poets described, and taught men to reject Homer
> and the other poets, and directed them to use reason [or the Word] to seek knowledge of the
> god unknown to them, saying "It is not easy to find the father and creator of all, or having
> found him it is not safe to declare him publicly."[21]

In the end, Plato's literary gifts and reputation, coupled with the shifting political, social, and cultural landscape of the ancient world, helped transform Socrates from a seditious crank into a secular saint. Long after the decline and fall of Greco-Roman civilization, future generations would read Plato's account of Socrates' final days and come to regard him as a tragic hero who not only stood his ground against an ignorant mob, but willingly sacrificed his life in defense of those principles he regarded as central to his definition of selfhood. Writing of the impact of Plato's rendering of Socrates' death, Lacey Baldwin Smith notes:

> To this day Socrates' performance—the cold deliberateness of his actions, the dramatic style
> of his death, and the purpose for which he died—has stamped and befuddled the history of
> martyrdom.[22]

SOCRATES AND THE HISTORY OF HEROISM

As we have already noted, by the standards of his contemporaries there was little about Socrates' life or death that would have been regarded as heroic. He was lacking in breeding, beauty, and wealth, uninterested in war, sport, and public office, and without any claim to fame save a Delphic pronouncement that he was a wise man. Further, in a culture where heroism was closely tied to considerations of honor and shame, Socrates had submitted himself to a humiliating public trial, been found guilty of serious crimes, and suffered execution as a common criminal. At his death, few mourned his passing, and no one accorded him posthumous honors.

Through the agency of Plato's literary imagination Socrates was rescued from historical oblivion and transformed into a figure worthy of remembrance and emulation. In his dialogues about his teacher's trial and death, Plato presented Socrates to posterity as a man of extraordinary wisdom charged by the gods to enlighten mankind. He also portrayed his mentor as an intellectual warrior athlete who contended with and vanquished ignorance; explored new realms of thought; promoted virtue among his countrymen; and voluntarily chose death over dishonor. While we cannot ascertain the degree to which this account of Socrates' final days actually influenced ancient thinking on the subject of heroic martyrdom, we do know that Plato's works were well regarded and much read by later generations of educated Greeks and Romans. Given this fact, it seems safe to assume that Plato's Socratic apology must have played some role in securing acceptance for the idea that in certain circumstances surrendering voluntarily to public disgrace and death was an act worthy of a hero's laurels.

Certainly, by the last century of the Roman Republic, if not before, the ancient public appears to have been increasingly willing to consider martyrdom in defense of an ideal or principle as noble and praiseworthy. This shift in opinion can be seen quite clearly in

Cicero's speech in defense of Gaius Rabirius Postumus in 54 BCE, where he holds out the possibility of honor even in the face of a humiliating trial and execution:

> How grievous a thing it is to be disgraced by a public court; how grievous to suffer a fine, how grievous to suffer banishment; and yet in the midst of any such disaster some trace of liberty is left to us. Even if we are threatened with death, we may die as free men.[23]

By the first centuries of the Common Era, according high honors to an individual who had shown exceptional virtue (or excellence) by dying in a "noble" fashion appears to have become commonplace. Evidence of this development can be found in works on epideictic rhetoric (the rhetoric of praise and blame) that were penned during this period. In Quintilian's *Institutio Oratoria* (1st century CE), and the *Progymnasmata* (rhetorical handbooks) of the second and third centuries of the Common Era, very specific rules of praise were delineated for each stage of a person's life, i.e., their origin and birth, nurture and training, and accomplishments and deeds. Particular attention in these accounts was paid to the manner and circumstances of an individual's demise, and if that death was (1) voluntarily chosen and freely accepted; (2) in defense of virtuous ends, e.g., justice, wisdom, piety; (3) beneficial to others; and (4) befitting a victor rather than a slave or a victim; it was regarded as a honorable and heroic way to die. According to these standards, Socrates and any other person who opted to die a martyr's death were entitled to a hero's laurels.[24]

The acceptance by the ancients of martyrdom as an act worthy of high honor and praise added a whole new dimension to the Western idea of heroism. Whereas, prior to Socrates, death had always dogged the heels of any would-be champion, and a courageous demise certainly burnished any heroic reputation, dying in and of itself had never been the principal grounds for according someone the status of a hero. To be sure, Plato had sought to portray his mentor as a conventional heroic figure — i.e., as an extraordinary, divinely favored pseudo-warrior intent on doing good for his people — and, in the future, the press agents of other martyrs would take a similar tack. This said, however, it was not Socrates' life that secured him heroic status in the West, but rather the circumstances and the manner of his death, and this would continue to be the case with others of his ilk down to the present day.

Acknowledging the praiseworthy nature of a martyr's death also considerably expanded the range of who might be considered heroic. As we have already noted, prior to, and well after, Socrates' death there was a presumption among the ancients that a hero was a nobly born champion or benefactor with exceptional abilities, resources, and a pleasing mien. Martyr heroes, however, transcended these criteria. Indeed, as long as a person was willing to bear witness to their beliefs by voluntarily suffering death, their gender, class, occupation, and appearance were irrelevant. Ironically, by transforming his mentor into a heroic martyr, Plato democratized the Western heroic pantheon.

Finally, Plato's success in winning Socrates a place among the honored dead and the martyrs that would follow him also insured the inclusion of non-conformists among the ranks of the West's heroes. In the centuries following Socrates' tragic demise, men and women of conscience representing all manner of principles and persuasions would share pride-of-place with Homer's warriors and Pindar's athletes. Prominent among these heroic dissenters would be the followers of the Jewish and Christian testaments and it is their place in the history of heroic martyrdom we will now address.

Hear O Israel the Lord thy God, the Lord Is One: Heroism in a Jewish Context

From the moment they first appeared in the Near East, the children of Israel were notable for their refusal to act in conformity with the generally accepted beliefs and practices of their neighbors. In particular, they were noted for their rejection of all gods save for a stern, jealous, temperamental, and highly vengeful desert deity named Yahweh, who claimed to be the author of creation and the master of the universe. The Israelite devotion to this omnipotent, omniscient, and omnipresent god was grounded in a conviction that he had selected them in the time of Abraham to be his chosen people, and that he had confirmed this election in the following centuries by delivering them from bondage in Egypt, giving them a law code at Sinai, and leading them to a promised land in Canaan.

In return for the honor of being their god's "own possession" (Ex. 19:3–6) among the peoples of the earth, the children of Israel bound themselves to a sacred covenant with Yahweh when they received his Ten Commandments at Mount Sinai. Under the terms of this agreement, the Israelites were not only forbidden to place any gods before their divine patron, but were also required to distinguish themselves further from their neighbors by strictly observing a regulatory regimen that included no idolatry; circumcision; dietary restrictions; modesty (no nudity); and observance of a Sabbath day. Compliance with this covenant was mandatory for all Jews and each generation was apprised by Yahweh's priests and prophets of both the favors Israel had received in honoring its provisions — freedom, homeland, empire — as well as the punishments that had been meted out to her for disregarding its strictures — enslavement, exile, and the destruction of Jerusalem. By the time of Socrates' death, this sacred contract had served as the constitution of the Israelite tribes, as well as the framework for the traditions, beliefs and institutions of Judaism, for almost a thousand years.[25]

This deep-seated belief among Israelites that they were bound by covenant to an all powerful deity exercised a profound influence on their thinking about heroes and heroism. Unlike the well-born, self-centered, vainglorious, and often impious heroes of the Greco-Roman world, the heroic figures of the Hebrew Testament were a profoundly pious lot that haled from every social stratum and all walks of life. They were shepherds (Moses, David), mothers (Debora), widows (Judith, Ruth), bandits (Jephthah), rogues (Samson), ascetic prophets (Samuel), self-made warlords (Joshua, Saul), eunuchs (Nehemiah), and priests (Ezra). And what bound this motley crew together was not a quest for the deathless glory that was so prized by their pagan peers, but a shared sense that they had been summoned by their Lord God to serve his chosen people in a time of need. Whether one is speaking of Moses liberating the Hebrews from bondage in Egypt, Debora leading her people to victory over the Canaanites, or Ezra rebuilding the temple in Jerusalem, the heroic champions of ancient Israel were first and foremost the pliant instruments of Yahweh, selected and shaped by him for the purpose of securing the physical and spiritual welfare of the Jewish nation.[26]

To be sure, the heroes of ancient Israel were not without pride and passion, and, as their biblical accounts make clear, it was not unusual for them to arouse the ire of their god. The anger of Moses caused him to be banned from the Promised Land, Samson was blinded, both literally and figuratively, by his lust, and the indiscretions of David were legion. Despite these human failings, however, these Jewish heroes were largely obedient to Yahweh and faithful to his covenant with Israel. Indeed, it was their submission to the will of their god and the selfless service they rendered their countrymen at his behest, which won for these biblical champions both their extraordinary powers — Moses' control over the forces of nature, Samson's phenomenal strength, David's military skill, the prescience of Debora, Samuel and Jeremiah — as well as the right to be remembered and revered for all time by those who honor the Hebrew Testament.

JEWISH MARTYRDOM
AND THE MACCABEAN ORDEAL

Self-sacrifice was implicit in the ancient Hebrew ideal of heroism, and a champion of Israel was expected to willingly submit to any hardship asked of him or her by Yahweh in the service of his covenant and people. As the Bible attests, the heroes of the Israelites often abandoned their homes, families, tribes, and livelihoods in obedience to the commands of their god. And as their encounters with vengeful pharaohs, Egyptian hosts, Philistine giants, mad kings, fiery furnaces, and lions' dens demonstrate, these intrepid individuals were equally willing to suffer the loss of life and limb in defense of their compatriots.

A willingness to sacrifice oneself in the service of Yahweh, however, did not necessarily translate into an acceptance of martyrdom by the Israelites. If the Hebrew heroes of the Bible suffered tribulations and/or the possibility of injury and death, they did so at the command of a god who was usually loathe to allow any real harm to befall them. Indeed, only two biblical heroes — Saul and Samson — actually requested or allowed their lives to be taken voluntarily, and in both of these cases this action was instigated out of a desire to preserve the personal honor of the men involved, rather than to defend their faith and nation.[27]

It is not until the end of the Old Testament period, during a time when Yahweh appeared to have withdrawn from the affairs of his chosen people, that we find accounts of heroic Jewish martyrdom. Written in the first and second centuries before the Christian era, these narratives recount the terrible suffering and grisly deaths in 167 BCE of nine defenseless Jews — an elderly scribe, Eleazar, a mother and her seven sons — at the hands of the Seleucid king, Antiochus IV Epiphanes. This tale of martyrdom is an integral part of an apocryphal, or noncanonical, collection of Jewish texts known as the First, Second and Fourth Books of Maccabees, which relate the history of both Antiochus IV's efforts to extirpate Judaism in the second century BCE and the successful revolt that was led against him by an Israelite patriot, one Judas Maccabeus.[28]

The origins of this efflorescence of Jewish martyrdom and the Maccabean insurrection that it sparked can be traced back to the meteoric career of Alexander the Great. In the course of his war against the Persians, Alexander acquired Judea, which was at that time a part of the Persian province of Coele-Syria. Following Alexander's death in 323, this territory was contested by the two Macedonian generals who divided up the eastern portion of his empire, i.e., Ptolemy I Soter who established himself as king of Egypt and Seleucus I Nicator who carved out a kingdom of his own in Asia Minor, Babylonia, and Persia's eastern principalities. After a series of hard fought campaigns, Ptolemy managed to assert control over Coele-Syria, an arrangement that lasted for the next 103 years until, in 198, it was wrested from Egypt by Antiochus III, the sixth ruler of the Seleucid dynasty.

Aside from an annual tribute, the Hebrew community in Judea enjoyed considerable autonomy under the Ptolemies and their first two Seleucid monarchs, Antiochus III and Seleucus IV. The high priest of the temple in Jerusalem was acknowledged by both dynasties as the spiritual and temporal head of the Jewish community, and it was left to this individual and his agents to maintain order, levy taxes, and collect the yearly revenues due Israel's foreign rulers. As long as this priestly aristocracy was able to preserve the peace and keep the tribute flowing, Ptolemy and Seleucid alike were content to allow the Jews to maintain their temple, practice their religion, and live in accordance with their own laws and customs.

A combination of external and internal crises during the early 2nd century BCE upset this equitable arrangement between Israel and her Seleucid overlords. In 190, Antiochus III suffered a shattering defeat at the hands of the Roman Republic at Magnesia, a site in what is now modern day Turkey. Under the terms of the peace imposed on him by Rome, Antiochus was compelled to cede Asia Minor, surrender his war elephants and navy, pay an enormous indemnity, and hand over hostages (one of which was his son the future Antiochus IV). When he died in 187, Antiochus left to his successors a kingdom that was bankrupt, internally unstable, and threatened by enemies on all sides — Romans to the west, Parthians in the east, and Egyptians to the south.

One of the sons of Antiochus III, Antiochus IV Epiphanes (175–163), set himself the task of rectifying the many problems bequeathed to the Seleucids by his father. After murdering his brother, Seleucus IV (187–175), and seizing the throne, Antiochus IV proceeded to pursue a number of policies aimed at securing the finances, unity and borders of his kingdom. In practice, this program of action entailed plundering the various temples of the peoples under Seleucid rule, fostering the adoption of a common Hellenic culture, encouraging the worship of the king as the visible manifestation of Zeus (thus Antiochus' name "Epiphanes" or "God Manifest"), and pursuing an aggressive foreign policy aimed at securing the kingdom's borders.

It was at this juncture in the history of the Seleucid Empire that internal tensions between culturally conservative Jews and those favoring the adoption of Greek practices and customs set the stage for the persecution and death of the Maccabean martyrs. Following the ascent of Antiochus IV to the Seleucid throne, the Hellenic party in Judea offered the new king 440 talents of silver and full cooperation with his policies in exchange for the office of high priest in Jerusalem. Only too happy to agree to this profitable arrangement, Antiochus deposed the legitimate high priest, Onias III, and replaced him with his brother, Jason, one of the leaders of the pro–Greek faction in Jerusalem. Three years later, Jason shared his brother's fate when, in exchange for a higher yearly tribute, Antiochus installed another member of the Hellenic party, one Menelaus, as high priest.

Under the rule of both Jason and Menelaus, Judea was subjected to an active policy of Hellenization. A gymnasium was established in Jerusalem, Greek sports and fashion were encouraged among young Jews, and rites honoring pagan gods were permitted within the precincts of Israel's holiest city. In order to pay for these activities, as well as the higher tributes they had pledged to Antiochus in return for their offices, Jason and Menelaus also expropriated and sold off sacred vessels from the temple in Jerusalem. Not surprisingly, these Hellenic practices and the despoliation of Judea's most sacred shrine shocked and angered conservative Jews, and in 169 they demonstrated their displeasure by joining in a bloody revolt against Menelaus, which was led, ironically enough, by his deposed predecessor Jason.

Angered and alarmed by these disturbances in his Judean province, Antiochus marched on Jerusalem in 169, plundered its temple and restored Menelaus to power. A year later, in the face of continued Jewish resistance to his high priest, Antiochus invaded Judea again, sacked Jerusalem a second time, massacred the city's population, and tore down its walls. In the aftermath of these atrocities, the Seleucid monarch also resolved to forcibly Hellenize the Jewish population by forbidding the practices of Judaism. This entailed outlawing the circumcision of infants, suspending regular sacrifices to Yahweh, banning the observance of the Sabbath, destroying copies of the law, and abolishing the Jewish dietary code. Pagan altars were also erected in the temple at Jerusalem and throughout Israel, and Jews were required to sacrifice unclean animals at these sites and eat their flesh on pain of death.

These decrees were soon followed by a veritable reign of terror against the Jewish community in Palestine. Individuals studying the Torah were slain. Sacred scrolls were shredded and put to the torch. Mothers who had circumcised their infants were paraded through the streets of Jerusalem and hurled headlong from the city's battlements with their children still clinging to their breasts. And faithful Jews who fled the cities and towns of Judea to practice their religion in the hills and deserts of the surrounding countryside were pursued by Seleucid troops and put to death.[29]

Initially, Jews were at a loss as to how to respond to this savage persecution. They lacked the arms and training necessary to resist the military might of Antiochus' professional army. Their leadership was divided into mutually antagonistic Hellenic and traditionalist camps. The high priest of the Yahwist cult in Jerusalem — the spiritual and temporal head of the Hebrew people since their return from the Babylonian captivity — was a creature of the man dedicated to extirpating Jewish identity. And the divinely inspired prophets and champions of Biblical times were nowhere to be found.

It was at this moment of Jewish national crisis that an elderly scribe and a fatherless family voluntarily embraced death rather than betray the tenets of their faith. These individuals were part of a group of Jews who were rounded up in 167 for the purpose of staging a public recantation of their faith before Antiochus IV. Specifically, the Jewish participants in this drama were ordered by the king to eat swine flesh that was consecrated and sacrificed to the Greek gods on pain of being broken on the wheel — a rather slow and painful way to die. As the meat in question was both pork and an offering to gods other than Yahweh, compliance with the command constituted a direct violation of Covenant ordinances governing diet and the Decalogue's stricture against idolatry. By compelling the assembled Jews to either obey the royal directive and live, or refuse to do so and suffer torture and death, Antiochus' advisers hoped to demonstrate to the Jewish community of the Seleucid Empire that there would be no retreat from the king's policy of forced Hellenization.

The first of this unfortunate group to be summoned before Antiochus "was a man named Eleazar, a priest by family and an expert in the Law, advanced in age and known to many of the king's court because of his philosophy."[30] When urged by the king to eat of the swine's flesh and save himself, Eleazar is reputed to have responded in the following fashion:

> I shall not violate the sacred oaths of my ancestors in regard to keeping the Law, not even if you cut my eyes out and burn my entrails. I am neither so decrepit, nor so ignoble, that reason should lose the vigour of youth in the cause of religion. So make ready your torturer's wheel, fan your fires to a fiercer heat.[31]

Enraged by this act of defiance, Antiochus ordered Eleazar savagely scourged with whips until "he was flowing with blood, and his sides were lacerated."[32] Despite the severity of this beating, however, and Eleazar's advanced age, the elderly scribe "endured the pain, despised the compulsion, prevailed over the torments, and like a noble athlete under blows outstripped his torturers."[33] Indeed, even when offered the opportunity to save himself further pain by pretending to "taste of the swine's flesh and be saved," Eleazar declined stating that:

> Contrary to reason indeed would it be, if having lived our lives in accordance with truth, and having, in keeping with the Law, guarded our reputation for so doing, we should now change and ourselves proved to be a model of impiety to the young by setting an example for the eating of forbidden food. Shameful indeed would it be, if, having but a short shrift of life remaining, we should become ludicrous in the eyes of all for our cowardice, and earn the tyrant's contempt as ignoble by failing to protect our divine Law unto death.[34]

This last expression of defiance was met by one final outburst of savagery in which the elderly scribe was brought to a fire where he was burned "with evilly devised instruments" and "consumed to his very skeleton."[35] It was during these cruel tortures that Eleazar died and, in so doing, left "his death as an example of nobility and as a precedent of valor to be remembered not only by the young but by the multitudes of his nation."[36]

Having failed to compel a man of learning and advanced years to recant his faith under grievous torture, Antiochus' advisers next selected from the crowd of hapless Jews a family of seven brothers and their mother, Hannah.[37] In an effort to sway these individuals to eat the unclean sacrificial meat, Antiochus ordered:

> That the instruments of torture be brought forward ... wheels and instruments for dislocating joints, racks and wooden horses, and catapults, and caldrons and braziers and thumbscrews and iron grips and wedges and bellows; and the tyrant then ... said: "Lads, be afraid; the justice which you revere will be indulgent to transgression under duress."[38]

Replying for his family, the eldest brother evoked the example of the recently martyred Eleazar stating that:

> If old men of the Hebrews have died for the sake of their religion, and persevering through torture have abided by their faith, it is even more fitting that we who are young should die, despising the torments of your compulsion, over which our aged teacher triumphed.[39]

This response, which was echoed by the other brothers and their mother, infuriated Antiochus who proceeded to subject the entire family — one after the other — to grisly tortures that included scourgings, scalpings, maimings, amputations of various body parts, and being fried in pans. As each family member expired, we are told by the chroniclers of their martyrdom that they reaffirmed their faith in the Covenant of their forefathers, offered their lives up as an expiation for the sins of Israel, warned of future punishment for their tormentors, and declared their belief that their sacrifice would be rewarded with a heavenly afterlife.

Whether or not Antiochus "and his whole council, were amazed at the constancy"[40] of these martyrs, as the author of Maccabees Four attests, their willingness to die in defense of their faith was certainly not lost on their countrymen. The news of how Eleazar, the mother and her seven sons had steadfastly refused to betray the Jewish Covenant, despite the most gruesome tortures, spread throughout Judea and helped fan the coals of resistance to Seleucid rule. Among those most inspired by the example of these martyrs was the House of Hashmon, the family of Judah Maccabeus, which, in the following year (166), launched a revolt against Antiochus that would last for twenty-one years and bring about the liberation of Israel from foreign rule.

THE MACCABEAN MARTYRDOM AND THE HISTORY OF HEROISM

In the aftermath of their tragic deaths, there does not appear to have been much debate among Jews regarding the heroic status of Eleazar, Hannah and her seven sons. While Judaism afforded its adherents considerable latitude in avoiding martyrdom — indeed, later rabbis would ordain that under threat of death most religious prohibitions might be disregarded — idolatry was a particularly egregious offense against the covenant with Yahweh.[41] As such, the decision of the Maccabean martyrs to sacrifice their lives rather than eat the flesh of an animal sanctified to pagan idols was regarded as a righteous action in defense of Israel's faith. Add to this exemplary act of piety the fact that these deaths also segued seamlessly into a popular and ultimately successful revolt against the Seleucid Empire, and it is not difficult to understand why these individuals were readily embraced as heroic figures by the Jews of the Greco-Roman world.

The heroic credentials of Eleazar and the family of Hannah were further burnished by the Jewish historians that made it their business to write about the Maccabean martyrdom in the years after their deaths. The narrator of Maccabees II, Jason of Cyrene, and the unknown author of Maccabees IV were well-educated, Greek speaking Jews who patterned their accounts of the Maccabean martyrs after the so-called "pathetic" histories of the Hellenistic period; a popular genre of Greek historical writing that entertained its readers with emotionally charged, melodramatic accounts of divinely favored long-suffering heroes.[42] In the pathetic narratives Jason and his colleague penned about the Maccabean martyrdom, Eleazar and his compatriots were transformed from a hapless elderly scribe and a nameless family into stalwart Israelite champions engaged in a battle royal against an evil "tyrant resolved to destroy the polity of the Hebrews."[43] Even the grisly tortures to which these unfortunates were subjected were transmogrified by these authors into heroic athletic contests in which:

> Eleazar was the prime contestant; but the mother of the seven sons entered the competition and the brothers too vied for the prize. The tyrant was the adversary, and the world and humanity were the spectators. Reverence for God was the winner, and crowned her own champions. Who did not marvel at the athletes of the divine legislation, who were not astonished by them?[44]

This image of the Maccabean martyrs as heroic athletes and warriors was further enhanced by the resemblance of their case to that of Socrates. Whether or not the chroniclers of the Maccabean martyrdom intended to draw parallels between the situation of their heroes and that of the 5th century Athenian dissident, any person educated in the Greek classics of this period could not help but see certain marked similarities between the heroic deaths recounted in Maccabees II and IV and Plato's account of the trial and death of his mentor. Like Socrates, the Maccabean martyrs were given a choice between betraying the principles by which they had lived their lives, and dying. Similarly, both parties opted for death and presented a spirited public defense of their self-sacrifice, which demonstrated the intellectual and moral inferiority of their persecutors. Both Socrates and his Hebrew counterparts turned a deaf ear to their supporters' cajoling, pleading, and offers of escape, and affirmed their belief in a divine order that rewarded the righteous and punished the wicked in a posthumous afterlife. And these martyrs all demonstrated their exceptional bravery by dying well.[45]

Whatever the reasons for the heroic status accorded to the Maccabeans, the deaths of Eleazar, Hannah and her seven sons marked the moment in the history of heroism when self-immolation on behalf of religion and nation was adjudged worthy of a hero's laurels. Whereas Socrates had opted for death in order to preserve his sense of selfhood and personal honor, the Maccabean martyrs offered up their lives in defense of an ideal that transcended their individual egos, i.e., Judaism and the Jewish national identity that was inseparably bound up in the practice of that faith. Indeed, in the accounts of their deaths, considerations of self and reputation were largely absent from the arguments that Eleazar and his compatriots made in defense of their embrace of martyrdom. In the place of pronouncements about the personal honor and glory their deaths would win for them, the Maccabean martyrs spoke instead of the necessity of demonstrating loyalty to the laws of their forefathers; of a desire to provide posterity with "an example of nobility" and "a precedent of valor;"[46] and of a belief that the suffering and death of a righteous individual can serve as a "ransom for sin" capable of assuaging the anger of God.[47] To be sure, the chroniclers of the Maccabean martyrdom tell us that these individuals were rewarded for yielding "up their bodies to suffering for the sake of religion."[48] However, this reward encompassed not only the admiration of mankind — the principal motivation for the heroic deeds of most Greco-Roman heroes — but the promise "of a divine portion"[49] in an eternal afterlife with God.

In addition to opening the heroic pantheon of the West to individuals who bore witness to their faith by sacrificing their lives, the Maccabean martyrdom established the bar against which all other religious (and in time national) martyrs would be judged. Further, the recounting of that martyrdom in Maccabees II and IV would serve as the principal literary model for the authors of all future martyr chronicles. As the Anchor Bible's translator of the Books of Maccabees, Jonathan A. Goldstein, notes, the accounts of the Maccabean martyrdom are:

> The direct source for the patterns that thereafter prevailed in Jewish and Christian literature [regarding martyrs]: the cheerful acceptance by the martyr of terrible pain rather than commit an act viewed by pagans as trivial; the dialogue between the martyr and his persecutors and tormentors; the vivid description of the torments; the martyr's persistent faith to the death;

the care to record both the anger and the admiration of the pagans as the tortures prove to be in vain; [and] the presentation of the martyr as an example to be followed by the rest of the faithful.[50]

Christians in particular were attracted to this Maccabean narrative of heroic martyrdom because they saw parallels between the plight of Eleazar and his compatriots and their own persecution at the hands of the Romans during the first three centuries of the Common Era. Church fathers, such as Gregory of Nazianz, John Chrysostom, Ambrose, and Augustine, regarded the Maccabees as "protomartyrs" and urged their flocks to emulate them when facing persecution. Indeed, the Books of Maccabees were not only incorporated into the canonical literature of the early Church, but the relics of Eleazar, Hannah and her sons were later displayed in the post-persecution Christian churches of Antioch, Constantinople, Milan, Rome, and Cologne.[51]

Christians were also drawn to "the extreme and wonderful suffering of the [Maccabean] martyrs,"[52] because their martyrdom appeared to prefigure the passion of Jesus of Nazareth. Just as the Maccabees believed their demise would earn both redemption for Israel and a "divine portion" for themselves, Jesus embraced his death in order to redeem humanity from sin and secure eternal life for those who would follow in his footsteps. For a great many Christians the lesson from both of these martyrdoms was quite clear — to embrace death in defense of one's faith was to win the acclamation of mankind, "the fame of pleasing God, and the prize of living for eternity."[53] And it is to these early Christian martyrs, eager for death and the glory that it would bring them, that we now turn.

Do This in Remembrance of Me: Jesus and the Birth of Christian Heroism

The man known to history as Jesus of Nazareth was probably born in 6 BCE into a respectable, albeit common, Jewish artisanal family. Jesus' physical appearance elicited no comments from his contemporaries, and, with the exception of one reference to his religious precocity at the age of twelve (Luke 2: 41–50), his youth and early manhood were equally non-descript. At the age of thirty, Christian tradition has it that Jesus joined the circle of an itinerant ascetic fire-eater named John the Baptist who preached an apocalyptic evangel of doom, damnation, and repentance. Following John's arrest and execution by Herod Antipas, Tetrarch of Galilee, Jesus embarked on his own career as a wandering holy man, preaching a gospel of personal piety, religious reform, love and forgiveness in the countryside, marketplaces, and synagogues of Judea. Over the course of this public ministry, which lasted no more than three years, Jesus acquired a reputation as a prophet and healer and attracted a motley following of Jewish and Gentile men, women and children, many of whom were considered godless and unclean. This ragtag "Jesus movement," coupled with Jesus' open disdain for what he regarded as a purely formalistic and hypocritical Jewish piety, aroused the ire of the religious and political authorities in Judea. In 30 CE, while celebrating Passover in Jerusalem, Jesus was arrested, tried for blasphemy and sedition, judged guilty of treason, and crucified under Roman law. In the aftermath of his death, belief in Jesus' resurrection from the dead became the focus of a new religion that developed and spread throughout the Roman Empire in the first three centuries of the Common Era.

With the exception of the story of his resurrection, there is little in the aforementioned biography of Jesus that would have set him apart as a hero in the first century Mediterranean world. As we have seen, Greco-Roman heroes were men who were nobly born, well-made, and divinely favored. They possessed extraordinary military, athletic, and/or intellectual abilities, were usually well-off, and sported resumes touting lifetimes of impressive achievements. In the case of Israel, even though Jewish heroes and heroines were more diverse in background and occupation than their Greco-Roman counterparts, they too tended to possess exceptional abilities and they also enjoyed the special favor of a powerful deity. Most importantly, all of these individuals — Gentile and Jew alike — enjoyed the respect of their compatriots, who showered them with honors both in life and after death.

On all of these counts, Jesus of Nazareth would have been found wanting. His family was common, his appearance unremarkable and his curriculum vita sparse. In the thirty-three years of his life, Jesus won no accolades for military or athletic prowess, left no body of scholarly work, and made no financial bequests to his countrymen. Aside from some sermons, parables, and cures that were later attributed to him, we have no first century physical evidence of Jesus' life at all; no writings, no inscriptions, and no monuments. While the Christian movement that grew up in the aftermath of Jesus' death claimed he was the son of God, the Jewish community in which he lived and died did not recognize him as either a Messiah or a divinely favored prophet. Indeed, the only laurels Jesus of Nazareth received during his brief life were a trial for treason, a crown of thorns, and a criminal's death on the cross.

The first Christians were well aware of the fact that the founder of their new religion was an unlikely candidate for either heroic or divine status. More to the point, as we will see below, they also knew that Jesus' message represented a repudiation of the Mediterranean culture of honor and shame on which the entire edifice of ancient heroism rested. As with Socrates and the Maccabean martyrs, however, Jesus was fortunate that the authors of his Gospels knew how to speak and write Greek, were steeped in the heroic literature of the Greco-Roman world, and were well-schooled in the conventions of classical rhetoric, particularly as it pertained to individuals regarded as worthy of a hero's laurels. In the hands of these "evangelists," the tragic tale of an impoverished, eccentric Jewish rabbi, tortured to death for treason and blasphemy, became the good news of a latter-day heroic *hemitheoi* sent by God to redeem mankind.

Indeed, as Gregory J. Riley and Jerome H. Neyrey have demonstrated in their works on the New Testament, one of the most striking features of the Gospels is how they transformed the biography of Jesus of Nazareth into that of a classical hero. As in the stories of Achilles, Hercules, and the other semi-divine champions of Greco-Roman mythology, Luke and Matthew present Jesus as the offspring of a union between a god and a virgin mother. Following Greek rhetorical conventions governing the recounting of a hero's life, these two evangelists also embellished their accounts of Jesus' childhood with all manner of signs and portents — the visit of the three Magi, Simeon's recognition of Jesus as the messiah during his circumcision, the young Christ holding court among the learned at twelve — that were intended to underscore his promise of future greatness. More evidence of Jesus' extraordinary nature is provided in the Gospels of Mark and John where readers are treated to accounts of him raising the dead, casting out demons, healing the blind and lame, changing water into wine, multiplying loaves and fishes, stilling storms, and walking on water. And just as the Homeric heroes were distinguished by the foes they challenged and bested, the narrators of the New Testament filled their Gospels with stories of Jesus doing battle with a host of enemies both mortal (the Pharisees, the Sanhedrin, Herod, Pilate) and divine (Satan and his minions).[54]

As for the shameful trial, torture and crucifixion of Jesus, the evangelists presented the execution of their heroic champion as a "noble" death that was divinely ordained, freely chosen and bravely met. The author of the Gospel of Matthew was particularly intent on presenting Jesus' passion in such a way as to demonstrate how it satisfied the classical criteria of a heroic demise, i.e., the ordeal was voluntary; benefited others; and was the death of a victor not a slave or victim. Matthew also embellished his account with a series of portents and prodigies that accompanied Jesus' death — the rending of the temple veil, the unleashing of earthquakes, the opening of tombs and raising of the dead — that the ancients would have interpreted as posthumous honors accorded by God to his son and champion. While not quite as dramatic as Matthew, the passion narratives of the other evangelists make it equally clear that the death of Jesus was not a cause for shame, but merely one more proof of his heroic and divine nature.[55]

Ironically, while the Jesus that emerged from the pages of the Gospels fits the classical profile of a hero, his "good news" represented a radical departure from all of the conventions by which heroes had been defined. As we have seen, to attain heroic status in the ancient Mediterranean world, an individual was expected to lay claim to this honor and win public acknowledgement of it by engaging successfully in a wide range of *agonistic* (competitive) behaviors that involved verbal and physical challenges, sexual aggression, lying, and even impiety. This heroic ethos applied not only to warriors and athletes, but to politicians, philanthropists, artists, and pedagogues who aspired to a hero's laurels. Even the pious and scrupulously honest martyrs that we have examined up to this point aggressively challenged their tormentors, accorded them no respect, spurned their offers of mercy, and died defiantly.

The ethos of Jesus of Nazareth departed markedly from this tradition of heroism. In the Sermon on the Mount (Matthew 5: 3–12) and the so-called Antitheses that followed it (Matthew 5: 21–48), Jesus forbade those who followed him from engaging in any of the behaviors deemed typical of the heroic individual. Instead of seeking public recognition and acclaim, Jesus called on his disciples to practice a private piety aimed at securing a heavenly berth for their eternal souls. Jesus also insisted that his followers foreswear violence, sexual lust, lying, and participation in the whole challenge-riposte culture of the Mediterranean world. Indeed, in the face of insult and injury, Christians were commanded to turn the other cheek (Matthew 5:39); share their belongings (Matthew 5: 40, 42); and love, bless, be good to, and pray for their enemies (Matthew 5: 44). Suffice it to say, in the first century of the Common Era anyone adhering to these precepts would have been "considered a weakling, a wimp, a worthless no-account who" could not "defend his honor, a person of whom one takes advantage, a man to be ashamed of."[56] In short, an individual who was not and could never be a hero.

Of course, Jesus' followers were not much interested in emulating the conduct of heroes past. As the adherents of a movement that believed the material world to be false, corrupt and fast approaching its end, the first Christians viewed the heroic quest for public honors and accolades as a futile exercise in empty and meaningless vanity. For devout Christians there was only one goal worth seeking and that was a place in heaven for eternity with Jesus and his divine father. And to attain this honor, Jesus' disciples believed a person needed to cultivate a profoundly personal relationship with God; renounce all purely formalistic displays of public piety; favor the spiritual over the material world; and live a life of service and self-sacrifice. For the members of the early Jesus movement, heroes were individuals who eagerly sought out and achieved such a "Christ-like" existence and, in so doing, secured for themselves the favor of God and his reward of eternal life after death.

Suffice it to say there was much about this Christian notion of heroism that was appealing to the inhabitants of the Mediterranean world. In a time when heroic honor was considered a limited commodity available only to a certain kind of person, Christianity held out the prospect that anyone — man or woman, Jew or Gentile, noble or commoner — could be adjudged a hero and enjoy all the perquisites attendant on that status. By acknowledging Jesus as the only begotten son of God and their spiritual father, Christians, no less than the *hemitheoi* of the past, could lay claim to a divine patron and parent. By embracing an ethos of personal piety, self-abnegation, charity, and forgiveness — an ethos which they believed to be divinely sanctioned — Christians could also lay claim to a lifestyle that was no less challenging and honorable than that of the traditional hero. And in making a good faith effort to follow in Jesus' footsteps while alive, Christians believed that they would be honored by their co-religionists in this life and by their God in the afterlife.

However, despite the fact that Christianity made possible a radical reconfiguration of the heroic ideal, early Christians still made a point of singling out from their ranks individuals that they regarded as extraordinary and worthy of respect, reverence, and emulation. These Christian heroes included both "protomartyrs," such as the Maccabees, as well as Jesus' family members, companions (e.g., Mary Magdalene), original apostles, and the principal proselytizer of his faith in the years following his crucifixion, Paul of Tarsus. In addition to these founding fathers and mothers, early Christians also lionized their comrades who were willing to offer up their lives in defense of the new faith. One of these martyred heroes was an elderly man by the name of Pionius.

Taking Up the Cross:
The Case of St. Pionius

In January 250 CE, against a backdrop of political unrest, barbarian invasions and a recent spell of famine, the Roman emperor Decius issued an edict ordering all citizens, save for those of the Jewish faith, to offer propitiatory sacrifices to the gods. This decree specifically singled out the Christian communities of the empire, ordering them to abjure their faith and make sacrifices before locally appointed commissioners, or face death. In late February of the same year, imperial commissioners in Smyrna, an ancient Greek city on the Aegean coast of present day Turkey, complied with Decius' decree by initiating a roundup of their community's Christian population with the aim of compelling them to participate in the city's Dionysia; a pagan celebration that coincided with the Jewish holiday of Purim and the yearly assizes (judicial sessions) of the Roman governor.

The majority of Smyrna's Christian population, including its bishop, cooperated with the commissioners and ate the roasted flesh of animals that were sacrificed in honor of Dionysus, his Olympian colleagues, and the official cult of the Roman emperor. A Christian elder named Pionius, however, and two of his companions, Sabina and Asclepiades, did not cooperate. Instead, they signified their intention to defy Decius' decree by fashioning three sets of woven chains and placing them around their necks in order to alert both the commissioners and the community-at-large that they were determined to be imprisoned, tried, and sentenced to death rather than abjure their faith. On the day of the Dionysia, Pionius and his colleagues were arrested, lead to Smyrna's forum and interrogated before a multitude that included both Greek and Jewish residents of the city. During this interrogation, Pionius acted as the advocate for himself and his colleagues and demonstrated both exceptional erudition and rhetorical skill. He referenced Homer, Deuteronomy and Proverbs in his comments to his fellow citizens, warned them about the impending end of the world, and displayed considerable courage in the face of the usual interrogatories and threats of torture and death.

In the face of Pionius' intransigence, Smyrna's authorities had no choice but to imprison him and his colleagues and await the arrival of the Roman governor who alone was empowered to render a verdict of death. While in prison, Pionius was visited by a great many Christians who sought his counsel, forgiveness for having lapsed from their faith out of fear, and intercession on their behalf with Christ when he entered heaven after his death. Even a considerable number of pagans paid Pionius a visit and pleaded with him to reconsider his position or pretend to make sacrifice. As in the case of Socrates and Eleazar, such pleadings were to no avail.

One final effort was made before the arrival of the Roman governor to compel Pionius and his companions to commit apostasy. They were alternately beaten, mocked, interrogated, and threatened. When these blandishments failed, a different tack was taken by a noted rhetorician and honored city father Rufinus — of whom more will be heard below — — who pleaded with Pionius to stop being a fool, show reason and choose life and the respect of his fellow citizens over an unnecessary death. Pionius rejected Rufinus' plea and justified his stand by invoking the example of a number of heroic pagan martyrs who had also been persecuted for their beliefs :

> Is this your rhetoric? Is this your literature? Even Socrates did not suffer thus from the Athenians. But now everyone is an Anytus and a Meletus. Were Socrates and Aristides and Anaxarchus and all the rest fools in your view because they practiced philosophy and justice and courage? [57]

On March 12, Pionius was brought before the Roman governor, Quintillian, who attempted to win his compliance to Decius' decree first through persuasion and then through a series of tortures that included hanging and tearing out his fingernails. These torments, however, were unsuccessful in breaking Pionius' spirit and Quintillian sentenced the Christian elder to be nailed to a gibbet and burnt alive. When this sentence was carried out, the chronicler of Pionius' martyrdom reported that the martyr gladly removed his clothes, eagerly stretched himself out on the cross, and, as the flames were rising around him, "pronounced his last Amen with a joyful countenance and said: 'Lord, receive my soul.'"[58] After the fire died down:

> Those of us who were present saw his body like that of an athlete in full array at the height of his powers. His ears were not distorted; his hair lay in order on the surface of his head; and his beard was full as though with the first blossom of hair. His face shone once again — wondrous grace! — so that the Christians were all the more confirmed in the faith, and those who had lost the faith returned dismayed with fearful consciences.[59]

In many respects, the foregoing account of the trials, tribulations, and terrible death of St. Pionius is typical of the heroic martyrologies of the early Christian Church. Like the Maccabean protomartyrs before him, Pionius is confronted with a clear choice — abjure your faith by eating the flesh of a pagan sacrifice or die. Rather than renounce his faith, Pionius openly embraces death, engages in a spirited and learned exchange with his persecutors, turns aside all offers of compromise, gladly endures a variety of gruesome tortures, and dies exceptionally well. In return for this extraordinary act of self-sacrifice, we are told by Pionius' admiring biographer that he achieved "victory in the great combat" with Satan, passed "through the narrow gate into the broad, great light" of heaven, inspired the faithful, and struck fear in the hearts of "those [Christians] who had lost the faith."[60]

Aside from reiterating the essential patterns of Judeo-Christian martyrologies, however, the narrative of St. Pionius' martyrdom also reveals much that was distinctive about the heroic martyrs of the early Church. A case in point is the exchange between Pionius and one of his pagan interlocutors, the rhetorician Claudius Rufinus. One of Smyrna's most honored citizens, Rufinus met all the criteria of a classical Greco-Roman hero. He was the scion of a well-respected family of scholars; a sophist of exceptional learning who had been granted an exemption from all local taxes and duties by the emperor; the elected general of Smyrna's citizen militia; and a generous benefactor who built and maintained public buildings at great personal expense. In recognition of his intellectual abilities and extraordinary civic engagement, the citizens of Smyrna showered Rufinus with honors. Coins were struck that acknowledged his good standing in the eyes of the emperor, a large clientele accompanied him on his outings in the city, he was acclaimed in the theater and at other public events, he was free of tax and service obligations, and his death would be honored with a public funeral, commemorative games and a lavish tomb. In the eyes of a man like Rufinus, Pionius' eagerness to die rather than honor the gods and the emperor was an incomprehensible repudiation of personal honor and civic virtue, as well as a foolish obstinate act.[61]

For Pionius, on the other hand, everything about Rufinus' life was empty vainglory. As his comments make clear in the record of his trial, Pionius was convinced the end of the world was near and that the only activity worthy of a Christian's attention in the time before this event was prayer, meditation and a Christ-like life. Only spiritual activity aimed at establishing a communion with Jesus and his divine father could secure both immortality and an honored place at the court of Christ in the world after death. Securing honor and glory in the material world, a world teetering on the edge of destruction, was both a waste of time and a monumental act of sinful hubris.

Considerations of Armageddon to the side, however, we also know that Pionius was unmoved by the reproofs of a pagan grandee like Rufinus because he was intent on following in the footsteps of another Smyrnan who he regarded as a true model of Christian heroism. That individual was St. Polycarp, a second century bishop of Smyrna and martyr for the faith (died 155 CE) who, while alive, was noted for his erudition, rhetorical brilliance, Christ-like patience and charity, and unstinting opposition to heresy and apostasy. Pionius became aware of Polycarp during his youth when he served as one of the copyists and distributors of a Greek text that described the particulars of his martyrdom. This account deeply moved Pionius and sparked in him a desire to emulate Polycarp in "the hope that the Lord Jesus" might gather him "too into the company of his elect in the kingdom of heaven."[62] Consequently, over the course of his life, Pionious also became a noted preacher, teacher and rhetorician, a fervent opponent of heretics and apostates, and an elder of the Smyrnan church. When he was arrested on February 23 — the same day that Polycarp had been burned to death ninety-five years earlier — Pionius was offered the chance to imitate not only the life of his hero, but his death as well. As we have seen, it was an offer he could not refuse.

Why this was so resides in the fact that for Pionius and his co-religionists "the most excellent Christians ... were the Christians whom pagans put to death."[63] Polycarp and others like him, who had chosen to die rather than succumb to pagan intimidation, were revered above all other Christian heroes because they were seen as most closely following in the footsteps of Jesus. Like the founder of their faith, these individuals voluntarily embraced death for the benefit of mankind, endured their torments bravely, and died well. Consequently, Christians regarded their martyrs as heroic "prizefighters," athletic champions, and unconquered warriors who were honored by God for their suffering with a complete remission of their sins, immediate entry into paradise, and an honored place at the right hand of Jesus.[64]

In addition to these spiritual laurels, those who chose the path of the martyr could anticipate a full measure of fame and deathless glory in the material world as well. Because Christians believed that martyrs enjoyed immediate access to paradise and a close proximity to Christ, they also assumed these individuals could intercede with the heavenly powers to obtain not only forgiveness of sins, but also cures for diseases, and respites from untimely deaths. Consequently, Christian martyrs acquired considerable clientele both in life and after death. As Tertullian noted, "no sooner has anyone put on bonds than adulterers beset him, fornicators gain access, prayers echo round him, and pools of tears from polluted sinners soak him."[65] This was certainly the case with Pionius, who, as we have seen, was besieged in prison by Christian petitioners seeking absolution for their sins.

After their deaths, Pionius and his associates became the "powerful dead" of the Christian Church, and latter day heroic cults grew up around their remains and/or places of interment. Just as the shades of these individuals were believed capable of securing their clients a place in heaven, so too were their bodies considered potent talismans that could ward off evil, restore health, and insure good fortune. This belief that power remained in the remnants of a martyr's corpse led the post-persecution Church to exhume, break up, and distribute the body parts of its martyred heroes to Christian communities throughout the empire. Over time, these relics of bone and skin would be adorned with silks and encrusted with jewels, churches and cathedrals would be constructed to house them, and rich bequests would be made to honor the memories of their former owners. In taking these actions, the early Church affirmed that in this life as well as the next its sainted martyrs occupied the apex of the Christian heroic pantheon.

From Criminals to Saints: The Triumph of Heroic Martyrdom

We do not know the exact number of Christians who were martyred during the first three and a half centuries of the Common Era. Whether they numbered in the thousands or the hundreds of thousands is impossible to know because of the paucity of historical evidence available to us. Most Christians who died in the persecutions of Nero and his successors were illiterate and undistinguished. Among those who could write, only a handful left behind personal accounts of their lives and final days. And while the churches of the western and eastern Roman Empires compiled hundreds of *Acta Martyrum* (*Acts of the Martyrs*) in the fourth and fifth centuries, which were ostensibly based on eyewitness reports, these chronicles were heavily embellished and followed a stereotypical narrative pattern that casts doubt on their authenticity.[66]

Whatever the actual numbers of Christian martyrs, their example made a great impression on the adherents of the early Church. The extraordinary bravery of these individuals in the face of torture and death reminded Christians of the self-sacrifice of Jesus, and their eagerness to die appeared to confirm the Christian belief that for the faithful, death was merely a gateway to paradise. Indeed, the apparent rewards of martyrdom — immediate access to heaven, a place in the inner circle of Christ, and the esteem and reverence of the living — were so attractive that a great many Christians sought out arrest and execution; a state of affairs that caused considerable consternation among Church fathers worried that such voluntarism might devolve into a form of suicide.[67]

Even pagans were often impressed by the steadfastness of the Church's martyrs, though they tended to perceive the actions of these individuals as representative of an irrational Christian passion for death. As the Church grew and popular misconceptions about its religious practices were dispelled, many pagans began to feel not only sympathy but admiration for Christians who were willing to die rather than renounce their faith. This tendency was only strengthened by Constantine's legalization of Christianity in the early fourth century, and the appearance of hundreds of martyrologies that represented martyrs not as hapless victims but as heroic athletes and warriors who accepted suffering "on their own accord for the sake of fame and glory."[68]

By the time Christianity becomes the official state religion of the Western and Eastern Roman Empires (380 CE), historical events — Socrates' trial, the Maccabean ordeal, the persecution of the early Church — coupled with a rich apologist literature — Plato, Jason of Cyrene, Tertullian — had succeeded in winning acceptance for the idea that martyrdom in defense of one's principles, national identity, and/or religion was an act worthy of a hero's laurels. Christians in particular were inclined to view their martyrs as heroes of the first rank, and, by the fifth century CE, the reputations of the Church's martyred men and women was so great that Theodoret, Bishop of Cyrrhus, a Syrian city near the present day Turkish border, felt justified in writing that:

> The philosophers and the orators have fallen into oblivion; the masses do not even know the names of the emperors and their generals; but everyone knows the names of the martyrs better than those of their most intimate friends.[69]

While this boast was something of an exaggeration, it nevertheless underscored the honored place the martyr would now occupy in a Western heroic tradition under Christian management. Indeed, in the future Christian kingdoms and empires that would supplant the pagan imperium of Rome, no one would question the heroism of individuals who willingly offered up their lives in the defense and furtherance of a just cause.[70]

Finally, by elevating the martyr to the forefront of the Western heroic pantheon, Christianity was also introducing a new set of expectations with regard to the behavior of more conventional hero types. While extraordinary ability and bravery in battle, on the playing field, and at the prow of a ship would continue to be grounds for awarding an individual the status of a hero, heroic "Christian" warriors, athletes, explorers, and intellectuals would also be expected to exhibit some of the traits of those saintly men and women who had offered up their lives in defense of Holy Mother Church. These characteristics included not only fearlessness and bravery, but also selflessness, charity, a deep personal piety, and a disregard for the honors and accolades of the material world. As we will see, the attainment of this Christian heroic ideal — at once sacred and profane — would preoccupy the princes, prelates, and knights of the medieval world for the next thousand years.

4

"Creatures of a Day"
The Hero as Athlete

Creatures of a day! What is a man? What is he not? A dream of a shadow is our mortal being. But when there comes to men a gleam of splendor given of Heaven, then rests on them a light of glory and blessed are their days.

— Pindar: *Pythian 8.* 95–7

The race of men is one thing, that of the gods, is another. There is a total difference in power, so that we are nothing — while the bronze heaven remains the gods' secure seat forever. But, nevertheless — we can become something like the gods, through excellence — excellence of mind or of body; even if we don't know from day to day — or night to night — what finish line fate has marked for us to run.[1]

— Pindar: *Nemean 6.* 1–7

One can get some sense of what it meant to be one of Pindar's athletic heroes, agleam in the "light of glory," by watching the chariot race in William Wyler's 1959 film version of Lew Wallace's novel, *Ben Hur: A Tale of the Christ*. In this memorable scene, the film's principal protagonists, Messala and Judah Ben Hur, confront each other for the last time in a Jerusalem hippodrome as contestants in a racing competition between nine charioteers representing cities and provinces from every corner of the Roman Empire. The ensuing contest takes up only eleven minutes of film but in that brief time span the viewer is treated to a realistic and breathtaking recreation of an ancient chariot race replete with throngs of cheering spectators, crashing chariots, trampled bystanders, and mortally injured drivers. At the end of this melee, the victorious Judah Ben Hur is crowned with a laurel of victory by an unctuous Pontius Pilate who, in the name of the divine emperor Tiberius, pronounces him the "one true God" of the race's ecstatic and worshipful spectators.

While there is much about Wyler's cinematic reimagining of the ancient world that is wrong — there were no hippodromes in the vicinity of Jerusalem; the emperor Tiberius was never deified either in life or death by the Roman Senate; and no pagan procurator would ever have haled a living mortal the "one true god" — his racing scene does afford the viewer a fairly accurate glimpse of Greco-Roman athletic culture. Save for Jerusalem, coliseums and hippodromes were a common feature of most Greek and Roman population centers, and large audiences of devoted, even fanatical sports enthusiasts flocked to these venues to see a wide range of athletic activities. These ancient sporting events included not only chariot racing, but horse and foot races; jumping; javelin and discus throwing; wrestling; boxing; and a brutal no-holds barred kind of "ultimate fighting" match called *pankration*. As Wyler's race scene also makes clear, these athletic competitions were conducted without recourse to the rules that govern contemporary sporting events, and, with the exception of certain kinds of Roman gladiatorial combat, team sports were completely absent from the ancient arena. Indeed, the sports of antiquity were spirited, often violent contests between individual athletes intent on proving themselves first and best in whatever sport they chose to compete.

Like the charioteers in *Ben-Hur*, these ancient athletes haled from all corners of the Mediterranean world and were representative of every social class, income bracket, and occupation. With few exceptions, these individuals were male professionals who were dedicated to attaining excellence and preeminence in their chosen sport or sports. Supported by wealthy patrons, city governments, or family incomes, these sportsmen trained from early childhood to develop the strength, stamina, and skills necessary to compete in and win local athletic contests, annual sporting events in large cities such as Athens, and, ultimately, the *periodos*, or circuit of "crown" games held in Greece at Olympia, Delphi, Corinth, and Nemea.[2]

Aside from a love of competition, athletes entered these different games because they offered a rich array of prizes to their victors. These awards ranged from leather coats and livestock in the more modest local games to precious metals and large quantities of costly olive oil in the athletic festivals of urban centers like Thebes, Megara, Ephesus or Pergamum. All of these prizes paled, however, before those which were given to the *periodoniki*, or "winners of the circuit games" of mainland Greece. Indeed, to be victorious in the Pythian, Isthmian, Nemean, and especially the Olympic contests was to be acknowledged a champion without parallel. And while these crown game champions may not have been declared "one true" gods, they were showered with laurels of victory, poems of praise, commemorative statues, and honors from their home communities such as triumphal parades, cash prizes, a lifetime of free meals, reserved seats in amphitheaters, and high civic offices. In some cases, these *periodoniki* were even regarded as *theios aner*, "godlike men," and honored with the cult of a hero after death.

In the following pages, we will be addressing these heroized champions of the Greek crown games. Neither dealers in death nor doomed proselytes, these "godlike" athletes were passionate about life and intent on achieving within its mortal coil a glorious moment of uncontested and unparalleled excellence through the *agones*, the "struggles," of the *periodos* contests. How these "creatures of a day" achieved this transcendent moment, what it meant to the athletes seeking it and the fans cheering them on to victory, and how this quest for personal excellence on the playing field influenced the history of the heroic ideal and the Western civilizing process are the questions to which we will now turn.

The Peculiarity of Greek Athletics

Sports in ancient Greece were regularly recurring physical contests between individuals. They included running events — sprint, distance, and *hoplite*, or races in armor; field events — discus, long jump, and javelin; combat events — wrestling, boxing, and pankration; and equestrian events — chariot and mounted horse races. What differentiated these athletic competitions from the sporting activities of other Mediterranean civilizations was the fact that they were ongoing — in some cases centuries-long — affairs that were regulated and held at specific times of the year throughout the Greek mainland, islands and colonies. The evidence that we have of wrestling, boxing, racing, and other kinds of athletic activity in Mesopotamia, Egypt, and Crete does not indicate that these sports were part of any formal recurring competitions. Even among the Romans, who were certainly familiar with Greek athletics and often staged Greek style games, sports were periodic activities that citizens engaged in for physical exercise or popular entertainment.[3]

Why these competitive sports events were found in Greece and not elsewhere remains a question that is still in search of a definitive answer. Many have argued that these contests were important to the Greeks because they were a central part of their religious life. All Greek sporting events, for example, were linked to religious festivals that celebrated and worshipped one or more gods. In the case of the *periodos* games, Olympia and Nemea were dedicated to Zeus, the Pythian contests at Delphi honored Apollo, and the Isthmian competitions at Corinth were sacred to Poseidon. Greek sporting events were also held in the vicinity of a temple or sacred sanctuary, sacrificial rites marked their beginning and end, and the various laurels of victory awarded to their winners were cut from trees or plants grown in groves dedicated to their patron deities.

While there definitely appears to have been a connection between Greek athletics and religion, there is nothing to indicate that this linkage was either peculiar to Greece or the principal impetus behind the Greek love of competitive sports. Athletic activity of one kind or another was often a part of the sacred cult practices of other Mediterranean cultures, and there is no evidence that Greeks flocked to their games out of any deep-felt religious fervor. Indeed, as Mark Golden notes, while sacred festivals and sacrifices at Greek sporting events may appear extremely religious from our point of view, there was really nothing exceptional about such practices "in a society in which every part of life was pervaded by cult activity and invocations of the gods."[4]

Warfare is another explanation that is often given for Greek competitive athletics. From the Archaic period through the rise of Macedon, raids, Persian aggression and city state conflicts were a near constant of Greek life. Survival in such an environment required the *poleis* to develop ways of ensuring that their citizens were physically fit and well schooled in the principles of combat. Greek sports, with their emphasis on stamina in running, equestrian proficiency, javelin throwing and brutal hand-to-hand fighting, were certainly well suited to the achievement of these ends. [5]

Nevertheless, while sports must have played some role in the military training programs of the Greek city states, it is doubtful that either the provenance or the purpose of these events was rooted in warfare. Literary evidence we have from this period indicates that from Homer to Plato Greeks made a clear distinction between competitive sports and military exercises. The games immortalized in both the *Iliad* and the *Odyssey*, for example, were sporting events between individuals for the purpose of honoring the dead, entertainment and demonstrating athletic excellence. Indeed, Epeius, one of the champions in the boxing contests of Achilles' funeral games for Patroclus, makes a point of distinguishing between warfare and sport when he notes:

I think no other here will take the mule [the prize of the contest] by whipping me. I'm best, I don't mind saying. Enough to admit I'm second-rate at war; no man can be a master in everything."[6]

This distinction between athletic ability and military prowess was further underscored by those writing in the centuries after Homer. Living in a world where warfare had shifted from hand-to-hand combat to clashes between massed, heavily armed citizen armies, Euripides dismissed the military usefulness of Greek athletics altogether, noting in his play *Autolycos* that no athlete could "fight with the enemy discus in hand or drive out their ancestral foe by striking through the shields with their hands. No one who stands near steel is so stupid."[7] Plato concurred, urging his compatriots to adopt new kinds of sporting events that would actually simulate combat.[8]

Religion and warfare to the side, perhaps the best explanation for the Greek attachment to competitive sports is that which was offered by Jakob Burckhardt over a century ago. Writing about the cultural history of ancient Greece, Burckhardt concluded that the wellspring of Greek creativity in art, literature, science, philosophy, and athletics could be attributed to a national character that drove the Greeks to compete with one another. While the notion that different nationalities have distinct character traits is highly problematic — particularly in light of the racist and genocidal policies that have been associated with the idea — most scholars of ancient Greece would concur that there were few areas of Greek public life that did not involve some kind of contest. Public building programs and religious festivals were underwritten by politicians and wealthy aristocrats vying against one another for the approbation of their fellow citizens. Artists and sculptors competed to win commissions to create the friezes and statues that graced the temples, baths and agoras of Greek cities. Plays and poetry were penned by dramatists and poets competing in yearly contests held throughout Greece. And musicians often composed songs for prize competitions that were held in tandem with festivals that also featured athletic events.

Why the Greeks were so competitive is another one of those questions for which there is no readily apparent answer. Pseudo-scientific notions of a competitive "national character" to the side, formal competitions appear to have served a number of useful functions in Greek society. These contests distinguished Greeks from non–Greeks, provided the communities that hosted them with a source of civic identity, pride, entertainment, and revenue, and unleashed individual creative energies.

Greek athletic contests certainly served all of these different functions. As we have already noted, these events were quite unique in the ancient world and they differentiated Greeks from other neighboring peoples. Competitive sports were also an integral part of the festivals that city states sponsored to honor their patron deities, celebrate their civic identities, and foster patriotism among their citizens. These contests were enormously lucrative enterprises as well, bringing in large numbers of participants and spectators who patronized a sponsoring community's local temples, shrines, victualers, innkeepers, craftsmen, artists, and prostitutes.[9]

Finally, competitive sports also acted as a kind of *cursus honorum*, or "ladder of honor," that fostered athletic excellence among the aspiring athletes of the Greek city states and their colonies. The first rung of this ladder was the local contest, which provided a training and testing ground, as well as a measure of financial support, for all young men intent on pursuing an athletic career.[10] Champions of these local sporting events moved up the ladder to compete in the prestigious and lucrative *chremata*, or "money" games, sponsored by powerful city states like Athens and Sparta. A victory in these contests not only garnered an athlete rich prizes but also established him as a sportsman worthy of note. Indeed, it was these seasoned athletes, these champions of both local contests and prize competitions who competed in the panhellenic circuit games of the Peloponnese — the final rung in the athletic *cursus honorum* of the Greek-speaking world. Out of these four contests came the best of the best, the champions without peer deemed worthy of honor in life and the status of a hero in death.

The Crown Games and Their Participants

Why of all the thousands of athletic contests held throughout the Greek-speaking world were the *periodos* games so prestigious? In part, their preeminence was due to their venerability. Not only were these four contests the most ancient of Greek sporting events, but they were all associated with first tier Olympian deities and much revered human heroes. This was certainly true of the most important of these contests, the Olympic games, which were held at the sanctuary of Olympian Zeus on the Alpheius and Cladeus rivers southeast of Elis in the northwest Peloponnesus. Whether these Olympian contests had their beginnings in the Bronze Age — as some archaeological evidence suggests — or actually began in 776 BCE— the traditional date given by Hippias of Elis for the first competition held at this site — they held pride of place as the first of the panhellenic crown games. Olympia's luster was further burnished by its association with a number of mythical founders that included Zeus, his half-human son, Heracles, and the legendary charioteer, king of Pisa, and ruler of the Peloponnese, the hero Pelops.

While not as prestigious as the Olympian games, the other three circuit contests were also distinguished from other athletic competitions by dint of their age and mythical origins. Established in 586 BCE, the Pythian games at Delphi were reputed to have been founded by Apollo to celebrate his triumph over the dragon Python. The Isthmian games of Corinth, which were founded in 582 BCE, claimed Theseus, the half-human son of Poseidon and legendary hero king of Athens, as their founder. And the Nemean contests, which were initiated in 573 BCE, attributed their origin to Heracles, who reputedly celebrated his capture of the Nemean Lion by establishing games at this site.[11]

Whatever the actual dates or mythical origins of these competitions, the *periodos* games recurred on a regular basis at specified times of the year for a millennium. Like clockwork, the Olympian and Pythian games were held every four years, separated from one another by the Isthmian and Nemean contests that were held every two years. An example of what this cycle looked like is reproduced below[12]:

Festival	Frequency	Time of Year
Olympics	Four Years	July/August 480
Nemean	Two Years	August/September 479
Isthmian	Two Years	April/May or June/July 478
Pythian	Four Years	July/August 478

Festival	Frequency	Time of Year
Nemean	Two Years	August/September 477
Isthmian	Two Years	April/May or June/July 476
Olympics	Four Years	July/August 476

The dependable regularity of these games, in tandem with their longevity and prestigious provenance, made them a lodestone for the Greek-speaking world's athletes and sports aficionados. Whatever the changing fortunes of the Greek city states, or the kingdoms and empires that dominated them, for over a thousand years these crown contests were a seemingly permanent fixture in the firmament of Hellenic athletic culture. As such, professional sportsmen and the fans that followed their careers could not help but take note of these games and, whenever possible, participate in them.

Another factor that contributed to the luster of these contests was their panhellenism. Whereas participation in many of the local games and some of the big prize competitions was limited to the inhabitants of a particular city and its allies, the *periodos* were open to any citizen of a Greek city state, and, by the fourth century BCE, to all Greek speaking individuals as well. This panhellenism was made possible by an *ekecheiria*, or truce, that was observed by all of the major Greek urban centers. Under the terms of this truce, the territories of the cities holding the crown games were declared inviolate for a period of time before and after the competitions they were sponsoring, and safe passage was guaranteed for all spectators and competitors traveling to and from these locales. While there were periodic violations of these truces — and the incessant warfare of the Greek city states was unaffected by them — they were largely respected by the different *poleis* and this made it possible for the circuit games to be truly international events that brought together athletic champions and sports enthusiasts from throughout the Hellenic world.

Not surprisingly, the fact that these games were open and accessible to all Greek speaking individuals made the *periodos* irresistible to the aficionados of ancient athletics. Spectators were drawn to these events because they offered an unparalleled opportunity to witness displays of extraordinary strength and skill in running, javelin and discus throwing, wrestling, boxing, and horse racing by the best sportsmen of Greece, Asia Minor, Africa, and western Europe. Athletes competed in these games because they afforded them the chance to test their mettle against peers from all parts of the Greco-Roman world, and to acquire a crown of victory that designated them as *world* champions in the sports of their choice. Indeed, for sportsmen the most alluring aspect of these circuit games was the prospect of besting the best before an international audience that would spread the news of their victory — and with it their renown — to the four corners of the Mediterranean.

As we have already noted, the athletic competitors in these crown games were professionals who were representative of all the different city states, social classes and occupations of the Greek world. Given the amount of time and expense involved in training and traveling to the crown contests, as well as the requirement at Olympia that athletes spend thirty days on the site before the competitions began, a great many of these competitors were aristocrats. This was certainly true of those competing in *periodos* equestrian events because only individuals with considerable wealth could afford to assemble and maintain the stables of horses necessary for these contests. Indeed, as the literary evidence attests, kings and tyrants such as Hieron of Syracuse, Theron of Akragas, Anaxilas of Rhegium, and Alcibiades of Athens were among the many prominent victors of horse races at Olympia (and in the case of Hieron, Pythia and Nemea as well).

While the wealthy were well represented at the crown games, there were also competitors who haled from non-aristocratic families and occupations. The first Olympic victor, Koroibos of Elis, for example, was reputed to be a cook. Other working class *periodos* champions included a goatherd, Polymestor of Meletus, who won the boys' 200 meter race at Olympia in 596 BCE; a cowherd, Melesias of Braca in North Africa, who won the Olympic wrestling contest in 460 BCE; and a farmer, Glaukos of Karystos, who won the boxing crown of all four games in 520 BCE. How these individuals, and others like them, were able to find the time and the resources to train and travel to these contests remains an open question. Legend tells us that Polymestor of Meletus practiced his running by racing rabbits and that Melesias of Braca wrestled the bulls in the cow herds that he tended. Less colorful competitors from among the common folk probably relied on prizes from local games and the *chremata* for support, or public funds that city councils made available for the training and maintenance of promising athletes. It is also possible that many localities followed the example of the people of Argos who pooled their money in 480 BCE in order to send a community chariot contestant to Olympia (who was also victorious in that event).[13]

The thousands of spectators who flocked to the circuit games were as diverse a lot as the athletes they came to see. These ancient sports fans haled from every corner of the Mediterranean basin and were representative of every social class and occupation. Kings, tyrants, aristocrats, and, in Roman times, even emperors rubbed elbows with artisans, farmers, herdsmen, prostitutes, unmarried women, priests, soothsayers, augurs, magicians, and thieves. Many of these people were drawn to the games because they saw them as an opportunity to make a religious pilgrimage or to earn some money catering to the many needs and desires of festival attendees. Some just came to participate in a weeklong party. The majority, however, attended these games because they wished to experience the "spontaneous, elementary, unreflective yet pleasurable excitement"[14] that occurs when watching superb sportsmen competing with one another for a crown of victory. And it was this desire by thousands of Greeks — and a great many non–Greeks as well — to share in the experience of these athletes, as well as to enjoy vicariously the thrill that victory would bring them, which ultimately made the *periodos* the premier sporting events of the ancient world.

Creatures of a Day: The Heroization of the Circuit Champion

We have noted that the athletes of the circuit games were professionals who participated in sports for the purpose of winning rich prizes. In the case of the crown competitions, however, the only prizes to be won were wreaths of victory — olive at Olympia, laurel at Delphi, celery at Nemea, and pine at Isthmia — which designated the winner a world-class champion in whatever sporting event he competed in and won. What made these simple circlets of wood and leaves the most coveted prizes in ancient athletics was the knowledge that a great many other honors and material benefits followed in their wake. These ancillary prizes, which were bestowed on a champion by his home community, patrons, and family, included:

- A victory procession known as the *eiselasis* in which the champion was borne into his city by chariot clad in a saffron colored or purple tunic known as the *xystis*. During this parade, the victorious athlete's ecstatic fans would shower him with garlands, ribbons (*tainiai*), leaves and fruit (*phyllobolia*).
- An *epinician* or victory ode;
- The privilege of lifelong feasting (*sitesis*) at the public expense in the *prytaneion*, or town hall of a city;
- Special seats of honor in the theater and games;
- Exemption from duties and taxes;
- Victor statues and commemorative coins (and if victorious at Olympia, a statue of oneself in the sanctuary of Zeus); and
- A special position of honor in military campaigns.

In addition to these parades, poems, and special privileges, a crown game champion might also be honored with a hero cult after his death.[15]

As we noted in our earlier discussion of the *hemitheoi*, prior to the Hellenistic period these hero cults were established to honor the semi-divine offspring of the gods, as well as to placate the potent shades of extraordinary individuals who had benefited their communities in life, e.g., city founders, lawgivers, and great warriors. The institution of such a cult was one of the highest honors a human being could receive because it secured for its recipient immortality, a privileged place in the underworld, and respect among the living for the hero's surviving family and descendants. In return for these benefits, the shades of heroized individuals were expected to help and protect the communities that venerated them. Given the benefits and responsibilities associated with such cults — as well as the time, trouble and expense to maintain them — their establishment often required oracular sanctions, official decrees of approval by city assemblies, and a commitment by a wealthy family or group of families to support the festivals, sacrifices, and rites necessary to honor the heroic individual.

Renowned as they were, the *periodoniki* were by no means guaranteed the honor of one of these hero cults. Milo of Kroton, a sixth century wrestler and legendary strongman, is a case in point. Over the course of his life, Milo won the wrestling crown at Olympia six times — once as a boy — seven times at Pythia, ten at Isthmia, and nine at Nemea. His feats of prowess outside of the arena were equally impressive. Challengers were unable to knock him off a greased discus, he could snap cords tied around his head by holding his breath, and his little finger could not be pried loose once his fist was clenched. This extraordinary strength was also accompanied by an equally legendary appetite. Milo reputedly consumed twenty pounds of meat a day, an equal amount of bread, and eight quarts of wine. On one occasion, he was said to have carried a bull the length of a stadium, after which he butchered the animal and ate it. Nevertheless, despite his athletic achievements, remarkable strength, and exceptional capacity for food and drink, Milo was never honored with a hero cult after his death.[16]

This was not so with the fifth century boxer Theogenes of Thasos. The winner of as many as 1400 crowns of victory, Theogenes won two at Olympia in both boxing and *pankration*, three at Pythia (one without competition), and nine each at Nemea and Isthmia. The undefeated boxing champion of the Greek world for twenty-two years, Theogenes also won the *dolichos*, or long race, at Argos and Phthia in Thessaly. Like Milo, Theogenes was also renowned for his appetite — it was said that he could eat a whole ox easily — and his strength — as a boy he was reputed to have carried a bronze statue from the agora of Thasos to his home. Unlike Milo, however, Theogenes' shade proved potent enough after his death to insure that his fellow Thasians would institute a hero cult in his honor.

As recounted by the second century CE travel writer, Pausanias, after Theogenes' death, an enemy vandalized the statue that the Thasians had erected to commemorate his many athletic triumphs. When the statue fell on the vandal and killed him, his family brought charges against it, won their case in court, and had the offending bronze thrown into the sea. Following this action, however:

> A famine beset the Thasians, and they sent envoys to Delphi, where Apollo instructed them to recall their exiles. They did so, but there was still no end to the famine. They sent to the Pythia a second time and said that although they had followed the instructions, the wrath of the gods still was upon them. The Pythia responded, "You did not remember your great Theogenes."[17]

Luckily for the Thasians, a fisherman was able to retrieve Theogenes' statue, which was re-erected in its former position. A hero cult was also instituted to honor the spirit of the offended athlete, the famine ended, and Theogenes was thereafter worshipped by both Thasians and others as a healing deity.[18]

The reason why some *periodoniki* were honored with hero cults and others were not is, like so much else in the history of Greek athletics, one of those questions that lack a definitive answer. Despite their strength, skill, and renown, many crown game champions appear to have been regarded as arrogant oafs unworthy of the semi-divine status that a hero cult would confer on them. This appears to have been the case with Milo whose ignominious death revealed both hubris and a lack of judgment. Coming across a felled tree that was partially split and held open by wedges, Milo is reputed to have tried to pull the trunk apart only to have the wedges fall out and the tree snap shut on his hands. Helpless and "as large and senseless a victim as the bull he had once consumed,"[19] Milo was devoured that night by a pack of wolves.

The example of Milo and other cultless *periodoniki* like him has led many scholars to conclude that athletic accomplishments alone were not sufficient to warrant the establishment of a hero cult for an individual. Rather, a heroized athlete was someone who had distinguished himself not only on the playing field, but also in other areas of activity such as war or administration. Absent such non-athletic achievements, the only other way for a sportsman to acquire a hero cult appears to have been through an oracular pronouncement in favor of such an honor or some kind of miracle attributed to an object that was associated with him.[20]

While this question of why some *periodoniki* enjoyed posthumous cults while others did not is a fascinating one, it obscures the fact that in all likelihood crown game champions were regarded as heroes while they were alive, and enjoyed this status because of their athletic achievements. Hero cult or not, the other honors that were showered on these individuals were a clear indication of how highly they were regarded by their countrymen and fans. The *eiselasis* or victory parade, for example, with its chariot and special robes, was an honor normally reserved for kings. Similarly, garlands, ribbons, leaves, and fruit were only showered on images of gods, military victors, great statesmen, and, according to legend, heroes such as Jason, Orestes, and Theseus. *Sitesis* or the right to lifelong feasting at the public expense, along with special seats at performances and games, and exemptions from taxes and duties, were exceptional honors visited only on individuals who had rendered extraordinary service to their communities. Monumental statues were usually erected to honor gods and heroes. And being accorded a special position in the front lines of a city's army was to be put on the same footing as kings and generals, as well as to be given an additional opportunity to achieve further glory in battle.[21]

Epinicians, or victory odes, which were penned for *periodoniki* between the end of the sixth and the middle of the fifth centuries BCE, provide additional evidence that these athletic champions were regarded as heroic figures in their own right while alive. Commissioned by an athlete or someone on his behalf to celebrate his success in the circuit games, these odes were choral poems set to music and performed at the victory party of the champion. Though most of these odes are lost to us, a considerable number of the *epinicians* penned by Pindar of Thebes survived and these attest to the heroic stature enjoyed by crown game victors.

In Pindar's extant odes, the listener is reminded that human beings are mortal, inconsequential, and little more than "a dream of a shadow."[22] In other refrains of his poems, however, Pindar also noted that on rare occasions some individuals were capable of achieving an excellence of mind or body that made them "something like the gods;"[23] and he underscored this point by including in his odes stories of ancient heroes whose deeds had secured them a place among the immortals. Aside from demonstrating that it was possible for mortals to be godlike, Pindar also inserted these heroic tales in order to draw parallels between the athletes honored by his odes and the heroes of old. Thus in *Olympian* 1, the *epinician* celebrating the equestrian victory of Hieron, tyrant of Syracuse, the victor is likened to the legendary charioteer and lord of the Peloponnesus, Pelops; in *Nemean* 10, the wrestler Theaius of Argos receives favorable comparison to Castor and Pollux; and in *Isthmian* 4 parallels are drawn between Heracles and the winner of the *pankration*, Melissus of Thebes. In these odes, and others like them, it is evident that Pindar and his audiences were quite comfortable with the idea of the crown game champion as a heroic figure.

These *epinicians* may have functioned as a kind of surrogate hero cult as well. As Pindar notes in his poem *Pythian* 3:

> We know of Nestor and Lykian Sarpedon, still the talk of men, from such echoing verses as wise craftsmen constructed. Excellence endures in glorious songs for a long time. But few can win them easily.[24]

Crown game champions were obviously among the "few" Pindar believed could win such enduring glory, and he made it clear in his odes that his intent in writing them was to insure that his patrons' renown would be recalled long after their deaths. Indeed, as David Young notes in his work on the Olympian Games, these *epinicians* were preserved by the families, friends and home communities of the athletes they honored. They were also copied, distributed and, in some cases, actually displayed in the temples and public spaces of a champion's city. And in time, these songs became part of that classical canon of literary work — Homer's epics, Hesiod's *Works and Days*, the dramas of the Athenian masters — which the Greek-speaking public read and listened to for centuries to come.[25]

Given the special honors, material rewards and paeans of praise showered on the crown game victors, it is obvious these individuals were regarded as heroic figures while they were alive and "for a long time" after death. Nevertheless, while it is evident the ancients regarded these athletes as *theios aner*, or "godlike men," there is still the question of why this was so. As we have noted in preceding chapters, the heroes of the ancient world tended to be demigods, warrior kings, city founders, wealthy philanthropists, and fearless martyrs, i.e., individuals who were both extraordinary and — intentionally or not — of service to their communities. The heroic status of athletic champions, however, does not appear to have rested on anything other than their performance on the playing field.

To be sure, some of these individuals were proficient at arms, but the vast majority of them were not renowned for their military prowess. Concurrently, with the exception of those *periodoniki* who were princes, there is little mention in the surviving sources of circuit winners who showered their cities with rich benefactions. And while martyrs were often equated with athletes, few — if any — professional sportsmen are known to have actually laid down their lives in defense of a cause or principle during antiquity. Indeed, as we noted earlier, this lack of achievement in anything save sports is one of the reasons many scholars believe athletic champions were denied hero cults. Why then did the ancient public heroize these sportsmen?

Perhaps the most obvious explanation for the heroic stature enjoyed by these ancient jocks is the simple fact that they had proven themselves to be both first and best in a competitive sport on the premier playing fields of Greece. Whether their victories were at one or all of the crown games, in a single sporting event or a combination of them, these individuals had pitted themselves against the top athletes of their world and defeated them before an international audience. In a culture where honor had to be claimed and won publicly, and *arête*, or excellence, was valued above all else, this demonstration of athletic prowess served to single these athletes out as extraordinary human beings worthy of high honor in life and after death.

Athletic prowess was also one of the distinguishing characteristics of the heroes celebrated in Greek myth, epic poetry, drama, and art. Sports were an important pastime of mythic heroes like Heracles, Jason, and Theseus, and the stories that were told about them underscored the fact that they were not only warriors and daring adventurers, but also passionate athletes who sponsored games, competed in them, and carried off their crowns of victory. Competitive sport figured prominently in the lives of the heroes celebrated in Homer's epics as well. In Book Twenty-three of the *Iliad*, all of the principal Argive champions compete for glory and rich prizes at the funeral games of Patroclus, and in the *Odyssey*, Odysseus participates in and wins the running, wrestling, jumping, discus, and boxing contests organized for his entertainment by the Phaeacians of Scheria. Greek heroic dramas also made reference to the athletic renown of their protagonists. In their various plays about Orestes, for example, Aeschylus, Sophocles and Euripides all made a point of highlighting their hero's reputation as a champion runner, wrestler, boxer and chariot racer. And no theme was more popular among sculptors and the painters of amphora and friezes than renditions of some heroic figure of legend engaged in athletic activity. Given the prominent place accorded to competitive sport in Greek heroic literature and art, it is not surprising that hero and athlete were often regarded as synonymous terms.

It is also likely that considerations of class figured in the readiness of the Greeks to regard the *periodoniki* as heroes. As we have seen, a great many of these athletes haled from the aristocracy, and among these noble competitors were a fair number of tyrants, kings, and princes. The prominent role played by these men of "quality" in the crown games not only contributed to the prestige of these contests, but also signaled to Greek society-at-large that victory in them was no "mean" achievement. And the lavish celebrations, *epinicians*, and monumental statues commissioned by these noble contestants to commemorate their circuit victories could not help but underscore the idea that crown game winners were extraordinary figures worthy of honor and emulation.

Whatever their social status, all circuit champions were hometown heroes. In a world in which people felt very much rooted in and shaped by their *polis*, the *arête* of crown game victors was proof of the excellence, the superiority of the places that had borne, raised, and nurtured them. As such, all of the compatriots of circuit winners basked in "the gleam of splendor given of heaven" to their native sons. Aside from being a source of great civic pride, the successes of these athletes also afforded their communities with opportunities to come together and celebrate their membership in a common body politic. As with the festivals and other activities honoring the heroes of old, the celebratory parades, poetic performances, statues, coins, and hero cults that were commissioned to honor the *periodoniki* served to affirm and strengthen communal identity and unity.

Finally, these athletic champions enjoyed a level of popular adulation that set them apart from the other kinds of heroes we have examined up to this point. Godly offspring, berserker warriors and fearless martyrs might be admired and revered, but their lives and actions were markedly different from those of ordinary folk. Mortal peasants, artisans, merchants, women, and slaves were largely uninterested in either toting up impressive body counts or submitting to humiliation, pain, and death in defense of a metaphysical principle. Sport, however, was a different matter altogether. From childhood on, almost everyone in the ancient world had engaged in some kind of play that involved a competitive game — racing, wrestling, fisticuffs, hurling objects, and, if from a wealthy enough family, riding horses. Consequently, a professional athlete performed before an audience that to some degree could understand the challenges he faced and empathize with the emotions he felt on the playing field. Add to this affinity the enormous pleasure that spectators enjoy when the tensions created by an athletic contest are resolved in the victory of one sportsman over another, and it is easy to understand why the champions of the crown games were lionized by their fans. Indeed, as Stephen G. Miller notes in his own ruminations on the popularity of these individuals:

> We look at them and see ourselves as we would want to be seen, and sometimes we fool ourselves that we might have been as good at games as they. They represent an undying hope that we have a share in immortality, and they allow us to step outside ourselves from time to time so that we can return refreshed and revived to our everyday lives.[26]

Athletic Heroism and the Civilizing Process

Whatever the reasons for the exalted status of the crown game champions, the contests in which they competed remained a fixture of Mediterranean life throughout antiquity. The circuit survived the Peloponnesian wars, the decline of the Greek city states, and the absorption of Greece into the Macedonian kingdom of Alexander the Great and his Antigonid heirs. When the Greek mainland passed under the rule of Rome, the crown games were held throughout the civil wars and internecine strife that destroyed the Roman Republic; and they continued unabated during the first two centuries of the Empire, enjoying the patronage and largess of Augustus and his imperial successors. Even in the face of the barbarian invasions and economic downturn of the third and fourth centuries of the Common Era, athletes continued to compete for the laurels of the *periodos* and the adulation of the sports enthusiasts who, in the face of great difficulty, still managed to make their way to these contests from throughout the Roman world.

In the end, it was neither warfare nor financial distress that terminated the crown games, but the religious zeal of a late fourth century Christian emperor. Intolerant of the circuit's ties to Zeus and his family, and intent on fashioning a new kind of athletic hero dedicated to winning heavenly glory through spiritual contests with Satan and his minions, Theodosius I issued an edict in 393 CE that closed the pagan sanctuaries and banned all games associated with pagan worship. A thousand year tradition of competitive sports and athletic heroism came to an end, not to be revived again until 1896 with the first modern Olympic Games in Athens.

While the Greek practice of competitive athletics would lie dormant for the next millennium and a half, the memory of these recurring contests and their "godlike" champions would loom large in a Western imagination nurtured on the epics of Homer, the poetry of Pindar, the dramas of the Athenian playwrights, and the sculpture of Myron and Polykleitos. Indeed, even though the popular mass sports of the last century — football, baseball, basketball, soccer, hockey — have been contests between teams, their competitive spirit and the adulation showered on their star players owe much to the example set by the ancient Greeks. When a Babe Ruth or a Michael Jordan lead their fellow players to world championships and shatter records for achievement in baseball and basketball, they are following in the footsteps of ancient athletes who, like themselves, were seeking to set the standards of excellence in their sports and acquire a deathless renown in the process. And when the peers and fans of these men treat them to ticker tape parades, induct them into "halls of fame," produce biopics about their lives, and write novels, poems, and biographies celebrating their careers, they are participating in a form of hero worship that has its beginnings in the crown games and heroic cults of the Greco-Roman world.

The prominent place accorded the victorious athlete in ancient Greek poetry, drama, sculpture, and painting also inspired succeeding generations of Western artists. From the epistles of Paul to the poetry of William Wordsworth and the novels of John Updike, writers in Europe, the Near East and the Americas have drawn on the imagery of competitive sport to communicate important lessons about character, struggle, excellence, beauty, victory, defeat, and the fleeting nature of human glory. Concurrently, much of the anatomical realism of later Greco-Roman sculpture and painting — a realism that would later serve as a model for the artists of the Renaissance and the modern period—was based on the painstaking efforts of classical Greek artisans to accurately reproduce in stone and paint the beauty of the athletic body at rest and in motion.[27]

Ironically, the *periodos* champion who was a godlike man to the Greeks and a model of exceptional excellence, extraordinary strength and skill, and great beauty for modern sports enthusiasts and artists, may also have helped advance the ideals of equality and meritocracy that lie at the heart of contemporary mass society. In a world characterized by gross inequities, the circuit games were open to all comers regardless of their social, economic, or political status. Aristocratic and non-aristocratic contestants alike acceded to a common set of rules governing the games in which they were competing. Any competitor judged in violation of those rules was subject to the same punishments, i.e., flogging and dismissal from the games. And whether tyrant or goatherd, all those participating in the crown contests did so in the nude on a common playing field before an international audience comprised of people from different social strata and every walk of life. In the end, the laurels of the circuit only graced the heads of those who had demonstrated themselves worthy of the honor, and their example would serve as a model for those later thinkers and activists who would argue for a society in which power and status was linked to demonstrable talent and achievement.

Whatever the impact of Greek competitive athletics on the struggle for equality in the modern world, the *periodos* definitely played a role in the ongoing democratization of the Western heroic pantheon. As we have seen, these games were open to all males of Greek descent, and any contestant with the right combination of strength, skill, and divine favor might win a "gleam of splendor" and, in so doing, "become something like the gods." Further, regardless of the birth, occupation, social standing, or posthumous cult status of these godlike champions, their fans and countrymen regarded them as heroes and showered them with the distinctions and material rewards attendant on that status. In honoring the *periodoniki* in this fashion, the ancients were not only expanding the range of who and what might be considered heroic—in this case, any man, noble or non-noble, who had competed with the best in a given sport, won its most prestigious crown of victory, and proven himself a superlative athlete without peer—but the right of the public-at-large—the spectators, fans, and compatriots of a sportsman—to heroize him and, in so doing, share in his glory. Both of these developments will make it easier in the future for anyone who is prominent in a profession or pastime that enjoys a popular following to be proclaimed a hero. Indeed, the heroization of the ancient athlete is the first step on a road that will take us to a world in which the idea of the heroic is increasingly conflated with the worship of celebrities who grace the covers of tabloids, specialty publications, and *People* magazine.

✣ PART TWO ✣

Soldiers and Servants of Christ: Heroism in the Middle Ages

I tell you, eating or drinking or sleeping hasn't such savour for me as the moment I hear both sides shouting "Get 'em!" and I hear riderless horses crashing through the shadows, and I hear men shouting "Help! Help!" and I see the small and the great falling in the grassy ditches, and I see the dead with splintered lances, decked with pennons, through their sides.

— Bertram de Born

It has been suggested that it is the function of saints in any era to go beyond the bounds of what is normally expected, to engage in extravagant, demonstrative, sensational deeds, which challenge people's common sense and provoke their response.

— Richard Kieckhefer: *Unquiet Souls*

"The more it changes," the French say, "the more it remains the same," and this is certainly an apt description for what happens when the Western heroic tradition finds itself under Christian management during the Middle Ages. Despite the fact that Europe becomes the center of a chiliastic religion celebrating charity, pacifism, piety, and disregard for the honors and accolades of the material world, its inhabitants continue to embrace a profane ideal of heroism that celebrates the deeds of worldly warriors hungry for gold and deathless glory. Indeed, whether one is speaking of Siegfried and Beowulf or Achilles and Odysseus, for most medieval folk the hero remains a noble champion who is highly skilled with edged weapons, extremely touchy about his personal honor, and all too fond of drinking, wenching, hunting, monster slaying, and stealing other people's property.

Nor was the continuing popularity of this heroic type all that surprising given the somewhat unsettled nature of this era. The Middle Ages or, as some irreverent wags refer to it, "the thousand years of camping out," was a time of considerable violence, danger, and movement for the peoples of western Europe. From the collapse of the Roman Empire in the West (476 CE) to the end of the tenth century, the peoples of this region experienced a veritable explosion of murder and mayhem as Germans, Huns, Muslims, Saracens, Magyars, and Vikings sacked and slaughtered their way across the continent. Even with the restoration of some measure of order and settled life during the late medieval period, warfare remained an endemic feature of everyday existence, and the fact that it was conducted by indigenous Christian princes did little to lessen its horror.

In such perilous times, a man-at-arms who could rally other warriors to his side, fend off invaders, maintain some measure of local order, and bring home both booty and bacon was a hero of the first rank. And from the tenth century on, this heroic fighter was increasingly a mounted warrior known as the knight. Secured to a horse by stirrups and bowed saddles, clad in armor, and sporting a deadly panoply of weapons—heavy lances, broad swords, spiked metallic maces—this fearsome cavalryman could charge his enemies at great speed and rain down on them blows of exceptional force. Indeed, for the better part of five centuries, this human missile on horseback dominated the battlefields of Europe and the Middle East.

Nevertheless, despite the fact that these mounted shock troops were Christian and practiced warfare in a way that was markedly different from the military operations of antiquity, they still shared many of the normative values of their pagan predecessors. Like the Greco-Roman and German warriors that preceded them, knights worshipped prowess and spent their lives seeking out opportunities for violent combat. They were also greedy for treasure, hungry for honor, loyal to their lords and liegemen, and eager for renown. And, as with their compatriots in the time of Homer, the heroes of these men were also professional freebooters who were reputed to be indomitable in battle, generous with their wealth, and courteous to their peers.

These cavalrymen and their pre–Christian notions of heroism proved problematic for the prelates and princes of Christendom. Knightly bellicosity, vanity, avarice, and glory seeking were completely at odds with Church teaching, and the inordinate fondness of these men for violence posed a very real threat to the peace and stability of Europe. In fact, much of the murder and mayhem of the high Middle Ages could be directly attributed to the private feuds, vendettas, and civil wars of knights seeking to hone their skills, acquire booty, or avenge some affront to their personal honor.

Whatever the faults of these warriors, however, they did constitute the principal military force in late medieval Europe. Rome required their services to defend Christendom from heretical movements at home and attacks by infidels from abroad. And Europe's crowned heads needed their muscle to expand, defend and preserve order in their territories. Consequently, considerable energies were expended at this time by both clerical and secular authorities to articulate and foster an ideal of knightly heroism and ethics that would make knighthood a more pious, pliant and pacific instrument of Church and state policies.

As the following section makes clear, these efforts at creating a heroic knight that was both an efficient killer and a paragon of Christian virtue met with mixed results. Knights had their own notions of what it meant to be a *Miles Christi*, or warrior of Christ, and these were often at odds with the formulations of the Curia and the men they anointed as kings. Nevertheless, out of this clash of clerical, courtly, and chivalric ideas about knightly conduct emerged a concept of the "gentle" man and woman that continues to inform Western thinking regarding what it means to be an ideal soldier, policeman, secret agent, courtier, and champion.

Though they are often regarded as the embodiment of medieval heroism, knights were not the only heroic figures of this period. Indeed, any discussion of this era's heroes would be incomplete without some mention of the Christian community of saints. An exceptionally varied lot, which included martyrs, scholars, hermits, missionaries, rulers, churchmen, mendicants, and mystics, these "servants of God" were venerated throughout Christendom because of their extraordinary piety in life and the miracles they were reputed to work on behalf of the living after death.

Literally thousands of these holy men and women were sanctified by local communities during the Middle Ages and venerated like latter-day *hemitheoi*. Splendid tombs and shrines were constructed to house their remains and personal effects. Special feast days, rituals and masses were celebrated in their honor. And streams of pilgrims visited the sites of their cults to seek salvation, remission of sins, cures, and good fortune in life.

While the Church was largely supportive of this *cultus sancti*, or "cult of the saints," these popular devotions were not without problems for both local bishops and the Curia in Rome. The laity often put forward candidates for sainthood the clergy deemed unworthy of Christendom's highest honor. Communities sometimes established saintly cults venerating not only martyrs and doctors of the Church, but pagan deities, murdered bar maids, and pious pets. And for most Christians a saint remained not so much a life to be emulated as a talismanic fetish to be appeased and tapped for divine favor.

Pressures from local clergy to address these issues eventually led the papacy to take a more active interest in the Church's community of saints. Beginning in the tenth century, the Holy See claimed the sole right to canonize a saint; established standards all nominees for sanctification were expected to meet; and initiated a lengthy judicial process to insure that every candidate for the *cultus sancti* satisfied papal criteria. While local communities were encouraged to continue bringing forward individuals they believed worthy of saintly status, Rome was increasingly disinclined to grant these candidates sainthood.

Behind the Curia's waning enthusiasm for popular saints was a desire to repopulate the Church's heroic pantheon with individuals who enjoyed something more than a reputation for wonder working remains. While posthumous miracles on behalf of the living continued to be a requirement for sanctification, Rome also wanted evidence that the life of a prospective saint was an imitation of Christ so "extravagant, demonstrative, and exceptional" that it inspired piety among the faithful and helped make Europe a more holy, orthodox, and Roman Catholic commonwealth. Increasingly, this shift in focus from saintly relics to saintly lives favored the canonization of a generation of mendicants and mystics — Dominic, Elizabeth of Hungary, Francis of Assisi, Catherine of Siena — who were as noted for their piety, learning, and good works as for the prodigies attributed to their intercession after death. Indeed, not only would the *imitatio Christi* of these "modern" saints redefine what it meant to be a "servant of God" in the medieval Church, but it would also generate a sacral idea of heroism that continues to inspire and inform the work of Western philanthropists, social activists, and religious zealots to the present day.

In what follows, we will examine in some detail these medieval soldiers and servants of Christ with an eye aimed at understanding how their ideals and actions influenced and shaped the development of the Western heroic tradition. The first chapter addresses the ways in which the moral principles of the Jesus movement — selflessness, charity, personal piety, and disdain for worldly honor — interacted with earlier Greco-Roman and northern European warrior traditions to produce that paragon of heroism in the West, the Christian knight. This exposition on the knightly hero is then followed by an examination of that other archetypal hero of the Middle Ages, the saint. Beginning with its initial use as a signifier for any follower of Christianity, this section explores how the term "saint" was transformed into an honorific applied only to the members of a very select group of semi-divine beings; a confraternity of friends and intimates of Christ that to this day embody what it means to be a hero for millions of Christians throughout the world.

5

Miles Christi
The Hero as Warrior of Christ

Lords, look at the best knight that you have ever seen.... He is brave and courtly and skilful, and noble and of a good lineage and eloquent, handsomely experienced in hunting and fal- conry; he knows how to play chess and backgammon, gaming and dicing. And his wealth was never denied to any, but each has as much as he wants...And he has never been slow to perform honourable deeds. He dearly loves God and the Trinity....And...he has honoured the poor and lowly.

— Girart

They fought each other ferociously, looting and burning in each other's territories and adding crime to crime. They plundered poor and helpless people, constantly made them suffer losses or live in fear of losses, and brought distress to their dependants, knights and peasants alike, who endured many disasters.

— Orderic Vitalis: *Ecclesiastical History*

You are proud; you tear your brothers to pieces and fight among yourselves. The battle that rends the flock of the Redeemer is not the militia Christi. Holy church has reserved knight- hood for itself, for the defense of its people, but you pervert it in wickedness...you oppressors of orphans and widows, you murderers, you temple defilers, you lawbreakers, who seek the rewards of rapacity from spilling Christian blood.

— Baldric of Dol

In the Lerner and Lowe musical *Camelot*, France's most formidable warrior, Lancelot du Lac, makes his way to King Arthur's court singing a tune entitled *C'est Moi*. The point of the song is to give Lancelot the opportunity to share with his audience what he thinks "a knight of the Table Round should be," as well as to assure it that he does indeed meet all of the criteria for membership in this very select circle. First and foremost, Lancelot tells his listeners, such a fellow "should be invincible." This entails being able to do an assort- ment of daunting deeds — scaling unclimbable walls, whacking dragons, swimming moats in armor — beyond the ken of most mortal men.

In addition to being a "Prometheus unbound," Lancelot also highlights in his song the self-restraint and extraordinary piety expected of anyone wishing to be counted among Camelot's heroic elect. The soul of such a person, he croons, should be exceptionally pure. Not only does he pay no heed to the temptations of the flesh, but his self-control is a thing that even the saints find admirable.

Mention is made of Lerner's musical rendition of chivalric virtues because it conveys the traits most of us expect to find in a heroic medieval knight. Like Lancelot, we too believe that such a person should be a redoubtable warrior — preferably on horseback clad in gleaming armor — who is skilled with lance and sword, and always eager to prove his prowess in jousts, tourneys, and wars. We also share the young Lancelot's expectation that a knight should be not only a formidable berserker, but also a deeply pious Christian; trustworthy, loyal, chaste, and willing to employ might only in defense of right.

This idea of the heroic knight as a kind of "bad" Boy Scout is a powerful and enduring trope in Western culture. Indeed, the knightly protagonist who is fierce, albeit modest, selfless, and restrained, figures prominently in modern historical literature, fantasy fiction, political propaganda, and action adventure films. He is the prototype of Sir Walter Scott's Wilfred of Ivanhoe, and the inspiration for the Riders of Rohan and the Dúnedain ranger, Aragorn, in J. R. R. Tolkien's fantasy epic *Lord of the Rings*. He is also an icon and model of conduct for law enforcement agencies, special military forces, the U.S. Marine Corps, and a variety of authoritarian leadership cadres such as the SS, KGB, and CIA. And in a galaxy far far away, he is the ancestor (or descendant depending on one's point of view) of George Lucas' Jedi knights; those humble, chaste followers of the Force, who loyally employ their skills in martial arts, light saber dueling, and fighter plane piloting to defend the Republic, its citizens, and assorted damsels, widows, orphans, and androids in distress.

Popular and compelling as this modern notion of knightly heroism may be, the epigraphs introducing this chapter — all of which actually hale from the Middle Ages — suggest that medieval knighthood was a decidedly more complicated affair than that celebrated in Lerner's lyrics or Lucas' *Star Wars*. "The best knight," for example, who is described in the passage quoted from the romance *Girart*, is not only a formidable warrior, but also a wealthy, worldly fellow, fond of games and gambling, and eager for glory and honor. Concurrently, the latter two quotations, from the ecclesiastical works of Odo Vitalis and Baldric of Dol, highlight a pattern of knightly violence, lust, and greed, which underscores how a medieval knight could be both Darth Vader and Obi Won Kenobi.

This dichotomy between past and current perceptions of knighthood stems in large part from the tendency of modern writers, artists and filmmakers to focus on a model of knightly behavior that was largely limited to a number of religious military orders — Templar, Hospitaller, Teutonic — that subscribed to a code of chivalry modeled on a monastic way of life and subject to the authority of the Roman Catholic Church. Though these priestly knights were respected and admired in the Middle Ages, their concerns and lifestyles were quite different from their more numerous secular confreres, who lived in and around princely courts and were intent on securing gold, glory, land, and profitable marriages. For these non-clerical knights, acquiring the status of a *preudome*, i.e., becoming a man of prowess, integrity, and experience, was a decidedly less religious affair.

To be sure, knights outside of the clerical military orders were often scrupulous in their devotions and just as concerned about the salvation of their souls as any member of the medieval Christian community. Further, as shown below, these individuals were also well aware of the fact that both their profession and their eagerness for worldly fame and honor were at variance with the nonviolence, humility, selflessness, and spirituality of their Savior. Nevertheless, as the heirs of both Greco-Roman and Germanic military traditions in which prowess, largesse, and loyalty were revered, and renown was counted the highest good, knighthood-at-large either paid piety short shrift or simply ignored clerical pronouncements that conflicted with what knights deemed necessary to be counted men of worth.

Pious or not, however, most medieval knights regarded themselves as both servants of Christ and members of a very select band of brothers joined together by a shared devotion to prowess. To be counted a hero of this *Militia Christi*, to be found worthy of inclusion in a "Table Round" or a *chanson de geste*, it was necessary to find a way to satisfy the demands of two very different masters, one a god of peace and love, the other a demiurge of bloodlust and vanity. Not surprisingly, attempting to achieve this end was a difficult, dangerous enterprise, and a key concern of knighthood in the Middle Ages was finding a code of conduct that would help its members attain great renown and honor in this life without jeopardizing their chances of a heavenly berth in the next.

This was a tall order and the search for a knightly ethic, or order of chivalry, that could define and justify knighthood to its acolytes, while also transforming them into redoubtable, god fearing, loyal, generous, and well-mannered warriors, was as complicated and contested an affair as any quest for the Holy Grail. Not only did such a code of chivalrous behavior have to contend with the obvious contradictions inherent in making a person both a savage cold blooded killer and a "gentle man," but it also had to pass muster with a number of medieval players who had a vested interest in knightly prowess and were eager to shape, control and channel it in ways that advanced their varied agendas. These actors included a Roman Catholic Church desperate for devout disciplined soldiers capable of defending Christendom from heretics at home and infidels abroad; a clutch of ambitious power hungry monarchs seeking to expand their authority over territories populated by restive and often unruly knights; and a knighthood-at-large comprised of aristocrats fiercely protective of their privileges and prerogatives. All of these prelates, princes, and potentates had their own ideas as to what constituted a perfect knight and all of them produced texts — histories, romances, *chansons de geste*, and manuals of conduct — that advanced codes of chivalry they hoped would realize their knightly ideals.

Not surprisingly, this varied chivalric literature presented its audiences with different and often conflicting notions of what it meant to be a heroic knight. In clerical texts he was an armed monk subservient to Rome. In romances and stories penned at princely courts he was a loyal and reliable retainer. And in books of chivalry written by actual knights he was something of a peripatetic freebooter, eagerly seeking out the battle scars, booty, and babes necessary to be regarded as a *preudome*, or man or worth. Indeed, for the medieval man-of-arms intent on becoming a knight worthy of the Table Round, there were many paths to Camelot.

The following pages explore in some depth these different pathways to heroic knighthood during the Middle Ages. Like the maps in an atlas, they seek to trace out the salient features of the clerical, royal, and aristocratic codes of chivalry, which constituted the principal means of access by which a medieval warrior made his way into both the order of knights and its pantheon of heroes. And just as a topographic map strives to reveal the structural relationships of the varied objects in a given terrain, this chapter likewise highlights the ways in which these distinctive prescriptions for knightly excellence intersect with one another, commingle, and metamorphose into that fusion of ideas, rituals, practices, and traits the modern world associates with the chivalrous knight.

Before we can begin this journey down the highways and byways of medieval chivalry, however, we must first ask how a common Carolingian soldier, a man-of-arms lacking in both lineage and lucre, was transformed into a *Miles Christi*, a warrior of Christ who was the very embodiment of good breeding, wealth, taste, and heroism. And, appropriately enough, the answer to that question is to be found a long time ago, in a place far, far away...

From Hired Hand to Castellan: The Origins of Medieval Knighthood

Prior to the researches of a number of twentieth century medieval historians, traditional accounts of the Middle Ages hewed to the line laid down by certain 11th century clerics that feudal society was divided into three orders — churchmen who prayed, aristocrats who fought, and commoners who labored.[1] In this tripartite social arrangement, knights were obviously included in the ranks of the brawling aristocracy, and within this order they were typically depicted as members of a hereditary noble elite who rendered homage and military service to a great lord — either a king, emperor, or higher nobleman — in return for a fief of land. Though medievalists acknowledge that knights might vary in wealth, with some being great landholders and others penniless hired hands, their noble status in society was accepted as a given.

More recent scholarship on feudal society by Marc Bloch, Georges Duby, Joseph Strayer, and others, has since revealed that knighthood and nobility did not become synonymous terms until the late twelfth century. Indeed, during the period of Frankish ascendancy in western Europe known as the Carolingian period (roughly 750–950 CE), *miles*, the Latin word used to signify a knight, was simply a term for a professional soldier who rendered military service to a patron or lord in exchange for some means of support. While these patron-client/lord-vassal relationships did distinguish men-at-arms from the peasantry, they did not transform them into aristocrats with hereditary titles and lands, the right to dispense justice, or the power to coerce and command.[2]

Despite their common social status, however, these early medieval Frankish warriors exhibited many of the qualities that would become trademarks of knighthood and its champions. Prominent among these was their devotion to prowess. As heirs to both Roman and Germanic military traditions, the fighting men of Charlemagne's empire recognized that it was physical strength, skill at arms, fearlessness, and discipline in battle that secured for a professional soldier the privileges, prizes and praise that set him apart from others. They also prized, as had their predecessors in Caesar's legions and Ariovistus' armies, loyalty to comrades and commanders, because the former covered your back going into battle and the latter looked out for your welfare when the fighting was over. And above all else, these fighters craved the renown and honor that was accorded to an individual who had distinguished himself with feats of arms.

The introduction of new technologies and techniques of mounted warfare in the late 10th and early 11th centuries afforded the cavalrymen among these Frankish soldiers with new opportunities for prowess, fame, and fortune. Stirrups made it easier for these horsemen to control and direct their steeds in battle, and the addition of improved bow saddles, armor and heavier lances allowed them to charge a foe at considerable speed and deliver blows of extraordinary force. Indeed, this new equipment essentially transformed these warriors into human missiles on horseback and, until the late Middle Ages, there was very little on a field of battle that could withstand their charge.[3]

Indeed, this new form of mounted shock combat effected a change in military tactics that essentially made the knight the most important player in medieval warfare. And the need to have a force of these fellows at one's command in the likely eventuality of aggression induced Europe's various princelings to elevate what had been a lowly *miles* into a separate military class with privileges and property of its own. In taking this step, knighthood's aristocratic employers were recognizing not only the newfound importance of these warriors on the battlefield, but also the simple fact that training and equipping them was a lengthy and costly affair. Consequently, by the end of the 11th century, it was fairly commonplace for the knightly retainers of a nobleman to hold title to a fief of land, to enjoy exemptions from taxation or other services expected of laborers, to participate in tournaments aimed at testing and improving their military skills, and to be inducted into the profession of knighthood through some kind of special "dubbing" ceremony.[4]

Knightly power and prestige was further enhanced by the breakdown of political order in western Europe during the 10th and 11th centuries. Following the death of Charlemagne, the empire he built was divided into three kingdoms whose rulers quickly fell to fighting amongst themselves. This internecine turmoil and violence was further exacerbated by invasions of the Frankish realm by Saracens from the south, Magyars from the east, and Vikings from the north. Bereft of a strong central authority and confronted by threats on all sides, the Carolingian aristocracy had little recourse but to rely on their armed retainers to maintain order and dispense justice in their territories. Knights responded to these new responsibilities by erecting fortified dwellings on their lands and exacting further rewards — titles, hereditary rights, arms, gold, good marriages — from their noble employers.[5]

If Europe's princes provided their knights with the wherewithal and authority that allowed them to become a new aristocracy of armed landholders, Catholic prelates advanced the legal and intellectual arguments that justified their aristocratic status. Confronted by the collapse of royal authority in the West, the invasion of Christendom by various non–Christian peoples, and a wave of knightly violence against Catholic parishioners, personnel and property, the Church launched a movement in the 10th century known as the "peace of God." Through sermons, synods, and clerical tracts, churchmen throughout Europe argued that Christian society was a threefold arrangement in which clerics tended to the spiritual needs of the people, warriors protected the Church and their fellow Christians from harm, and commoners toiled in the fields and towns to produce the goods and services necessary to the survival of both themselves and the other two estates. Knighthood in this social scheme was pronounced a sacred order of *miles Christi*, or "warriors of Christ," whose mission was to uphold justice by protecting the weak, defending the Church, and waging war on the enemies of Christianity, particularly those of the Muslim persuasion. As we will see below, while this clerical effort at reining in and channeling the aggressive tendencies of the knightly class was only partially successful, it nonetheless succeeded in establishing the idea of the knight as a noble, almost sacral, figure.[6]

Finally, the contemporary literature of this time also played an important role in the process by which a common cavalryman was transformed into the very embodiment of the Christian aristocratic ideal. During the 11th and 12th centuries, troubadours, poets, and historical chroniclers penned *chansons de geste*, romances, and histories that celebrated the deeds of noble knights. In works such as *The Song of Roland*, *Tristan and Iseult*, and the Arthurian romances, low and high born audiences alike were treated to stories about mounted warriors with impeccable lineage, comely looks, extraordinary prowess, great piety, and good manners. While these tales related a world of make believe, it was a realm that most medieval boys (and quite a few modern ones as well) yearned to enter.[7]

Whatever the reasons behind this metamorphosis of a medieval mercenary into a "gentle man" of wealth and taste, by the 12th century a new kind of warrior known as the knight had taken his place on the European stage. Made possible by changes in military technology and tactics, brought to the fore by the political and military crises of the 10th and 11th centuries, blessed by the Church, and enshrined in the literature of the day, this figure was unquestionably the heroic ideal of his time. Of course, what that ideal entailed in terms of a knight's lifestyle and behavior was a much contested subject, and it is to this debate over knightly conduct that we will now turn.

Becoming a Man of Worth: The Three Faces of Chivalry

Chivalry is derived from *chevalier*, the French word for an armored cavalryman, and it was initially used to signify nothing more than a band of mounted warriors or the occupation of a knight. However, as historians of knighthood are quick to point out, between the 11th and 15th centuries, this term came to mean other things as well. Clerics and lawyers, for example, used it to describe a form of land tenure for which military service was expected. Writers and troubadours employed it as a kind of shorthand in literary texts, like *The Song of Roland*, for a knight's prowess in battle and his good behavior at court. And from the 12th century on, many people associated it with knightly codes of social and ethical conduct.[8]

The following pages are largely focused on this last usage of chivalry, i.e., as a compendium of moral principles and profane practices that were designated by various parties in the high Middle Ages as mandatory for a knight to be adjudged worthy of his heroic calling. As mentioned in the introduction to this chapter, the central importance of the knight in medieval society as both a guarantor of order and an agent of disorder, coupled with the tensions inherent in a profession that simultaneously worshipped violence and a god of peace, necessitated some kind of ethic to inform the training of new knights and the actions of those already inducted into the order. The particulars of such a code of conduct, however, the various things that a knight should or should not do in his quest to become a man of worth, were subject to the agendas of individuals and groups who were often at odds with one another about what constituted ideal knightly behavior. And nowhere were these conflicts over the meaning and practice of chivalry more pronounced than in the efforts of Rome to create a knightly warrior whose lifestyle and actions were consistent with the teachings and needs of Holy Mother the Church.

God's Good Servant: Clerical Chivalry

From the moment they first appeared on the European scene, knights proved problematic for medieval Christendom's Catholic caretakers. Though nominally Christian, these mounted warriors behaved in a manner that was completely contrary to the life and teachings of Jesus of Nazareth. Whereas Christianity's founder had preached non-violence, meekness, humility, and unconcern for the ways of the world, knighthood was bellicose, boastful, arrogant, vain, and eager for gold and glory. Nor did these warriors appear to be much concerned about what was supposed to be front and center in every Christian's life, namely the salvation of their immortal souls. Indeed, most of these men-at-arms lived pretty much as they pleased until the hour of their death, at which time, a nearby cleric was usually coaxed or compelled to absolve them of their many sins.

Nothing illustrates the tensions between the knightly and clerical orders of this time better than the whole knotty business of jousts and tournaments. For knights, these armed contests were not only essential training for their profession, but they were also a means of acquiring a reputation and catching the eye of potential employers. Further, because the victors in these games were also awarded both the person and property of the vanquished, these events were an important source of rich booty — steeds, armor, and weapons — as well as ransoms from the families and friends of the defeated warriors.

One can get some idea of how important these contests were to knights by considering the career of a man who many regard as the premier knight of the Middle Ages, Sir William the Marshall. Though he would end his days a regent of England charged with the care and education of Henry III, Marshall began his life in considerably more humble circumstances. The fourth son of a rural baron of middling means, William's only sources of support were his prowess and ability with arms, both of which he amply proved at a young age by taking part in every tournament that came his way. His success in these games, as well as at war, brought him to the attention of Henry I of England who made him a member of his inner circle and the guardian of his son Henry II. This rise into the ranks of royalty, however, never stopped Marshall from tourneying; and, in 1177 alone, over a span of ten months, he captured in tournaments and put up for ransom one hundred and three knights. These feats not only enriched him greatly but also won him the attention and support of new patrons, among them the Count of Flanders and the Duke of Burgundy. Clearly, for any man seeking a career in knighthood, and ambitious for power and prestige, jousts and tourneys were essential.[9]

The Church had a distinctively different take on what St. Bernard of Clairvaux referred to as "those accursed tournaments."[10] From the clerical point of view, jousts and tourneys, which celebrated violence, promoted greed, and encouraged vanity, were the very embodiment of the kinds of sinful behavior that Christianity sought to combat in the world. Churchmen also regarded these events as a form of gluttony because of the vast resources — food, horses, equipment, costly clothing, lodging, and festivities — required to both mount the games and support the heralds, minstrels, squires, grooms, armorers, and smiths that accompanied the knights fighting in them. Quoting St. Bernard once again:

> What then, O knights, is this monstrous error and what this unbearable urge which bids you fight with such pomp and labor, and all to no purpose except death and sin. You cover your horses with silk, and plume your armor with I know not what sort of rags; you paint your shields and your saddles; you adorn your bits and spurs with gold and silver and precious stones, and then in all this glory you rush to your ruin with fearful wrath and fearless folly.[11]

Considerations of sin to the side, the principal reason behind the Church's hostility to tournaments was the simple fact that they encouraged and valorized a cult of knightly violence that was very much a threat to the internal and external security of Christendom. Not only did these events result in unnecessary waste and bloodshed, but they also generated enmities that could spark private wars between knights; wars that invariably resulted in murder, mayhem and misery for the clerical and laboring populations of the Christian community. Further, with Europe threatened on all sides by pagans and infidels, the Church strongly believed there were far better targets a Christian knight might direct his prowess against, than the shields of his fellow men-at-arms.

Of course, in the end, no amount of clerical condemnation could wean knighthood away from its attachment to tournaments, and, in the early 14th century, Rome lifted its various strictures on these events. In taking this step, the Curia was acknowledging a number of realities with regard to these men-at-arms. First, that theirs was a profession predicated on "bloody, sweaty, muscular work done with lance and sword."[12] Second, that these individuals required some means of both learning their trade and demonstrating their bona fides as warriors. Third, that the Church had no physical means to compel a knight to obey its edicts against these contests. And finally, that this tourney loving knightly crowd was the only armed force the clerical order could call upon in the event of any internal or external threats against Christendom.

It was this latter point, i.e., the dependence of the Roman Church on knights for both the defense of its physical existence and the enforcement of its spiritual authority, which made churchmen so keen on the idea of a clerical chivalry. Indeed, long before the Curia finally accepted the tournament as a necessary evil of medieval military culture, its clerics were busy at work delineating a set of principles and practices aimed at transforming the knight into a Christian warrior whose might was used only in ways deemed rightful by the Church. Out of this effort came a tradition of holy warfare, pilgrimage, militant monasticism, and chivalric literature that both strengthened the Christian elements within secular knighthood-at-large, and celebrated the idea of the heroic knight as a powerful, pious, and pliant son of Holy Mother Church.

Among the different elements of this clerical chivalry, probably none was more efficacious in elaborating what it meant to be a *miles Christi* than the Crusades. Initiated by Pope Urban II at the end of the 11th century, these military expeditions were organized with the aim of liberating Jerusalem and the shrine of the Holy Sepulcher from Muslim control. The papacy also hoped these campaigns would bring knighthood under the direct control of the Catholic Church; drain knightly violence from Europe by directing it against non–Christian peoples; and provide employment for the younger sons of knights, who, because they lacked opportunities for advancement at home, were prone to private warfare and brigandage.

Between 1095, when the First Crusade was launched, and 1291, when the last Latin outpost in Palestine was expelled, there were eight of these Middle Eastern incursions; and knighthood flocked to them with gusto. In part, knightly enthusiasm for these expeditions stemmed from their substantial spiritual benefits. As both holy wars and pilgrimages to sacred sites, participation in the Crusades could win for a knight expiation of his sins while he was alive, as well as a berth in heaven should he die in battle. Knights also viewed these campaigns as an opportunity to practice their trade largely free of royal or religious interference. Once in Palestine, a crusader could essentially hack, hew, pillage, plunder, and rape as he pleased, and the fact that many of his victims were defenseless civilians and Christians to boot was immaterial. Indeed, for a young knight eager to acquire the battle scars and booty necessary to be deemed worthy of his profession, the chance to engage in such untrammeled hooliganism was irresistible.[13]

Though there were marauders aplenty during the Crusades, it should also be noted that there were a great many knights who were deeply religious, committed to the spiritual aims of the crusading movement, and eager to become warriors of Christ. These folks banded together in military-religious orders that combined the dedication, discipline, and organization of monasticism with the practice of knighthood. The first of these Christian knightly brotherhoods was the Poor Knights of Christ and of the Temple of Solomon, more commonly known as the Knights Templar. Founded by a French knight, Hugues de Payens, in 1119, the Templars took vows of poverty, chastity, and obedience, lived together in their own communities, and pledged themselves to the service of the Church. The Knights Templar also provided admirable and courageous service as the guardians of pilgrims making their way to holy sites throughout Palestine. When they were formally recognized by Rome in 1128 — and provided with a rule of life by no less a figure than St. Bernard of Clairvaux — the numbers of the Templar order increased rapidly. In time, they became one of the most powerful organizations in the Crusader states; building and maintaining castles, providing levies to defend Jerusalem, transporting and guarding monies raised to support the crusades, and enforcing papal directives throughout Christendom.[14]

Other knights that followed the example of the Templars were the Order of the Hospital of Saint John of Jerusalem, i.e., the Knights Hospitallers, and the Fraternal House of the Hospitallers of Saint Mary of the Teutons in Jerusalem, also known as the Teutonic Order. Founded around 1130, the Hospitallers organized and operated a hospital for sick pilgrims and wounded knights near the Church of St. John in Jerusalem. As a religious military order, the Knights Hospitaller, followed a monastic rule of life, cared for the sick and poor of the Holy Land and waged war on the Muslims. Following the fall of Acre in 1291, the Hospitallers moved their order to Cyprus, then Rhodes, and finally to Malta, which they managed to hold against repeated assaults by the Turks until 1798 when Napoleon Bonaparte conquered the island. The brother order of the Hospitallers, the Teutonic Knights, was founded in 1190 as a charitable organization associated with a German hospital, also in Jerusalem. In 1198, this group assumed a military character and under the leadership of its Grand Master, Hermann von Salza, relocated its operations to eastern Europe, where it conquered and converted pagan Prussia.[15]

The knights of these religious military orders were the embodiment of the clerical ideal of heroic knighthood, fusing together martial virtues — prowess, loyalty, largesse, courtesy — with an ecclesiastical way of life. Like their clerical counterparts in monasteries, these Christian warriors lived simple lives, performed charitable deeds, abstained from the ways of the flesh, and obeyed the commands of the Grand Masters who were the heads of their orders (and were themselves subject to the authority of Rome). And when these men-at-arms committed violence, it was only at the behest of the Church against the enemies of Christendom, i.e., heretics, apostates, schismatics, pagans, and infidels, with all the booty from these "just" wars flowing back to the Curia's coffers.[16]

In return for their loyalty and good works, the Church rewarded these most Christian knights with a wide array of benefits both sacred and profane. As warriors of the Church militant, they were granted plenary indulgences that remitted all temporal punishment in Purgatory for sin. If slain in battle, their souls were guaranteed a one way ticket to heaven. Special liturgies — sword blessings, purification baths, and clerical dubbing ceremonies — sacralized their induction into knighthood. Neither secular nor ecclesiastical authorities — save for the Pope — could command or punish them. Castles, lands, and gold were given to them both for their support and the continuation of their charitable acts. Indeed, to paraphrase Mel Brooks, it was good to be a knight who was dubbed a hero of Holy Mother Church.

Outside of its crusading military orders, the Church's chivalric ideals also found expression in certain works of literature authored during the 12th and 13th centuries by clerics or men educated in Church schools. A series of romantic fables relating the quest of Lancelot, Galahad and Percival for the Holy Grail celebrated the idea of the knightly hero as a crusading pilgrim in search of salvation over worldly glory. *The Order of Chivalry (Ordene de chevalerie)*, a poem penned by an anonymous priest or monk sometime around 1220, articulated the particulars of a clerical induction ceremony for knighthood that was meant to remind aspiring knights of their Christian duties and responsibilities. Included in this ritual was a bath to remind the knightly acolyte of baptism and to cleanse him of sin; a bed to signify "the repose of paradise" to be won by his deeds; white and scarlet cloaks — one to underscore the importance of cleanliness, the other the necessity of shedding one's blood in defense of the Church; brown stockings as a reminder of life's finitude; a belt of white signifying the need to be chaste; gold spurs to remind the candidate that he must be swift in following God's commandments; and a sword symbolizing the unity of justice and loyalty, as well as the need for every knight to defend the poor and weak against oppression. *The Order* also laid out four commandments every Christian knight was expected to follow throughout his life, i.e., be honest and never commit treason; honor and protect the weaker sex; attend Mass every day; and fast on Fridays in remembrance of Christ's passion.[17] Similar statements regarding the Christian symbolism of a knight's weapons and garb, as well as other reminders of the articles and obligations of his faith, were also central elements in the popular and much read manual of chivalry, *The Book of the Order of Chivalry (Libre del ordre de cavayleria)*, written between 1279–1283 by the Catalan mystic and poet, Ramon Lull.

Monastic military orders, Grail literature, and Christianized dubbing ceremonies to the side, exactly how successful was this clerical attempt to shape the lifestyle and practice of European knighthood-at-large? As Maurice Keen, Richard Kaeuper, and other historians of chivalry have noted, while knights initially flocked to the Crusades and welcomed the sanctification of their profession by the Church, outside of the military brotherhoods, Rome was largely unsuccessful in exercising control over knightly culture. This was most apparent in the area of warfare. As the whole conflict over tournaments demonstrated, *Chevalerie* regarded the practice of violence to be their special province and reserved to themselves the right to determine when, where, and how to ply their trade.

Further, the kind of chivalric ideal embodied by the Templars, Hospitallers, and Teutonic Knights was completely removed from the concerns and pastimes of their more secular counterparts. Knighthood as a whole lived not in monastic communities, but in and around the courts of kings and princes. In these places, fleshly concerns trumped those of the heavenly kingdom to come. Indeed, clerical nostrums of poverty and humility were of little use to men who lived and moved in an environment where questions of wealth, reputation, rank, style, manners, and personal appearance were paramount. And chastity was completely at odds with a society that valued good marriages, discreet infidelity, and courtly love romances.

Clerical chivalry was successful, however, in its efforts to infuse a religious dimension into what was largely a secular vocation of violence. Throughout the Middle Ages, the Crusades loomed large in the knightly imagination and any man seeking to be counted a heroic knight believed it necessary to engage in some form of crusading and pilgrimage. Concurrently, the sacralization of knighthood through the blessing of its swords and banners, and the introduction of Christian elements into its induction ceremonies, all served to remind knights of their "higher" calling to defend the personnel and property of the Church, to protect those weaker than themselves — women, orphans, the oppressed — and to strive to lead a moral life characterized by loyalty, honesty, courtesy, and faith. Indeed, there were few medieval accounts of knightly heroism that did not give some kind of lip service to the ways in which the knight in question was a good son of the Church. However, as we will see, the piety practiced by the chivalrous class was always more in keeping with its own needs than those of the Curia.

The King's Good Servant: Royal Chivalry

Unlike the clerical order, Europe's ruling families enjoyed a relationship with knighthood that was both personal and practical. The kings of France, Britain, and Spain, the Dukes of Burgundy and the Italian city states, and the Holy Roman Emperor were all men-at-arms schooled in mounted combat. These individuals were also inducted into the knightly *ordo* through some kind of dubbing ceremony, patronized and often participated in tournaments, worshipped prowess, hungered for fame, were fond of warfare, and organized crusades. And to the courts of these men came the minstrels, troubadors, and poets who gave voice to the *chansons de geste*, courtly love romances, and historical chronicles that defined what it meant to be a knight.

Aside from being actual members of the knightly family, as well as patrons of its lifestyle and literature, Europe's princes were also dependent on knighthood for the manhood and muscle necessary to defend their domains. Medieval monarchs were confronted by the same external threats as the Church — Northmen, Magyars, Saracens, Turks — and turning back these invaders required armed, trained and loyal bands of knights. Concurrently, because most of these rulers initially lacked the wherewithal to support either professional armies or bureaucracies, they were also beholden to their knightly vassals to maintain order and dispense justice in the manors and demesnes allocated to them for their support.

However, despite these bonds of class, culture, and mutual self-interest, knighthood proved to be as troublesome for princes as it was for prelates. While knights acknowledged the superior social status of their royal employers, they also regarded these rulers as firsts among equals and expected them to respect the privileges and prerogatives of their fellow men-at-arms. And among these knightly perquisites, none was more important than the right to engage in whatever kind of private warfare a knight deemed necessary to uphold his honor and fortune.

Not surprisingly, medieval monarchs and their administrators were less than enamored with knighthood's claim of an untrammeled right to commit violence at any time and place of its own choosing. Aside from the fact that such a prerogative completely undermined royal authority, the feuds, vendettas and turf wars that ensued from its exercise encouraged murder, fostered mayhem, and disrupted commerce within a princely realm. There was also the problem that any knight injured or killed in one of these private conflicts was one less man-at-arms a lord could call upon in the event of an insurrection in or invasion of his territories. Indeed, no less than the Church, European royalty was very much intent on controlling and channeling the prowess of its knights.

Being men of the world, however, monarchs favored an ideal of knightly behavior that was decidedly less spiritual than the chivalrous conduct favored by Rome. A Richard the Lion-Heart or Saint Louis IX of France, for example, took pride in their prowess, participated in tournaments, waged wars, led Crusades, and enjoyed the ways of the flesh. They were also loyal to their companions and retainers, generous to their servants, well educated, courteous to friend and foe alike, quick to anger, sensitive to slights, and capable of great cruelty. In short, these kings were the very embodiment of a chivalry with which most secular knights could easily identify.

Nevertheless, while Richard and Louis shared the passions, pursuits, and prejudices of their knightly men-at-arms, they also expected a degree of loyalty, service, and obedience from them that was not always to their liking. These kings accepted that a knight should glory in his strength and military skills, seek fame and riches, and enjoy profane pleasures, but they also insisted that it was their right to determine when and where a knight's arms could be used, what booty was his to lay claim to, and with whom he might play. Neither the Lionheart nor the pious Louis tolerated private wars in their royal domains, and they exacted from their retainers what they regarded as their due, whether this took the form of taxes and/or military service either at home or in the Holy Land. Indeed, for these monarchs, the heroic knight was first and foremost a loyal liegeman who was always at the beck and call of his lord.

Medieval monarchs like Richard and Louis were also in a much better position than the Church to compel compliance with their chivalric ideals. As the actual sources of law, legitimacy and largesse within their realms, these rulers could reward a loyal and pliant man-at-arms with titles, lands, and legal authority over his vassals and dependents. Concurrently, a knight who dared invoke the displeasure of these princes faced a very real risk of finding himself outlawed, stripped of rank, reduced to penury, sent into exile, or condemned to the gallows. However irksome knights might find their royal employers, it was usually to their political, social, and material advantage to comply with their wishes, or at least appear to do so.

Support for strong kingship and knightly fealty to one's lord also found support in the chivalric literature of this time. In works of the Arthurian cycle such as *Lancelot du Lac*, the *Story of Merlin*, and Thomas Malory's late 15th century prose account, *Le Morte Darthur*, various characters spoke directly to the importance of kings as the guarantors of peace, harmony and the knightly order. And all of these stories addressed the dire consequences — strife, warfare, famine, plagues — that befell a kingdom whose knights challenged or betrayed their monarch.

Aside from these tales of Arthur's knightly fellowship, ideals of royal chivalry also figured prominently in a series of 14th century *chansons de geste* relating the deeds of the legendary outlaw Robin Hood. Skilled with horse, sword and bow, generous to all in need, courteous to low and high born alike, devoted to the Virgin, a protector of women, orphans, and the poor, and the courtly lover of Maid Marian, this bandit warrior was the very paragon of virtuous knighthood (and in later retellings of his tales, he was actually recast as a noble knight, Robin of Locksley, the Earl of Huntington). In addition to his many virtues, Robin was a fiercely loyal liegeman to his king — Edward in early versions, Richard the Lionheart in later ones — in whose name he commits acts of banditry and insurrection against such unchivalrous and disloyal villains as the Sheriff of Nottingham, Sir Guy of Gisborne, and Richard's scheming brother, John Lackland. Indeed, to the present day, there is no better exemplar in literature of a king's good and true knight than the champion of Sherwood Forest.[18]

This chivalric literature, however, also underscores many of the practical difficulties confronting any king seeking to shape and control the behavior of his knightly retainers. In the case of Lancelot, for example, while Camelot's most chivalrous knight was deeply devoted to Arthur and accepted him as his suzerain, he also brooked no interference with his right to behave in a manner he deemed fitting for a noble man-at-arms. As such, he felt free to cuckold his king, wage war on his fellow knights, embark on any adventures that caught his fancy, and even plunge the realm into civil war. Similarly, Robin Hood's long campaign against his enemies was not undertaken at his king's behest, but because he deemed such behavior necessary to uphold his honor and, almost as an afterthought, that of his liege. Nor should it be forgotten that in some variants of the Robin Hood story, the protagonist tires of life at court and opts instead to return to a life of banditry in Sherwood Forest.

Indeed, knighthood remains a royal headache right up until the early modern period, when a combination of reliable revenue streams, salaried armies, and heavy artillery finally afford monarchs the wherewithal to bring these mounted warriors to heel. To be sure, where a medieval throne was occupied by a strong, forceful king flush with money and eager for war, knights could be persuaded to forego their private warfare and direct their prowess against the enemies of their lords. And, as Richard Kaeuper notes in his work on royal chivalry, these same warriors were often willing to loyally and faithfully serve their crowned masters in a variety of non-military capacities as well.

They also gave essential and unpaid help in law and administration; they sat on juries and inquests, on commissions of oyer and terminer, on commissions of roads and dikes, or of array; they acted as tax assessors and collectors. Some served as sheriffs, some as justices.[19]

These many services to the side, however, as the seemingly endless conflicts of the Middle Ages attest, knights largely behaved in a manner consistent with their own sense of what was necessary to be adjudged a man of worth; whatever the commands of their prelates or princes, whatever the consequences for public order. Why they felt compelled to do so goes to the very heart of what chivalry, what heroism actually meant to knighthood-at-large, and it is to that complex of ideas and practices we now turn.

The Good Servant of Prowess: Knightly Chivalry

Whether we are speaking of clerical or royal chivalry, we are talking about codes of conduct that heroized the knight who was above all else a good and obedient servant of either the Church or the state. Yet, as we have seen, neither popes nor princes were completely successful in bending knighthood to their will. Insofar as service to a cleric or a king was beneficial to them, knights were happy to serve in their crusades and dynastic wars, as well as to render them valuable assistance in civil matters during peacetime. Otherwise, knights reserved to themselves the right to determine how a knight should behave and who among their brotherhood was worthy of being dubbed a hero.

This said, what exactly did chivalry and heroism mean for most knights? As already noted, looking to chivalric literature for an answer to this question is problematic because so much of this material was produced by churchmen, clerically trained writers, or troubadors and storytellers singing for their suppers at court. Consequently, the *chansons de geste*, romances, and chronicles that were authored and/or performed by these scribes and singers tended to reflect their patrons' predilections for plots featuring protagonists who were, above all else, pious, virtuous, and loyal to their lords. While we know that knighthood was familiar with this material, and in many cases tried to emulate the warriors in these stories, we also know from the evidence of knightly behavior that knights probably focused more on the adventures and swordplay in these tales than on their more vaunted themes.[20]

A better indicator of what knighthood-at-large regarded as chivalrous/heroic behavior lies in the various manuals of chivalry that were penned during the Middle Ages by actual knights, and of these works, probably the best is a 14th century book of chivalry authored by one Geoffroi de Charny. A veritable knight's knight, Charny was a man-of-arms who actually lived and died in the saddle. Born sometime before 1306, in the middling ranks of elite French society, Charny acquired through two good marriages lordship of Pierre Perthuis, Montfort, Savoisy and Licey. His martial career began in 1337 with the commencement of the Hundred Years War between the Plantagenet and Valois kings of England and France and continued without interruption until 1356 when he perished defending his sovereign, Jean le Bon (John the Good), at the battle of Poitiers.[21]

In the intervening years between the commencement of his military service and death, Charny was the very embodiment of the redoubtable warrior. Service in Gascony in 1337 was followed by active campaigning against the English at Tournai in 1340 and Brittany in

1341. Knighted in 1343, Charny took advantage of a lull in the conflict between France and England to take part in the unsuccessful crusade of Humbert II, dauphin of Viennois, against the Turks at Smyrna in Anatolia from 1345 to 1347. Upon returning to France, he promptly re-entered the Valois/Plantagenet conflict, attempting to recover Calais from the English in 1349; an effort that resulted in his defeat and capture by Edward III.

Upon his accession to the French throne in 1351, Jean II ransomed Charny from captivity, made him a member of his new order of chivalry, the Company of the Star, and commissioned him to write up a chivalric code for his band of royal knights. Upon recommencement of hostilities with England, Jean named Charny keeper of the French king's standard, the sacred Oriflamme of St. Denis. It was in this capacity as his monarch's standard bearer that Charny met the heroic demise at Poitiers described below by the medieval chronicler Froissart:

> There [at Poitiers] Sir Geoffroy de Charny fought gallantly near the King. The whole press and cry of battle were upon him because he was carrying the King's sovereign banner. He also had before him on the field his own banner, gules, three escutcheons argent [three silver shields on a red background]. So many English and Gascons came around him from all sides that they cracked open the King's battle formation and smashed it; there were so many English and Gascons that at least five of these men-at-arms attacked one [French] gentleman. Sir Geoffroy de Charny was killed with the banner of France in his hands.[22]

While Charny was without question a loyal liegeman to the king he died defending, as well as a good son of the Church — aside from hearing mass every day before sunrise, he had the right to a portable altar, enjoyed the services of a personal confessor, and was the first recorded owner of the Shroud of Turin — his book of chivalry makes it clear that he viewed himself first and foremost as a fighting man whose principal concern in life was perfecting his trade and acquiring honor. This is stated in the very first pages of his work, where Charny asserts that the business of knighthood is "deeds of arms" and the aim of its individual members is to acquire the prowess — the strength, skills, and experience — necessary to perform these martial feats *exceedingly* well. "All deeds of arms" Charny asserts:

> Merit praise for all those who perform well in them. For I maintain that there are no small feats of arms, but only good and great ones, although some feats of arms are of greater worth than others. Therefore, I say that he who does more is of greater worth.[23]

Doing more for Charny entailed distinguishing oneself in a variety of martial contests, each more difficult and dangerous than the one preceding it. For it was only through the constant practice of one's craft in ever more challenging circumstances that a warrior could acquire the muscle, stamina, dexterity, discipline, knowledge of warfare, and, most importantly, courage, necessary to win the honors, i.e., the reputation, titles, revenues, marriages, and places at court, which made one knight "of greater worth than others."

Charny's manual also provided his readers with a guide to the kinds of combat an aspiring *preudome*, or man of worth, was expected to engage in during his life; and, in keeping with his idea that some feats of arms were more worthy than others, he assigned to these varied acts of violence different quotients of honor. In peacetime, for example, men-at-arms were expected to distinguish themselves in jousts and tournaments, though those participating in tourneys deserved higher praise than their comrades who limited themselves to jousting, because group combat was more dangerous and required a higher level of military skill than contests between two men alone. Those who won distinction on the tournament circuit, however, had to give pride of place to their colleagues who had seen action and won honor for service in local or private wars. And those who only participated in local conflicts were considered of lesser worth than knights who "at great expense, hardship, and grave peril undertake to travel to...distant countries" and "perform great deeds of arms" in those places.[24]

The best knights for Charny were those individuals we might call natural born killers, i.e., those men

> Who, from their own nature and instinct, as soon as they begin to reach the age of understanding...like to hear and listen to men of prowess talk of military deeds, and to see men-at-arms with their weapons and armor and enjoy looking at fine mounts and chargers.[25]

Charny noted that without prodding or encouragement these young devotees of knighthood advanced from one martial activity and honor to the next. As soon as they reached the appropriate age they engaged in jousts, enjoyed them, and then learned to bear arms in tournaments. Participation in tourneys demonstrated to them there is greater honor to be had in group combat and so they would opt to do more tourneying than jousting. In time, they realized that "men-at-arms who are good in war are more highly prized and honored than any other men-at-arms,"[26] and this realization would lead them ineluctably to study and practice warfare both at home and abroad.

Charny also believed that in addition to an aptitude for violence, those who were born to rumble shared common motives as well. They wished to maintain the honor of their name; they hungered for earthly renown; and they were eager to win "booty or prisoners or other profit from the enemies of those on whose side they fight."[27] With regard to the latter of these considerations, Charny reminded his audience that:

> In this vocation [knighthood] one should therefore set one's heart and mind on winning honor, which endures for ever, rather than on winning profit and booty, which one can lose within one single hour. And yet one should praise and value those men-at-arms who are able to make war on, inflict damage on, and win profit from their enemies, for they cannot do it without strenuous effort and great courage. But again I shall repeat: he who does best is most worthy.[28]

What is striking about this passage, and others like it in Charny's book of chivalry, is his unequivocal acknowledgement that knights are first and foremost servants of prowess, i.e., men who "make war on, inflict damage on, and win profit from their enemies." As such, life for these individuals is an ongoing round of violent conflicts—jousts, tournaments, local feuds, dynastic wars, crusades—which hone their fighting skills and afford them opportunities to win the respect of peers, worldly fame, and last, but certainly not least, prisoners and plunder. Indeed, Charny even treats non-martial activities as forms of combat training, admonishing his readers to avoid soft beds, rich foods, and too much wine; to keep fit through hunting, hawking, and regular jousting; to play games in moderation; to dance and sing so as to stay in good spirits; and to listen to old knights when they recount their war stories. As for love and romance, while Charny accepts that matters of the heart are a normal and healthy part of any warrior's life, their principal benefit lies in the fact that they "inspire knights, men-at-arms, and squires to undertake worthy deeds that bring them honor and increase their renown."[29] In short, Charny's most worthy knight is a man whose every waking hour is spent in service to his profession.

Further, because prowess and its exercise are so central to knighthood, Charny acknowledges few limitations on a knight's efforts to learn, master and excel at his craft. Highway robbery and theft are "forms of ill doing" if done "for no good reason."[30] Murder "in a bad cause" is also to be avoided, as are "seizing, plundering, and robbing others without any challenge and without any wrongdoing on the part of the persons attacked."[31] And violence against the personnel and property of Holy Mother Church are cited as evil deeds because they prevent the clergy from carrying out the noble services by which a knight is shriven of sin and made ready for his eternal reward. Otherwise, Charny leaves his fellow men-at-arms essentially free to ply their trade as they see fit, or as he puts it "to wage war on their own behalf in order to defend their honor and inheritance."[32]

To be sure, Charny's book of chivalry does call on his fellow warriors to engage in deeds of arms that are of service to others. He stresses the worthiness of knights serving "in the wars to defend the honor and inheritance of their rightful lord who maintains them."[33] And he also argues that

> No one can and should excuse himself from bearing arms in a just cause, whether for his lord or for his lineage or for himself or the Holy Church or to defend and uphold the faith or out of pity for men or women who cannot defend their own rights. In such cases they should commit themselves eagerly, boldly, and gladly to such deeds of arms and adventures, fearing nothing.[34]

This admonition to the side, Charny nevertheless leaves to knights the right to determine when, where, and how their arms are to be employed. And he does so out of a sincere belief that most of his fellow men-at-arms will use their prowess properly because they are members of a noble Christian order, which surpasses all others save the service of God. Indeed, Charny asserts that knights are in many ways superior to their clerical confreres because there is "nothing in comparison with the suffering to be endured in the order of knighthood."

> For, whoever might want to consider the hardships, pains, discomforts, fears, perils, broken bones, and wounds which the good knights who uphold the order of knighthood as they should endure and have to suffer frequently, there is no religious order in which as much is suffered as has to be endured by these good knights who go in search of deeds of arms.[35]

In addition to this physical agony, knights suffered from spiritual torments because they faced the very real prospect of dying suddenly without recourse to the last rites of the Church. Consequently, Charny argues:

> One could well say that of all the men in the world, of whatever estate, whether religious or lay, none have as great a need to be a good Christian to the highest degree nor to have such true devoutness in their hearts nor to lead a life of such integrity and to carry out all their undertakings loyally and with good judgment as do these good men-at-arms who have the will to pursue this calling...wisely and according to God's will.[36]

While there were probably few knights as deeply pious as Geoffroi de Charny, it is likely that knighthood-at-large agreed with his portrayal of them as *miles Christi* whose prowess reflected God's grace, and whose suffering served as both a form of penance and even martyrdom. It is also quite clear from what we know of the Church's efforts to promote its own code of chivalry that these men-at-arms did not accept Rome's claim of authority over them, and were very much in accord with the sentiments expressed by their comrade William the Marshall on the occasion of his death:

> The clerks are too hard on us. They shave us too closely. I have captured five hundred knights and have appropriated their arms, horses, and their entire equipment. If for this reason the kingdom of God is closed to me, I can do nothing about it, for I cannot return my booty. I can do no more for God than to give myself to him, repenting all my sins. Unless the clergy desire my damnation, they must ask no more. But their teaching is false — else no one could be saved.[37]

Both Marshall's deathbed salvo against the clergy and Charny's ruminations on chivalry tell us a great deal about the kind of warrior knighthood-at-large dubbed a hero. He was from first to last a good servant of prowess; a man skilled with edged weapons and experienced in all forms of combat. As such, his life was one spent in an unceasing pursuit of opportunities for violence — single combat, tourneys, private wars, dynastic conflicts, crusades — aimed at honing his martial abilities, taking captives, and appropriating other people's property. In short, this heroic man-at-arms was the medieval equivalent of an American gunslinger, i.e., a gifted freebooter with a record number of kills, holdups, and shakedowns for which he was adjudged worthy to receive respect from his peers, obedience from his inferiors, and rich bounties from his employers.

Beyond his proven prowess, the knightly hero was also a man noted for his generosity, manly bearing, and loyalty to lords and liegemen. He could read, write, and recognize a story that was well told; behave appropriately at court; show good table manners; marry well; sire male children; engage in discreet infidelities; and properly pleasure whoever happened to be in his bed. In matters of religion, he deemed his vocation a holy order, his feats at arms a sign of God's favor, and his many wounds and hardships a form of penance. And at his discretion and on his terms, the heroic knight also participated in pilgrimages, crusades, and other kinds of sanctified combat aimed at protecting the Church and its flock. Above all else, however, this "supreme man of worth" (*un homme plus soulvereinement preux*) was a person who answered to nothing and no one save his own often prickly sense of honor.

Sunset of a Dream: Knighthood in Decline

In the fullness of time, the different elements of clerical, courtly, and knightly chivalry fused together to produce the ideal of heroic knighthood celebrated in the modern period. Indeed, one could argue that there was always something of a consensus among medieval churchmen, monarchs, and knights about the principal characteristics of what they dubbed a *preudome*, or worthy man-of-arms. For example, whether such a warrior served popes, princes, or prowess, he was always expected to be a lean, mean fighting machine eager for combat and fearless in battle. And whether he was an errant mercenary or the liegeman of a lord, all of chivalry's commentators agreed that in order to win deathless glory a knight had to follow some kind of honor code, which, at the very least, required him to be loyal to his employers, forthright with his peers, generous with his wealth, protective of women, orphans, and the weak, and a servant of Christ.

Of course, by the end of the 16th century, questions about who a knight should serve and how that service should be rendered were largely irrelevant. The rise of dynastic states supported by armies of infantrymen equipped with guns and cannon insured that in the modern period knights would kowtow to the occupants of Europe's various thrones. Backed up by superior firepower, regular tax revenues, and a pliant clergy, European monarchs were able to make and enforce the claim that they alone possessed the right of licit violence in their territories, and that they alone were empowered to determine who enjoyed honor and privilege in their domains. Slowly, begrudgingly, knighthood acquiesced to these monarchical claims, and their royal masters rewarded this submission with commands, commissions, and courtly appointments. Indeed, this quid pro quo, this *ancien regime*, would remain in place throughout most of Europe until the end of the First World War.

The decline of knighthood as an independent fighting force, however, does nothing to diminish the prestige of its warriors. From the early modern period to the present, the medieval knight remains one of the most revered figures in the Western heroic pantheon. Professional soldiers look to him as the model of the ideal man-at-arms; skilled in warfare, steadfast in combat, obedient to the chain-of-command, and ever solicitous to the needs and welfare of those committed to his or her care. Would-be gentle men and women follow his example when they cultivate the art of conversation, practice good manners, dance well, and behave in a gallant manner to the objects of their romantic affection. Self-styled champions of justice fancy themselves his direct descendants when they fight for the rights of those they deem distressed and in need of rescue. And contemporary cinema is awash with his fictional counterparts — Luke Skywalker, Batman, James Bond — who, like Lancelot and his knights of the Table Round, are licensed to kill; expert in mounted shock combat (albeit of a type wedded to a very different kind of horse power); skilled in all manner of weaponry; driven to act out of a deeply personal sense of morality and honor; impossible to control; and conversant in the delights of dry vodka martinis shaken not stirred with a twist of lemon.

6

Imitatio Christi
The Hero as Saint

It is the same with the saints in Paradise as with the counselors of kings ... whoever has business with an earthly king seeks, in effect, to know who he holds in high regard and who, having his ear, is able to approach him successfully. He then seeks out this favoured person and begs him to convey his request. It is the same with the saints in paradise who, being the friends of Our Lord and his intimates, can invoke him in all confidence, since he cannot fail to listen to them.

— St. Louis IX

In the Church militant, two things are required before someone can be regarded as a saint: virtue of morals and truth of signs, that is, works of piety in life and evidence of miracles after death.

— Innocent III

Pound pastrami, can kraut, six bagels — bring home for Emma.
— J. Walter Miller, Jr.: *A Canticle for Leibowitz*

In 1993, while conducting research at the Deutsches Literatur Archiv in the vicinity of Stuttgart, I was invited by two of the archive's librarians to accompany them on a sight seeing trip to the Bavarian city of Würzburg. Nestled in the northern tip of Franconia, Würzburg is an ancient Catholic city famous for its Romanesque, Gothic and Baroque cathedrals. Indeed, most of our time that day was spent exploring these churches, which, aside from their prominent architectural features, are also notable for their many richly decorated altars, shrines, reliquaries, paintings, wood carvings, and sculptures celebrating the life of Christ and his community of saints.

During our visit to these Catholic holy sites, my companions — a German Jewish survivor of the Holocaust and the daughter of an East German Evangelical Protestant minister — expressed their discomfort with the rich trappings, icons, and statues that filled these places of worship. Not only did they feel there was just too much "stuff" in these cathedrals, thus contributing to an overwrought and claustrophobic environment, but it also seemed to them that all of the paintings, sculptures and shrines were an obvious violation of the Decalogue's strictures against both false gods and the making and honoring of idols and graven images. I found their objections of interest because, as the scion of a devout Catholic family who had spent most of his youth in similar, albeit less splendid, churches, my own reaction to these interiors was markedly different. What my colleagues found crowded, for example, made me feel warm and even cozy. And the images, relics, and inscriptions that struck them as idolatrous were, in my eyes, little more than a kind of much loved scrap book filled with photos, mementos, and news clippings relating key moments in the lives of close relatives and well regarded friends.

As I explained to my fellow sight seers, much of the visual material in these churches was commissioned in centuries past by a Roman episcopate trying to familiarize largely illiterate populations with the life of Jesus, the tenets of his faith, and the acts of assorted Christians deemed heroes of the Church. While worthy of respect, these images and relics were intended not as objects of worship — though certainly more than one Christian had treated them as such — but as heuristic devices whose aim was to edify and inspire their visitors. As such, everything in these sacred precincts — stonework, carved wood, stained glass, canvas, body parts — functioned as primers to educate the faithful about the major events in the life of Christianity's founder, as well as the deeds of Christ's relatives, colleagues, and assorted devotees who were counted among the Church's *cultus sancti* or "cult of the saints."

Having mouthed the Church's official line on holy iconography, however, I also felt it necessary in the interest of full disclosure to acknowledge to my companions that, whatever Rome's pedagogical aims, a great many Catholics — as well as Eastern Orthodox Christians, Anglicans, and even some "high church" Lutherans — do indeed treat the simulacra and remains of the sainthood with what can only be described as pagan-like devotion. Indeed, it is not an unusual sight in Catholic churches to find communicants clustered around saintly shrines saying prayers, offering up assorted gifts — candles, incense, flowers, money — and making secret vows in the hopes of securing some kind of heavenly assistance. People behave in this manner because they believe that the extraordinary sanctity (*fama sanctitatis*) of these individuals in life secured for them not only an honored place in heaven among Christ's counselors, but the power to work miracles on behalf of the living as well.

Another reason church visitors are drawn to these cults is because they believe that the saints honored by them often use their mojo to advance the petitions of supplicants associated with certain causes and/or vocations dear to them when they were alive. Folks who find themselves in desperate straits, for example, frequently flock to the corner of a church dedicated to St. Jude Thaddeus, an apostle and martyr with a penchant for lost causes. Similarly, married couples unable to have children may light a candle at the shrine of St. Anne, the mother of Mary, who ostensibly looks out for the infertile because she conceived and gave birth to her own daughter late in life. And for individuals who make a living driving cabs, or who dream of growing prize winning roses, it never hurts to offer up a prayer to St. Fiacre, a medieval herbalist and healer reputed to take a special interest in gardeners, taxi drivers, and all who suffer from hemorrhoids.

Whatever the reasons for their devotion to the altars, likenesses, and remains of the saints, Catholics have identified, sanctified, and venerated scores of these individuals over the last two millennia of the Common Era. In addition to the apostles and martyrs, scholars, hermits, missionaries, rulers, bishops, popes, mendicants, and visionaries have been inducted into this company of holy men and women. And because these sainted folk were Christ like in life and imbued with magical *virtus* in death, they have also been honored, like the pagan heroes before them, with public cults featuring splendid tombs, shrines, works of art, gifts, endowments, feast days, festivals, and special liturgical rituals. Indeed, as John Lennon would say of the Beatles in 1966, these figures have been, and in many segments of the Christian world still are, "more popular than Jesus."

Suffice it to say, this cult of the saints represented a radical departure from the ideals and practices of early Christianity. As noted in our discussion of martyrdom, the Jesus movement initially eschewed the whole notion of heroes and their cults, as well as the idea that there could be any intercessor between God and his people save the Christ. Insofar as it was used, "saint" connoted either any member of a Christian congregation, or someone who was martyred for the faith and honored by his community with a respectable grave and a mass of remembrance.

All of this changed, however, when, following Constantine's Edict of Milan, Christianity extended its sway over Greco-Roman and Germanic populations that were wedded to tutelary deities, semi-divine heroes, talismans, and magic. It was these newly converted peoples, in conjunction with priests and bishops recruited from their ranks, who transformed what had been a term of respect for fellow co-religionists and martyrs into a signifier for the members of a very select community of semi-divine beings. Drawing on traditions taken from both pagan heroic death cults and early Christian commemorative ceremonies for the martyred, early medieval communities began to identify and designate as saints churchmen, missionaries, and anchorites noted for their exceptional sanctity in life and, most importantly, for the purported ability of their bodies to work miracles after death. Indeed, it was this conviction that the physical remains and personal effects of the sainted were "power traps" of supernatural energy, which provided the initial impetus for a *cultus sancti* replete with enshrined tombs, feast days, and special religious ceremonies.

This cult of the saints proved to be very popular with both the laity and clergy during the Middle Ages. The notion that there was a heavenly community of Christian heroes overseeing and protecting its earthly clientele meshed well with pre-existing beliefs and superstitions. Saintly feast days also provided clerics with a ready made means of inculcating Catholic orthodoxy and controlling popular religious devotion. Churches with saints' tombs and relics were enriched by the gifts supplicants left when paying their respects to these sites. Dynasties and communal authorities found these cults could be used to foster loyalty, unity and patriotism among their subjects. And local economies benefited from servicing the needs of pilgrims visiting their holy shrines.

Not surprisingly, the proliferation of these cults, their widespread popularity, varied functions, and obvious profitability also attracted the attention of Rome. While the Curia was not opposed to a cult of the saints, and in fact recognized the many pedagogical, political, social, and economic benefits of a Christian heroic pantheon, it was concerned that local communities might sanctify pagan deities, heretics, or people of questionable virtue. Further, there was also some unease among the church leadership about the fact that these popular devotions were more centered on the slavish veneration of saintly remains than on what could be learned from the lives of the relics' former owners.

Consequently, beginning in the 10th century and continuing through the end of the Middle Ages, the Roman Curia moved to assert control over the whole business of saintly canonization. While communities were encouraged to continue bringing to the attention of their clergy holy men and women believed worthy of a saintly cult, the papacy claimed sole right to canonize their nominees. Rome also established stricter criteria for those elevated to the sainthood, as well as a lengthy and expensive judicial process to evaluate the merits of those brought forward for this honor. Though regions, cities, and towns continued to create cults to venerate various individuals whose remains were believed to be imbued with supernatural power, the Church's officially sanctioned *cultus sancti* required more of its members than an ability to act as Christianized jujus. Increasingly, a prospective saint's advocates needed to demonstrate that their candidate not only had miracle-working bones, but also a life that had been so Christ like it inspired piety among Christians and helped advance the interests and causes of Holy Mother Church.

This new papal canonization process transformed the Christian cult of the saints from a warehouse of talismanic relics into an actual community of heroic figures with exceptional lives deemed worthy of emulation by the faithful. Moreover, in its efforts to focus more attention on the saint's life rather than the magical properties of his remains, Rome began to canonize men and women whose lives were closer, in some cases contemporaneous, with those of Christians living in the late Middle Ages. This "modern" sainthood included such luminaries as Francis and Clare of Assisi, Thomas Aquinas, and Catherine of Siena, as well as other men and women who were as renowned for their sanctity, learning, and orthodoxy, as for the miracles they worked on behalf of the faithful after death.

In what follows, we will address this medieval *cultus sancti* with an eye aimed at illuminating the various ways in which it represented both a continuation of ancient pagan heroic traditions and an attempt to create a new ideal of heroism rooted in an *imitatio Christi*—a life of exceptional piety in thought, word and deed. Beginning with its initial use as a descriptor for any follower of the Jesus movement, the succeeding pages explore how the term "saint" became an honorific accorded only to those who, in the words of St. Louis IX quoted above, were adjudged "the friends of Our Lord and his intimates," the men and women who were both Jesus' counselors and humanity's intercessors in heaven. As this chapter will detail, who these special pals of Christ were, how they got identified as such, what this meant for them in the way of public and popular devotion, and what was expected of them in return for this veneration, were questions that both laity and clergy wrestled with throughout the Middle Ages. Their answers to these queries created a rather remarkable collection of souls, a cult of saints whose example informs what it means to be a Christian hero to the present day.

New Wine in Old Bottles: The Rise of the Cultus Sancti

In his reverent send up of Catholic sainthood, *A Canticle for Leibowitz*, J. Walter Miller, Jr., imagines a possible future where a community of monks struggles to preserve knowledge in a post-apocalyptic America populated by illiterate "simpletons" who burn books and murder the people who read them. The founder of Miller's imaginary monastic order is Isaac Edward Leibowitz, a Jewish electrical engineer who converts to Catholicism in the aftermath of the nuclear holocaust that destroys civilization. Fearing the extinction of learning, Leibowitz organizes a Christian sodality of "bookleggers" dedicated to saving printed matter and smuggling it to safety. Unfortunately, as so often happens during dark ages in history, he is rewarded for his troubles with a martyr's death at the hands of a mob, which roasts him alive over a pile of texts he was trying to save.

Miller relates in the first part of his novel how Leibowitz's booklegger brotherhood regard him as a hero, revere him as a saint, and press the papacy to follow their example by officially canonizing him. After centuries of patient lobbying, this canonization is finally achieved when a young monk miraculously stumbles upon a fallout shelter, which contains some personal papers of Leibowitz that help to confirm his sanctity. These precious relics — a schematic for an electric circuit, several handwritten notes, and a shopping list quoted in this chapter's third epigraph — are exhumed, illuminated, and translated to "New Rome," where they take their place amid the other enshrined remains of the Church's community of saints.

Mention is made of Miller's sci-fi classic because the particulars of its title character's life, death and canonization are illustrative of how sainthood emerged and developed during late antiquity and the early medieval period. Like Leibowitz, a great many members of the early Jesus movement were converted Jews whose advocacy of the new faith often led to rather gruesome deaths. In the eyes of their fellow Christians, these martyred souls were an exceptional lot because of their great fortitude and the assured place of honor their demise had earned for them in Christ's kingdom. Consequently, during the persecutions, it became customary in Christian communities to regard these individuals as especially holy men and women, or "saints."

Following the legalization of Christianity by Constantine, congregations continued to show deference to their martyred brethren. In addition to honoring them with the rubric of saint, communities initiated the practice of exhuming their remains and translating them into tombs thought more appropriate to their dignity. Local clergy presided over these translations, offering up a mass of remembrance that was repeated in following years on the anniversary of the martyr's death.

Though initially a purely communal affair aimed at honoring neighbors who had died for the faith, these saintly cults became a Church-wide phenomenon in late antiquity. Communities compiled and exchanged accounts of the lives and deaths of their saints, and these vitae in turn won for many of their subjects — Lawrence of Alexandria, Perpetua, Felicity, and Cyprian of Carthage, Martin of Tours — a popular following that extended well beyond the boundaries of their home towns. Indeed, by late antiquity, it was not uncommon for local liturgical calendars to feature feast days and special masses commemorating martyrs from all corners of the Roman world.

Aside from encouraging the growth of an increasingly catholic community of saints, the end of official persecution also ushered in an expanded notion of sanctity. While congregations still regarded a willingness to die for the faith as the surest sign of a person's saintliness, they also began to sanctify folks who demonstrated their devotion to Christianity in less lethal ways than martyrdom. Doctors of the Church, such as Augustine, Jerome, and John Chrysostom, for example, achieved sainthood because of the role they played in defining Christian orthodoxy and defending it against pagans, heretics, and schismatics. Hermits like Paul of Thebes and Anthony of Egypt, on the other hand, were canonized for renouncing the world and living holy lives of solitude, poverty, and self-mortification. And various bishops — Leo I of Rome, Aignan of Orleans, Loup of Troyes — acquired saintly status for ably defending their episcopates against barbarian invasions.[1]

Whatever the reasons for their sanctification, all of these holy men and women were extremely popular with the recently converted peoples of the Roman Empire and the Germanic kingdoms. In part, this was due to the fact that whether they were martyrs, confessors, hermits, or militant clerics, these Christian saints did not appear all that different from the demigods, warriors, lawgivers, and athletes pagan communities had heroized and venerated for centuries. Like their earlier counterparts, saintly folk also enjoyed divine favor, possessed special abilities and powers, were accorded places of honor in the afterlife, and could intervene in the affairs of the living. And, as we noted in our examination of martyrdom in the ancient world, the early Church encouraged these comparisons by both underscoring the semi-divine nature of Jesus, and likening those martyred in his name to the pre–Christian champions of antiquity.[2]

New converts were also attracted to the *cults* of these Christian saints. The practice of translating the bodies of individuals sanctified by their communities into respectable tombs and shrines played well with populations that believed the shades of departed heroes continued to reside in their bones and belongings. Similarly, the veneration of saintly remains with special masses and yearly feast days also coincided with the pagan belief that the heroic spirits resident in relics were powerful and in need of placation.

Indeed, for peoples who haled from religions replete with guardian spirits, sacred sites, talismans, incantations, and necromancy, perhaps sainthood's biggest draw was the possibility that the corpses and personal effects of its members might be induced to work assorted favors and miracles on behalf of the living. For if, as the Church insisted, the actions of those sanctified while alive had won for them both a special gift of grace and a place among Christ's heavenly counselors, then:

> Once dead, saints became even more of a source of power than during life, a power available to be trapped and controlled ... by possession of relics which served as reminders of their human existences, and in the care of corporeal remains that contained the essence of their force as intercessors.[3]

This notion that the remains of saints were power traps of supernatural energy helped transform sainthood during the early Middle Ages from an expression of respect for a congregation's exceptionally pious members into a kind of Christianized heroic death cult. Communities bought, sold, traded, exchanged, and even stole sanctified body parts and effects, and, like the documents of Miller's fictitious Saint Leibowitz, illuminated these items with gold, jewels and precious wrappings. Congregations also ensconced these remnants in elaborately decorated crypts, altars and reliquaries, and these sites became the foci of popular devotions aimed at tapping the talismanic power of their relics for health, protection, and good fortune.

Not surprisingly, this obsession with saintly charnel also began to play an important role in the canonization process. The decision to sanctify a person increasingly began to hinge not so much on what he or she had done in life to defend and advance the faith, as on the prodigies their relics were capable of working on behalf of the living after death. In time, this fixation on miracle making bones actually made it impossible to achieve sainthood without them. Indeed, even after sanctification, a saint's status — the size of their following, the ubiquity of their images and hagiographies, the numbers of churches, confraternities and children bearing their name — continued to depend on the ability of their remains to deliver bonafied benefits to the faithful. Saints that failed to attend to the needs of their supplicants faced the prospect of seeing their relics publicly humiliated, sequestered in less prestigious quarters, and shunned by the pilgrimage-going public.[4]

What kinds of people were honored with these early medieval death cults? Some were popular pagan gods and heroes who were simply Christianized by their communities. Cornély of Carnac, for example, the patron saint of horned beasts, was very likely a canonized version of Brittany's Celtic deity Cernunnos, the horned god of the hunt. Similarly, Saint Brigid of Kildare, patroness of blacksmiths and scholars, may have been a Christian facsimile of the Irish goddess of fire and poetry who shared the same name. As for the actual Christians who were canonized at this time, these included the twelve apostles, martyrs for the faith, early Church fathers, holy hermits, militant bishops, and successful missionaries such as Patrick of Ireland, Columba of Scotland, Remigius of the Franks, and Boniface of the Germans.[5]

Regardless of their provenance, these saints were very much like the other heroic figures we have examined up to this point. They tended to hale from well-to-do backgrounds; enjoyed some education; displayed exceptional abilities as lawgivers, warriors and champions; and were notable for their fortitude, courage, intellect, and piety. And, like the savior they served, these Christian heroes were also reputed to have worked wonders while alive — healing the sick, vanquishing demons, driving serpents out of Ireland, vanquishing "Nessie."

Given these characteristics, it is not unexpected that lay Christians believed these individuals to be, literally, saintly material. Nor were they discouraged in this view by their clergy. Local bishops investigated and confirmed the sanctity of the people their episcopates deemed worthy of inclusion in the Christian heroic pantheon. They also presided over the exhumation and translation of the bodies and personal effects of these individuals, created special offices, or rituals, to commemorate their lives, and celebrated the anniversaries of their deaths with masses and feast days.

Clergy participated in this *cultus sancti* for reasons both sacred and profane. Like the laity, they too enjoyed a limited understanding of the natural world and believed that it coexisted with a supernatural realm full of angels, demons, restless shades, and powerful spirits, which were capable of influencing the affairs of the living. And as good Christians, churchmen also considered it an article of faith that Jesus did indeed bless certain people with special gifts of grace, including the power to work miracles and to secure for the faithful berths in heaven. Consequently, it required no great stretch of the imagination for Christendom's clerics to believe that individuals were tapped by Christ to work his will in life and after death.

On a less metaphysical level, clergy were aware that these cults were extremely popular with recently converted Christians and helped secure their loyalty and devotion to the Church. Communal attachments to saints also fostered patriotism and could be used to rally the faithful in times of crisis. And, if a congregation was lucky enough to have relics with a widespread reputation for working wonders, sainthood provided local businesses and churches with a ready source of revenue.

Finally, clerical engagement in the *cultus sancti* also insured some measure of official control over who was inducted into the Church's sacral community and why. As we will see in the following section, such a gate keeping function was particularly important during the Middle Ages when a veritable mania for sainthood had "every community; the smallest town, soon even the tiniest village" wanting "a patron saint of its own."[6] Indeed, meeting this demand and insuring that those sainted were found worthy of Christendom's highest honor would bring Rome into the canonization process and make sanctification a church wide concern.

Before turning to Rome's involvement in sainthood, however, it should be noted that well before the tenth century of the Common Era, Christians had established a pantheon of saints populated with individuals who were largely well born and enjoyed reputations for piety in life and miracle working after death. The candidates for this heroic community were put forward by the Church's lay population and their sanctity was confirmed by local clergy who collected evidence that these nominees had indeed led exceptionally pious lives and possessed mana filled bones. Following clerical confirmation of their worthiness for sainthood, the remains of these folk were exhumed and translated into formal shrines where they became the focus of public cults replete with liturgical feast days and special masses. And to these saintly sites flowed streams of devoted pilgrims seeking remission of sins, salvation, cures, protection, and favorable outcomes for enterprises great and small.

From Vox Populi *to Papal Canonization: Rome and the* Cultus Sancti

Because ecclesiastical authorities regarded saints as models of Christian heroism worthy of veneration and emulation by the faithful, they were intent on insuring that these sanctified men and women were proper Christians who had led suitably holy lives. Clerical efforts to control sanctification, however, often ran afoul of a lay public that entertained more expansive notions of holiness than those of their clergy. Martyrdom was a case in point. While everyone agreed that martyrs were the very stuff of saintliness, and the Church was willing to sanctify any individual who sacrificed their life in defense of the faith, the populace-at-large was often willing to extend sainthood to people whose deaths were simply unjust or unmerited. Counted among these popular pseudo martyrs were young, beautiful and virtuous women murdered by their husbands; charitable maidservants slain by wolves and brigands; honest workmen lynched by mobs for crimes they did not commit; defenders of political causes executed by tyrannical princes; and adolescents believed to have been killed by the Jews.[7] In addition to folks who died in especially tragic circumstances, local communities were equally fond of sanctifying pagan deities and demi-gods, legendary heroes, fictitious figures, and, in one rather odd case, a dog named Guinefort.

Venerated by the inhabitants of Villars-les-Dombes, a community in the south of France, this holy hound was the faithful hunting dog of a knight with a castle in the vicinity of Lyons. Left alone with the knight's infant son, Guinefort saved the child by killing a serpent that threatened his life. However, when Guinefort's master returned to find the nursery in chaos, the baby missing, and the greyhound's jaws covered in blood, he assumed the animal had devoured his son and cast him into a well where he died. Upon discovering his error, the knight was filled with remorse for his pet's unmerited death and turned his watery grave into a commemorative shrine. Following a number of miracles attributed to his bones, Guinefort was declared by the locals to be a martyr and saint specializing in infant protection, and his tomb became the center of devotions that attracted a considerable number of pilgrims. Though this canine cult was never recognized by the Church, and was actually prohibited on a number of occasions, it continued to be celebrated well into the twentieth century.[8]

Suffice it to say, both local bishops and the Curia were not amused by the prospect of a *cultus sancti* populated with pagan gods, assorted victims of homicide, and faithful dogs. As long as canonization was a communal affair, however, and the *vox populi* selected those who were to be sanctified, clergy often felt they could do little more than ratify the cults of the saints their parishioners elected to revere. Consequently, in the decades preceding the first millennium of the Christian era, Europe's prelates began to pressure the papacy to take steps aimed at insuring the worthiness of the people's choices for admission into Christendom's community of saints.

Rome's initial response to this whole question of who should be canonized and why was rather desultory. Indeed, the first official canonization of a saint by the Holy See was in 993 when a Roman synod of bishops asked John XV to formally ratify sainthood for Bishop Ulric of Augsburg. Other such canonizations followed, but no pope actually claimed an exclusive right to canonize saints until a century and a half later in 1171. In that year, Alexander III asserted that it was not permitted to publicly venerate King Eric of Sweden, a notorious drunkard who died in a stupor, "without the authorization of the Roman Church."[9] This papal prerogative was reaffirmed in 1200 by Innocent III who declared "the approval of the Roman pontiff is necessary before anyone can be deemed a saint."[10] Thirty-four years later, Innocent's stricture was written into church law by Gregory IX.

In tandem with this assertion of papal proprietorship over sainthood, the Curia was also busy at this time developing a formal set of canonization procedures aimed at insuring the sanctity of those nominated for inclusion in Christendom's community of saints. Initially, this process was fairly simple and straightforward. Petitioners for a would-be saint presented Rome with a Vita of the candidate and, most importantly, a list of witnesses attesting to the miracles performed on their behalf by the candidate's blessed remains. Barring any objections from the local clergy, sanctification was usually pro forma.

By the beginning of the 13th century, however, Rome began to demand more of a saint than just a reputation for wonder working bones. In addition to asserting his sole right to canonize saints, Innocent III insisted that the proponents of a would-be *sanctus* speak more to what their candidate had actually done in life to live piously and advance the interests of Holy Mother Church and her flock. In taking this step, Innocent was not only acknowledging that miracles were difficult to verify, could be staged, and might even be the work of the devil, but also underscoring the limits of saintly remains — no matter how well endowed with supernatural power — to act as models for emulation by Christians in their daily lives.

This insistence on a more holistic and rigorous canonization process essentially transformed what had been a fairly informal local affair into a church-wide judicial proceeding. While the laity was still welcome — even encouraged — to bring forward candidates for induction into the *cultus sancti*, the Holy See now expected these nominations to be accompanied by a more formal petition for sanctification from the metropolitans of the areas where the nominated "servants of God" lived and died. In these petitions, bishops, along with other interested members of the local leadership, were expected to lay out a case for sainthood that was based on solid evidence of a nominee's reputation for sanctity in life (*fama sanctitatis*), as well as proof of miracles attributed to their intercession after death.

Upon receiving one of these petitions, a sitting pope selected three commissioners (one of whom was normally a bishop) to initiate a *processus*, or independent inquiry, aimed at evaluating the merits of the candidate for sainthood. Following their formal appointment, these examiners visited the final resting place of the prospective saint, convened public hearings, and collected, transcribed, and notarized testimony regarding the candidate's life and miracles. During this discovery process, the tribunal examined the nominee's written works to insure that they were in keeping with Church teaching and canon law. They also asked for evidence of the postulant's "heroic virtues," i.e., how their lives embodied the three theological virtues of faith, hope, and charity and the four cardinal virtues of fortitude, justice, prudence, and temperance. And they looked closely at the circumstances of the nominee's life and death to see if he or she had endured extraordinary suffering — abuse at the hands of pagans, schismatics, and heretics; assaults by demons; extreme asceticism — that might be construed as a form of martyrdom for Christ and his Church. Finally, the pope's emissaries closely scrutinized the various prodigies attributed to the servant of God after death. This part of the process was especially focused on thaumaturgical miracles and involved collecting proof that individuals healed by the saint's intercession had actually suffered from an ailment for a considerable length of time and been cured permanently.

Once their investigation was complete, the pope's commissioners would send their findings to Rome, where yet another panel comprised of one or more cardinals was convened to further examine the evidence and prepare a final report for the pontiff. The findings and recommendations of these senior prelates were then shared in two secret consistories — one comprised of cardinals, the other of bishops and archbishops — where all were encouraged to voice an opinion about the candidate for sainthood. Following these councils, the Holy Father would convene yet a third consistory, this one in public, where he would announce his decision on the petition for sanctification. In the event of a favorable finding, the servant of God was formally inscribed in the Catholic Catalogue of Saints, and a papal bull was issued announcing the canonization and assigning the new saint a feast day. This proclamation also included three prayers — collect, secret, and post communion prayer of thanksgiving — to be said at the masses celebrated in the saint's honor.[11]

It goes without saying that this lengthy and rigorous papal canonization process acted as an effective check on the future population growth of Christ's saintly court. Indeed, following the implementation of these judicial procedures in the 13th century, no more than 35 saints were canonized between 1198 and 1431.[12] To be sure, local communities continued to single out individuals for sanctification, but, absent official confirmation of their saintly status, these popular choices for sainthood were relegated to the ranks of the so-called *beati*, i.e., "blessed" folk deemed worthy of private veneration but not the full panoply and honors of a public cult.

Papal Canonization and "Modern" Sainthood

During the late Middle Ages what kind of person actually won admission into the Church's official community of saints? As André Vauchez makes clear in his monumental work on late medieval sainthood, individuals canonized by the Holy See at this time were well born, well situated, and well suited to the needs of the papacy. As in the period prior to papal canonization, Christendom's saintly heroes were overwhelmingly aristocratic in their social origins. Between 1198 and 1431, 60 per cent of the folks canonized by Rome were of noble birth and the majority of these individuals haled from Europe's reigning dynasties. Among those falling outside of this group, 17 per cent were members of wealthy bourgeois families, 8 per cent were peasants who overcame the obstacles associated with their birth by entering the clergy, and 14 per cent were of unknown social origin. Even the "common" saints in this group were far from ordinary.

> Of the three saints of modest origins canonized, one was a pope (Celestine V), another a regular Mendicant (St. Nicholas of Tolentino) and the third an eleventh-century hermit (St. Sebald), who was in any case presented by his fourteenth-century hagiographers as the son of a king of Denmark.[13]

The preponderance of aristocrats among Christ's heavenly counselors reflected both the popular prejudices and socio-economic realities of the time. Peasants and popes alike agreed that being born into prosperous circumstances signaled the presence of divine favor. Add to this fortunate birth the fact that these people actually owned land, dispensed justice, and enjoyed the power to coerce and command, and it is not difficult to understand why nobility was often seen as a prerequisite for saintly status. Indeed, while scripture might declare it easier to pass a camel through the eye of a needle than for a wealthy man to get into heaven, it was still the rich and powerful of Christendom who defended the faith, built churches, endowed monasteries, and distributed alms to the poor. And with the initiation of a lengthy and expensive canonization process, only these folks enjoyed the resources necessary to push forward a candidate — usually one of their own — for sainthood.

A person's zip code also played an important role in determining who was sainted in the late Middle Ages. Two-thirds of those canonized by the Church between 1198 and 1431 were situated in one of three countries, England (31 per cent), Italy (25 per cent), or France (17 per cent). The remaining third of those sanctified haled from German (14 per cent), Scandinavian (5 per cent), and Eastern European (5 per cent) countries. No one from Iberia, the Low Countries, or Northern Germany was recognized by Rome at this time.

To a large degree, these geographical disparities were simply a function of the proximity of certain countries to the Curia. Whether we are talking about Rome or Avignon — the seat of the papacy during the 14th century — it was much easier for French and Italian communities to lobby papal authorities on behalf of their candidates for sainthood. The fact that the overwhelming majority of this period's popes were also from France and Italy, and often familiar with the popular cults of their countrymen, made it even more likely that Christ's "friends and intimates" would hale from these countries.

England's success in getting its candidates canonized can be attributed to the country's strong monarchy and well organized episcopate. Unlike other countries at this time that left the canonization process largely in the hands of local communities, the kings and bishops of Plantagenet England tended to put forward nominees for sainthood that enjoyed "national" support. Aside from giving a certain heft to the candidacies of English postulants, this church-state collaboration also made it possible to hire and maintain full-time envoys and procurators whose sole job was to lobby the Curia on behalf of Britain's saintly aspirants.

As for the seeming dearth of saints with addresses in Central and Eastern Europe or the Iberian peninsula, it appears that proximity, local tradition, and politics worked to the detriment of candidates from these areas. Not only were northern Germany, Scandinavia, and the Slavic countries distant from the Curia and largely peripheral to its concerns, but communities in these areas tended to be satisfied with older more established cults and less interested in promoting or adopting new ones. As for Iberia, conflicts between the Holy See and the Aragonese court were commonplace in this period and Spanish cases for canonization suffered as a result.[14]

Finally, the official saints of the late Middle Ages tended to be "modern," or near contemporaneous folk whose lives and actions were well-suited to the needs of the papacy. Most of the individuals sanctified by the Holy See between 1198 and 1431 lived and died in the 13th and 14th centuries and, while alive, were supportive of the Curia in its many struggles against the self-aggrandizing monarchs, infidels, heretics, and schismatics of this period. Thirteen of those sainted at this time were bishops and/or popes who, like St. Thomas Beckett in the 12th century, stalwartly defended church prerogatives against the Hohenstaufen emperors of the Holy Roman Empire and the Plantagenets of England. In addition to these church magnates, there were thirteen monks and mendicants, such as Dominic, Francis of Assisi, and Thomas Aquinas, whose pious lifestyles, preaching, and written work proved effective against Catharism and other popular heresies. And among the lay men and women of this cohort, were counted monarchs (Louis IX), noblewomen (Elizabeth of Thuringia, Hedwig of Silesia), and daughters of prosperous bourgeois families (Catherine of Siena) who demonstrated their allegiance to Rome by launching crusades, rooting out heresy, and combating schismatics.[15]

Aside from the support this modern community of saints rendered Rome against its enemies foreign and domestic, its lay and mendicant members were also exemplars of an engaged, practical piety embraced by the papacy in the centuries immediately following the first millennium of the Christian era. Like the pontiffs who canonized them, late medieval sainthood's friars and lay religious folk were inspired and shaped by a church wide reform movement in the 12th century that sought to offer the faithful models of Christ like behavior and activism in everyday life. Towards this end, these individuals lived lives of poverty, chastity and obedience outside of the cloister; spread the gospels; acted as good Samaritans by feeding the hungry, clothing the naked, caring for the sick, and burying the dead; suppressed sinful desire through ascetic practices; and sought a personal communion with God through constant prayer and meditation on the life and suffering of Christ.[16]

Among those sanctified by the Holy See during this period, probably the two that best exemplified both this practical Christianity and the other qualities of modern sainthood discussed here were Francis of Assisi and Catherine of Siena. While not aristocrats, both of these individuals were from prosperous bourgeois families, haled from Italy, and were personally known by the popes who canonized them. They were also obedient servants of the

Holy See whose efforts to imitate Christ did not call into question either the orthodoxies of the Church or the authority of the Curia.

Of these two saints, Francis was the one who best embodied the new piety of the late 12th and early 13th centuries. Born in 1181 into a family of well-to-do cloth merchants, he was a worldly youth who spent his early years fighting in the armies of Assisi and the papacy. A series of dreams and visions of Christ caused Francis to abandon his military career, material possessions, and family ties and take up the life of an impoverished solitary outside his home town. On February 24, 1208, on the feast of St. Matthias, he listened to a gospel according to Matthew in which Christ told his Apostles:

> Preach saying, the kingdom of heaven is at hand. Heal the sick, cleanse the lepers, raise the dead, cast out devils: freely ye have received, freely give. Provide neither gold, nor silver, nor brass in your purses, nor scrip for your journey, neither two coats, neither shoes, nor yet staves: for the workman is worthy of his meat.[17]

Francis took these words to heart and opted to become a latter day disciple of Jesus. He dedicated himself to poverty, began preaching to the people of Assisi, attended to all who were poor and in need of assistance, cast off his shoes, dressed himself in coarse homespun, and dined only on the simple fare provided to him by charitable Christians.

Though Francis only wished to live a holy life consistent with the message of the gospels, his self-appointed apostolic mission happened to coincide with one of those periods in Christian history when the laity was disaffected with the worldly ways of its clergy and yearned for a return to the primitive Christianity of the early Church. Consequently, in the years following 1208, Francis found himself at the center of a circle of young idealistic city boys, who, like himself, were also seeking a more personal form of religious experience centered on an *imitatio Christi*. Following his lead, these "poor brothers" (*fratres minores*, or friars minor) abandoned their careers, distributed their possessions among the poor, dressed in rough cloaks, walked barefoot, lived on whatever food was given to them by their countrymen, and preached a message of salvation through penance.

Unlike many of the other groups of poor wandering preachers at this time — Waldensians, Humiliati, Beguines — that often found themselves at odds with the Church, Francis managed to avoid trouble with the Curia by seeking approval for his brotherhood from the Holy See. In 1210, he walked barefoot to Rome and asked Innocent III to declare his Friars Minor an official order dedicated "to follow the teachings of our Lord Jesus Christ and to walk in his footsteps." Though Innocent had some reservations about ratifying a movement that eschewed private property and embraced a daily regimen of severe asceticism, he sanctioned the Franciscan rule and allowed Francis and his band of mendicants to continue their lives of poverty and preaching as an official Catholic community.

Armed with Innocent's approbation of their rule of life, the Franciscan movement spread like wildfire across Europe. By the time Francis died in 1226, his brotherhood numbered in the thousands and boasted three orders, one for full time male mendicants, one for women — the so-called Poor Clares — and one for religious men and women who could not leave their families, the Order of the Brothers and Sisters of Penance. Francis' followers also established permanent missions in Italy, France, Germany, England, Ireland, Bohemia, Hungary, Poland, and the Holy Land; and staffed them with mendicants who were from every social strata in Christendom — aristocrats, commoners, clergy, illiterates, and university graduates. In sixteen years, the Franciscans went from a small circle of itinerant evangelists preaching in the area around Assisi, to an organization that was the very embodiment of the Nicean ideal of "one holy, catholic, and apostolic church."

The dramatic success of the Franciscans also benefited their Roman sponsors. The Friars Minor and the other mendicant orders that followed in their wake — Carmelites, Dominicans, Augustinians — afforded the Holy See with a means of addressing the many discontented Christians who were yearning for a spiritual life that was more in keeping with the ideas and practices of early Christianity. By offering these folks the rule of Francis and his confreres, the papacy was able to channel these discontents into an officially sanctioned and supervised form of pietism that allowed its practitioners both to emulate Christ in their everyday lives and remain faithful to the precepts and practices of the official Church.

In addition to serving as safety valves for the anger many Christians harbored towards Rome at this time, these new religious sodalities provided the papacy with a ready made army of Church militants. Preaching friars propagated the official Catholic line throughout Europe and combated heretical teaching wherever they found it. They also served willingly as missionaries spreading Christ's evangel among the adherents of Islam and the pagan inhabitants of newly discovered lands.

As for the man who founded this movement of militant mendicants, Francis eventually withdrew from the actual running of his Friars Minor in order to evangelize the Muslims. Joining the Fifth Crusade against Egypt in 1219, he managed to cross enemy lines at Damietta and preach to Sultan al-Kāmil. Though Francis failed to convert his Muslim host, he did win permission to visit the various holy places under his control in Palestine.

Returning to Europe in 1220, Francis worked with the papacy to promulgate a new rule for his rapidly growing order, after which he retired from the leadership of the Friars to pursue a solitary life of prayer and meditation in the mountains around Assisi. At this time, he penned his canticles of the sun and the creatures, poems expressing his love of all God's creations great and small; preached sermons to birds and animals; and, in 1224, received the stigmata, or wounds of Christ, ostensibly from a winged Seraph. In 1226, wracked with pain and almost blind, Francis died at the Porziuncola, the church below Assisi where, in 1208, he heard the gospel of Matthew that launched his career. Legend has it that the donkey which carried him throughout his life wept at the moment of his death.

Of all the men and women inducted into the Church's official community of saints over the centuries, Francis of Assisi is without question the one who is most well known, admired and loved. Even before his death, Francis had been dubbed the "second Christ," and his acts of voluntary poverty, fraternal charity, penance, preaching, and proselytizing were certainly an *imitatio Christi* without peer both in his time and our own. Add to this incredibly pious life an equally impressive reputation for miracles — talking to birds, converting wild animals, taming a savage wolf, the stigmata, healing the sick — and one can understand why Gregory IX felt it necessary to place Francis' body under papal guard lest it be torn apart by mobs seeking a piece of what everyone agreed would be wonder working remains. Indeed, less than two years after his death, Francis was canonized a saint, assigned a feast day on October 4th, and named patron of animals, nature, and Italy. A Basilica of St. Francis was erected in Assisi in his honor, and in 1230 his remains were exhumed and translated to a tomb in the lower part of this church. To this day, thousands continue to pay their respects at this resting place of the man who is arguably Christendom's greatest hero.[18]

In many respects, Catherine of Siena (1347–1380) was a 14th century female counterpart of Saint Francis. Like the *povarello* of Assisi, she was born into a respectable bourgeois cloth merchant's family, experienced visions of Jesus in her youth, and opted to lead a nonconventional religious life. Towards this end, she consecrated her virginity to Christ, joined a lay order of the Dominicans — the Sisters of Penitence of St. Dominic — and retired to a small room in her father's home where she engaged in constant prayer, fasting and mortification of the flesh.

In 1366, Catherine experienced an epiphany that caused her to abandon this solitary existence and become actively engaged in the world. According to her account of this event, she was the recipient of a vision in which Christ presented her with a wedding band made from his circumcised foreskin. During this "mystical marriage," Jesus also instructed Catherine to leave her cell and live a life that was consistent with the message of his gospels.

Catherine complied with her heavenly husband's command and over the next fourteen years dedicated her life to caring for the sick, especially those who were dying or afflicted with disfiguring diseases such as leprosy. She also attracted a sizable following of men and women, and, in contravention of social norms and canonical strictures, traveled with these companions throughout northern and central Italy preaching the gospels, advocating the reform of the clergy, working for peace among the warring Italian city states, and calling for a new crusade. In addition to this apostolic activity, Catherine continued to experience visions and trances in which she traveled to Heaven, Hell and Purgatory, drank from the wound inflicted on Jesus by a Roman spear at the crucifixation, exchanged hearts with Christ, and experienced a kind of mystical death.

Not surprisingly, all of this unconventional behavior earned Catherine the ire of a great many churchmen, and in 1374 she was summoned to Florence by the Dominicans to answer charges of possible heresy. During the ensuing interrogations, Catherine acquitted herself well and successfully established that she was a faithful daughter of the Church willing to accept the Curia's lead in all matters of faith and doctrine. She also assuaged Rome's concerns at this time by accepting as her confessor and spiritual mentor, Raymond of Capua, a prominent and orthodox Dominican theologian who would later become one of her most devoted disciples, as well as her principal biographer.

Catherine demonstrated her orthodoxy in other ways as well. From 1375 (the year in which she is reputed to have received the Stigmata of Christ) through 1378, she worked tirelessly to end a war that had broken out between Florence and the Papal States. Though she was unsuccessful in her efforts at mediating this conflict, Catherine did befriend Pope Gregory XI and was successful in convincing him to leave Avignon and return the Holy See to Rome in 1377. Following Gregory's death and the outbreak of the Great Schism in 1378, Catherine carried on a lively correspondence with various monarchs, aristocrats, and church leaders throughout Europe in an effort to win support for his successor, Urban VI.

When Catherine died in 1380 of a "mysterious agony of three months, endured by her with supreme exultation and delight,"[19] she was already regarded by both the Curia and her countrymen as a model of modern sainthood. Like Francis of Assisi, she had struggled to imitate Christ in her daily life through acts of asceticism, penance, and charity. And in her capacity as a healer, preacher, prophetess, and peacemaker, Catherine had in fact helped ease the suffering of the sick; inspired the faithful to greater piety; generated a rich spiritual literature; and advanced the cause of Christian comity. It goes without saying, that her death was also accompanied by the usual plethora of miracles.

Ironically, for a Church intent on canonizing saints who could serve as examples of practical Christian action in life, Catherine's career as a social activist, church reformer, and international diplomat was given short shrift in the process that led to her sanctification. As Karen Scott notes in her examination of the hagiography of Catherine, which was written by her confessor and advocate, Raymond of Capua, much of the case for her sainthood was focused on her mystical marriage with God, a union in which she served as the weak and willing vessel of the Lord's divine grace and instruction. Indeed, insofar as her charitable work and diplomacy was addressed during her *processus*, it was always framed within this traditional medieval conception of the ideal woman — whether married mother or virgin saint — as first and foremost a dutiful wife carrying out the commands of her spouse. While a man like Francis of Assisi could find his own way to an apostolic mission in God's service, his sister in Siena, burdened by her weak physical constitution and sinful irrational sex, still required what was in essence a divine guardianship.[20]

Of course, in Raymond's defense, by stressing Catherine's spiritual espousal with Christ, he was also underscoring her extraordinary virtue and the profound holiness of her actions in life as an activist, author, and peacemaker. Such a rhetorical strategy may have reinforced popular prejudices regarding women at this time, but it also served to dispel any suspicion that Catherine's rather unorthodox life was in any way unnatural or heretical. In the end, whatever Raymond's reasons for writing Catherine's hagiography in the way that he did, Rome was satisfied with his work and formally admitted his candidate into the Church's heroic pantheon in 1461. In the years following her canonization, Catherine of Siena was named patroness of the ill and the nurses who treat them, those who suffer ridicule for their piety, folks suffering sexual temptation (admittedly most of the human population), and, along with Francis of Assisi, Italy. In 1999, John Paul II also added Europe to her saintly portfolio.[21]

From Relic to Avatar of Christ: The Saintly Hero

In his fascinating study of hagiography in the Middle Ages, Thomas Heffernan notes that the churchmen writing these sacred bios did not consider their subjects to be heroes. While such an appellation might have been appropriate for pagans seeking fame and deathless glory, it was not regarded by these writers as an accurate description of a Christian confraternity whose members were contemptuous of the world and hungry only for salvation. Even the extraordinary strength, fortitude, wisdom, and preternatural powers of the saints — traits that were the very stuff of heroism in antiquity — were portrayed in the saintly vitas of this period as gifts of grace from God, rather than as evidence of exceptional natures worthy of special honors.[22]

As the foregoing makes clear, however, whatever the rhetorical reservations of the folks writing about saintly lives, the medieval public — lay and clerical alike — regarded these holy men and women as heroic figures and afforded them much the same treatment as their pagan counterparts. Throughout the Middle Ages, Christian communities singled out certain individuals — many of them Christianized facsimiles of ancient deities and demi-gods — and declared them "sacred" because of their exceptional deeds in life and miracle making *virtus* in death. Like the heroes of the pre–Christian era, the shades of these saints were believed to be potent, capable of acting on the living, and resident to some degree in their physical remains. And public cults replete with special crypts, shrines, rituals, and feast days were initiated to honor, placate and tap into the supernatural powers of these holy souls.

The assertion of papal control over canonization during the latter part of the medieval period did little to change the particulars of this locally based *cultus sancti*. Whether the Curia approved of their cults or not, communities continued to venerate individuals — and in the case of St. Guinefort, animals — they regarded as holy, and a saint's status among the masses remained tied to the reputation their relics enjoyed for working miracles. At a period in its history when the Holy See was contending with far greater threats to its authority than a popular penchant for uncanonized bones, Rome found it advisable to tolerate these unofficial devotions.

Nevertheless, while the papacy was not completely successful at this time in bringing the community of saints under its control, the creation of a centralized canonization process did afford the Church an opportunity to define more clearly the contours of what it meant to be Christendom's heroic ideal. Though there remained an expectation that such a person was someone who could and would work wonders on behalf of the faithful after death, this individual was now expected to be more than a talismanic magnet of divine energy. Ironically, for the princely prelates of the Curia — men who lived in palaces, patronized art, and draped themselves in fine raiment and costly jewels — this modern sainthood increasingly entailed living a life that was as perfect an imitation of Christ as humanly possible.

Moreover, as the cases of Saints Francis of Assisi and Catherine of Siena demonstrate, the Christ being imitated here was not the water walking, miracle working, dead raising son of the one true God, but the all too human Jesus of Nazareth. The *poverello* of Galilee who preached an evangel of penance and salvation, walked with the outcast, cared for the sick, experienced doubt, and suffered unspeakable agony for the advancement of the faith Rome believed had been entrusted to the care of Peter and his successors. It was, in short, an ideal of Christian heroism that would survive the crackup of Christendom and inspire countless generations of missionaries, teachers, caregivers, and civil rights activists, among them Albert Schweitzer, Mohandas Gandhi, Mother Teresa, and Jimmy Carter.

❦ PART THREE ❦

Rebels, Rogues, and Reprobates: Heroism in the Modern World

Not earthly are the poor fool's meat and drink. His spirit's ferment drives him far, and he half knows how foolish is his quest: From heaven he demands the fairest star, and from the earth all joys that he thinks best; and all that's near and that's far cannot soothe the upheaval in his breast.

— Goethe: *Faust*

I teach you the Superman. Man is something that should be overcome. What have you done to overcome him?

— Nietzsche: *Thus Spoke Zarathustra*

Everyone is a hero in birth, where he undergoes a tremendous psychological as well as physical transformation from the condition of a little water creature living in a realm of amniotic fluid into an air-breathing mammal which ultimately will be standing.

— Joseph Campbell: *The Hero's Adventure*

Up to this point in our narrative, we have examined notions of the hero that were rooted in traditional rural societies with fairly rigid social hierarchies and subsistence economies. In this world, a small elite of predatory princes and ostensibly prayerful priests bullied and bilked a much larger peasant population, which was consigned to a hard scrabble existence centered on cultivating enough food to stay alive. The only other group of any note in this social arrangement was a growing bourgeoisie of merchants, craftsmen, and assorted artists that resided in a handful of largish cities and catered to the needs of the countryside and its rulers for financial services, markets, finished goods, and entertainment.

Heroism in these stratified societies was largely about taking actions aimed at protecting, preserving, or transcending this centuries-long status quo. Consequently, the people who were billed as heroes tended to be either fighting men who turned back invaders, suppressed rebellions, and protected the civilian population from oppressors, or especially holy men and women that worked miracles and were headed for heaven. And because all of this praiseworthy fighting and praying required a considerable amount of free time, these heroic individuals tended to be folks who haled from families with fortunes and good pedigrees.

A new science coupled with political, industrial, and information revolutions undermine and eventually sweep away the traditional social arrangements described above, and bring into being the mass, socially mobile, democratic societies in which we live and work today. In this modern world, the remaining princes of the West are figureheads; fighting men are now the recruits and draftees of regimented armies with weaponry that makes individual combat the stuff of video games; miracle working clerics are in short supply; and most folks accept the idea that every individual life has merit and all individuals should have the opportunity to explore and realize their full potential.

Not surprisingly, this shift from a closed corporate social order to a more democratic and fluid society has had a profound impact on the Western ideal of heroism. Whereas the rubric of hero was once largely limited to warrior princes, righteous priests, and Olympian athletes, the heroic pantheon is now open to all individuals able to distinguish themselves through extraordinary ability and/or action in any field of human endeavor. Indeed, as the following section demonstrates, throughout the 18th, 19th, and early 20th centuries, intellectuals, scientists, artists, writers, and political revolutionaries were all identified as heroes by their adoring publics.

This democratization of the Western heroic ideal, however, has also been accompanied by what might be described as a demonization of the hero. Over the course of the last two centuries, a number of hero-worshipping movements — Romanticism, Fascism, Bolshevism — and a slough of self-styled heroic leaders — Mussolini, Hitler, Stalin — led many in the post World War II period to treat heroes and ideals of heroism with great wariness. Increasingly, the modern public has become enamored with an anti-heroic tradition that celebrates picaroons, survivors, slackers, indeed any individual who demonstrates how mundane, inglorious acts like tending your garden, keeping your head down, and trying to stay alive really are the better part of valor.

The following pages examine in some detail both the heroic and anti-heroic traditions of the modern era. The first two chapters address how natural philosophers, explorers, aesthetes, and rebels pushed their way into one of history's most exclusive clubs. This discussion is then followed by a rather lengthy examination of the hero worshipping crackpots, dreamers, madmen, artists, revolutionaries, and dictators of the early 20th century who attempted to realize a latter-day heroic age; a project that brought forth instead a generation of SS "black angels" and Communist "new men" whose efforts to refashion humanity covered the world in blood and set the stage for the triumph of the anti-hero, the subject of this section's concluding chapter.

7

"To boldly go where no one has gone before"

The Hero as Explorer

It is possible to arrive at knowledge which is most useful in life, and that, instead of speculative philosophy taught in the Schools, a practical philosophy can be found by which, knowing the power and the effects of fire, water, air, the stars, the heavens and all the other bodies which surround us ... we might put them ... to all the uses for which they are appropriate, and thereby make ourselves, as it were, masters and possessors of nature.

— Descartes: *Discourse*

Sitting in the gaudy radiance of those windows hearing the organ play and the choir sing, his mind pleasantly intoxicated from exhaustion, Daniel experienced a faint echo of what it must be like, **all the time,** *to be Isaac Newton: a permanent ongoing epiphany, an endless immersion in lurid radiance, a drowning in light, a ringing of cosmic harmonies in the ears.*

— Neal Stephenson: *Quicksilver*

The Greeks made the Argonauts ... into demigods; but are they worth ... as much as the assistants who accompanied you [Maupertuis]? The Argonauts became divinities, and you? What is your recompense? ... Rest assured that the approbation of the thinking beings of the eighteenth century is far beyond the apotheosis of Greece.

— Voltaire to Maupertuis, May 22, 1738

These [Natural] philosophers ... penetrate into the recesses of nature, and show how she works in her hiding places. They ascend into the heavens: they have discovered how the blood circulates, and the nature of the air we breathe. They have acquired new and almost unlimited powers; they can command the thunders of heaven, mimic the earthquake, and even mock the invisible world with its own shadows.

— Mary Shelley: *Frankenstein*

During various trips that I have taken over the last decade to such places as Chichen Itza, Machu Picchu, and the Valley of the Kings, I have been struck by how often Indiana Jones comes up in conversations. Whether scaling a pre–Columbian temple, hiking along the Inca Trail, or descending into the burial chamber of Tut's tomb, people invariably reference the film adventures of George Lucas' intrepid, wisecracking archaeologist. Comments such as "Wow, this terrain is right out of an Indiana Jones movie"; or "Can't you just see Indy exploring this temple"; or "All that's missing is the rolling boulder and the lost

107

ark"; are not uncommon. Nor are these observations limited to unsophisticated tourists. I have heard historians, anthropologists, Egyptologists, classicists, and not a few scientists make similar remarks during these excursions.

I suspect that the association of Indiana Jones with these places can be traced to a number of clever creative choices on the part of George Lucas and Steven Spielberg. First, many of the scenes in their movies were actually shot in the neighborhood of these archaeological sites. Secondly, their character is a larger-than-life version of the men — Edward H. Thompson, Hiram Bingham, Howard Carter, among others — who actually uncovered the ruins, treasure troves, human remains, and mummies that were found at places like Chichen Itza, Machu Picchu, and the Valley of the Kings in the late 19th and early 20th centuries. And finally, Indy is an amalgam of all those heroic explorers — mythical and real — that we associate with the discovery of unknown lands, lost civilizations, rare artifacts, and new science. Indeed, as Lucas' intellectual mentor, the late Joseph Campbell would say, Indiana Jones is very much a "hero of a thousand faces." He is at one and the same time an ancient Argonaut seeking legendary treasure in uncharted territories; a motorized, gun toting, whip wielding knight errant on a quest for sacred relics; and a latter-day natural philosopher bringing the concepts, theories, and methods of the sciences to the search for the remains of the human past.

I bring up Lucas and Spielberg's fictitious protagonist and the tendency of people to associate him with some of archaeology's greatest finds because I believe he exemplifies the traits that have come to be associated with a heroic explorer in the modern era. Like Indy, such a person is expected to be — Lara Croft Tomb Raider notwithstanding — a male scholar-scientist who brings to the task-at-hand genius, wide erudition, a skeptical attitude, excellent observation skills, a passion for puzzles, a burning desire to unlock the mysteries of life, and a deep seated belief that all discoveries should be applied to the benefit of humanity and whatever place the explorer calls home. Concurrently, there is also an expectation that this seeker of new frontiers should be someone who possesses the strength, stamina, fortitude, single mindedness, and eagerness for fame that were characteristic of the ancient and medieval warriors who journeyed into the unknown searching for golden fleeces, holy grails, and buried treasure.

In what follows, I argue that this contemporary notion of the heroic explorer as an all-around scientist, adventurer and warrior has its beginnings in the 17th century with the advent of the "new science." At this time, a rather motley crew of aristocrats, courtiers, religious dissenters, alchemists, and military men that included, among others, Francis Bacon, René Descartes, Galileo Galilei, and Isaac Newton, set themselves the task of looking at nature through eyes unclouded by the prejudices of either the past or the present. Out of the varied musings and experiments of these "natural philosophers" emerged an epistemology predicated on skepticism, doubt, direct observation, and testing, as well as a view of the Earth as a sun-circling, gravity propelled motion machine comprised of parts that could be analyzed, understood, and controlled. In addition to revolutionizing Western thinking as to how the world works and should be studied, these students of nature envisioned — and in Bacon's case actually wrote about — a future in which the natural philosopher would become a Promethean-like figure; boldly exploring unknown and forbidden territory, questioning accepted verities, and, to paraphrase the words of Descartes' *Discourse* quoted above, striving always to find and exploit knowledge that would make humanity "masters and possessors of nature."

The work of these early "prophets of science" and their elevated view of the natural philosopher were enthusiastically embraced by the philosophes and saloniers of the Enlightenment. Indeed, for these self-styled citizens of Europe's 18th century Republic of Letters, the principles, practices, and tools of 17th century natural philosophy were critical weapons in their struggle to combat ignorance and harness the power of nature to improve the lot of humanity. And, as Voltaire makes clear in this chapter's opening epigraphs, in this monumental struggle between the forces of light and darkness, the "thinking beings of the eighteenth century" were also in agreement that the adepts of the new learning were nothing less than the modern equivalent of the ancient world's semi-divine Argonauts.

Voltaire's rather high opinion of people doing the new science was also shared by his contemporaries who were actually working in natural philosophy during the eighteenth century. Savants like Pierre-Louis Moreau de Maupertius, Alexander von Humboldt, Joseph Priestly, Antoine Lavoisier, and Benjamin Franklin did regard themselves as members of a very select confraternity of the mind. No less than the ancients who sailed off into the unknown, these men were also eager for fame, intent on acquiring esoteric knowledge, and willing to confront and overcome any challenges that blocked their access to it. Indeed, two members of this brotherhood, the aforementioned Maupertius and von Humboldt, actually styled themselves "explorers"—a term normally associated with soldiers who conducted highly risky reconnaissance in unfamiliar territory—because they traveled to remote and unmapped corners of the Earth to conduct scientific research in difficult, inhospitable, and often dangerous conditions. This military connection was further underscored in the published and widely read accounts of their expeditions, where descriptions of the physically challenging and exotic nature of the environments in which they moved and worked demonstrated how their vocation combined both the erudition of the scholar and the stamina, fortitude, and yen for adventure of the warrior.

This association of the natural philosopher with ancient Argonauts and undercover military men was important because it helped to establish the bona fides of the new science and it practitioners at a time when societies were male dominated, hierarchical, corporate, and extremely status conscious. In fact, as we will see below, Enlightenment savants spent a considerable amount of time and effort during this period establishing an institutional framework for their work and articulating standards of excellence for their nascent profession. This entailed securing royal patronage, organizing professional societies and journals, founding academies, attending salons, sponsoring competitions, meting out awards and titles of honor to peers, and creating and peopling a pantheon of heroes for the new sciences.

While these efforts to elevate and institutionalize natural philosophy and its acolytes were certainly of great importance, it was the scientific discoveries of the 19th and 20th centuries and their enormous impact on how Westerners lived and worked, which made scientists (a term first used in 1834) positively glamorous. The steam engine of James Watt, for example, saved labor, cheapened production, and made possible revolutionary advances in manufacturing and transportation. Louis Pasteur's experiments in immunology led to techniques for destroying germs and set the stage for dramatic advances in disease prevention and control. Gregor Mendel's studies of the inheritance of specific traits in pea pods laid the foundations of genetics. And the work of Einstein, Bohr and other physicists at the turn-of-the century made possible everything from transistors and lasers to atomic bombs.

In tandem with these remarkable breakthroughs in the natural sciences, the 19th and 20th centuries also witnessed yet another wave of travel to various uncharted areas of the Earth. Sir Richard Francis Burton, a gifted polymath, Arabist, and former officer of the Indian Army, reached Lake Tanganyika and sought out the headwaters of the Nile. Amateur geologist and medical missionary, David Livingston, explored and mapped Central Africa, and was the first European to see Victoria Falls, which he named in honor of his queen. Norwegian Roald Amundsen sailed the fabled Northwest Passage, was the first to reach the South Pole, and later flew across the Arctic Basin. And American, Robert E. Peary, claimed the distinction of being the first to reach the North Pole and plant the Stars and Strips on it.

As with the Argonauts of the 18th century, these individuals also penned accounts of their travels and sold them to a public eager for stories of unknown lands and the hardships attendant on exploring them. Unlike their Enlightenment colleagues, these explorers were also accompanied by the representatives of a sensationalist mass press. Recognizing early on that exploration sells newspapers, large urban dailies often underwrote expeditions to Africa and the poles and assigned reporters to cover them. These journalists in turn acted as something akin to heralds, writing columns that accented the challenges and dangers of these journeys and playing up the heroic features of the latter-day knights errant who led them. Indeed, long before Tom Wolfe coined the phrase "the right stuff," late 19th and early 20th century press accounts were portraying Livingston, Amundsen, and others of their ilk as members of a very select circle of men who were exceptionally brave, strong, willful, competitive, smart, and intent on the acquisition of knowledge and fame at any cost. And these news stories also played up the idea that, like their crusading brethren before them, these individuals were combating ignorance and falsehood, spreading Western civilization, and enriching their native countries.

This fixation on scientists as Promethean fire givers and larger-than-life heroic explorers full of manly virtues was not without its problems. Not the least of these was the reduction of the Scientific Revolution to the deeds of a handful of brilliant thinkers, inventors and adventurers. As historians of science have noted, in addition to individual genius, there were a great many other factors — Protestant millenarianism, the English Civil War, the wheels of commerce, royal patronage, advances in tool making, better printing presses, the Enlightenment *Encyclopédie*, to name a few — which contributed to the development and success of the new science. Nor did accounts of godlike geniuses lost in ongoing epiphanies, lurid radiance, and ringing cosmic harmonies — to paraphrase this chapter's opening quote by the novelist Neil Stephenson — do justice to the painstaking, often boring, and frequently fruitless round of experiments, observations, note taking, and testing that is the actual lot of those who toil in the vineyards of science.

Concurrently, as we will see later when we turn to the heroic ideal in a totalitarian context, the idea of the scientist as a latter-day *hemitheoi* capable of gifting humanity with the wherewithal to become gods was profoundly dangerous. More than one tyrant in the 20th century seized on this notion and attempted to put it into effect by using science and its disciples to plan, design, and launch murderous programs of social and racial engineering. Unfortunately, while a great many scientists rejected these "god building" schemes as little more than latter-day hubris, all too many of their confreres — Josef Mengele and Trofim Lysenko come instantly to mind — proved unable to resist the temptations of absolute knowledge and power.

Indeed, perhaps we should rejoice that in the contemporary period a figure like Indiana Jones is the model of the heroic explorer. Whatever his gifts as a scholar, scientist and swashbuckler, Indy always ends his adventures with the recognition that there are no "final solutions" in science. Or as physicist Brian Green puts it:

> To be a scientist is to commit to a life of confusion punctuated by the rare moments of clarity. When I leave the office at night, the confusion comes with me. Ruminating over these equations, seeking patterns looking for hidden relationships, trying to make contact with hidden data — it's all uncertainty and possibility engaged in an endless chaotic dance. Every so often the blur resolves, but the respite is short lived; the next puzzle demands focus. This really, is the joy of being a scientist. Established truths are comforting, but it is the mysteries that make the soul ache and render a life of exploration worth living.[1]

How this science-centered "life of exploration" came into being and what it has meant to be adjudged one of its heroes are the principal questions to which we now turn.

The New Atlanteans: Galileo, Bacon, Descartes, and Newton

Our examination of modern exploration and its heroic exemplars takes as its starting point the lives and achievements of four 17th century natural philosophers who revolutionized the field of science, i.e., Galileo Galilei, Francis Bacon, René Descartes, and Isaac Newton. We begin our inquiry with these individuals because their observations, experiments, instruments, and discoveries established principles of scientific inquiry that undergird much of the last four centuries of exploratory work in everything from astronomy and physics to geography and folklore. Further, the manner in which these men comported themselves in life, their political and cultural prejudices, and their sense of what natural philosophy was and how it should be practiced also influenced and informed the behavior of succeeding generations of savants, gentleman scholars, gifted amateurs, inventors, researchers, and professional scientists intent on making a name for themselves as explorers and discoverers of new knowledge. Indeed, as the following pages demonstrate, these gentlemen were the prophets, precursors, and first heroes of a scientific revolution that continues unabated to this day.

Of these four men, Galileo Galilei (1564–1642) is probably the best known because of his conflict with the Roman Catholic Church over the issue of heliocentrism (the idea that the Earth and its sister planets revolve around the sun). Well before this clash, however, Galileo was already a noted mathematician, physicist, philosopher, inventor, and "public intellectual" whose methods and findings were known and respected in learned circles throughout Italy and Europe. His achievements included groundbreaking theoretical and experimental work on the motion of bodies; the invention of refracting telescopes and

compound microscopes; improvements in the design of the compass; and a series of astronomical discoveries — sunspots, satellites around Jupiter, mountains on the moon, the phases
of Venus — that refuted Aristotelian notions of an immutable motionless universe and
confirmed the heliocentric theories of Copernicus, Kepler, and Brahe.[2]

Galileo's impressive corpus of work was the end result of a rigorous *modus operandi*
that he followed when investigating and attempting to explain the operations of the natural world. This process involved (1) close observation of any phenomenon selected for study;
(2) inductive reasoning aimed at formulating general explanations for what had been
observed; and (3) testing those generalizations with experiments and mathematical measurements that could be replicated by others. To maintain complete objectivity during this
period of fact finding, analysis, and experimentation, Galileo also ignored prior prejudices,
assumptions, and shibboleths surrounding the objects of his inquiry.[3]

It was this last aspect of Galileo's "scientific method," i.e., his insistence that when dis-
cussing "physical problems we ought to begin not from the authority of scriptural passages,
but from sense experience and necessary demonstrations,"[4] which got him into trouble with
Rome. Though a great many churchmen at this time, including a reigning pontiff, Urban
VIII, respected Galileo's intellect, admired the integrity of his work, and even concurred
with his findings, they were also sensitive to the ways in which both his discoveries and the
process by which he arrived at them could foster further confusion and dissent in a Christendom already riven by a Protestant Reformation and conflicts that would culminate in a
Thirty Years War. Galileo's astronomical work, for example, clearly demonstrated that the
Aristotelian idea of a motionless Earth in a changeless universe — a view of the cosmos
which had been embraced by Christians for centuries — was nonsense. And his insistence
that science should be conducted free of any scriptural references or clerical dogmas was
particularly problematic for a Church that was facing challenges to its doctrinal authority
from Protestants, skeptics, free-thinkers, and heretical philosophers throughout Europe.

For the clerics charged with defending Catholic orthodoxy and authority in matters
of faith and reason, i.e., the Holy Office of the Inquisition, Galileo's discoveries and methods were more than just problematic, they were downright dangerous. Unlike Galileo's
more liberally minded admirers in the Curia, the churchmen of the Inquisition regarded
the Copernican doctrine of a sun-centered solar system as false, absurd, heretical, and contrary to Scripture, and they got this written into Church law in 1616. These clerical inquisi-
tors also rejected the notion that science might operate independently of religion and they
made this quite clear to Galileo by formally forbidding him in the same year they outlawed
Copernicanism from teaching the "erroneous" idea that the earth moves.

Following this ban, Galileo found ways to circumvent inquisitorial strictures on his
work by publishing his findings in countries less subject to Church control than Italy, and
presenting the idea of the earth rotating around the sun as a supposition rather than a fact.
In 1633, however, he abandoned these maneuvers and published *Dialogue on the Two Chief
World Systems*, an elegant, witty, and widely read affirmation of Copernican heliocentrism.
Whether he took this step out of a conviction that his friend Urban VIII would protect
him, or simply because at 68 he was weary of trying to accommodate men he believed to
be fools, the decision to publicly embrace a world system the Curia had declared contrary
to Church teaching got him arrested, dragged before the Inquisition, tried, and found guilty

of disobedience and heresy. Under threat of torture and being burned at the stake, Galileo recanted his errors and was placed under house arrest where he remained until his death nine years later. Apocrypha have it that following his recantation, Galileo muttered under his breath *"Eppur si muove,"* "And yet it moves."[5]

Whether these words of defiance were actually uttered or not, Rome's persecution of Galileo transformed him into the first martyr and hero of the Scientific Revolution. In the years following his condemnation, natural philosophers throughout Europe came to regard him as a prophet and treated his works as something akin to canonical texts. This saintly status was confirmed in the 18th century when Florence constructed a shrine around Galileo's tomb in the Basilica of Santa Croce that quickly became a place of pilgrimage for Enlightenment era savants, poets and philosophes. And in the 20th century, he was proclaimed "the father of science" by Albert Einstein and Stephen Hawking; his trial became the subject of a play, film, and several television documentaries; and various moons, spacecraft, global satellite navigation systems, and units of acceleration were named after him. Even the Holy See eventually embraced Galileo as a heroic son of the Church. Bans on his ideas and publications were gradually lifted by the Curia throughout the 18th and 19th centuries; and, in 1939, Pius XII declared him to be among "the most audacious heroes of research."[6]

Suffice it to say that all of this attention helped make Galileo a model of what it means to be counted a great scientist. Indeed, from the time of his death to the present day, any candidate for induction into the heroic pantheon of the natural sciences is expected to exhibit Galileo's insatiable curiosity, as well as his burning desire to "penetrate into the recesses of nature, and show how she works in her hiding places."[7] And in these efforts to uncover the workings of the world, all prospective heroes of science are also supposed to demonstrate the brilliance, erudition, devotion to scientific methodology, and indifference to dogmas, sacred or secular, of their 17th century predecessor.

Important as Galileo was in establishing the standards by which future champions of science would be judged, he was not alone in this enterprise. René Descartes (1596–1650) and Isaac Newton (1642–1727) also played key roles in shaping the modern ideal of the heroic explorer. Like their Italian contemporary, these two men were highly inquisitive natural philosophers who were intent on exploring and explaining the operations of nature. They were also brilliant, well-versed in a great many fields of human inquiry, and committed to conducting their investigations of the cosmos and life in a scientific manner free of reliance on, or reference to, theological and classical authorities. They were, in short, "heroes of research" in the Galileian mould.

Of these two men, Isaac Newton is without question the most well known and revered because of his many significant discoveries. From 1666 to 1686, he invented infinitesimal calculus; articulated a theory of light and its colors that pointed the way to modern optics; and formulated the law of universal gravitation, which is the foundation of present day space travel. The book in which he laid out the proofs of his gravitational theories, *Mathematical Principles of Natural Philosophy*, also known as the *Principia* for the first word of its Latin title, is regarded as the single most important work in the history of modern science.[8]

The implications of Newton's findings in all of these areas were enormous. By demonstrating that mathematical laws could be used to calculate everything from the rates of change to the movements of planets in the heavens and those of apples falling to the earth,

Newton created a new cosmology in which the universe was a uniform and regulated machine. Such a world system was not only stable, orderly and predictable, but it also held out the promise that future scientists gifted with Newton's genius and daring would be able to isolate, study, comprehend, and even manipulate its various mechanisms.

Suffice it to say that these achievements guaranteed that Newton would be regarded as a hero of the new science and he has in fact been idolized by learned and lay publics alike for the last four centuries. He was the first scientist to receive a knighthood and the only one to be buried in Westminster Abbey. And his stature was so great in his own time that the poet Alexander Pope penned the following lines just a few decades after the publication of his *Principia*:

> *Nature and nature's law lay hid in night;*
> *God said, "Let Newton be!" and all was light.*

While Descartes' scientific discoveries were not as spectacular as Newton's — in physics, he was the first to perceive the distinction between mass and weight; and in mathematics he founded analytic geometry — his reveries on the nature and acquisition of knowledge shaped the way in which succeeding generations of scientists perceived themselves and their work. Starting from the premise that our senses often deceive us, Descartes argued for an epistemology that treated all received authority with skepticism until it was proven to be valid by those purest expressions of human reason, mathematics and science. As laid out in his most widely read work, *Discourse on Method* (1637), individuals intent on finding "certain" knowledge about the world should be guided by four principles: (1) accept nothing as true unless clearly recognized as such; (2) solve problems systematically by analyzing them part by part; (3) proceed from simple to more complex considerations; and (4) review everything thoroughly to make sure that nothing has been omitted.[9]

This epistemological method had important implications for science and its practitioners. By enshrining doubt as the starting point for all inquiry, and accepting as true only that which could be proven by logic, deductive reasoning, and empirical study, "Cartesianism," as it came to be known, further undermined orthodox views of the universe and man's place in it, and privileged scientific knowledge over the doctrines and speculations of more metaphysical philosophies. Descartes' epistemology also worked to transform individuals who were versed in science and mathematics into the equivalent of modern magi. For in a Cartesian world, only scientists could *truly* see, understand and manipulate the mechanisms that held the world together and made it work.[10]

Like Galileo and Newton, Descartes' work in mathematics and philosophy won him the approbation of learned folk throughout Europe, including such notables as Richelieu, Louis XIV, Princess Elizabeth of Bohemia, and Queen Christina of Sweden. Even those critical of Descartes' approach to science, such as Isaac Newton, acknowledged the originality and importance of his methods and discoveries (indeed, Descartes' efforts in algebra and geometry laid the foundation for Newton's calculus). Consequently, in the years following Descartes' death, his name was affixed to a school of philosophy; varied circles, coordinates, diagrams, products, and graphs; an optical law of refraction; a crater on the moon; and an asteroid. He was also dubbed the father of modern philosophy and analytical geometry, and his tomb in St. Germain-des-Prés in Paris became a popular pilgrimage site for generations of students, philosophers, and scientists who admired his many contributions to Western intellectual life.[11]

This "trinity" of 17th century natural philosophers set the standard against which all future heroes of the new science would be judged. To follow in the footsteps of these three titans would require genius, great erudition, a burning desire to explore and explain the unknown, and an unswerving devotion to science and its methods. Their successors would also need to display a healthy skepticism towards all received knowledge, as well as a willingness to challenge any assertion or authority not verified by reason and empirical study. And above all else, those seeking a place in history alongside Galileo, Newton and Descartes would need to demonstrate their mettle with discoveries that increased human knowledge of and control over the world.

The heroic example set by these extraordinary explorers was further reinforced by the writings of Sir Francis Bacon (1561–1626). Though not a great scientist himself, Bacon was without question the chief propagandist and herald of the new science in the 17th century. Indeed, his fictional work *New Atlantis* inspired generations of literate Westerners with its vision of a science-centered utopia governed by a benevolent fellowship of natural philosophers.[12]

In Bacon's "fable," scientists occupy the highest level of society and function as something akin to Plato's philosopher kings. They also live and work together in a scientific foundation known as Salomon's House whose mission is:

> The knowledge of causes, and secret motions of things; and the enlarging of the bounds of human empire, to the effecting of all things possible.[13]

In this temple of wisdom, there are great laboratories, observatories, workshops, kilns, pools, zoos, aviaries, orchards, and gardens where the resident scientists employ the rules and methods of the new science — observation, inductive reasoning, experimentation — to conduct researches into the operations of nature. The findings of these never ending research projects are made public and used to benefit society-at-large by improving agriculture, industry, manufacturing, art, craft, and trade.

Though Salomon's House is a collaborative enterprise, it is also corporate and hierarchical. The foundation's natural philosophers run the place and are assisted in their various projects by novices and apprentices seeking admission into their ranks. Under these scientists-in-waiting are "a great number of servants and attendants — men and women"[14] — who do the daily drudgery of cooking, cleaning, and mending. As for the folks at the top, they too are differentiated from one another by titles, duties, and honors. Twelve "Merchants of Light" are charged with exploring the outer world, others known as "Depredators" collect and try out new experiments, and three "Dowry-men or Benefactors" focus on the practical applications of the House's many discoveries. The scientists who are most highly regarded, however, are the inventors. As the narrator of the tale notes:

> For upon every invention of value we erect a statue to the inventor, and give him a liberal and honourable reward. These statues are, some of brass, some of marble and touchstone, some of cedar and other special woods, gilt and adorned, some of iron, some of silver, and some of gold.[15]

And the statues of these heroic figures are placed in a "very long and fair" gallery where the "ordinances and rites" of Salomon's House are conducted and future generations of natural philosophers can be inspired by their example.

One natural philosopher who was very much inspired by Bacon's ideal society and its heroic inventors was the chemist Robert Boyle. In 1660, Boyle and eleven other adherents of the new science—a group that included Bishop John Wilkins, the philosopher Joseph Glanvill, the mathematician John Wallis, inventor and microscopist Robert Hooke, and the architect, Christopher Wren—formed their own version of Salomon's House, the Royal Society of London for Improving Natural Knowledge. This organization, which was granted a royal charter by Charles II in 1662, was openly Baconian in its aims. It attempted to conduct research and gather knowledge about every aspect of nature with an eye aimed at using this information to benefit humanity. The Society's members also assisted the government in its efforts to rebuild London in the aftermath of the great fire of 1666 by providing technical advice, blueprints for new construction, and a "political arithmetic" that we now describe as social statistics.[16]

Aside from becoming a clearinghouse for research on natural phenomena, the Royal Society of London also took a number of steps aimed at providing both a public forum and standards of excellence for their fledgling profession. These included publication of the first professional scientific journal, *Philosophical Transactions*, in 1665; the institution of lectures where working scientists were invited to discuss and demonstrate their research; the establishment of official criteria for membership in the Society; and the practice of offering medals and other prizes to honor significant discoveries in the natural sciences. Among the 17th century luminaries who were made fellows of the Society, participated in its forums, and received its honors were Isaac Newton and Robert Halley.

Mention is made of England's Royal Society because it becomes the model for similar scientific academies and foundations throughout the West. Indeed, by the turn of the 17th century, these organizations are to be found in France, Holland, Sweden, the Germanic states, and Russia. Like their English counterpart, these groups function as something akin to both a Baconian House of Salomon and an Arthurian fellowship. They bring together their countries' best and brightest in the natural sciences, provide these folks with an opportunity to "strut their stuff," publicly honor them for their achievements, and articulate, disseminate, and enforce a code of conduct they are expected to follow in their explorations, experiments, and exchanges with one another. All of these groups also enshrine through plaques, statues, busts, inscriptions, galleries, or pantheons the memory of those individuals foreign and domestic who they regard as heroes of scientific exploration and invention. And, not surprisingly, Galileo, Newton, Descartes, and Bacon are always counted in the front ranks of these "new Atlanteans" of science.

The New Argonauts

The spectacular discoveries of natural philosophers in the 17th century generated a genuine enthusiasm, even a reverence for science among the educated elites of the Enlightenment era. Not only had these scientists come up with new and convincing solutions to age-old problems in mathematics, astronomy, physics, chemistry, and anatomy, but they had also demonstrated that the world was a stable, orderly, and predictable place; a highly comforting finding in a period characterized by dissent, disorder and near constant conflict.

Moreover, the rational practices these men utilized in their investigations — observation, inductive and deductive reasoning, mathematical equations, experimentation, indifference to received authority — were free of the superstitions, creeds, dogmas, and ancient prejudices that many of this period's literate folk believed were at the root of human ignorance, misery, and violence. Indeed, science offered the citizens of the 18th century's "Republic of Letters" a surrogate religion with its own cosmogony — the universe as divinely created tinkertoy — sacred texts — *Principia, Discourse on Method, The Starry Messenger, Novum Organum, On the Fabric of the Human Body*— priests and rituals — scientists and their methods — and promise of paradise — albeit one in the here and now made possible by the practical applications of scientific research.

This religious zeal of the West's learned laity for science was shared in equal measure by its practitioners. As the immediate successors of Galileo and his contemporaries, eighteenth century students of natural philosophy saw themselves as the *avant garde* of what many were coming to regard as an Age of Scientific Revolution. These individuals were among the first both to fully understand their predecessors' work and appreciate its implications for other fields of inquiry. As such, they functioned very much like the missionaries and doctors of an emerging religion, both spreading the "good news" about the new science to the public-at-large and engaging in research and writing that dramatically expanded knowledge about the operations of nature and human society. Indeed, it was as proselytizers and scientific explorers that these 18th and early 19th century savants and gentleman scholars earned a place for themselves in both science and society's "very long and fair gallery" of heroes.

Achieving this distinction initially presented a number of challenges to those who were determined to follow in the footsteps of the 17th century titans discussed in the previous section. Aside from the fact that these individuals were working in the shadows of the founders and lawgivers of the Scientific Revolution, they were also trying to make their mark in a nascent profession that was still in the process of defining and justifying itself. Unlike warfare, sport and religion, natural philosophy lacked a pedigree distinguished by extraordinary feats of fortitude, sacrifice, and service. And until the latter half of the 17th century, scientists also lacked princely patrons, professional institutions, and a public interested in their activities and achievements.

This situation changed with the formation and propagation of scientific societies and academies throughout Europe and America during the Enlightenment era. Modeled after England's Royal Society and France's Royal Academy, these institutions helped to foster a sense of corporate identity among natural philosophers and, "even though these men operated within different contexts and traditions," they also laid the foundations for a new career in the sciences with "characteristics, obligatory stages, [a] *cursus honorum*, and goals."[17] They achieved this by bringing together and organizing the natural philosophers of their respective countries, regions, and communities; establishing criteria for the election of new members into their ranks; adopting logos and icons to distinguish natural philosophy from other professions; collecting and disseminating scientific research; organizing public lectures and collaborative scientific enterprises; and sponsoring international competitions with prizes and honors for scientists who solved specific questions and problems in such fields as physics, mathematics, astronomy, and chemistry.

These societies also "ennobled" science by winning royal charters and support for their activities. In this, they were helped enormously by Louis XIV who recognized early in his reign the many practical benefits to be gained from scientific research, particularly in the area of warfare. His decision to found, sponsor and subsidize a French Royal Academy of Sciences was imitated by princes throughout Europe who were eager to emulate France's grand monarch. In turn, all of this princely patronage helped to transform what had been a minor, even plebeian profession into a pastime worthy of men and women of "quality."

The elevation of natural philosophy into a prestigious enterprise was also advanced by the efforts of Enlightenment era natural philosophers and their devotees to heroize science and its practitioners. D'Alembert and his fellow contributors to the *Encyclopédie*, for example, portrayed Descartes and his contemporaries as geniuses who had boldly ventured into the unknown and demonstrated great courage by challenging the authority of the ancients and the forces of the Church. Other 18th century scientists went a step further and actually combined the abstract intellectual labor of their scientific research with travel that involved the kinds of physical exertion, discomfort, and dangers associated with heroic warriors and explorers.

As historian Mary Terrall has demonstrated in her very insightful work on these peripatetic natural philosophers, these men were well aware that in the aristocratic societies in which they lived and labored heroic status and its perks tended to be the preserve of nobly born warriors who had rendered some kind of extraordinary service to king and country. Consequently, they consciously emulated soldiers and their mythic counterparts by embarking on expeditions to unknown, distant and difficult territories to bring back data, specimens, and maps that could solve knotty scientific problems, uncover new knowledge, and possibly enhance the prestige, power and wealth of their patrons and sovereigns. On their return home, these traveling scientists also took advantage of the growing publishing industry to pen, print and sell travel narratives that represented their trips as adventures requiring not only intellectual prowess, but also great daring and stamina.[18]

Devotees of the new science among the literate laity also played up the heroic nature of these expeditions and their scientific researchers. In speeches, pamphlets, and other kinds of tracts, 18th century philosophes such as Voltaire referred to these traveling scientists as "new Argonauts," and made a point of highlighting their bravery by dwelling on the challenges attendant on entering an unknown country where, to paraphrase the secretary of the French Royal Academy, Bernard de Fontenelle, there were vast swamps, forests without roads, inaccessible mountains, and few towns.[19] As Terrall notes, by portraying these individuals as adventurers who were "venturing out into the unknown to find the golden fleece that would resolve a pressing scientific question," these commentators transformed them into heroes who "had to overcome obstacles as Jason and his companions had" with all the "cleverness, bravery, and stamina" required for such feats of derring do.[20]

This Enlightenment myth of the scientist as heroic explorer was well received in the salons and princely courts of Europe and, by the end of the 18th century, science and the folks engaged in it were *à la mode* throughout the West. Accounts of mapping and measurement expeditions were best sellers. Gazettes and the first daily newspapers published detailed accounts of the activities of scientific academies and societies, as well as reports on the competitions and debates between noted scientists. Experiments in electricity, especially those performed by Benjamin Franklin, were conducted before packed audiences. And thousands of people from all strata of society followed the exploits of the men conducting Europe's first aerostatic hot air balloon flights. Indeed, the new Argonauts and their varied explorations were so popular that the French dramatist and writer, Louis-Sebastien Mercier, exclaimed:

> The reign of letters has passed; physicists replace the poets and the novelists; the electric machine supplants the play.[21]

While Mercier's declaration of literature's demise at the hands of science proved premature, there was certainly no question but that "scientific culture" had come "to take a rightful place in the intellectual education of the modern urban elites" of this time.[22] More to the point of this study, the growth and spread of scientific foundations, coupled with the physically demanding explorations of distant and dangerous locales, also allowed 18th century natural philosophers to "claim membership in the scientific lineage" of "the great thinkers of the seventeenth century" who "had shown courage by questioning the authority of the ancients, or of the church."[23]

Who were these Enlightenment champions of science and what was the nature of the *cursus honorum* that they climbed to fame and glory? With the exception of self-made men like Joseph Priestly and Benjamin Franklin, most of the 18th century's scientific celebrities were the scions of well-to-do families, many of which belonged to the lower ranks of the European aristocracy. Their lives also tended to follow a common trajectory, i.e., study at one or more universities; a tour of the capitals of Western science — London, Paris, Berlin — to meet and hobnob with fellow students of natural philosophy; frequent attendance at salons; victories in competitions sponsored by scientific societies; participation in a scientific expedition and/or receipt of a prestigious academic appointment; research, discoveries, and publications; and official heroization by the state and professional associations of science.

Exemplary of the Enlightenment era savants who successfully mounted this scientific ladder of honor, and were acclaimed heroes of science in their lifetime, were the Italian and French mathematician, Joseph Louis Lagrange (1736–1813) and the Prussian naturalist, Alexander von Humboldt (1769–1859). Of these two men, Lagrange's career hewed closest to the life arc outlined above. The son of the treasurer of the king of Sardinia, he attended the College of Turin where he developed an enthusiasm for mathematics after a chance reading of Edmund Halley's work on the use of algebra in optics.

Though largely self-taught in mathematics, Lagrange's early work in this field showed such promise that he was appointed in 1755 at the age of 19 to a mathematics professorship at the Royal Artillery School in Turin. The following year, he was also elected to the Berlin Academy for his application of the calculus of variations to mechanics. And in 1757, he formed a scientific society with his pupils — later incorporated as the Turin Academy of Sciences — which published several volumes of transactions that highlighted his groundbreaking work on the propagation of sound, the theory and notation of the calculus of variations, and the general differential equations of motion.

Having demonstrated his brilliance as a physicist and mathematician, in 1763 Lagrange embarked on a tour of Basel, Berlin and Paris, where he conferred with colleagues in his field and other areas of natural philosophy. In Paris, he befriended the philosophe and mathematician Jean d'Alembert — an association that would prove most advantageous to his career — attended all of the city's major salons, and entered a competition sponsored by the Royal Academy of Science on the libration of the Moon, i.e., the motion of the Moon that causes the face that it presents to the Earth to oscillate causing small changes in the position of its features. He won the prize for this competition in 1764, as well as another Academy prize in 1766 for work on the orbits of Jupiter's satellites. Other Royal Academy prizes followed in 1772, 1774, and 1780.

In 1766, on the recommendation of his Director of Mathematics at the Berlin Academy, Leonhard Euler, and his good friend, the abovementioned philosophe, Jean d'Alembert, Frederick II (the Great) wrote to Lagrange expressing his wish as "the greatest king in Europe" to have "the greatest mathematician in Europe" at his court. Specifically, Frederick offered Lagrange the mathematics directorship that Euler was vacating to take a post in St. Petersburg. Lagrange accepted this prestigious position, and at the age of 30 embarked on a twenty-year period of highly original, even daring scientific research and discovery. During this time, he produced papers on the three-body problem; differential equations; prime number theory; the number-theoretic equation; probability; mechanics; and the stability of the solar system. In 1770, he published a "Reflections on the Algebraic Resolution of Equations" that took algebra in new directions and inspired later work in group theory.

Following the death of Frederick, Lagrange accepted Louis XVI's invitation to come and work in Paris. In France, he was given special apartments in the Louvre and made a member of the Royal Academy of Science. These honors and distinctions continued during the revolutionary period. Indeed, at the height of the Terror, he was made chairman of the committee to standardize the Republic's weights and measures and appointed to a mathematics professorship at the new École Polytechnique, the school that would educate France's elites for the next two centuries. He was also lionized during the Empire. In 1808, Napoleon named Lagrange a Grand Officer of the Legion of Honor and made him a *Senateur* and a *Comte de l'Empire*. The French emperor also awarded him the *Grand Croix de l'Ordre Impérial de la Réunion* in 1813, and, after Lagrange's death in the same year, interred him in the Pantheon as a father of France.

It should be noted before moving on to Humboldt, that the heroization of Lagrange continued long after his death. Streets were named for him in Paris and in Turin where he was born; he was one of 72 prominent French scientists commemorated on plaques during the first stage of the Eiffel Tower; Italy declared him an "Italian" scientist and hero of the nation following its unification in 1868; and, like Galileo and Descartes, his name was affixed to a lunar crater.[24] All in all, an impressive list of honors for a man who was said to be extremely shy, retiring and uninterested in anything save mathematics.

Unlike Lagrange, Friedrich Wilhelm Heinrich Alexander von Humboldt was neither shy nor retiring, and his interests were legion. Whereas Lagrange was in many respects the embodiment of the modern specialized "professional" scientist, Humboldt was very much the gifted amateur, curious about and conversant in everything from technology and mining to geography, volcanism, ethnology and botany. And where his French counterpart was a sedentary fellow whose explorations were confined to problems, papers and mathematical measurements, Humboldt was something of an Enlightenment era Indiana Jones; scaling mountains, crossing oceans, peering into volcanoes, plunging into unexplored jungles, and navigating unmapped rivers.

As was the case with other heroic Enlightenment savants, Humboldt was born into a well-to-do family. His father was a royal chamberlain at the Prussian court and his mother was the wealthy widow of a baron. He also attended a number of universities and academies — Frankfurt an der Oder, Göttingen, Hamburg, Freiberg in Saxony — where he developed a passion for botany, mineralogy, geology, anatomy, and astronomy. As a student, he impressed both his peers and his teachers with his prodigious memory and seemingly inexhaustible reserves of energy. While studying mining at the University of Freiberg, for example, he spent mornings in the mines surrounding the city, afternoons in class studying minerals and geological formations, and evenings collecting botanical specimens.

From 1792–1796, Humboldt worked for the Prussian mining service as an assessor. In this capacity, he invented and personally tested a new safety lamp, as well as a rescue apparatus for miners in danger of asphyxiation. In addition to these inventions, he founded and funded a school to train miners in both practical technology and mineralogy. Perhaps most remarkable, however, was the fact that he managed to carry out all of these official duties while still attending to his scientific research. This included publication, in 1793, of a book on the subterranean vegetation of the Freiberg mines; inspection tours of salt mines in Austria, Czechoslovakia, and Poland; and a geological and botanical trip through northern Italy and the Swiss and French Alps where he studied altitude effects on climate and plants and developed an interest in geomagnetism.

The considerable estate that he inherited from his mother following her death in 1796 allowed Humboldt to leave the Prussian civil service and dedicate himself to a life of travel and scientific exploration. Unfortunately, the upheavals caused by the Napoleonic wars at the turn-of-the-18th century made it impossible for him to immediately embark on scientific expeditions outside of Europe. Consequently, from 1796–1799 he traveled to different cities on the continent for the purpose of meeting with his fellow savants and acquiring a thorough knowledge of those fields he felt would be useful for future trips to unexplored areas of the globe. This tour took him to Jena where he became a member of Goethe and Schiller's Weimar circle, studied galvanism, and learned how to make geodetic and geophysical measurements; Vienna and Salzburg where he studied West Indian plants and practiced taking geographic bearings with the geologist Leopold von Buch; Paris where he conducted research at the Royal Academy on the interactions of oxygen and nitrogen gases, gave lectures, and set up galvanic and chemical experiments; and Spain where he headed a measuring expedition that produced a relief map of a substantial portion of the Iberian Peninsula.

All of the information and skills gleaned from this three-year hiatus stood Humboldt in good stead when he was finally able to set out in June 1799 on a research expedition to Spain's American colonies with the French botanist Aimé Bonpland. In what has been called "the scientific discovery of America," over the next six years these two men traveled on foot, pack horse, native canoe, and sailing vessel to Venezuela, Cuba, Colombia, Peru, Ecuador, and Mexico. As Humboldt's biographer, Kurt Biermann notes, despite great hardships, which included dense jungles, stifling heat, swarms of insects, wild animals, poisonous snakes, hostile tribes, and altitude sickness,

They recorded, sketched, described, measured, and compared what they observed, and gathered some 60,000 plant specimens, 6,300 of which were hitherto unknown in Europe. Humboldt made maps and amassed exhaustive data in countless fields — magnetism, meteorology, climatology, geology, mineralogy, oceanography, zoology, ethnography.[25]

Highlights of their expedition included an exploration of both the course of the Orinoco River and the Andes from Bogotá to Trujillo, Peru. The river trip, which lasted four months and covered 1,725 miles of largely uncharted, inhospitable, and uninhabited territory, proved there was a connection between the Orinoco and the Amazon. On the Andean hike they climbed a number of peaks including all of the volcanoes in the area around Quito, Ecuador without ropes, crampons, or oxygen supplies. Indeed, Humboldt's ascent of the Chimborazo volcano (20,561 feet) to a height of 19,280 feet, which was just short of the summit, set a world mountain-climbing record for nearly 30 years. During this part of their journey, Humboldt was the first to correctly diagnose the cause of altitude sickness as a lack of oxygen in the rarefied air of great heights.

After a brief trip to the United States, where Humboldt met and conversed with President Thomas Jefferson about his expedition and was elected a member of the American Philosophical Society, the two men returned to France in 1804 with an immense amount of information. Humboldt was given a hero's welcome in Paris where he read the first of what would be a long series of reports on his expedition to the Royal Academy. Indeed, Humboldt would spend the next 23 years of his life in the French capital sifting through his data, evaluating his findings, and publishing a voluminous journal of his travels.

This travel journal, which featured 34 volumes published over 25 years, would never be completed. Each volume offered its readers copperplate engravings of maps and illustrations prepared by Humboldt, as well as invaluable information about a mind-boggling array of topics. As Biermann points out, in these journals, Humboldt:

> Developed climatology as a science in itself; established the fields of plant geography and orography; formulated the fissure theory of volcanology; specified vegetation types; set forth concepts such as plateau, mean height of a pass, mean height of a summit, and mean temperature; and introduced the isotherm in meteorology.[26]

Humboldt's oeuvre was so impressive that Robert G. Ingersoll, a 19th century American politician and orator, felt justified in declaring that "he was to science what Shakespeare was to the drama."

At the age of 58, Humboldt returned to Berlin where he lived until his death at 90. Though these years were not as adventurous as those of his youth, he remained incredibly active. He served as science tutor to the crown prince of Prussia, taught physical geography at the University of Berlin, delivered lectures to the lay public, and organized an international scientific collaboration that succeeded in measuring the earth's magnetic storms and determining that they were caused by the periodically changing activity of sunspots. He also mounted and led at age 60 an expedition to Siberia and Central Asia that collected, measured, and compared geographical, geological, and meteorological data about an area of the world that was still relatively unknown. And during the last 25 years of his life, Humboldt became something of a 19th century Carl Sagan, by writing and publishing four volumes of a highly popular book entitled *Kosmos*, which attempted to present a comprehensible account of the universe as then known, as well as to communicate the joys of scientific exploration and discovery.

Suffice it to say that Alexander von Humboldt was and continues to be counted among the great heroes of science. His contemporary, Charles Darwin — a scientific hero in his own right — declared him "the greatest traveling scientist who ever lived. I have always admired him: now I worship him." This sentiment was also shared by Darwin's colleagues who rushed to honor the Prussian naturalist by awarding him honorary doctorates — Frankfurt an de Oder (1805), Dorpat (1827), Bonn (1828), Tübingen (1845), Prague (1848), and St. Andrews (1853) — memberships in their academies, titles — royal chamberlain to the King of Prussia, chancellor of the peace division of the order of the *pour le mérite*, president of the Société de Géographie in Paris — and awards such as the Royal Society of London's 1852 Copley medal for "outstanding achievements in research in any branch of science, and alternates between the physical sciences and the biological sciences." He has also had several species of flora and fauna named after him, as well as a number of geographical features, cities, towns, universities, and colleges. His grave site in the Schlosspark Tegel in Berlin continues to draw visitors from around the world.[27]

Coda: Heroic Exploration in the Enlightenment Era

If the new Atlanteans of science — Galileo, Newton, Descartes, Boyle — were the revolutionaries who radically shifted the "paradigms" natural philosophers had used for centuries to study and make sense of the universe, the savants of the Enlightenment were what might be called the first revolutionary cadre of modern science.[28] Like the ancient explorers who made use of Iron Age breakthroughs in metallurgy, ship building, and navigation to build vessels that allowed them to sail off into the unknown and uncover new knowledge and civilizations, these 18th century scientists were a new breed of Argonauts who took the findings and tools of their 17th century predecessors and used them to launch an equally daring series of investigations into the operations of the natural world. Out of their explorations emerged not only groundbreaking discoveries about the cosmos and life, but also a *cursus honorum* with models and standards of excellence for those wishing to win a place in the heroic pantheon of the new sciences.

As the preceding section demonstrates, attaining this status did not require the titan-like paradigm shifting of Galileo and company. Nevertheless, to be counted worthy of inclusion in the ranks of these giants still required considerable erudition, brilliance, professional dedication, stamina, daring, and no small amount of imagination. Further, the increasing professionalization of natural philosophy in the 18th century also obliged would-be champions of science to prove their scientific chops through research, travel, sociability, discoveries, publications, and prizes. Like reputation hungry medieval knights on the tourney circuit, glory seeking modern savants also had to demonstrate their mettle by successfully plying their trade among fellow professionals.

Unlike knightly heroes, however, these new Argonauts wielded instruments of science rather than the edged weapons of war and their voyages of discovery were imaginative exercises of the mind conducted, more often than not, in the safety of their private rooms. Armed only with pens, paper, and polynomials, a Joseph Lagrange or a Carl Friedrich Gauss could trace the orbits of moons and predict the behavior of gravitation, electricity and magnetism. To be sure, there were actual traveling scientists like Alexander von Humboldt and Pierre Louis Moreau de Maupertius who could be and were associated in the popular mind with both knights errant and mythic explorers. These men were as strong, daring and brave as warriors past or present and their trips took them to places as remote and alien as any visited by an Odysseus or a Sinbad. Nevertheless, as with their more sedentary colleagues, their fame was ultimately predicated not on the slaughter of native peoples or the acquisition of holy grails and golden fleeces, but on the successful collection and interpretation of scientific data that explained the workings of the world and set the stage for a cohort of heroic scientists many would liken to the fire-giver Prometheus.

The New Prometheans

By the end of the 19th century and the beginning of the 20th, there was every reason to believe that Francis Bacon's dream of a science-centered world was being realized. State subsidized science academies, professional associations of scientists, and scientific instructional programs in both vocational schools and private and public universities were commonplace features of Western life. Science was not only an established field of inquiry with its own mission, methods and marks of excellence, but its practitioners enjoyed, as they did in Bacon's new Atlantis, the respect and high regard of their societies. Monarchs, presidents and parliaments relied on them for recommendations on everything from waging warfare to improving national health, industry, and commerce. Businessmen and entrepreneurs looked to them for discoveries that might improve old, or create new product lines. Poets and writers from Wordsworth and Byron to Jules Verne and Sinclair Lewis lauded them as prophets and high priests of a New Jerusalem.[29] And everyone — farmers, factory laborers, artisans, tradesmen, and white collar workers — were in some way touched, for better or for worse, by the inventions and innovations their scientific research made possible.

As the profession of science became more important and prestigious, greater numbers of people entered its ranks. At the beginning of the 20th century, in addition to the many amateurs in the field, there were some 15,000 trained scientists in Western Europe and the Americas; in the latter half of the century, their numbers had swelled to more than half-a-million.[30] As with other professions, those opting for a career in the new sciences did so for varied reasons. Most viewed their occupation as a secure meal ticket with good hours, high wages, and great benefits. Many were motivated by a desire to use scientific methods and discoveries to improve the lot of humanity and build a better world. Some simply saw science as a calling they were both powerless to resist and eager to embrace.

Whatever their motivations for pursuing science, a number of these individuals made their way into Bacon's "long and fair" hall of heroes in the 19th and 20th centuries. Among the members of this heroic cohort were to be found paradigm shifters in the mould of Galileo, Newton, and Descartes; researchers, theorists, and traveling scientists like Lagrange and Humboldt; and representatives of a group as yet unnoted in these pages, i.e., inventors. As with their 18th century predecessors, these post–Enlightenment champions of science were almost exclusively male and haled from comfortably situated upper and/or middle class families. They were also an equally motley crew of learned amateurs, gentleman scholars, adventurers, and trained professionals. And their path to fame and fortune followed the same course of honor as their savant brethren, i.e., years of study, participation in professional societies, research, discoveries, publications, prestigious appointments and/or expeditions, prizes, and official recognition as a player of some significance in their field/s of inquiry.

In keeping with the increasingly specialized nature of science over the last 200 years, quite a few of these latter-day heroes of scientific exploration were heroized for work that either redefined older sciences or laid the foundations for new ones. Among these paradigm shifters and founding fathers were:

- Michael Faraday (1792–1867), English natural philosopher who discovered benzene, constructed the first electric motor, and revealed the relationship between electricity and magnetism;
- James Clerk Maxwell (1831–1871), Scottish theoretical physicist and mathematician whose electromagnetic field theory was named "the second great unification in physics" after the first one carried out by Newton;
- Dmitri Mendeleyev (1834–1907), Russian chemist who created the periodic law and periodic table;
- Charles Darwin (1809–1882), English naturalist whose *Origin of the Species* and *Descent of Man* laid the foundations of evolutionary biology;
- Louis Pasteur (1822–1895), French chemist and proponent of germ theory credited with founding the field of microbiology;
- Gregor Mendel (1822–1884), Austrian monk whose studies of the inheritance of specific traits in pea pods laid the foundations of genetics;
- Max Planck (1858–1947), German physicist who founded quantum theory; and
- Albert Einstein (1879–1955), German physicist and *Time Magazine*'s "Man of the 20th Century" for his theories of special and general relativity.

Like their predecessors in the 17th century, all of these men were insatiably curious, brilliant, critical of received authority, and gifted with that rare ability to imagine the world, or at least those parts of it they were exploring, in novel ways. They also came up with radically new paradigms of studying and explaining the operations of nature, and their findings were often greeted with either skepticism or, in the case of someone like Darwin, outright hostility. In time, their experiments, findings, and theories were accepted by their colleagues, and they were accorded great honors including a well-deserved place alongside the giants of the 17th century.

The 19th and early 20th centuries were also good times for those scientists who were seeking fame and fortune by traveling to as yet unexplored areas of the globe. Large parts of Africa and the polar regions were still *terra incognita*. The reading public continued to be enamored with stories about difficult and dangerous journeys into remote and little known territories. And the British and American press were willing to underwrite scientific expeditions to unexplored places on the planet for the purpose of generating travel tales that would sell newspapers.

Indeed, there was no better way for a scientific explorer of this time to achieve heroic status than to be involved in an expedition covered by the mass press. Just as Voltaire and d'Alembert heroized the traveling scientists of the Enlightenment, the reporters of the penny press — Henry Morton Stanley, William Henry Gibbs, Joseph Pulitzer, among others — served as the heralds and mythographers of late 19th and early 20th century explorers. These men covered and in many cases accompanied the amateurs, adventurers, and professional researchers who traveled to the world's remaining uncharted regions. And in their accounts of these trips, they underscored the sublime and exotic features of the territories through which these scientists traveled; the many discomforts and dangers they endured; and the various personality traits that marked them out as extraordinary men.[31]

While these newspapermen played a key role in heroizing the explorers of this period, the scientists heading up these expeditions were in fact a remarkable lot. The men who sought the headwaters of the Nile (Sir Richard Burton and John Hanning Speke); explored the interior of subtropical Africa (David Livingston); journeyed to the South Pole (Roald Amundsen); traversed the ice caps of Greenland (Fridtjof Nansen); and reached the North Pole (Robert E. Peary) did indeed have what Tom Wolfe would later term "the right stuff." They were brilliant and exceptionally erudite. Burton, for example, was fluent in 40 languages (counting dialects); Livingston was a physician as well as a geologist; and Nansen was conversant in zoology, oceanography, ethnography, and all manner of travel technology. These folks were also strong, courageous, fearless, and daring. In addition to taking a Somali spear through his cheeks during an expedition to east Africa, Richard Burton faced all manner of dangers when he disguised himself as a Moslem pilgrim, traveled to the sacred cities of Medina and Mecca, and measured and sketched the mosque and holy Muslim shrine, the Ka'bah. Fridtjof Nansen and a colleague survived for a year in the northern Arctic islands in a hut of stone with a roof of walrus hides on a diet of polar bear and walrus meat with only blubber as heating fuel. And Robert Peary lost all but two toes to frostbite during his Arctic adventures, commenting at one point that "a few toes aren't much to give to achieve the Pole."[32] Small wonder such men were honored heroes in the annals of science.

Another group of scientific explorers who came to the fore in the modern period were those actually honored in Francis Bacon's imaginary hall of heroes, i.e., inventors. Though most of the natural philosophers, mathematicians, and travelers addressed in the preceding pages made no distinction between applied and theoretical science, some of these folks were nonetheless gifted with a special knack for applying the equations and experiments of the sciences to "the structures of everyday life." Like their more theoretically inclined colleagues, these inventive individuals tended to be men who were extremely bright, curious, and willing to take risks. They were also distinctly different from their confreres in that they were often self-taught and self-made engineers, artisans, and entrepreneurs who, in the words of Thomas Edison, "worked for the silver dollar."

Without meaning to downplay the contributions of the other heroic figures in science addressed up to this point, it was ultimately the work of these dollar hungry inventors at the turn of the 19th century that made science appear to be an all-purpose panacea and its practitioners a race of new Prometheans. Thomas Edison's incandescent light bulb, for example, was literally a gift of fire that illuminated the whole world. Alexander Graham

Bell's telephone allowed near instant communication with people otherwise separated by time and space. Sir Charles Parson's steam turbine engine made cheap and plentiful electricity possible and revolutionized marine transport and naval warfare. Indeed, new inventions in scores of different fields made possible cheaper production, easier transportation, more food, better information, and improved products in everything from dyes and textiles to fertilizers, pharmaceuticals, and explosives.

Of the many Prometheans who revolutionized modern life, the one who most embodied what it meant to be a heroic inventor was the abovementioned Thomas Alva Edison (1847–1931). Born into a struggling working class family, Edison's formal education consisted of three months in an elementary school at the age of seven; a stint which ended when he was expelled by a schoolmaster for being "retarded." Fortunately, his mother was a former schoolteacher who tutored him, introduced him to natural science, and encouraged him to set up a small chemical laboratory in the basement of their home.

At age 12, Edison went into business for himself by selling newspapers and candy on trains running between Port Huron and Detroit, Michigan. During this time, he set up a laboratory in a baggage car, mastered telegraphy, and read every scientific journal he could find. After a period as a "tramp telegrapher," Edison secured a position as a Western Union night telegraph operator in 1868. Over the next twelve months, he read Michael Faraday's *Experimental Researches in Electricity*, conducted all of the Englishman's experiments, and decided, at the age of 21, to become a full time free-lance inventor.

Over the next ten years, Edison embarked on a series of researches and experiments that produced inventions which changed the world. Using the fortune he made for the invention of a Universal Stock Printer and a quadruplex telegraph, he set up the first professional science research laboratory, or "invention factory," in Menlo Park, California. Like Bacon's House of Salomon, Edison's "scientific village" brought together clockmakers, machinists, electrical engineers, and theoretical physicists to make inventions to order and invent devices that would satisfy the real needs of people in their daily lives. This lab, which was stocked with "every conceivable material" including "eight thousand kinds of chemicals, every kind of screw made, every size of needle, every kind of cord or wire, hair of humans, horses, hogs, cows, rabbits, goats, minx, camels,"[33] churned out some 400 patents, developed a carbon-transmitter that improved the operations of Bell's telephone, produced the phonograph, and developed the incandescent electric light bulb.

In his later life, Edison founded the General Electric Company that manufactured and distributed his new lamps and also designed and produced the electrical station equipment needed to power them. He also set up an even larger research laboratory in West Orange, New Jersey that employed over 5000 specialists in different fields. At this lab, Edison generated an even wider array of products than those he developed at Menlo Park, including an improved phonograph with wax records, the mimeograph, fluoroscope, alkaline storage battery, dictating machine, and the motion picture camera and projector. By the time he died in 1931, he held 1,093 patents in the United States, as well as patents in Britain, France, and Germany.

Not surprisingly, Edison is regarded as one of history's most prolific inventors, and is probably *the* outstanding genius in the history of technology. Towns, colleges, high schools, companies, a U.S. naval destroyer and a nuclear submarine bear his name. Places associated with his life and work are now museums and memorials. The oldest and highest award in the field of electrical science, engineering, and arts, which is presented by the American Institute of Electrical Engineers, was named after him and instituted in his lifetime (1904). Edison was also listed first in *Life* magazine's 1997 issue featuring "The 100 Most Important People in the Last 1000 Years." And the United States Congress declared his birthday, February 11, National Inventor's Day.[34]

Doubtless, Sir Francis Bacon would have approved.

"Now I am become Death, the destroyer of worlds": Scientific Heroism in the Atomic Age

Robert Oppenheimer's quotation from the Bhagavad-Gita on the occasion of the first detonation of an atomic bomb at Socorro, New Mexico on July 16, 1945 serves to remind us that the gifts of our latter-day Prometheans have not come to us without cost. Indeed, the findings and inventions of the scientific explorers examined in this chapter have often been exploited in ways that have caused considerable human misery and suffering. Newtonian science, for example, markedly improved the ability of modern artillerymen to hit their targets. Expeditions like those of David Livingston and Henry Morton Stanley helped open up non–Western areas of the world to the depredations of European imperialists. The invention of steam engines, spinning jennys, railroads, chemicals, and steel made possible industrial revolutions that destroyed traditional ways of living, crowded millions of men and women into vast urban slums, and degraded the environment necessary for human survival. Nuclear physics gave us weapons that could, and may yet, destroy all life on the planet. And Darwin's work on evolution was twisted into a racist, pseudo-scientific eugenics movement that sent millions to their deaths in concentration camps and death centers.

These "byproducts" of the Scientific Revolution did not go unnoticed and in the aftermath of the 20th century's two world wars many began to view scientists in a less heroic light. This shift in attitude was particularly pronounced in popular culture where researchers, inventors and explorers were often portrayed as either outright villains or dangerously naïve fools. In films such as *Metropolis*, *Frankenstein*, *The Thing from Another World*, and *Jurassic Park*, the man and/or men of science — even in the movies science remains a manly vocation — are the willing toadies of tyrants, megalomaniacs with delusions of godhood, amoral opportunists, or hapless Cassandras doomed to sound warnings that will never be heeded. Similar portrayals can also be found in various television series, comic books, sci-fi novels, and horror fiction. The Baconian vision of the scientist as "new Atlantean" seems quaint indeed.

Increasingly, the public expects of its heroic explorers not only genius, daring, and the approbation of his or her peers, but also evidence that they are aware of the ramifications of their work and committed to improving the human condition. To be sure, most of the heroes of science we have examined up to this point were in fact deeply concerned about the political and social issues of their day and engaged in efforts aimed at addressing them. Bacon was Lord Chancellor of England. Newton supported the Glorious Revolution of 1688, was a member of Parliament, and served as Warden of England's Mint. Humboldt was a committed democrat who was fiercely opposed to anti-semitism and slavery. Edison was a noted philanthropist and proponent of nonviolence. And Einstein and Oppenheimer were both concerned about the proliferation of nuclear weapons and agitated for disarmament. These noteworthy activities to the side, however, the heroization of these men was predicated first and foremost on their achievements as researchers, travelers, and inventors, not as social activists.

This is not to say that scientists of the future who have shifted paradigms, explored the universe, or invented new technologies should be deprived a spot in science's hall of heroes because they were insufficiently zealous about the issues of their times. As mathematician and biologist, Joseph Bronowski, famously reminded us in his television documentary, *The Ascent of Man*, Auschwitz was a crime of arrogance and dogma committed by people — many of whom were in the sciences — who were zealously involved in political and social movements that aspired to achieve absolute certainty in human affairs and godlike omnipotence. Rather, we should continue to heroize those intrepid explorers who have taken to heart the following recognition by one of modern science's first great heroes, Isaac Newton:

> I do not know what I may appear to the world, but to myself I seem to have been only like a boy playing on the sea-shore, and diverting myself in now and then finding a smoother pebble or a prettier shell than ordinary, whilst the great ocean of truth lay all undiscovered before me.[35]

8

"The road of excess leads
to the palace of wisdom"
The Hero as Romantic Rebel

Let us sate the fervors of passion in depths of sensuality! ... Let's plunge into the torrents of time, into the whirl of eventful existence! There, as chance wills let pain and pleasure, success and frustration, alternate; unceasing activity alone reveals our worth.

—Goethe: *Faust*

But soon he knew himself the most unfit
Of men to herd with Man; with whom he held
Little in common; untaught to submit
His thoughts to others....
He would not yield dominion of his mind
To spirits against whom his own rebell'd;

— Byron: *Childe Harold (Canto III, Stanza XII)*

Prince! What you are, you are by circumstances and by birth. What I am, I am through myself. Of princes, there have been and will be thousands. Of Beethovens there is only one.

— Beethoven to Prince Lichnowsky

A suicide establishes a man. Alive one is nothing; dead one becomes a hero."

—Louis Reybaud: *Jérôme Paturot*

If there is a Beverly Hills of the dead, it is probably France's Père Lachaise cemetery. The largest necropolis in Paris, it has served as the burial ground of choice for the crème de la crème of French and Western cultural life for the last two centuries. Actress Sarah Bernhardt, dancer Isadora Duncan, painter Eugène Delacroix, author Honoré de Balzac, composer Frédéric Chopin, and opera singer Maria Callas are just a few of the many prestigious figures who have selected this exclusive boneyard as their final resting place.

The presence of all these departed artists and writers has also helped make Père Lachaise one of the most popular tourist spots in the world. Thousands of people flock to this cemetery every year to visit the gravesites of various celebrities from yesteryear that have touched their lives in some fashion. And just as the rich and famous above ground enjoy varying degrees of popularity with the general public, so too are some of the residents of Père Lachaise more "in" than others. The burial place of France's "little sparrow" of the slums,

Edith Piaf, for example, continues to draw large crowds of adoring fans even though she died in 1963 and her music is largely unknown to the millenials of the 21st century. The mass grave of the 147 workers who were executed and buried together during the suppression of the Paris Commune in 1871 still serves as a rallying point for the mass parties and movements of the French left. And the crypt of the irrepressible Oscar Wilde who was prosecuted and imprisoned for "the love that dare not speak its name" remains a popular gathering spot for the cemetery's many gay and lesbian visitors.

Of all the gravesites in Père Lachaise, however, probably none gets more attention than the "funeral pyre" of rock star Jim Morrison. Ever since the heroin overdose that landed him here in 1971 at the age of 27, the burial place of this self-styled "Lizard King" of the Sixties has drawn a steady stream of visitors. Like medieval pilgrims at the shrine of a popular saint, these fans have covered Morrison's grave with lighted candles, flowers, and personal belongings. They have also celebrated his memory by staging a 40 year rock and roll wake at his graveside complete with the kinds of drinking, dancing, and drug use he was so fond of while alive.

Figuring out why Morrison enjoys such sainted status has engaged the energies of more than one pop culture maven. While he was certainly young, beautiful and talented, and led a highly publicized hedonistic lifestyle, his oeuvre was uneven at best. A handful of largely unknown short films, five slim volumes of poetry — most of them privately published — and a discography that includes everything from soulful psychedelic melodies to pop singles sporting bubble gum lyrics.

Sympathetic biographers of Morrison, such as Daniel Sugerman and Jerry Hopkins, argue that his allure both in life and death stemmed from the fact that he was a "god," a latter-day Dionysus whose poetry touched and transformed his audiences.[1] Filmmaker Oliver Stone, who chronicled Morrison's seven-year stint as a rock star and pop icon in his 1991 movie, *The Doors*, believed the singer was not so much a divinity as a shaman, i.e., an ecstatic holy man who existed in two worlds, one sacred, the other profane. In his film, Stone suggests that Morrison entered a trance state during his performances that allowed him and his audiences to "break on through" to an alternative plane of existence. Other less adulatory commentators have simply noted that Morrison was the perfect poster child for a self-indulgent tumultuous time that was in love with troubled, tormented pretty boys who lived fast and died young.

Whether they worship him as the reincarnated Bacchus or diss him as just another Sixties bad boy, all of these chroniclers of Morrison's life agree that his fan base was largely drawn from people with a pronounced fondness for "romanticism," that amalgam of lifestyles and aesthetic practices characterized by "emotional exuberance, unrestrained imagination, and spontaneity in both art and personal life."[2] Though this romantic tendency originated in the late 18th century as a kind of contra Enlightenment, it has continued to exercise an enduring hold on the Western imagination for the better part of three centuries. Indeed, a considerable number of the West's most notable poets, painters, actors, authors, musicians, and revolutionaries — many of them interred at Père Lachaise — have counted themselves adherents of this sensibility.

What follows is an effort to arrive at some understanding of the meaning and salient features of this romantic movement, as well as why someone like Jim Morrison is counted among its heroes. Answering either of these questions poses a plethora of problems and one of the most prominent of these can be instantly deduced by taking a look at the epigraphs introducing this chapter. Though penned by noted romantics, these statements reveal a wide range of seemingly unrelated and often conflicting sentiments. Goethe's Faust, for example, reveals himself to be a sociable fellow dedicated to ceaseless striving, experience, and hedonism. Byron's Childe Harold, on the other hand, shuns the company of men in favor of a solitary individual existence lived solely according to principles of his own choosing. Beethoven echoes Byron in his rather unkind riposte to his patron, Prince Lichnowsky, and Reybaud suggests that suicide is preferable to living because it's the surest way for a man to acquire a measure of deathless glory. Discerning a uniquely "romanticist" position in any of these comments is difficult and that difficulty is only compounded by the fact that we know the adherents of romanticism were also fond of a great many other "isms"— naturalism, medievalism, historicism, nationalism — as well.

Further confusion ensues when one tries to delineate the traits of a romantic hero from the lives of these epigraphs' authors. Louis Reybaud to the side, few would disagree that Johann Wolfgang von Goethe, George Gordon Lord Byron and Ludwig van Beethoven should figure prominently in any *Who's Who* of romanticism. Nevertheless, it is hard to imagine three more different personalities. While he was a *Sturm und Drang* poet in his youth, as well as the author of the romantic classic, *The Sorrows of Young Werther*, Goethe was a comfortable bourgeois, a noted scientist, and the chief counselor of the Grand Duke of Saxe-Weimar. Similarly, Beethoven may have been a bold experimental musical genius of deep feeling, but he was also a devotee of the Enlightenment and the protégée, albeit a difficult one, of more than one enlightened despot. And Byron was both a rebellious litterateur and a peripatetic aristocratic wastrel who was regarded by friend and foe alike as "mad, bad, and dangerous to know."[3]

Insofar as romanticism does have a common core of convictions and an ideal of heroism, they are rooted in the response of two remarkable generations of artists in the late 18th and early 19th centuries to the scientific, political and economic revolutions that were reshaping Western life. The first of these generational cohorts was largely comprised of German and English writers who were dissatisfied with the Enlightenment fixation on rationality, order, restraint, and classicism in the arts. Though these poets and novelists were not hostile to reason or science, they were convinced that authentic knowledge and beauty were best found through explorations of the "unclassifiable" in human existence, i.e., through intuition, emotion, imagination, mystery, exoticism, and, most importantly, sublime nature. And they expressed this conviction by producing a literature filled with sentimental, emotionally intense characters living their lives in an unconventional manner.[4]

The successors of these early romantics came of age during the American, French and Industrial revolutions. Though they fully subscribed to their forerunners' critique of the Enlightenment, and adopted the same aesthetic sensibility in their work, these artists also embraced lifestyles and attitudes that embodied their reaction to the political, social and economic tumult of their times. Some of these folks were horrified by the excesses of the French Revolution, the Napoleonic wars, and the social suffering and environmental degradation caused by industrialization. Feeling powerless to address these ills, they retreated into self-centered aestheticism and/or reveries of an idealized medieval past. Others in this cohort were excited by the dual revolutions reshaping the West, seeing in them an opportunity to create a new world order with poets acting as "the unacknowledged legislators of the world." These individuals celebrated rebellion in their poems, paintings, and music, manned barricades, and participated in movements of national self-determination. Whether they were reactionaries or revolutionaries, however, all of the aforementioned romantics were staunch individualists, unyielding critics of the bourgeois society that succeeded the *ancien régime*, and prolific producers of an artistic oeuvre that was unconventional, bold, expressive, colorful, and frequently full of sound and fury.

Not surprisingly, the heroes of these early romantics reflected their values. Passionate, willful, and doomed outlaws, wanderers, and other assorted members of the damned figured prominently in their poems, novels, and paintings. In real life, they lauded self-made "world historical" personalities like Napoleon Bonaparte who exhibited emotional intensity, genius, creativity, and disdain for any social stricture or convention not of their own making. And among themselves, they heroized artistic types that mirrored their own take on the modern world. For those seeking escape from democratic industrial mass society, this was the aesthete or "dandy" interested in nothing save beauty, sensation, and the transformation of his own life into a work of art. For others of a more activist bent, it was the *l'homme engagé*, the engaged artist determined to use his or her work to transform the world into a place more agreeable to the romantic sensibility.

The sentiments of these 18th and 19th century poets, painters, and musicians continue to inform romanticism in its later incarnations. When actors emote, artists impress or express their feelings in their work, and revolutionaries execute some terrible act of violence intended to precipitate a secular second coming, they all follow in the footsteps of these early romantic rebels. Indeed, much of modern aesthetics, and all of the various "isms," are suffused with the ideas and practices of these individuals.

The foregoing précis on the romantics and their heroes highlights the principal points that are addressed in greater depth below. In the sections that follow, we examine the origins of romanticism, the dreams and delusions of its adherents, and the lives and work of certain artists considered representative of both the romantic movement and its heroic ideal. And we begin this examination in the storm and stress of a revolutionary age.

Things fall apart; the center cannot hold: Romanticism and Revolt

Romanticism has been characterized as a revolt against the "fixities and definities" of modern Western civilization.[5] And most of the people who study this romantic rebellion tend to agree that it began in the late 18th century when a group of German writers and poets — the most prominent of whom were Johann Wolfgang von Goethe, Friedrich Schiller, Jakob Lenz, Friedrich Klinger, and Johann Herder — challenged the Enlightenment era assumption that the whole of human experience could be understood and explained through reason and science. Often referred to as the *Sturm und Drang* ("Storm and Stress") group, these men argued instead that the wellspring of human behavior, creativity and even knowledge was to be found not in the head but in the heart, i.e., in such noncorporeal unclassifiable faculties as intuition, feeling, emotion and imagination.

This conviction found its most forceful expression in *Sturm und Drang* literature, the best example of which was Goethe's *The Sorrows of Young Werther*. One of the canonical texts of romanticism, this novel relates the story of a young bourgeois artist named Werther who is intent on living an unpretentious, honest life consistent with his sentiments and feelings. Rather than affect the mannerisms and fashions of Enlightenment high society, he speaks in a straightforward manner, wears his hair long, and dresses in a simple blue tail coat with a yellow waistcoat. He also abandons city life in order to take up residence in a small village populated by solid commonplace peasant folk who live in a traditional manner. And he shows his disdain for convention by falling madly and hopelessly in love with another man's fiancé. Misunderstood by his neighbors, who share neither his artistic sensibility nor his fashion sense; shunned by the local gentry; and obsessed with a woman who will never be able to requite his love; Werther ends his life by shooting himself in the head.

While Goethe's *Werther* is little read today except in college classes on European literature, it was a best seller in it own time (Napoleon admitted to reading the book seven times). The novel's critique of aristocratic culture, unabashed love of nature, and advocacy of feeling, freedom and natural goodness resonated well with 18th and 19th century readers disaffected with both the *ancien régime* and its Enlightenment savants. The book's fans were also wild about the title character.

> There was a Werther epidemic: Werther fever, a Werther fashion — young men dressed in blue tail coats and yellow waistcoats — Werther caricatures, Werther suicides.... And all this continued, not for a year, but for decades; and not only in Germany but in England, France, Holland and Scandinavia as well.[6]

Goethe's protagonist was also well received among his fellow romantics, many of whom regarded him as the perfect poster boy for their movement. Werther's characteristics — youth, artistic sensibility, emotional intensity, disaffection with the "fixities and definities" of society, unconventional behavior, love of nature, fondness for folk culture — were all consistent with the contra–Enlightenment stance of romanticism. And the character's sorrows and suicide were not only a further indictment of the enlightened society that shunned him, but a testament to the exceptional feeling and sensitivity of the romantic rebel as well.

The sentiments voiced in Goethe's *Werther* and the other works of the *Sturm und Drang* literati also loomed large in the thinking of such British writers as William Blake, William Wordsworth, Samuel Taylor Coleridge, and Walter Scott. These men too were critical of Enlightenment assumptions about reason, science and art, and they concurred with their German confreres' conviction that feeling was the true source of creativity and beauty in human affairs. In their work, they abandoned classical conventions of speech in favor of ordinary language, criticized the mechanistic materialism of 17th and 18th century thought, and worshipped nature as an organic living realm filled with divine force. Some sense of this early British romanticism can be gleaned from the following lines of Wordsworth's poem *The Prelude*:

> To every natural form, rock, fruit or flower,
> Even the loose stones that cover the high-way,
> I gave a moral life, I saw them feel,
> Or link'd them to some feeling: the great mass

Lay bedded in a quickening soul, and all
That I beheld, respired with inward meaning.[7]

The poetry and prose of these early British romantics also featured protagonists who, like Goethe's Werther, were at odds with the status quo. These included Coleridge's outcast mariners and drug addled dreamers seeking salvation and a glimpse of the divine. Scott's historical outlaws, rebels, and knightly freebooters championing individual freedom and revolting against centralized authority. Wordsworth's pantheists rejecting deism in favor of nature worship. And Blake's great rebel Satan opting, like Milton's Lucifer, for a life in hell over an existence of servitude in heaven.

This romantic idea of the hero as an emotionally intense outcast in revolt against society might have remained little more than a fictional contrivance if not for the outbreak of the French and Industrial Revolutions at the end of the 18th century. These two events not only reshaped the political, social, and economic contours of Western life, but they also transformed romanticism from a largely British and German literary affair into a mass movement in the arts with its own distinctive aesthetic principles and practices, audiences, and real life heroes. As Eric Hobsbawm notes in his *The Age of Revolution*:

> We might say that the French Revolution inspired him [the romantic artist] by its example, the Industrial Revolution by its horror, and the bourgeois society, which emerged from both, transformed his very existence and modes of creation.[8]

The dramatic changes unleashed by this dual revolution — the deposition of the French *ancien regime*, the dramatic rise to power of Napoleon Bonaparte, mass warfare, increased social mobility, urban expansion, bourgeois society — were indeed without parallel, and classical themes and artistic practices seemed woefully inadequate to capture the tenor of the times. Consequently, artists began to cast about for an alternative way to address the clangor and tumult of the world being born around them. And a movement like romanticism, which was both opposed to classicism and supportive of a new "modern" art predicated on feeling and revolt, appeared to offer just such an approach.

Indeed, the period stretching from the French Revolution to 1848 is often regarded as *the* "Romantic" era in the history of Western art. A new generation of writers — George Gordon Lord Byron, Percy Bysshe Shelley, Mary Wollstonecraft Shelley, Victor Hugo, Georges Sand, Alexander Pushkin — came to the fore at this time and penned a consciously romantic poetry and prose that was personal, passionate and peopled with young rebels, wanderers, nature lovers, obstreperous titans, and soulful monsters. Their counterparts in the visual arts also subscribed to the notion that a creative work should reflect the inner life of the artist, be original, and express warmth, emotion, and movement. Consequently, painters such as Caspar David Friedrich, Eugène Delacroix, and Joseph William Malford Turner filled their canvases with color, remote and exotic subjects, and scenes depicting nature's power, terror, and mystery. As for the aural arts, a generation of romantic composers including, among others, Frédéric Chopin, Franz Liszt, and Ludwig van Beethoven, revolutionized music by tripling the size of their orchestras and using percussion, wind instruments, strings, brass, and contrasting tones and themes to bring their listeners to a state of ecstasy and hysteria.[9]

Though these artists are regarded as the first non-fictional heroes of romanticism, they were not altogether different from the protagonists found in early romantic poetry and prose. Most of them were, like Werther and company, quite young when they made their mark on the Western artistic scene. All of them were exceptionally talented and innovative, and many of them were considered by their contemporaries to be "geniuses." Whatever their social rank, these folks also tended to be rebels of one sort or another who were fond of flouting conventions and behaving in an eccentric, often scandalous manner. And, in keeping with one of the central precepts of the romanticist sensibility, these artists all lived lives of emotional intensity. For most of them, this involved a lot of drugs, drink, sex, and the inevitable drama that usually accompanies these pastimes. Others in this group suffered from various kinds of mental disorders, and quite a few of them committed suicide.

Another thing that these romantic artists shared in common with their literary counterparts was a committed fan base. As Hobsbawm noted in the passage from his history quoted above, in addition to providing these individuals with inspiration and subject matter for their various media, the dual revolution provided them with an audience as well. Bourgeois society was literate, leisurely, interested in culture, and eager to patronize the arts. It was also subject to repressive political conditions, chronic social unrest, economic insecurity, and a cultural environment characterized by corsets, crinolines, and cant. With its emphasis on innovation, freedom, mobility, and unconstrained feeling, romanticism afforded a great many of these bourgeoisie with a means of demonstrating their artistic sophistication, expressing their displeasure with the status quo, and experiencing, even if vicariously, a life not boundered by traditional mores.

This romantic/bourgeois nexus was and still is extraordinarily complicated. On the one hand, this new largely urban audience provided romantic artists with both the financial wherewithal they needed to live and work, and the public approbation that transformed them into heroic figures. On the other hand, they embodied everything romanticism was against in modern life. The same professional middle class that purchased novels, paintings and tickets for musical and theatrical performances also provided the personnel for ministries and police departments that enforced restrictions on individual freedom, censored the press and the arts, and imprisoned those dissenting against the status quo. Bourgeois businessmen picnicked in the countryside and lived in luxurious rural settings, while underwriting enterprises that degraded the natural environment and filled cities with teeming slums. And for every bourgeois devotee of artistic work that honestly and frankly addressed human feeling, sexuality and/or the social inequities of the times, there were far more "philistines" who were ignorant of the arts and openly hostile to the men and women who produced and supported them.

While the relationship between modern artists and their middle class audiences was a troubled one, it nonetheless brought forth a rather colorful cadre of romantic heroes. These figures were young, creative, at odds with past aesthetic conventions, and eager to produce artwork that was both personal and original. They also tended to be at loggerheads with the political, social, and economic arrangements of their societies, and were subsequently sympathetic to ideas and movements aimed at altering the status quo. Their personal lives were stormy and marked by substance abuse, promiscuity, mental distress, and self-immolation. And they were dependent for their livelihoods on a mass audience they often despised.

Though these romantic heroes were a rebellious, contrary lot, they responded to the historical circumstances in which they found themselves in markedly different ways. Some sought to transcend the troubles of their time by transforming themselves and the stuff of their lives into art. Others, however, were intent on using their artwork and the power of personal example as weapons in a greater struggle aimed at liberating humanity from suffering and injustice. And it is to these two distinct, albeit related faces of romantic heroism that we now turn.

"To wake and sleep before a mirror": The Romantic Hero as Dandy

All heroes are selfish to some degree. As we have seen, heroic warriors, athletes, explorers, and scientists are notorious for their egos, as well as their unstinting efforts to insure that their names and deeds are remembered and celebrated long after they are dead. Even martyrs, saints, and revolutionaries, the selfless servants of great collective causes, are drawn to their vocations out of a desire to insure a berth for themselves in the paradises and pantheons — sacred or secular — of the movements they serve. Nevertheless, while all of these individuals are self-serving, their heroic status, like any other honor, still remains a claim of worth that requires acknowledgement from a public that expects something — defense, enrichment, enlightenment, rapture — in return. In the history of heroism, as with everything else in life, there are no free lunches.

The advent of romanticism markedly changes this heroic quid pro quo. Because it is a movement that celebrates creative individuals who are self-centered, emotionally intense, and unconventional, romanticism's heroes tend to be rebellious artists or artist wannabes who are focused first and foremost on living their lives in a manner that is faithful to their personal interests, needs, and desires. Insofar as service figures into this process of heroic self-realization, it does so *not* because society expects it, but because the romantic hero deems it necessary to his or her own development. As for public approbation, these romantic rebels neither need nor desire it. Indeed, as we have already noted, in both fiction and real life these folks tend to be social pariahs.

Nothing embodies the self-centered nature of romanticism's heroic ideal better than the so-called dandies of the 18th and 19th centuries. Though the etymology of their moniker is unclear, we know who these people were and what they did because "dandyism" was a subject of particular interest to such notable writers as Charles Baudelaire, Barbey d'Aurevilly, and Honoré de Balzac. Their accounts reveal that these individuals were usually male, comfortably situated, extremely sensitive, and very creative. They were also scornful of elite and bourgeois society and rejected whenever and wherever possible the prevailing conventions and taboos of the communities in which they lived and worked. This disdain for conventional society, however, did not translate into either love for the masses or commitment to social action. Rather, these dandy rebels responded to industrialized mass society by beating an epicurean style retreat into a world of their own making, a world populated only with people they deigned to name friends and equals. And within their domains, these dandies focused, not on the burning issues of the day, but on finding answers to questions about taste, style and pleasure.[10]

The heroic lion of this dandy set, the man whose life set the standard by which all other dandies would be judged, was George Bryan Brummell, more commonly known as Beau Brummell. Born in 1794, Brummell was the son of the secretary to Lord North, the author of the Tea Act that helped precipitate the American Revolution. At his father's death, Brummell inherited a fortune that enabled him to resign his commission in the British army and set up a bachelor establishment on Chesterfield Street in Mayfair, London.

Once ensconced in his new digs, Brummell essentially created an alternative lifestyle within the confines of Regency England's high society. Rather than wear the lavish wigs, brocaded jackets, and knee stockings of the 17th century fops, Brummell opted for a restrained understated look that involved wearing his hair long and dressing in fitted dark suits with full-length trousers and elaborately knotted cravats. He also filled the rooms of his townhouse with tasteful well crafted furniture that was both functional and pleasing to the eye. And he avoided the collector mania of this period that left most homes looking like curio cabinets stuffed with all manner of bric-a-brac.

Brummell was also extremely fastidious about his personal hygiene and appearance, spending as much as five hours a day getting dressed. This toilette included shaving, bathing, and cleaning his teeth, which, in a country and a time not noted for attention to either cleanliness or dental care, was considered rather eccentric behavior. He also polished his shoes with champagne and devoted an inordinate amount of time to his ties, working and reworking them forty or fifty times until he attained a look of "spontaneous perfection."[11] Indeed, Brummell's success in this latter pastime was such that his biographer William Jesse later noted that his "tie became a model that was imitated, but never equalled."[12]

In addition to being "king of the dandies" in matters of taste, elegance, and personal appearance, Brummell was noted for his rapier sharp wit and well-turned phrases. His contemporaries delighted in his bon mots — at least those that were not on the receiving end of them — and future exemplars of dandyism such as Oscar Wilde would emulate these witticisms in their own spoken and written discourse. Nevertheless, though he fancied himself a writer and was certainly capable of crafting clever repartee, Brummell's celebrity had less to do with his literary output than his reputation for tasteful suits and well appointed rooms.

Indeed, for a time, Brummell's dandy lifestyle made him the unofficial leader of fashion in Britain at the start of the 19th century. And because he counted among his personal friends no less a personage than the future George IV, his personal example and pronouncements in matters of dress, décor, and decorum were received with the utmost seriousness. Unfortunately, gambling and extravagant spending eventually bankrupted Brummell, and some rather ill-advised acerbic remarks about his royal patron served to alienate him from a great many of his high society friends and patrons. Hounded by creditors, and persona non grata in the social circles he once dominated, England's dandy king fled to France in 1816 where he died penniless and insane in a charitable asylum in 1840.

Whatever the nature of Brummell's notoriety while alive — his tasteful bachelor digs, exquisite grooming, witty repartee, and well heeled friends — it is difficult to imagine a more unlikely candidate for heroization. The entirety of his life was spent literally waking and sleeping in front of a mirror and gratifying his every personal whim. He was blithely unconcerned about the many political, social, and economic issues of his time, and he treated the world outside his Mayfair townhouse as little more than a quarry to be mined for the furniture, wallpaper, carpets, clothes, and cravats that made him an arbiter of fashion and the prototype of dandies everywhere. Even his tragic end, which was something of a requirement for any would be romantic hero, was less an indictment of an uncaring bourgeois society than the culmination of an extraordinarily selfish life.

All of these considerations to the side, Beau Brummell remains one of the prominent heroes of the romantic movement. His life has been the subject of a stage play, operetta, two Hollywood films, and a BBC television docu-drama. He figures as a character in any number of novels and his name graces colognes, rock bands, and the lyrics of assorted pop songs and Broadway musical numbers. There is a statue of Brummell on London's Jermyn Street; and the British Federation of Clothing Manufacturers presents the person they select as the year's Best Dressed Man with the George Bryan Brummell Award for sartorial elegance.[13]

Why Brummell enjoys such prominence is an intriguing question. Part of the answer to this query appears to lie in the fact that much of modern culture, be it elite or mass, is market based and focused on the gratification of personal desires. For the better part of two centuries, Western societies have been bombarded by novels, plays, films, television programs, and marketing campaigns counseling us to explore and realize our inner needs and yearnings, as well as to make some sort of personal statement about who we are. For many of the people and industries making this pitch, and certainly for the audiences receiving it, the consumption and ostentatious display of clothing, accessories, and cosmetics, as well as the frequent refurbishing of one's home, are the principal ways in which this exploration and development of the self is realized. Small wonder then that the West's first fashion guru and home remodeler par excellence would figure prominently in the modern heroic pantheon.

Another explanation for Brummell's heroic stature is suggested by a 60s mod named Marc Bolan who explained in a 1962 *Town Magazine* interview that Brummell "was just like us really, you know, came up from nothing."[14] Despite the fact that this romantic dandy was the heir to a small fortune and most certainly not like everyone else in early 19th century Britain, he is nonetheless viewed by many in modern democratic mass societies as a kind of self-made everyman. Rather than focus on Brummell's comfortable social situation and patrician lifestyle, people have opted instead to fixate on the fact that he haled from an untitled bourgeois family and used his inheritance to create a distinctive identity and way of living that was admired and emulated by his aristocratic betters. What they revere about Brummell is that he holds out the hope that any person can reinvent him or herself and become significant "players" over the course of their lives. Seen in this light, one could argue that the life of Beau Brummell was history's first reality TV show.

If Brummell's heroic stature rested on the independent and eccentric manner in which he lived his life, other dandy-like aesthetes were revered as romantic heroes because of the manner in which they ended their lives. Perhaps the two best examples of this heroic tendency were the 18th century poet and forger Thomas Chatterton and the early 20th century Dadaist Jacques Vaché. Born in 1752, Chatterton was a bright moody solitary young man who spent most of his life ensconced in one attic or another penning pseudo-medieval poetry, eclogues, lyrics, operas, and satires, none of which won him either fame or fortune.

Penurious, isolated, depressed, and furious at a world that refused to recognize his genius, he downed a draught of arsenic at the tender age of seventeen, died horribly, and was buried in a pauper's grave.

Though Chatterton's suicide went largely unnoticed at the time of his death, within a generation he "had become the supreme symbol of the Romantic poet."[15] His youth, emotional intensity, dedication to his art, rejection by the critics, solitary unconventional lifestyle, and, most importantly, self-murder made him emblematic of what many romantics considered their agonized existence within a philistine world that did not understand them. Poets such as Wordsworth, Coleridge, Shelley, Keats, and Rossetti lauded Chatterton's "genius," castigated the society that failed to recognize his gifts, and celebrated his decision to die young rather than live on into a middle age characterized by infirmity and declining creative powers. Chatterton also received posthumous plaudits from artists in other fields as well. Playwright Alfred de Vigny penned a drama recounting the poet's short life and death in 1835; Harry Wallis immortalized Chatterton's suicide in his famous 1856 painting *The Death of Thomas Chatterton*; Peter Ackroyd wrote a novel about the boy in 1987; and a number of composers—John Wall Callcott, Ruggiero Leoncavallo, Matthias Pinscher, Matthew Dewey—tried to capture the young artist's agony in music and opera. Chatterton also enjoys a "Wiki" page on the internet and rates a special collection of "Chattertoniana" in the British Museum in London.[16] As Reybaud wryly noted, suicide can indeed establish a man and make him a hero.

Chatterton's 20th century counterpart, Jacques Vaché, is neither well known nor highly regarded. Indeed, if it were not for Vaché's published war letters, his friendship with the founder of Surrealism, André Breton, and his rather novel suicide, we would know next to nothing about him. What little we do know is that he was born in 1895 and lived a rather twisted Brummell-like existence until his death in 1919. During this brief 24 year stint, he studied art, read widely and deeply, and dedicated himself to a life of idleness and "umore" (the French word for humor without the h). This "humorous" existence was largely fixated on men's fashion, drawing and painting postcards, hosting the occasional tea party, and "arranging" his girlfriend.

> He lived with a young woman whom he obliged to remain motionless and silent in a corner while he was entertaining a friend, and whose hand he merely kissed with ineffable dignity, when she served the tea.[17]

During World War I, Vaché served on the Western Front, suffered a leg wound in 1916, and was remanded to a military hospital in Nantes. While recovering, he met Breton who was taken by the fact that "every morning he spent a good hour arranging one or two photographs, some saucers, a few violets on a little lace-top table within reach of his hand."[18] Once he was able to walk, Vaché also took to parading about the city outfitted as different characters—hussars, airmen, cowboys, doctors. A year later he was brandishing a loaded revolver at the opening night performance of French poet Guillaume Appollinaire's play *Les Mamelles de Tirésias*.

During this period in which he was acting out his fantasies, Vaché decided to commit suicide at a time and place of his own choosing. In taking this step, he also resolved to:

> Die with somebody else. To die alone is boring. I should prefer to die with one of my best friends.[19]

And this is exactly what he did. In 1919, he administered lethal doses of opium to himself and two friends who were unaware they were joining him on a one way trip. As writer Al Alvarez notes in his study of suicide, "it was the supreme Dada gesture, the ultimate psychopathic joke: suicide and double murder."[20]

While Vaché's brief life and "umoresque" death were not celebrated with statues, paintings, operettas, films, BBC specials, or plays — though the author of this history once contemplated writing such a drama — his example was extraordinarily influential, particularly among the artistic avant garde of his time. Typical of this influence was the following statement from André Breton's first surrealist manifesto in 1924:

> In literature, I am successively taken with Rimbaud, with Jarry, with Apollinaire, with Nouveau, with Lautreamont, but it is Jacques Vaché to whom I owe the most.[21]

Much of Vaché's charm for Breton and company was that he embodied the ideal of the completely detached aesthete existing only for the sake of his own creative urges. Indeed, Vaché was not only indifferent to conventional society, but disdainful of the avant garde as well. Rather than follow in the footsteps of his romantic predecessors and carve out some kind of niche for himself as a fashion maven, alienated artist, or aesthetic activist, he abandoned the world altogether, seeking instead to translate his subconscious desires and imaginative fantasies into the actual stuff of his day-to-day life. That this exercise resulted in psychotic behavior, suicide, and murder obviously did not trouble him in the least. Nor did it bother a great many romantics who viewed Vaché's "umore" as the road of excess William Blake insisted all needed to travel in order to achieve the palace of wisdom — or, what one of Vaché's direct descendants interred at Père Lachaise would call, the "other side."

"Call out the instigator": The Romantic Hero as Rebel

The overwhelming majority of romantic artists in the 19th and 20th centuries rejected the rarefied aestheticism of the dandies. Though these romantics were as individualistic, passionate, unconventional, and rebellious as a Brummell, Chatterton or Vaché, they also recognized, as had Donne before them, that "no man is an island, entire of itself." Whether they liked it or not they were "a part of the main" and the political, social and economic conditions extant in their nations and communities directly impinged on their ability to live and work as they pleased. Indeed, it did not take any great perspicacity on the part of these artists to realize that state censors and policemen could suppress their art and take away their liberty; that modern industrial development was destroying the natural environment they revered and looked to for inspiration; and that all too many of their colleagues were impoverished and suicidal because close minded parochial audiences shunned artwork that did not follow classical canons. In the face of such realities, flight into some secret garden or imaginary dream world seemed quixotic at best.

Nevertheless, while most romantic artists opted to address the issues of the day, they did not follow the tack taken by Western politicians, parties, and social movements during the 19th and early 20th centuries. Whereas these latter groups opted for strategies of political and social action rooted in regimented organizations, hierarchies, and mass mobilization, romantics embraced an aesthetic activism that was anarchic in nature and largely centered on personal example and provocative artwork. To be sure, one could also find these individuals manning barricades, marching in demonstrations, signing petitions, and raising money, but they were almost always more fellow travelers than actual adherents of the various groups with which they made common cause.

Perhaps the best example of this engaged romanticism is to be found in the life and work of the man who is in fact the prototype of all romantic heroes, George Gordon Lord Byron. Born in 1788 into an upper class English family, Byron inherited both a title and sizable estates from a great-uncle at the age of 10. As with Beau Brummell, having the good fortune to inherit a fortune afforded Byron the freedom to do pretty much what he pleased, and, in his early years, this involved behaving like a naughty young dandy. He lived extravagantly, drank heavily, wracked up huge debts, traveled in the East, and, like some latter day Goth, dressed only in black. He also delighted in flouting the conventions of his class by engaging in love affairs with married and unmarried women, various male friends, and his half sister Augusta Leigh, with whom he may have had a child.

The scandal surrounding Byron's relations with his sister, coupled with a rather nasty separation from his wife, resulted in his departure from England in 1816. This self-imposed exile proved to be permanent and over the remaining 8 years of his life, Byron lived and worked primarily in Italy. Though this change in locale did nothing to assuage his appetites for drink and married women, it did inspire him to produce his greatest works of poetry and satire. During this time, he wrote *The Prophecy of Dante*, *Marino Faliero*, *Sardanapalus*, *The Two Foscari*, *Cain*, *The Vision of Judgment*, and his epic masterpiece *Don Juan*. It was in this latter work, which celebrated the life and loves of the legendary Don Juan, as well as in an earlier poem, *Childe Harold's Pilgrimage*, which was also completed at this time, that Byron presented his readers with his vision of the romantic protagonist. Like its creator, this "Byronic hero" was a flawed individual of great ability and passion who was "unfit to herd with man" because of his rebellious, self-destructive nature, and disdain for society and its conventions.

Aside from writing, wenching, and celebrating the peccadilloes of romantic bad boys like himself, Byron's Italian period was also characterized by a growing awareness of and support for the struggles of various peoples for national self-determination. The first of these groups to win his sympathy were the Armenians. Following a visit to the Mekhitarist monastery on the Venetian island of St. Lazarus in 1816, Byron developed a passion for Armenian culture that remained with him for the rest of his life. He learned Armenian language and history, helped compile an English-Armenian grammar and dictionary, translated a number of Armenian texts into English, and voiced support for the reconstitution of an Armenian nation.

He also became a proponent of Italian nationalism at this time, a cause he was introduced to, appropriately enough, by his married 19 year old mistress, the Countess Teresa Guiccioli. The countess haled from a long line of Italian patriots and her father and brother were also members of a secret society known as the Carbonari, which was dedicated to driving the Austrians out of northern Italy and achieving the unification of the peninsula. These two men initiated Byron into this revolutionary band and the poet returned the favor by purchasing arms for the Carbonari and supporting their uprising against the Austrian occupation. When this rising was suppressed, Byron and his Guiccioli co-conspirators were forced to flee Venice and take up residence in nearby Pisa.

The nationalist cause, however, with which Byron is most associated was the struggle for Greek independence. In 1823, while living in Genoa, he was approached by members of the London Greek Committee and asked to lend his support to their war of national liberation against the Ottoman Empire. Byron eagerly agreed, chartered a boat to Greece, spent £4000 of his own money preparing the Greek fleet for sea service, and then sailed to Messolonghi in the Western part of the country where he joined the army of Prince Aléxandros Mavrokordátos.

Byron participated in planning the attack on the Turkish fortress of Lepanto, employed a fire master to prepare the Greek army's artillery, and paid for and commanded a portion of the rebel forces. While engaged in all of this activity, he also managed to find the time to woo his page, a young Greek boy named Loukas Chalandritsanos. Unfortunately for Byron, both his campaign for military glory and Loukas' affections were cut short by a bad cold, high fever, and a round of "therapeutic" bleeding that resulted in his death at 36 on April 19, 1824.

Though Byron's sudden demise was less than glorious, it nonetheless sealed his reputation as a courageous freedom loving, tyranny hating heroic rebel. The Greek patriots whose cause he adopted declared him a national hero and later named a suburb of Athens after him. He was also lauded by Armenian and Italian nationalists for his dedication and contributions to their struggles for national self-determination. Even his fellow countrymen, long scandalized by his sexual licentiousness and unconventional lifestyle, were shocked by the news of his death; and when Byron's body arrived in England, it was placed on view in London for two days to allow the public to pay its last respects.

Despite his widespread popularity with the public-at-large, Byron continued to engender considerable hostility among members of the British establishment long after his death. Though he was regarded as the embodiment of English romanticism, and his poetry later became required reading for generations of public and private school students, his scandalous life proved an impediment to various efforts that were made to honor him in his native country. A statue commissioned by Byron's friends remained in storage for over a decade because it could not find a home in any of Britain's premier institutions. And efforts to have Byron honored with burial in Westminster Abbey were similarly rebuffed. In fact, the poet's devotees would have to wait 145 years until 1969 to see a memorial to him finally placed on the floor of the Abbey's Poets Corner.[22]

Of course, all of this official disdain only enhanced Byron's stature among the adherents of romanticism. The very things that the powers that be did not like about him — his poetry that celebrated carnal love and non-conformity, open passionate nature, disregard of sexual taboos, sympathy for the oppressed, support of revolution — all underscored for these folks the degree to which he had achieved the romantic ideal of an authentic existence lived according to one's own values and precepts. And the fact that he found a way to conjoin his unconventional lifestyle and work with the greater struggle for human emancipation and freedom helped make him a model of engaged romantic heroism for generations of rebellious artists who came after him.

Indeed, as the history of modern Western culture attests, there has certainly been no dearth of "Byronic heroes." From George Sand and Isadora Duncan to Ernest Hemingway and Norman Mailer, the last two centuries have been replete with writers, dancers, painters, and musicians who have produced deeply personal, original art; flaunted social conventions; embraced alternative ways of living and loving; and participated in various efforts aimed at making the world a freer and more just place. And when these individuals have behaved in this fashion, whether they are aware of it or not, they are following in the footsteps of that romantic instigator par excellence, George Gordon Lord Byron.

A Life Not Ordinary: The Romantic Hero

We began this chapter wondering why Jim Morrison, a young attractive singer with an uneven body of work, an insatiable appetite for sex, drugs, and drink, and a tragic death brought on by a heroin overdose at 27, rates a latter-day hero cult. Part of the answer to this question is that he fits the heroic profile of romanticism, a movement in the arts that came to the fore of Western life in the 18th century. Because the adherents of this tradition believe that individual feeling, intuition, and imagination are the wellsprings of truth and beauty, they have tended to heroize emotionally intense, self-indulgent, iconoclastic artists like the late Lizard King of rock and roll.

Nevertheless, while Morrison's mojo was sufficient to land him a place of honor in romanticism's hall of fame, there remains the question why he, or any of the other rebels addressed in the preceding pages, are admired by so many people who are neither artists nor iconoclasts. As already noted, these romantic heroes do not play by the rules observed by the other heroic types examined up to this point. Because their raison d'être is personal exploration and development, they feel no obligation to serve society-at-large, and are ostensibly indifferent to public opinion (ostensibly because they are none too pleased when the public is indifferent to them). Consequently, these folks often behave in an offensive manner; produce work that is, at least initially, inaccessible to all save the members of an esoteric avant garde; and revel in their personal flaws and foibles, which they see as roads of excess leading to the "palace of wisdom."

To be fair, like the explorers addressed in the last chapter, a number of these romantic artists were able to associate themselves with more conventional heroic types. For example, Lord Byron actually did become something of a warrior over the course of his life. He armed the Italian Carbonari and commanded a wing of the rebel Greek army; actions which won him kudos and a hero's laurels from the peoples of Italy and Greece. Similarly, Oscar Wilde's 1895 conviction and incarceration on charges of "gross indecency," i.e., sex with other men, transformed him into a martyr to the cause of gay rights.

These examples to the side, however, most of the romantics addressed in these pages were heroized not for conspicuous deeds of martial valor, self sacrifice to a cause, or even for the superb art many of them produced, but because they lived, worked, and usually died in an unconventional manner. Indeed, for many in the middle and working classes of the 19th and 20th centuries, what was alluring about these romantic rebels was the fact that they appeared to achieve the kind of individual freedom and self-realization that liberal capitalist society promised to all but delivered only to a few. And because so many of these iconoclasts were either bourgeois in origin or rogue aristocrats, their liberated lifestyles appeared attainable to any individual brave enough to emulate them.

The sense that these romantic rebels are, as Beau Brummell's mod devotee put it, "just like us," continues to inform our thinking about these figures, and to demonstrate this, I will end our discussion of romanticism and its heroes with a reference to my own adolescent adulation of the rock star who has figured prominently in this chapter, Jim Morrison. While there were a great many musicians whose work I enjoyed and admired while growing up in the 60s, I was drawn to Morrison because I felt an affinity with him on a number of different levels. His dissatisfaction with middle class society, lack of respect for established authority, countercultural lifestyle, eclectic tastes in literature and philosophy, and love of emotionally intense performances were all things with which I could identify. It goes without saying that his death saddened me deeply — though it also seemed a fitting way for someone of Morrison's sensibility to check out — and many years later, on a trip to Paris in 1985, I too would visit his gravesite and share a bottle of his favorite Jameson's whiskey with other folks who had come to pay their respects.

Reflecting back on all of this, I realize that Morrison was nothing like me at all. He was the scion of an admiral who grew up in well-to-do enclaves in Florida and San Diego, while I was the son of a sheet metal worker living in a small town outside Louisville, Kentucky. While chemically educated, I never consumed the quantities of hallucinogens that Morrison used routinely in his quest to break on through to the other side. And aside from air guitar and stereo — volume being my particular forte — I have no musical talent whatsoever. Nevertheless, what drew me to Morrison as a youth, and keeps me listening to his music as a middle-aged man, is that he represented the promise of a life that need not be ordinary. And in a mass democratic society where quests are the stuff of video games, martyrdom a weapon for terrorists, and ping pong passes for a sport, such a life is heroic indeed.

9

Black Angels and New Men
Heroism in a Totalitarian Context

I teach you the Superman. Man is something that should be overcome. What have you done to overcome him?
All creatures hitherto have created something beyond themselves: and do you want to be the ebb of this great tide, and return to the animals rather than overcome man?
What is the ape to men? A laughing-stock or a painful embarrassment. And just so shall man be to the Superman; a laughing-stock or a painful embarrassment.

— Nietzsche: *Thus Spoke Zarathustra*

My pedagogy is hard. The weak must be hammered away. In my castle of the Teutonic Order a youth will grow up before which the world will tremble. I want a violent, domineering, undismayed, cruel youth. Youth must be all that. It must bear pain. There must be nothing weak and gentle about it. The free, splendid beast of prey must once more flash from its eyes. I want my youth strong and beautiful. In this way I can create the new.

— Adolf Hitler: *Mein Kampf*

Man will become immeasurably stronger, wiser, and subtler; his body will become more harmonized, his movements more rhythmic, his voice more musical. The forms of life will become dynamically dramatic. The average human type will rise to the heights of an Aristotle, a Goethe, or a Marx. And above this ridge new peaks will rise.

— Leon Trotsky: *Literature and Revolution*

In the original *Star Trek* series of the 1960s, there is an episode entitled *Space Seed* in which the crew of the *Enterprise* comes across a derelict spaceship carrying 84 humans in a state of suspended animation. As the story unfolds, Captain Kirk and his intrepid colleagues discover that this ship was built in the 1990s during Earth's so-called Eugenics War, a worldwide conflict sparked by the efforts of a group of genetically altered "supermen" to seize control of the planet and reshape its biological destiny. Kirk and company also find out that the folks on this ship are a band of these bionic *Übermenschen* who were unaccounted for at the end of this war, and that their leader, a striking Sikh named Khan Noonien Singh — played with great brio by Ricardo Montalban — was the superman par excellence of this time period; governing, at the height of his power, over a quarter of the Earth's surface. Handsome, brilliant, incredibly strong, overweeningly ambitious, stern, hard, amoral, ruthless, and cruel, this Kahn is the embodiment of the eugenics ideal, a warrior prince committed to the creation of a new breed of super humanity at any cost. Indeed, Khan is so markedly different from the "normal" crew of the *Enterprise* that the ship's resident historian — a young woman with a romantic hankering for the great men of Earth's more colorful past — declares him a magnificent specimen worthy of the company of a Caesar, Napoleon or Leif Eriksson.

Mention is made of this episode in the ongoing *Star Trek* space opera because Khan — his personality traits, abilities, and ambitions (succinctly summed up at the end of the story by his acceptance of exile on an inhospitable planet because it offers him "a world to win, an empire to build") — is a perfect simulacrum of a heroic ideology that came to the fore in the West during the late nineteenth and early twentieth centuries. Often called "heroic vitalism,"[1] this philosophy of heroism was an odd amalgam of illiberal politics, romanticism, violence, and utopian reveries. Its proponents — a motley crew of hero worshipping crackpots, dreamers, madmen, artists, revolutionaries, and dictators — believed that Western civilization was morally bankrupt, disintegrating, and drifting towards degeneration, war, and chaos. These heroic vitalists also believed that they could reverse this dire state of affairs by sweeping away the liberal bourgeois capitalist societies of the West and replacing them with a "new order" created and governed by a "race" or, if of a more leftwing political persuasion, "cadre" of energetic, gifted, willful, amoral, and merciless heroes. Unhindered by Judeo-Christian ethical qualms, interest group party politics, or the capitalist preoccupation with profits, vitalists believed this heroic elite would restore order, win worlds and build empires, divine what was necessary for the common good, and initiate policies aimed at creating new "human types" capable of rising "to the heights of an Aristotle, a Goethe, or a Marx."

Ironically, this heroic faith with its deeply pessimistic view of modern civilization arose at a moment in time when Westerners could look back on a hundred years of unparalleled progress in every area of human endeavor. Throughout the nineteenth century, natural scientists in Europe and America had made groundbreaking discoveries and technological breakthroughs in engineering, metallurgy, chemistry, electricity, and biology. Enterprising entrepreneurs and industrialists on both continents had exploited this scientific work and launched a second industrial revolution, which had generated a wide array of new products, industries, markets, transportation systems, and jobs. These scientific and industrial advances had also meant more manufactured goods, better diets, longer life spans, increasing literacy, and some measure of formal schooling for Westerners of all nationalities and classes. And in the political realm, peasants, Jews, ethnic minorities, skilled and unskilled laborers, and even women were enjoying more freedom and control over their lives as the institutions and practices of bourgeois liberalism — parliamentary democracy, the right to petition and assemble, religious toleration, and a free press — took root throughout Europe. Indeed, taken together, all of these achievements in science, industry, society, and politics appeared to point to a future free of ignorance, poverty, disease, tyranny, and war. A world, in short, where each individual life could be realized, every anxiety tranquilized, and all boredom amused.

For heroic vitalists, however, the *fin-de-siècle* offered evidence that "nature was red in tooth and claw," human beings were fundamentally irrational, and liberal civilization was unjust, discordant, and detrimental to individual freedom and creativity. Darwin's theory of evolution and Freud's work on the unconscious, for example, seemed to confirm that human development and behavior were governed neither by God nor sweet reason, but by processes of natural selection rooted in primordial, deeply emotional and often vicious struggles for survival among the species. In philosophy, Hegel, Marx, and Schopenhauer had essentially consigned individuals to the role of helpless pawns in an amoral and often violent game of "world spirits," warring social classes, and primal biological "life forces." On the economic front, capitalism and its industrial revolutions had resulted not only in the "constant revolutionizing of production," but also in an "uninterrupted disturbance of all social conditions, everlasting uncertainty and agitation,"[2] pollution, teeming urban slums, and millions of dislocated, impoverished and embittered European workers. In politics, the advance of liberalism had meant not only more individual freedom, but also divisive party politics, mass movements on the right and left and revolutionary acts of terrorism. And on the world stage, rivalry among the great powers had transformed Europe into two heavily armed camps drifting inexorably toward a cataclysmic war. All of these developments convinced vitalists that they were living not in the "best" but the "worst of times" and that the future promised only the prospect of a long and very violent "winter of despair."

Paradoxically, though they saw the world to be a nasty, brutish, and amoral realm where endless tumult was the order of the day and human perfectibility a hopeless pipedream, vitalists also believed that existence was subject to the manipulation and control of certain willful, creative, "vital" individuals. They were also convinced that it was mankind's heroes, i.e., those extraordinary men and women who had defied the conventions of their time and gone beyond the frontiers of what was known and accepted, who were the true agency of historical development and human creativity. It was not masses in motion, class conflicts, or market manipulations that created empires, promulgated law codes, charted the heavens, and defined the sublime, but history's Alexanders, Caesars, Galileos, and Leonardos. Consequently, if the West was to avoid its impending winter of despair and experience a "spring of hope," vitalists believed it would require a new generation of heroes.

Creating these extraordinary individuals, however, would require nothing less than the repudiation of modern Western civilization. Such a drastic course of action was necessary vitalists believed, because the ethics, politics, economics, and social arrangements of the *fin-de-siècle* worked together to tamp down, if not make impossible, the emergence of bold unconventional heroic personalities. Judeo-Christian morality, for example, preached meekness, humility, and submission to the will of God and the needs of the many. Liberalism encouraged interest group politics, equalitarian thinking, and mass parties. Capitalism reduced everything to the worship of wealth and the acquisition of profits. And urban society leveled social distinctions and packed people together in anonymous crowds.

In the place of this morally constrained Mammon worshipping mass society, vitalists proposed a new heroic age that was reactionary — atavistic actually — in its political and social arrangements, and wildly utopian in its aims and aspirations for the human future. Parliamentary democracies and hereditary monarchies with their competing special interests and agendas were to be replaced by heroic despots whose right to rule would be based on their extraordinary strength, intellect and talent, as well as their ability to intuit the needs of the many. Society would be organized into guilds, orders, corporations, and collectives where contented workers, peasants and, in certain scenarios, slaves would work at those tasks best suited to their abilities and receive whatever recompense their governing *Übermenschen* deemed necessary to meet their needs. And markets would be replaced by planned economies in which the goods and services produced by the laboring classes would be those their heroic masters regarded as necessary for the maintenance of the common good, the scaling of "new peaks" of human achievement," and the creation of a humanity "immeasurably stronger, wiser, and subtler" than its predecessors.

To be sure, the proponents of this vitalist future were a varied lot with often radically different ideas regarding the particulars of the heroic world they had in mind. The three men quoted in this chapter's epigraphs are a case in point. Friedrich Nietzsche was a German classical philologist, musician, and iconoclast who idealized pre–classical Greece, castigated Christianity, and despised both nationalism and racism. In the heroic future he envisioned, a contented neo–Buddhist slave caste was to be ruled by amoral, albeit benign supermen who haled from every nation, tribe, and ethnic group. Nietzsche's countryman, Adolf Hitler, was an ill-educated Austrian rabble rouser who preached a virulent gospel of anti–semitism and Pan-German racial superiority. In keeping with his racist ideology, Hitler called for a new order where "violent, domineering, undismayed, cruel" and Aryan "beasts of prey" governed an enslaved Europe purged of Jews and other baneful racial influences. On the other end of the political spectrum, Leon Trotsky, a Russian Jew, brilliant Marxist theoretician, and member of Lenin's inner circle, imagined a classless communist utopia where, under the careful guidance of Russia's heroic vanguard party, every good worker and peasant might become an extraordinary being who could "hunt in the morning, fish in the afternoon, rear cattle in the evening, [and] criticize after dinner."[3]

Vitalists were also often at odds as to how any of these utopian reveries were to be realized. The more politically inclined among these hero worshippers believed that a generation of Aryan *Führers* or Bolshevik *bogatyri* (warrior princes) would appear on the scene and instigate revolutions that would sweep away liberal bourgeois society. Others of a more mystical bent put their faith in some kind of apocalyptic *Götterdämmerung*, or Twilight of the Gods, that would burn away the old order and leave behind a band of hardy horny heroes intent on repopulating and renewing the world. Most vitalists, however, were willing to let history take its course because they believed that the West was sloughing off one way of life for another, and that in such moments of historical transition "a rough beast, its hour come round at last," always "slouches towards Bethlehem to be born."

Under normal circumstances, all of these musings about supermen, new human types, and millenarian moments would have been little more than grist for the mills of lunatics, poets, and science fiction writers. The outbreak of World War I in 1914, however, catapulted this vitalist creed from the fringe to the mainstream of Western culture, society, and politics. The horrors of the First World War coupled with the chaos that ensued in the period following it, undermined the widespread belief at the turn-of-the-century that the West was progressing towards a more rational, benign and prosperous future. Fearful of another world war and weary of the chronic political instability and economic uncertainty of the 1920s and 30s, increasing numbers of Europeans abandoned the liberal credo of democratic government and free market capitalism and turned instead to the movements of demagogic self–styled *Übermenschen* who promised order, reliable train schedules, full bellies, secure jobs, peace, and a future filled with heroic deeds. Some of these "supermen" actually came to power in a number of European countries during the first half of the twentieth century and established dictatorships that were bent on realizing the vitalist vision of a "stronger, wiser, and subtler" humanity led by amoral, willful, and ruthless heroes.

The results of this totalitarian effort to translate a fanciful philosophy of hero worship and human engineering into the stuff of modern statecraft were nothing short of catastrophic. Millions lost their lives in government sponsored programs of social improvement and racial purification. Much of Europe and Asia were laid waste in a second world war launched by dictators intent on being counted among history's heroic conquerors. And the very idea of heroism was degraded by the acts of SS "black angels" and Communist "new men" whose only claim to distinction was their extraordinary capacity for cruelty.

The following pages attempt to arrive at an understanding of how an idea of the hero and heroic action came to be both a catalyst and an apologia for dictatorship, total war, and genocide. To achieve this end, this chapter progresses along two axes of inquiry. The first of these examines the origins and development of "heroic vitalism," that grab bag philosophy of the nineteenth century whose roots are to be found in the works of Nietzsche and Carlyle, the *völkish* pessimism of the *fin-de-siècle*, and the religious mysticism, folklore, and voluntarism of the Russian revolutionary tradition. The second line of inquiry addresses the influence of this vitalist tradition on the ideals of heroic leadership and action that were celebrated and practiced in the twentieth century's two most notorious totalitarian regimes — Nazi Germany and Bolshevik Russia. This latter investigation into the interrelationship of vitalism, fascism and communism involves a close analysis of what heroism meant in a National Socialist and Communist context; who and what these ideologies singled out as exemplary of their heroic ideals; and how the Nazi and Soviet regimes set about cultivating cadres of revolutionary heroes to serve as models of ideological purity, defenders of state security, and architects of their respective new world orders.

What follows is an account of one of the strangest episodes in the history of Western heroism. It is a modern horror story full of fantasy, fear, and dreadful crimes, and, as is so often the case with tales of terror, its authors were as different from the heroes they celebrated as Edgar Allan Poe and H.P. Lovecraft were from the monsters they imagined. A case in point are the men whose work castigated liberal Western society and called for a new heroic age of blood, iron, and "beasts of prey." And it is to this odd band of misfits and misanthropes that we now turn.

Sowing the Seed: Heroic Vitalism during the Fin-de-Siècle

THE PROPHETS OF HEROISM: CARLYLE AND NIETZSCHE

The term "heroic vitalism" makes its first appearance in a 1947 study of late nineteenth century hero worship entitled *The Cult of the Superman*. The author of this work, British playwright and literary critic Eric Bentley, coined this expression as a convenient catchphrase for an ideology of heroism that he claimed was widespread during the *fin-de-siècle* and subscribed to by such luminaries as George Bernard Shaw, Richard Wagner, Oswald Spengler, Stefan George, and D. H. Lawrence. While Bentley acknowledged that the individuals he labeled "heroic vitalists" were not part of any formally constituted intellectual or artistic circle, and were in fact often at odds with one another on many of the critical political, social and cultural issues of the day, he still treated them as ideological bedfellows because their varied works advanced, in one way or another, the idea that heroes were the *raison d'être* of human existence and the engine of historical development.

While there is much that is problematic about Bentley's attempt to tease forth a coherent philosophy of heroism from the musings, manifestos, and assorted manuscripts of a highly diffuse and unaffiliated group of thinkers and artists, his contention that there was a widespread cult of heroism during the *fin-de-siècle* was not without merit. There were in fact a great many educated Westerners at the turn-of-the-century who believed that human development was dependent on a select group of people who were gifted with a "vital" life force. Nor were these individuals limited to any particular philosophical school, political ideology, or artistic movement. Indeed, as we will see below, the idea that heroes made history and were also essential to human evolution was embraced by right wing reactionaries and communist revolutionaries, atheists and believers, materialists and mystics, fauves and futurists.

However, insofar as we can speak of Bentley's catchphrase as an ideology, we are largely talking about the ideas of two nineteenth century thinkers, Thomas Carlyle and Friedrich Nietzsche. Both of these men loathed the time in which they lived; glorified past periods they deemed more heroic than the present; lauded history's "great men;" and preached the coming of the superman. And while neither man left a unified corpus of work with a carefully reasoned clearly articulated philosophy of life, they were, nonetheless, prolific writers who penned a wide array of essays, historical analyses, and literary works that argued in favor of what could be called a heroic vitalist *Weltanschauung*.

In Carlyle's case, this vitalist viewpoint was very much a natural outgrowth of the experiential landscape of his youth. Eccelefechan, the rural Scottish village into which he was born in 1795, was a circular world boundered by traditions, customs, and ancient prejudices. Most of the inhabitants of this community, including Carlyle's family, were small landholding peasants whose way of life — tending the hearth, tilling the soil, and attending religious services in the local meetinghouse — had remained largely unchanged for centuries. These folk knew their place in the world and what was expected of them, accepted social inequality as a largely unalterable fact of life, and were loyal monarchists. They were also faithful Presbyterians who bowed their heads in reverence to a stern God who had decided that only a small elect — easily identifiable by their thrift, industry, prosperity, and extraordinary ability — would be favored with his saving grace. By all accounts, coming of age in this traditional setting left a lasting imprint on Carlyle's character, and also informed his rejection of Enlightenment thinking on social egalitarianism, human perfectibility, and historical progress.[4]

Whatever the influence of Eccelefechan on Carlyle's later hero worship, his immersion in this community's religious life, coupled with his family's desire that he pursue a career in the ministry, led him to take up theological studies at the University of Edinburgh in 1809. Over the next twelve years, he suffered a crisis of faith, developed a passion for German literature and philosophy — particularly the works of Goethe and Fichte — and tried his hand, unsuccessfully, as a teacher. In 1821, following a period of intense spiritual struggle, Carlyle opted to pursue a career as a professional writer, and it was in this capacity that he achieved financial security, a measure of fame, and a reading public that included such notables as Matthew Arnold, John Ruskin, Ralph Waldo Emerson, and Otto von Bismarck.

Intellectually curious, possessed of a wide learning, and never at a failure for words, Carlyle penned a considerable body of work. This corpus included translations of German novels (Goethe's *Wilhelm Meister's Apprenticeship*), satire (*Sartor Resartus*), history (*The French Revolution*), biographies (*Oliver Cromwell's Letters and Speeches, With Elucidations* and *A History of Fredrick II of Prussia*), and a number of critical commentaries (*Signs of the Times, On Heroes and Hero Worship and the Heroic in History, Past and Present, An Occasional Discourse on the Nigger Question*, and *Latter-Day Pamphlets*). And while these titles command only a limited and highly specialized readership in the present day, during Carlyle's lifetime, they were veritable Book-of-the-Month Club selections, going through repeated printings and enjoying a wide and extremely diverse audience.

Throughout this writing, Carlyle preached an evangel of cultural pessimism, political reaction, and unabashed hero worship. Enlightenment verities were rejected out–of–hand as naïve and completely wrong about both human nature and social progress. Modern society was condemned for its crass commercialism, heartless utilitarianism, and soulless ideologies. The Middle Ages was lauded as a period in which human and spiritual values were unified and communities were integrated and organic. Heroic leadership was considered essential to the development of human societies, and history was declared to be the collected biographies of its great men.

Out of these works also emerged the outlines of a philosophy of heroic vitalism. Though Carlyle had lost the Christian faith of his childhood, he nonetheless adhered to a view of existence that has been labeled "supernatural naturalism,"[5] i.e., a belief that the universe was governed by a vital life force, which, like the God of his forefathers, was intelligent, cruel, inexorable, and always in a state of becoming. This force pitted its creations against one another in a struggle for survival that encouraged constant change, mutation, and the evolution of higher and more perfect life forms. And out of this war of one against the other, humanity had emerged to take its place in the universe as the crown of creation. Nevertheless, despite our vaunted place in the natural scheme of things, human beings and their various societies remained organic and finite, subject to the same cycle of birth, life, decay, and death that all living and non–living matter experienced in the course of its existence.

In the face of this ceaseless conflict and flux, Carlyle offered only one constant, heroes. What differentiated these individuals from other human beings was the fact that they were especially imbued with the vital energy of the life force; and the special talents and abilities that accompanied this gift of grace made it possible for them to wield disparate forces together, create order out of chaos, and master the events of their times. Indeed, when Carlyle spoke of human civilization, law, science, and art, he was talking about the benefactions of a Solon, Caesar, Mohammed, Shakespeare, Goethe, Oliver Cromwell, or Frederick the Great. Take these great men (and greatness in Carlyle was always a decidedly male prerogative) out of the equation of life, and existence was nothing more than a short, nasty, brutish struggle for survival.

Not surprisingly, Carlyle's Hobbesian view of the world, coupled with his conviction that the hero was the essential guarantor of peace, order, and progress in human affairs, inclined him towards authoritarian arrangements in society and politics. Though Carlyle was not terribly fond of the ruling elites of his time, and in fact despised aristocratic privilege that was based on nothing more than the accident of birth, he nonetheless believed that feudal autocratic societies were more likely to maintain order and foster heroism. And of Europe's many "ancient regimes," he was particularly fond of Prussia, a militaristic, authoritarian nation whose soldier kings, Junker aristocracy, efficient bureaucracy, and limited franchise had produced a strong stable state, a unified Germany, and the only contemporary Carlyle regarded as a hero, Otto von Bismarck.

Prussia was no less admiring of Carlyle and in 1874 the Hohenzollern dynasty awarded him their country's highest civilian honor, the Order Pour le Mérite for Sciences and Arts (*Orden Pour le Mérite für Wissenschaften und Künste*).[6] Carlyle's Prussian patrons also insured that his works were translated, published and disseminated throughout the Second Reich that Bismarck had so recently created with blood and iron. Indeed, by the time Carlyle died in 1881, a broad cross section of the German speaking world — kaisers, kings, aristocrats, military men, school teachers, pastors, and poets — had read his books and were familiar with his vitalist views. Thirty-three years later, on the eve of the First World War, the Carlylean doctrine of hero worship was a mainstay of German intellectual life and a central element in the thinking of a *völkish* movement that would nurture, among others, Adolf Hitler.

Before turning to Carlyle's many admirers on the German right, however, it is necessary to consider the contribution to heroic vitalism of one of his younger contemporaries, Friedrich Nietzsche (1844–1900). The facts of Nietzsche's biography are well known and correspond with those of Carlyle in many ways.[7] Like his Scottish counterpart, Nietzsche too was born and raised in a tradition bound, highly conservative world. His father, a Lutheran minister with strong monarchist sympathies, christened Nietzsche Friedrich Wilhelm after Prussia's reigning king of the time, Friedrich Wilhelm IV. Röcken and Naumburg, the two small east Prussian towns where Nietzsche spent his childhood, were, like Carlyle's Eccelefechan, circular communities centered on farming, family, faith, and fatherland. Growing up in such a deeply religious, socially stratified, and politically illiberal environment very likely informed many of Nietzsche's later pronouncements against democracy, social convention, and Christian orthodoxy.

Nietzsche was also a highly gifted student with a varied academic career. He was accepted into Pforta, one of the most distinguished boarding schools in Germany, where he showed a marked talent for music and languages. Following his graduation from Pforta, Nietzsche decided to follow in his father's footsteps and enrolled at the University of Bonn to study theology. During his first year at Bonn, however, Nietzsche suffered a crisis of faith, which resulted, much to his family's chagrin, in his turning away from a career in the Lutheran ministry.[8] Soon thereafter, Nietzsche enrolled at the University of Leipzig where he took up the study of classical languages under the noted scholar Friedrich Ritschl. While his work in philology was highly regarded at Leipzig, Nietzsche found the field rather dull, antiquarian and completely indifferent to the problems and concerns of real life. Philosophy, particularly that of Arthur Schopenhauer, is what fired his imagination at this time, as well as the music of a man who would loom large in his life and work, Richard Wagner.

Ironically, despite his disdain for the study of classical languages, Nietzsche was regarded as a "phenomenon ... who will one day stand in the front rank of German philology."[9] These comments, part of a letter of recommendation written by Ritschl in 1869, won for Nietzsche, at the age of twenty-four — without either a completed doctorate or any teaching experience — a chair in classical philology at the University of Basel in Switzerland. During the ten years he taught at Basel, Nietzsche was, by all accounts, a dedicated teacher and he carried a heavy instructional workload. Philological research, however, was not at the forefront of his interests, and, when he was not teaching, Nietzsche spent most of his time during this decade working with Wagner and writing *The Birth of Tragedy Out of the Spirit of Music*, the first of what would be a series of controversial works.

In *The Birth of Tragedy*, Nietzsche first articulated a number of ideas that would become central elements in his own vitalist view of life. He characterized, a la Schopenhauer, the world as a godless amoral realm in which an irrational "will to live" was the raison d'être of existence. Unlike Schopenhauer, however, Nietzsche did not see this reality as a cause for despair, nor did he feel that the non–rational "Dionysian" forces underlying human actions needed to be suppressed. Instead, citing ancient Greek tragic drama as an example, he argued that it was possible to both confront the uncertainty and suffering inherent in existence and manipulate it in ways that could unleash great creativity and beauty. He also noted in this work that the rational "Apollonian" tendency embodied by Socrates and his later followers, while important to the development of civilization, had attained an unhealthy dominance in human affairs suppressing the wellsprings of imagination, art, and individual genius. What the modern world needed, Nietzsche concluded, was an "artistic Socrates," a heroic figure who combined in one person philosophy and passion, reason and poetry, science and music. And, at least at this point in his life, Nietzsche appears to have believed that Wagner was the embodiment of this Apollonian-Dionysian synthesis.

Suffice it to say, Nietzsche's academic colleagues were not much enamored with these highly speculative ruminations, particularly when they were devoid of such scholarly trappings as philological method and footnotes. For his part, Nietzsche was not particularly concerned about academe's opinion of his work and in 1879 he resigned from the University of Basel pleading poor health. Living on a modest pension that was provided to him by his former employer, Nietzsche spent the next ten years of his life as an itinerant litterateur penning a varied collection of tracts on a wide range of topics. The principal works in this corpus included *Thus Spoke Zarathustra* (1883–85), a four part "book for everyone and no one" in which Nietzsche declared god dead and preached the coming of the superman; *Beyond Good and Evil* (1886) and *The Genealogy of Morals* (1887), two books in which he castigated Christianity and its "slave morality;" *Twilight of the Idols* (1888), a work in which he praised great men — Caesar, Napoleon, Goethe, Dostoevsky, Thucydides — while at the same time critiquing philosophical and religious "otherworldliness," German culture, and a number of European intellectuals[10]; *The Anti-Christ* (1888), a tirade against Christian morals and a call for an anti–Christian morality; *Ecce Homo* (1888), an autobiography of sorts in which he reflected on his own historical significance; and *Nietzsche con-*

tra Wagner (1888), a summation of his respect for the great composer, as well as his despair with Wagner's Christianity, Aryanism, and anti–semitism. In 1889, Nietzsche suffered a mental collapse that spelled the end of his intellectual career. Over the next eleven-and-a-half years he was hospitalized in an asylum, then placed in his mother's care, and finally moved to Weimar where his sister, the anti–Semite and pan–German nationalist Elisabeth Förster-Nietzsche, cared for him until his death by pneumonia in 1900.

As the brief descriptions regarding the content of the abovementioned publications makes clear, Nietzsche's intellectual interests encompassed a great many subjects. While often brilliant, his pronouncements on these topics tended towards rambling disjointed collections of aphorisms, allegories and polemics characterized by acerbic, bold and sometimes outrageous statements that challenged many of the core beliefs of Western civilization. Attempting to discern a clear philosophical worldview from this material is extremely challenging, but, as Bentley and others have demonstrated, there is a core of what could be called heroic vitalist thinking in Nietzsche's oeuvre.

Central to that thought was the conviction that there was no rhyme or reason to the universe save the "will to power." Nietzsche rejected not only all notions of a divine presence in the world, but also Carlyle's supernatural naturalism, life after death, moral law, and Platonic speculations about "ideal forms" underlying our material reality. Instead, he believed existence was a state of being characterized by bitter and unequal struggles for survival and mastery. This was the natural order of things and in this schema humanity counted as merely one life form among many struggling to live in and master its surroundings. Consequently, human civilizations — their social arrangements, cultures, moralities, and states — were not evidence of mankind's divinely ordained place in an orderly chain of being, but adaptive strategies adopted by human beings over time to address primal urges, needs, and fears that were part and parcel of our struggle to survive.

This portrayal of existence as a godless, essentially meaningless affair, in which organisms of varying complexity struggled for life and power, was certainly nothing new with Nietzsche. Schopenhauer had made similar arguments in his work and Darwin's evolutionary theories pointed to similar conclusions. What was different about Nietzsche's pronouncements on this subject was his refusal to see such a state of being as a cause for pessimism or despair. While existence might be nothing more than a struggle for survival and mastery, Nietzsche believed this will to power also held out the possibility of life evolving into more complex, intelligent, creative, and beautiful forms. Indeed, such change was imperative, for life that did not "overcome" itself, that did not "create something beyond itself," was doomed to stagnation and death.

For Nietzsche, the idea of existence as an ongoing unconstrained process of mutation and change was a source of great joy; and why this was so goes to the heart of his thinking on heroism. In the absence of any existential metanarrative save a will to power, Nietzsche argued that humanity was at last free to create its own destiny. More to the point, this scenario also made it possible for a new generation of heroes — or *preparatory men* as Nietzsche called them — to liberate themselves from the constraints of convention and custom and "*live dangerously!*"[11] To paraphrase Nietzsche, in their drive to overcome themselves, these heroic individuals, these "lovers of knowledge" could now feel empowered to build cities under Vesuvius; sail ships into uncharted seas; live at war with their peers and themselves;

and be robbers and conquerors when they could not be rulers and owners.[12] The untrammeled actions of these daring "beasts of prey" would, in turn, lay the groundwork for a new "master-morality" that would bring forth the *Übermensch*, the superman whose destiny was to overcome man and usher in a golden age.

The "man" that Nietzsche was so eager to supersede was the enlightened Christian Westerner of his own time. As we have already noted in our brief discussion of Nietzsche's *Birth of Tragedy*, he believed that the decline of the creative Dionysian will to power in the West had its beginning with Socrates who exalted reason over emotion and introduced the idea of a transcendental changeless realm outside of mortal existence. Christianity had made matters worse with its fixation on the afterlife and its fostering of a "slave-morality" in which weakness and self-denial were deemed good, while strength, power, pride, command, and all other traits formerly associated with nobility and heroism were deemed evil and sinful. Though human history continued to produce heroic figures such as Cesare Borgia, Leonardo da Vinci, Michelangelo, and Napoleon — men who were rooted in this world, indifferent to the conventions of their time, and far above the common herd in their intellect, talent, and ability — the West remained in thrall to rationality and Christian morals. As for the various "isms" of his own time — liberalism, socialism, communism — Nietzsche saw in them merely a continuation of the Christian resentment of the weak against the strong, which had destroyed the spirit of Homeric Greece and relegated heroism to the bloodless pages of epic poetry, fantasy, and fairy tales.

Nietzsche acknowledged that the surpassing of rational Christian man would be a tumultuous and violent affair, a veritable *Götterdämmerung* that would sweep away Western civilization in an ocean of blood. He was somewhat vague, however, as to the nature of the new order that would emerge in its place. Unlike Carlyle, Nietzsche was neither a Hobbesian nor a Prussophile. His supermen were an amoral, self-centered lot largely unconcerned with the maintenance of order or any particular status quo, nation, or race. Insofar as these *Übermenschen* were concerned with other human beings, that concern was focused solely on how they could be used to satisfy their desires and advance their schemes. Indeed, the future Nietzsche appears to have had in mind was some kind of global caste system in which everyone's purpose and place in life was determined by their degree of usefulness to the *homo superiors* sitting at the apex of society. Rather than resenting their subordinate position vis-à-vis their new masters, Nietzsche seems to have believed that a de-Christianized humanity would embrace this arrangement as one that ultimately benefited them. Just as the military prowess of Homer's heroes and the exquisite artistry of Athens' dramaturges had enriched and elevated their countrymen, so too would the enhanced "life-feeling," or *Lebensgefühl*, of these fully realized supermen trickle down to their inferiors and ultimately improve all of humanity.

This supply-side heroism to the side, Nietzsche's critique of modern society, as well as his *Lebensbejahung*, or affirmation of life and human volition, were enthusiastically received at the end of the nineteenth century by many different individuals and groups, often for wildly divergent reasons. As Thomas R. Hinton has pointed out in his own work on Nietzsche's reception in Germany before the war, one was as likely to find young working class socialists among the philosopher's devotees as reactionary aristocrats.[13] Living in a self-styled postmodern period where, as free-floating, fully volitional individuals, we quarry with abandon the fragments of the last century's metanarratives, it is perhaps difficult to appreciate the impact of Nietzsche's pronouncements on the imaginations of various thinkers, artists, and assorted non–conformists during the *fin-de-siècle*. Nevertheless, in the intellectual landscape of that time, a landscape dominated by philosophies which left the individual helplessly entangled in a web woven by world spirits, warring classes, and primal biological drives, Nietzsche's view of the world as a realm whose operative principles were subject to the manipulation and control of willful, vital, and creative individuals was nothing short of liberating. The insistence of Nietzsche's Zarathustra that his followers remain "true to the earth," while striving to go beyond themselves, offered to many of his contemporaries a philosophy that was both rooted in the material realities of the given historical moment, and open to the possibility of human evolution into some higher state of being.

While Nietzsche's vitalist vision was more optimistic and cosmopolitan than Carlyle's, the two men concurred on a number of points regarding the nature of the world and the role of heroes in it. Both men agreed that existence was a godless amoral affair characterized by an ongoing, brutal, and unequal struggle for survival and mastery. They were equally convinced that humanity was part of this existential scenario; that human beings were governed by ineradicable predatory instincts, which pitted them against one another; and that human civilizations were transitory affairs subject to the same cycles of birth, life, decay, and death as the people who created them. And for both men, the only thing that justified this vale of tears was the hero, that vital, courageous, talented, hard being whose actions made possible all they felt worthwhile in human existence.

This belief in the hero as a kind of life redeemer also informed one other area of mutual agreement between Nietzsche and Carlyle, their disdain for modern Western civilization. Both men were convinced that the dominant religious, economic, social, and political tendencies of their time were not only unsuited to the cultivation of heroes, but guaranteed to produce both sedentary societies and mediocre personalities. Western Christian ethics, for example, celebrated modesty, selflessness, and humility rather than the worldly honor, glory, and greatness Nietzsche and Carlyle believed to be the very stuff of heroism. Capitalism was equally problematic because it reduced everything to considerations of profit; fostered the standardization of material and social life; and laid the foundations for mass consumer-centered societies in which the only distinction between human beings would be the financial assets they commanded and the level of conspicuous consumption they could afford. And while neither Nietzsche nor Carlyle were particularly fond of their era's governing elites, liberal democracy with its egalitarianism, checks on the privileges and prerogatives of the powerful, and utilitarian public policies was anathema to them. That the Christian ethics, capitalist entrepreneurialism, and democratic movements they castigated were also the impetus for some of history's most daring feats of exploration, scientific breakthroughs, and progressive legislation was an inconvenient fact that both men were either blind to or chose to ignore.

This rejection of the values and practices of liberal Western society, coupled with the idea of existence as a pool of primal predatory energies waiting to be tapped and exploited by a gifted and unfettered vanguard, was the essence of Carlyle and Nietzsche's philosophy of heroic vitalism. While it was riddled with inconsistencies and contradictions, and was completely dismissive of the standards of common decency that make civilization possible, this doctrine of hero worship played well with the malcontents of the *fin-de-siècle*. Indeed, it was perfectly suited to a century where a great many avant-garde artists, terrorists, revolutionaries, reactionaries, and romantics claimed exemption from social and moral authority because they fancied themselves the destined harbingers of a New Jerusalem.

FÜHRERS AND BOGATYRI: HEROIC VITALISM IN ITS GERMAN AND RUSSIAN GUISES

Among this motley group of rebels and visionaries, none were more enthusiastic about Carlyle and Nietzsche's vitalist ideas than the adherents of Germany's *völkish* ideology. A loose association of small groups drawn largely from the Second Reich's middle class youth, farmers, small shopkeepers, white collar workers, and "academic proletariat," i.e., men who held doctorates but were teaching below the university level, this movement embraced the notion that each national group was a *Volk* with a distinctive nature, or soul, that was rooted in and shaped by the organic natural surroundings within which its history had unfolded. Germans were one such *Volk* whose historical development in the forested landscapes of Northern and Central Europe had made them an intuitive, emotional, and creative people. While not all *völkish* groups were racist, the ideology lent itself easily to racialist thinking and by the outbreak of the First World War most of its devotees viewed themselves as members of both a German *Volk* and a superior Nordic/Aryan race that was locked in a biological battle for supremacy with Jews, Slavs, and other inferior non–Aryan peoples. Not surprisingly, these individuals were also extreme chauvinists who believed all Germans belonged together in a greater German Reich destined to dominate Europe if not the world.[14]

Heroic vitalism was attractive to these folks for a number of reasons. Like Carlyle and Nietzsche, *völkish* ideologues were disturbed by the factories, urbanization, and party politics of modern Western society. Industrialization destroyed the landscape from which Germandom derived its essence and pushed people away from the *volk* nurturing soil of the countryside into the soulless concrete jungle of the city. Within these urban areas, a deracinated German *Volk* was losing its identity, mingling with alien races — read here Jews — and becoming a mongrel people incapable of creativity. They were also being infected with foreign political ideas that encouraged the development of mass parties and interest groups, which divided and pitted Germans of different religions, regions, classes, and occupations against one another. For the *völkish* movement, all of these developments constituted a crisis that threatened the extinction of the German people.

While this was utter nonsense — the German Empire at the end of the nineteenth century was a super power with a rich cultural life and a science and industry that was the envy of the world — a great many Germans bought into this *völkish* fear mongering and were eager to address the dangers they imagined to be threatening Germany's survival. Their solution to the various ills of German life was a "conservative revolution" that owed much of its inspiration to heroic vitalism, particularly Carlyle's reactionary racist variant of it.[15] In the place of modern society with its environment destroying industries, vast cities, and undifferentiated anonymous crowds, *völkish* ideologues proposed a return to a medieval world in which the majority of people would once again derive their living from the land, small towns would replace large urban metropolises, guilds would control and regulate the production of goods and services, and the nation would be ruled by an aristocracy of heroic Teutonic knights. These knightly heroes would maintain order, dispense justice, defend the *Volk* from foreign invaders, expand the Reich's boundaries, and purify the Nordic race of all pests, parasites, and "usurious vermin," i.e., Jews.[16]

With regard to how this Germanic wonderland was to be realized, *völkish* thinkers took a cue from Nietzsche, i.e., they would be preparatory men — *Trommlers und Sammlers*, "drummers and ralliers" was how they described this role — laying the groundwork for an *Übermensch*, a heroic German *Führer* who would rise up and save Germany in a moment of crisis, and then lead the nation's grateful *Volk* into the medieval racially pure paradise they envisioned for the future. Like Nietzsche's Zarathustra, this *völkish* leader would be a ruthless man of action and instinct, uninhibited by reason or morality, deeply intuitive, and completely committed to the preservation and advancement of his people. And against the enemies of the *Volk*, both foreign and domestic, he would be merciless.

It is difficult to gauge how large the audience was for this rubbish. *Völkish* ideas were largely disseminated through small gatherings and publications, and while many conservative politicians were sympathetic to these notions, no large scale political organization actually adopted them into their party platforms during the life span of the Second Reich. Nevertheless, German historians largely agree that *völkish* ideology was widespread in *fin-de-siècle* Germany and constituted an important set of *idées fixe* in the mental equipment of its educated middle class. Certainly the works of noted *völkish* ideologues like Paul LaGarde, Julius Langbehn, and Moeller van den Bruck were best sellers and, as we have already noted, there were few educated Germans in the late nineteenth and early twentieth centuries that were not familiar with Carlyle and Nietzsche. Whatever the actual numbers of people who counted themselves among the *völkish* faithful, we do know that Adolf Hitler, Heinrich Himmler, Joseph Goebbels, Alfred Rosenberg, and a great many other members of the future Nazi leadership were steeped in these ideas, and, as we will see below, they were also intent on realizing them whatever the cost to Germany and the world.

Rightwing Teutonophiles were not the only hero worshippers of the late nineteenth century. Heroic vitalism also enjoyed a considerable following among the varied anarchists, populists, socialists, and communists who comprised the left end of the political spectrum. And among these varied and factious folk, none were more convinced of the efficacy of heroic action in transforming the world than the Russian revolutionary intelligentsia.

Why Russian leftists were such enthusiastic hero worshippers is a complicated question. A partial answer to this query is to be found in the complex of ideas and popular prejudices, peculiar to Russia, which had shaped the mental landscape of its revolutionaries, and inclined them to think of the world as a place that was subject to the manipulation of strong, vital, and willful men and women. Key among these indigenous notions and traditions was Orthodox Christianity, the religion within which most of these people had been raised. Not only did Russian Orthodoxy teach its charges that the universe was a repository of divine energies in a constant state of becoming, but it also inculcated within them the idea that humans were a part of this cosmic flux and, under the right circumstances, capable of transfiguration into holy Christ-like beings. Indeed, a good part of the Russian religious year was spent honoring a pantheon of heroic saints who had achieved this higher state of being by overcoming their weaknesses and temptations and dedicating their lives to the service of Orthodoxy and its adherents.[17]

In addition to this deeply rooted Orthodox faith was a centuries long tradition of autocratic rule that had encouraged the idea of the hero as a princely ruler who was both a *batiushka* or "little father," just and concerned about the welfare of his people, and a semidivine figure of dread, merciless and cruel to his opponents. One result of this "naïve monarchism," as some historians have termed it, was a widespread admiration for strong leaders, such as Ivan the Terrible and Peter the Great, as well as a tendency on the part of the Russian populace to rally around tsarist pretenders or other self-styled *Khozyains* ("masters") during times of unrest and rebellion. While this devotion to absolutist rulers who were actually responsible for much of the misery, oppression, and injustice endured by the Russian population was perplexing and misguided, the notion that the country's redeemer should be a stern, unchecked autocratic hero was, nonetheless, an article of faith for many among Russia's revolutionary ranks.[18]

This naïve monarchism was also bolstered by Russia's popular folklore, especially the many tales of the heroic warriors known as the *bogatyri*. Recounted in *Bylinys*, or oral stories, these *bogatyri* legends highlighted the lives and deeds of medieval Russian aristocratic knights who were dedicated to the service of the tsar and the defense of Russia and its peoples. While each *bogatyr* displayed distinctive qualities such as great courage, craftiness, or strength, all of them were generous and loyal to their companions-in-arms, hard in their dealings with their enemies, and willing to take whatever steps necessary, no matter how morally questionable, to achieve their ends. These *bogatyri* tales not only reinforced traditional Russian ideas of the hero as a hard, often cruel, strongman, but, as we will see below, they resonated well with Bolshevik notions of leadership and were actually used as models of heroism in Stalin's Soviet Union.[19]

In addition to these longstanding religious and aristocratic notions of heroism, nineteenth century Russian revolutionaries drew inspiration from a heroic pantheon of their own, which was populated with radical writers, such as Alexander Pushkin, Nikolai Chernyshevsky, Alexander Herzen, and I. A. Goncharov, as well as young terrorists who had distinguished themselves through acts of violence against the Romanovs and their agents. Among these lionized literati and assassins, perhaps the most influential in terms of Russia's revolutionary history was Chernyshevsky. His work *What Is to Be Done?* (1863) inspired generations of leftists including Nicolai Lenin, who took its title for his own seminal essay on the subject of revolutionary vanguard parties. In his book, Chernyshevsky castigated Western liberal society and called for its replacement with a collectivist paradise of communes and cooperative workshops peopled by a generation of new men and women who were willful, vital and voluntarist, i.e., willing to offer themselves in any capacity to insure the transformation of mankind into a higher state of being. Indeed, the fictional heroes of *What Is to Be Done?* served as models for many of the young Russian students, including Lenin's brother Alexander, who selflessly sacrificed themselves in various conspiracies and terrorist acts during the latter half of the nineteenth century.[20]

All of these Russian heroic traditions, reactionary and revolutionary, informed the Marxism of Nicolai Lenin and his Bolshevik colleagues. Unlike Georgi Plekhanov, Julius Martov and other Russian Social Democrats who favored Western style mass parties that engaged in the parliamentary process and were open to coalitions with other leftists and progressives, Lenin favored a conspiratorial, tightly organized vanguard party of professional revolutionaries who were highly disciplined, smart, and willing to take whatever steps were necessary to prepare the working class for the revolution and the ensuing dictatorship of the proletariat. While this notion of an elite band of revolutionaries taking the lead in the effort to overthrow the capitalist system was based on an honest appraisal of the very real difficulties facing the development of a revolutionary consciousness in Russia, it also reflected the influence on Lenin and his associates of a Russian heroic tradition that believed change was best effected by autocratic leaders and specially trained bands of voluntarist warriors who were intelligent, strong, dedicated, hard, and, most importantly, ruthless.

Before taking our leave of this Russian variant of heroic vitalism, mention also needs to be made of the widespread currency of Friedrich Nietzsche's ideas among Russia's *fin-de-siècle* revolutionary intelligentsia. Not only were educated Russian leftists familiar with Nietzsche's works, but they found much in them that resonated with their own intellectual and cultural prejudices. Nietzsche's pronouncement that man was something to be overcome and replaced with a higher type was consistent with Orthodox Christian ideas of sainthood and transfiguration that every Russian, Christian or not, had been exposed to from youth. His atheism, as well as his belief that existence was an amoral struggle for power, were in sync with the conviction of most Russian anarchists and Marxists that religion was an opiate and class conflict was the engine of historical development. Nietzsche's call for a generation of preparatory men who were hard, daring and cruel also resonated well with both a Russian revolutionary tradition of heroic voluntarism and the Leninist idea of a vanguard party of Bolshevik *bogatyri*. And the Zarathustrian vision of a post–Christian faith rooted in the real world and dedicated to the creation of the superman, inspired a whole generation of radical Russian artists and Marxists—Alexander Bogdanov, Anatoly Lunacharsky, and Maxim Gorky, to name a few—who believed that Marxism should be a secular religion of "god builders" dedicated to the creation of a new breed of super humanity. Indeed, as we will see, the heroic vitalism of Nietzsche combined with the promethean tendencies in Marxism inspired a whole generation of self–styled "new men and women" who were strong, daring and willing to commit any act, no matter how monstrous, to usher in a Soviet paradise.[21]

Reprise

It is important to reiterate here that at the turn of the nineteenth century none of the individuals, movements, or political factions discussed in the foregoing would have styled themselves "heroic vitalists." Nor did these individuals have much, if anything, to do with one another. Carlyle died in 1881 and was not acquainted with either Nietzsche or his work. Nietzsche was familiar with Carlyle through his writing and dismissed him as a dyspeptic romantic intent on replacing Christianity with hero-worship. Germans of a *völkish* bent saw leftist movements and philosophies as the Enlightenment *in extremis*. Marxist-Leninists, who regarded themselves first and foremost as revolutionary scientists, would have rankled at the suggestion that they had anything in common with reactionary Carlylean hero worshippers or Central European mystics.

Their dissimilarities to the side, however, these individuals did share a common set of views about existence, Western society, and heroes. Whether they were mystics who believed the universe was filled with intelligent design, or hard nosed positivists who regarded the cosmos as a meaningless composite of raw energy in a constant state of permutation, all of these folks accepted the idea that life was an ongoing struggle for survival and power. They also tended to agree that if humanity was to survive this state of affairs and evolve into ever higher forms of being, there was a need for heroic figures, i.e., extraordinary individuals who could divine the needs of their time, wield people together, and take the necessary steps, no matter how hard, that were required to usher in new ways of looking at, thinking about, and living in the world. Finally, there was also a consensus of opinion among these individuals that the liberal values, Judeo-Christian ethics, and capitalist economic arrangements of the West were both detrimental to humanity and ill-suited to the cultivation of heroic personalities.

This complex of ideas, which some scholars have termed heroic vitalism, also inclined these individuals to embrace utopian schemes that were amoral, authoritarian, and cruelly indifferent to human life. Backward looking Carlylean *völkish* fanatics as well as forward looking Nietzschean Marxists both agreed that liberal Western society needed to be swept away, whatever the cost in blood and treasure. They were also of one mind on the need for future governing arrangements that vested all power in the hands of a heroic vanguard elite willing and able to take whatever steps it deemed necessary to defend and advance the interests of those entrusted to its care. And if those steps entailed repression, ethnic cleansing, population "transfers," and/or mass murder, so be it.

In the end, it was this idea of the hero as an amoral, hard, ruthless leader that was most common to all of the people this chapter has labeled heroic vitalists. While Western heroes had often been leaders, were frequently called upon to make difficult decisions, and were certainly no strangers to death, from the Middle Ages on heroism in the West had entailed not only exceptional ability and power but extraordinary responsibility as well. To be deemed a hero, an individual was expected to serve his or her people, and heroic honor was predicated on deeds — defending the homeland, championing the faith, expanding the frontiers of knowledge, creating beauty — that directly benefited the hero's community. Further, while heroism might be muscular, within the context of Western Judeo-Christian culture it was never supposed to be cruel, and violence was always an act taken only as a last resort. Heroic vitalism turned this traditional understanding of the heroic on its head. The heroes of Carlyle, Nietzsche, the *völkish* movement, and the Leninist left were leaders accountable to no one and their heroic stature came not from the people they ostensibly served, but from the guns they commanded and were all too willing to use.

Under normal circumstances, this vitalist vision of an illiberal de–Christianized West governed by bands of heroic outlaws would have been little more than a pipedream. Unfortunately, the outbreak of World War I helped to move what had been a *fin-de-siècle* fantasy to the forefront of Western life. Sixteen million men died in the First World War and another 20 million were maimed and wounded. The experiences of these soldiers in the trenches and pitched battles of this conflict scarred an entire generation, haunted the imaginations of artists and writers years after the war's end, and undermined the widespread belief at the end of the nineteenth century that Europe was progressing toward a scientific and technological utopia. Indeed, both the pointlessness of this war and its extraordinary savagery confirmed for many of the millions that experienced it the idea that life was little more than an amoral, brutal struggle for power. And it also brought to the fore the idea of the hero as a fearless warrior who was first and foremost a remorseless and efficient dealer in death.

More to the point, this First World War and the chaos that followed it sparked revolutions that toppled the thrones of Germany, Austria-Hungary, Turkey, and Russia. In two of these countries — Germany and Russia — men and movements steeped in heroic vitalist thinking came to power and set themselves the task of launching a new heroic age. Who these German black angels and Russian new men were, what they did, and why they were regarded as heroes by the regimes they served are some of the questions to which we will now turn.

Reaping the Whirlwind: The Heroic Ideal in a Totalitarian Context

Working Towards the Führer: Heroism in the Third Reich

Any consideration of heroism in Nazi Germany must have as its starting point the man who articulated and embodied the National Socialist heroic ideal, Adolf Hitler. In his autobiography and exposition of Nazi ideology, *Mein Kampf*, Hitler made clear his belief that history was an ongoing struggle between a superior "Aryan" race — responsible for all art, science, and technology — and other inferior races that were parasitic and destined for extermination and/or enslavement. From this observation, Hitler also concluded:

> A philosophy of life which endeavors to reject the democratic mass idea and give this earth to the best people — that is, the highest humanity — must logically obey the same aristocratic principle within this people and make sure that the leadership and the highest influence in this people fall to the best minds. Thus, it builds, not upon the idea of the majority, but upon the idea of personality.[22]

What Hitler meant by the idea of personality was the notion advanced by Carlyle, Nietzsche, and the other vitalists of the late nineteenth century that history was really the collective biographies of its great men, and that:

> All inventions are the result of an individual's work. All these individuals, whether intentionally or unintentionally, are more or less great benefactors of all men. Their work subsequently gives millions nay billions of human creatures, instruments with which to facilitate and carry out their life struggle.[23]

This being the case, Hitler surmised that one of the central tasks of the National Socialist state was to raise "the best minds in the national community to leading positions and leading influence"[24] and to insure that these individuals were vested with whatever authority was necessary to achieve the tasks for which they were given responsibility. Hitler considered this *Führerprinzip* (leadership principle) as not only more reflective of the state of nature where the strong dominated the weak, but also essential to the creation of the new order he envisioned where a race of Germanic *Übermenschen* dominated the world. Indeed, Hitler was convinced that only a new Nazi aristocracy based on talent and ability would be capable of making the hard decisions necessary to carry out his mission, i.e., the defeat of the Western democracies, the destruction of Bolshevik Russia, and the extirpation of world Jewry.

How these National Socialist heroic leaders were to be cultivated and identified was through a process of intense competition and struggle centered on working towards the Führer. What this meant in theory and practice was that those Germans who really "got" Hitler, who understood his aims, anticipated his needs, and came up with innovative and effective ways of realizing his vision were Germany's natural leaders. In short, to be worthy of inclusion in the Nazi leadership cadre and pantheon of heroes, a person had to essentially become a Hitler personality.[25]

Given the centrality of Hitler to National Socialist notions of leadership and heroism, it is important to briefly consider why people thought him worth emulating, as well as what kinds of behavior actually set his "personality" apart from others. With regard to the first part of this question, Hitler enjoyed the admiration of a great many folk because his life was a remarkable rags to riches success story. Born into a lower middle-class Austrian family, Hitler's childhood and youth were completely uneventful and gave no indication that he would one day be a significant historical figure. Upon finishing secondary school, he fancied himself an artist and something of an architect, but he failed twice to gain admission to the Academy of Graphic Arts in Vienna. For five years after this rejection, he was an aimless drifter doing odd jobs, immersing himself in *völkish* tracts, and leading a bohemian existence in the Austrian imperial capital. In 1913, he moved to Munich to escape conscription in the Austro-Hungarian army and enlisted in the German military as an infantryman at the outbreak of the First World War. He distinguished himself during this conflict, winning the Iron Cross first class for bravery, but he failed to win promotion because his superiors felt he lacked leadership qualities. Indeed, for 32 years of his life there was nothing about Adolf Hitler that distinguished him from his peers or indicated he was destined for anything save a fringe existence.

From 1921 on, however, Hitler's life trajectory was nothing short of astounding. Lacking in social connections, higher education, administrative experience, and even German citizenship, Hitler managed to rise from a Munich beer hall rabble-rouser to leader of Germany's most powerful political party, chancellor and dictator of the German Reich, and master of Europe in less then twenty years. By any standards, these achievements set him apart from not only ordinary people, but also from most of the politicians, leaders, and statesmen with whom he interacted — and usually bested — during this time.

While much of this extraordinary success was owed to historical circumstances outside of Hitler's control — Germany's humiliation at Versailles; the instability of the Weimar Republic; the Great Depression; the complicity of the German ruling class; Europe's war weary populations; and the lackluster leadership of Great Britain and France — there were a number of personality traits that allowed Hitler to capitalize on the many opportunities Fortuna threw his way in the years before Stalingrad. His extraordinary oratorical ability, as well as his unshakeable belief that he was a messiah tapped by Providence to realize the *völkish* idea, conferred on Hitler a charismatic quality completely lacking in the colorless career politicians he competed with in his rise to the chancellorship. His willingness to take whatever steps necessary, no matter how ruthless, to gain untrammeled personal power made it easy for him to dispose of anyone — friend or foe — who opposed him. His abiding faith in his gut instincts, coupled with a willingness to gamble recklessly, also freed him to consider courses of action — the remilitarization of the Rhineland; the annexation of Austria and Czechoslovakia; an armored thrust through the Ardennes during the campaign against France — that his more rational and cautious advisors and generals would never have entertained. And a complete lack of morals made it possible for Hitler to engage in conduct — breaking promises; violating treaties; ignoring the rules of war; terrorizing civilian populations; enslavement and mass murder — that his counterparts in other countries found shameful and criminal.[26]

Despite the fact that much of Hitler's world view was irrational and his conduct often unethical — indeed, even sociopathic — in the years before World War II, supporters and opponents alike tended to regard his remarkable rise to power and subsequent domestic and foreign policy successes as evidence that he was a "great man" destined to be remembered as one of history's movers and shakers. Certainly, for the overwhelming majority of Germans at this time, their Führer was without question a heroic figure who had rescued the fatherland from political and economic chaos, erased the shame of Versailles, and restored Germany to its rightful place as a great power. Indeed, it was precisely this widespread adulation of Hitler, this sense of him as a kind of demiurge who against all odds had arrived on the stage of Europe and made the whole world hold its breath, which encouraged his henchmen to think of him as the mould from which all present and future Nazi heroes should be cast.

This equation of heroism with Hitler worship made for a rather circumscribed notion of what National Socialist heroes should look like and how they should behave. In keeping with Hitler's racist philosophy of life, any candidate for inclusion in the Nazi heroic pantheon had to be Aryan — preferably of the tall, blonde, and blue-eyed Nordic variety — and completely committed to the realization of the *völkish* idea of a racially purified greater Germanic empire. These individuals were also expected to share Hitler's nonchalant attitude toward death; indifference to the moral strictures of Judeo-Christianity; willful and instinctive nature; disdain for intellectualism; and willingness to be hard, cruel, and completely ruthless in the struggle against the ideological (Liberals and Marxists) and racial (Jewish) enemies of the Third Reich. Finally, to be a hero of Hitler's new order one was also expected to be an "aligned" personality, i.e., an extraordinary individual who was also completely in sync with the German *Volk*, capable of intuiting their needs, and willing to do anything on their behalf.

At first glance, this Hitler-centered heroic ideal appeared to offer any German with the proper racial pedigree the opportunity to become a Nazi hero. After all, women no less than men, as well as any German peasant, worker, tradesman, or professional, could embrace *völkish* ideals, dedicate themselves to the service of the German nation, and behave in an appropriately Führer-like manner. And to some extent, this was true. German women, for example, who were expected to return to their traditional roles as homemakers and brood mares, were regarded as heroic, and honored as such, if they abandoned the workplace, tended the hearth, and gave birth to lots of children. Peasants and workers who produced foodstuffs and industrial goods beyond the targets set by the state were also deemed heroes of the fatherland, as were industrialists and professionals who rendered valuable services to the Nazi state. This said, however, the Nazi heroic pantheon, like the *Volk* community it served, was a highly stratified place in which heroism was treated as a largely male prerogative, and the most honored heroes were men in uniform.

This preference for heroes who were military men was not surprising given the fact that the Nazi Party was a *völkish* movement with a vitalist view of existence as an unremitting racial struggle. In a world where warfare was regarded as the rule rather than the exception, National Socialists believed that heroic warriors would be critical to the *Volk's* survival, and Hitler reinforced this idea by declaring the army to be both the bulwark of the nation and the model par excellence for its organization and governance. In addition to these ideological considerations, the party's membership, particularly in its early years, was also largely comprised of male veterans who regarded their World War I *Fronterlebnis* (front experience) as the most significant and life affirming moment of their existence. This sentiment was also shared by the Nazi leadership, many of whom — Hitler, Röhm, Göring, Hess — fought in the First World War and considered it the most unforgettable, indeed, the greatest time of their lives.

One consequence of this Nazi adulation of the warrior was that long before Hitler's party assumed power it had already laid the foundations for a National Socialist mythology based on martyred military and/or paramilitary men. These early Nazi martyr heroes included the young German soldiers who had died at Langemarck, a Belgian town in Flanders, during the battle of Ypres in 1914-15; Albert Leo Schlageter, a freebooter executed by France in 1923 for sabotaging railway lines during the French occupation of the Ruhr; the sixteen Nazis who were killed during Hitler's abortive Beer Hall Putsch in November 1923; Horst Wessel, a Nazi storm trooper, thug and pimp gunned down by the Communists in 1930; and Herbert Norkus, a Hitler Youth member who was stabbed to death in a 1932 Berlin street brawl with his Communist counterparts. All of these individuals were singled out as heroic figures by Hitler and his henchmen because of their single-minded devotion to the *völkish* idea, fearlessness, and, most importantly, willingness to sacrifice their lives in the struggle against those the Nazis deemed enemies of the Reich, i.e., the Western democracies, the Weimar Republic, and "Judeo-Marxist" Communists. In the years following the establishment of the Nazi dictatorship, these individuals were also elevated to the status of national heroes and honored with burial ceremonies and memorial days with mass rallies. Their heroic stature was further reinforced by Nazi Propaganda Minister, Joseph Goebbels, who commemorated, in a highly hagiographic manner, their lives and deeds through architecture, monuments, paintings, music, literature, poetry, and films.[27]

Other than these freebooters and paramilitary types, the uniformed men who best embodied the Nazi heroic ideal were the "black angels" of the SS. Little more than Hitler's bodyguard and personal police force when the Nazis took power in 1933, following the purge of Ernst Röhm's SA in 1934, the SS increasingly became the Führer's executive arm; first in the areas of political security and police work and finally as the agents of Hitler's racial warfare. These duties required a sizable organization and by the time the regime collapsed in 1945 the SS was a state within a state, controlling factories, laboratories, schools, concentration camps, death centers, and even armed divisions.

The founder of this SS imperium, Heinrich Himmler, was the embodiment of the Orwellian concept of double think. He could be, simultaneously, a Grand Inquisitor and a petty bourgeois, a ruthless, ideological fanatic and a polite, amiable middle class father.[28] The efficient organizer, whose scientific approach to problem solving brought him to Hitler's notice and earned him his rank within the Nazi hierarchy, was also a *völkish* mystic. He believed in "glacial cosmogony, magnetism, homeopathy, mesmerism, natural eugenics, clairvoyance, faith healing, and sorcery. He sponsored experiments in obtaining gasoline by having water run over coal and in producing gold out of base metals."[29] A murderer of millions, he loved children and loathed hunting, once remarking to his masseur, Felix Kersten:

> How can you find pleasure ... in shooting from behind cover at poor creatures browsing on the edge of a wood, innocent, defenseless, and unsuspecting? It's really pure murder.[30]

Insisting that his men be sexual puritans, with eyes only for their loving fraus and large families, Himmler maintained a household for his personal secretary and mistress, Hedwig Potthast, who bore him a son and a daughter.[31]

Nowhere were these contradictions more apparent, however, than in Himmler's attempt to turn what was essentially a police force into an order of chivalry. Toward that end, Himmler modeled his SS after the Jesuits of the Counter-Reformation. Like Loyola, who was advised by four assistant generals on various questions of faith, Himmler divided his SS into separate departments to assist him in all matters pertaining to the sacred mission of National Socialism. Each department was headed by its own Gruppenführer and responsible for a particular area of concern to the SS, i.e., race, security, justice, education, operations, personnel, economics, and administration. Himmler also tried to imbue his order with the Loyolan principles of obedience, sacrifice and duty by laying down rigid conditions for membership in the SS, requiring oaths of absolute devotion to the Führer, and setting down a regimen of training and education, which candidates for the specialized divisions of the organization had to undergo. He even established special castles where his men were trained in "comradeship, duty, truth, diligence, honesty, and knighthood."[32]

Himmler also radically altered the membership of the SS during the early thirties in order to insure that it would become a reservoir of German society's "best and brightest." Beginning in 1933, the Free-Corps men, the lower middle-class party members and the crackpot intellectuals (with the exception of the Reichsführer of course) were weeded out of Himmler's SS order. In their place, came the aristocracy (60 percent of the senior SS posts were occupied by members of the German nobility), the lawyers, intellectuals, and technocrats of the upper middle-classes, as well as the middle-class section of the Reichswehr officer corp. By the outbreak of World War II, the SS was well on its way to becoming the leadership cadre of the party and the nation[33]

The irony of these efforts to make the SS into an elite quasi-religious Arthurian knightly order lay in the fact that the "sacred" mission of the organization was completely contrary to the ideals of chivalry or Loyolan Catholicism. That mission had, as its end result, not the protection of the weak, the defense of life or the glorification of God, but the enslavement of whole peoples and the selective slaughter of millions of men, women and children in order to satisfy the twisted pronouncements of one man. Such a mission was best accomplished not by knights dedicated to truth, altruism and chivalry, but by amoral sociopaths versed in the ways of falsehood and greed.

As a devotee of National Socialism, however, Himmler regarded his prisons, concentration camps, ethnic cleansing campaigns, and death centers as the front lines of a titanic political and racial struggle against the enemies of the German *Volk*, i.e., Marxists, Jews and the Slavic "hordes" of the east. The SS charged with running these operations were in his eyes truly latter-day Teutonic Knights, and, as such, he believed they could in fact torment, murder and despoil millions in an honorable correct manner. Indeed, Himmler was so intent on insuring that SS crimes were done properly that he actually promulgated a law code for his order that laid down rather strict prohibitions against sadism and corruption. Tellingly, humanitarian considerations had nothing to do with either of these strictures.

Himmler considered sadism a menace, not because of the needless suffering it inflicted on the victims of the SS, but because he felt it might undermine the psychological health of those responsible for incarcerating and eliminating the enemies of the Reich. When, in 1942, the SS Legal Department requested from Himmler clarification as to how the unauthorized killings of Jews were to be handled, he replied: "If the motive is purely political, there should be no punishment unless such is necessary for the maintenance of discipline. If the motive is selfish, sadistic or sexual, judicial punishment should be imposed for murder or manslaughter as the case may be."[34] What constituted a politically motivated killing, as opposed to one committed for sadistic reasons, remained an open question. In practice, this determination was left to the commanders in the field who usually could not be bothered with such legal niceties. After all, what was one murder committed in an unauthorized manner when one's mission was the extermination of some eleven million souls.

Corruption, on the other hand, was considered by Himmler to be a threat, not only to the individual members of his order, but to the entire German race. Probably no other crime was more abhorrent to Himmler than theft. It offended both his petty bourgeois sense of propriety and his *völkish* mysticism. As James Weingartner noted in his work on law and justice in the SS:

> The Reichsführer SS was convinced that diminished respect for public and private property was a measure of the degree to which the German people had wandered from their roots in ancient Germanic society in which theft was regarded as the most heinous of crimes.... Alien influences had diluted respect for property rights, Himmler believed, and it was part of the mission of National Socialism and its militant vanguard, the SS, to restore this element of Volk consciousness to health.[35]

Himmler continually admonished his SS elite on the necessity of remaining untainted by corruption and he left them with no doubts as to what would transpire should they ignore his blandishments. In October 1943, he informed his SS generals at a conference in Posen that "we have no right to enrich ourselves by so much as a fur, a watch, a mark or a cigarette or anything else. I shall never stand by and watch the slightest rot develop or establish itself here. Wherever it forms, we shall burn it out together."[36] As with sadism, however, once put into a completely lawless environment, Himmler's black angels tended to ignore his restrictions and took every opportunity to feather their nests with the property they plundered from their victims.

Among Himmler's many deputies, the one that came closest to his SS heroic ideal was "the Third Reich's evil young god of death," Reinhard Heydrich.[37] Tall, blonde, and blue-eyed, Heydrich was the physical embodiment of the Aryan racial type so admired by Hitler and his colleagues. An accomplished violin player and a champion athlete in fencing, skiing, swimming, and horseback riding, he was also something of a Nazi Renaissance man. And, unlike the Reichsführer he served, Heydrich was also a decorated German war hero with two Iron Crosses for his exploits as a fighter pilot in at least sixty combat missions during World War II.

With regard to Heydrich's ideological convictions, a lot has been written about the fact that he was not really a *völkish* fanatic in the mould of the men he served; that he was instead little more than an efficient technocrat interested only in the accumulation and exercise of power. While it is certainly true that he had little use for the intellectual pretensions, ideological ramblings, and mystical pastimes of Himmler — something that could also be said of most of the Reichsführer's colleagues in the Nazi leadership — Heydrich's single-minded drive to acquire the means necessary to realize Hitler's various aims was perfectly consistent with National Socialist leadership principles. Certainly, no one worked more successfully towards his Führer, and did so with more amoral hardhearted ruthlessness, than Heydrich did during his tenure as Himmler's second-in-command.[38]

Indeed, whether it was a question of consolidating and securing Hitler's power, realizing National Socialist racial objectives, or keeping subject populations quiescent, Reinhard Heydrich was the man the Nazi leadership often turned to for answers during the 1930s and early 40s. It was Heydrich, for example, who took the first steps towards creating an effective totalitarian state by gathering together all the various police agencies of the Reich — the Gestapo, the German criminal police (*Kripo*), and the SD (*Sicherheitsdienst* or Security Service) — into one central Reich Security Main Office under the direct control of Hitler and his SS minions. In racial affairs, it was also Heydrich who ordered the concentration of Polish Jews in ghettoes and, when the decision was taken for a "final solution of the "Jewish Question" in Europe, it was this "blond beast" who was tapped to chair the infamous Wannsee Conference, which drew up the plans for the deportation and extermination of European Jewry. And when Czech resistance threatened the flow of important war materials and foodstuffs to the German front lines, it was Heydrich who was named Reichsprotektor of Bohemia and Moravia (the former Czechoslovakia) and charged with restoring order; a task he achieved through the application of a policy of "whip and sugar" in which brutal terror was combined with increased food rations, pension payments, and unemployment insurance benefits for those who collaborated with his regime.

Heydrich's achievements as the Reich's premier secret policeman, mass murderer, and "enlightened" despot, insured that he was elevated to the highest tier of the Nazi heroic pantheon following his assassination by Czech partisans in 1942. At his two-day state funeral — an elaborate event with honor guards, flags, and flaming urns that was intended to serve as a model for all future burials of SS heroes — Himmler lauded his adjutant as loyal, brave, pure, incorruptible, and obedient to "the Aryan racial imperative." The Reichsführer SS also noted that Heydrich had carried out every task charged to him in an efficient and determined manner and that his example would serve to inspire his fellow SS knights in their war against the political and racial enemies of the German *Volk*. Himmler was followed by Hitler, who declared Reinhard Heydrich "one of the best National Socialists, one of the strongest defenders of the German Reich, one of the greatest opponents of all the enemies of this Reich." Hitler also posthumously bestowed on Heydrich the highest grade of the German Order and the Blood Order Medal, and then escorted his coffin to Berlin's cemetery of heroes, the Invalidenfriedhof.[39]

One final tribute to Heydrich, which was positively Homeric in its savagery, was the vengeance Hitler and Himmler exacted on his assassins and their ostensible supporters among the Czech population. Following the funeral, 10,000 Czechs were arrested and at least 1300 were shot including all the male inhabitants of Lidice, a village near Prague where Heydrich's assailants fled. The arrested women were deported to Ravensbrück where many died doing hard labor, while their children were either "Aryanized," i.e., placed under the care of SS families, or transported to death centers for gassing. The village of Lidice itself was razed to the ground and its ruins (including its cemetery) bulldozed. Two weeks later a similar vengeance was exacted on the small village of Ležáky.

In addition to this Czech "funeral pyre," Heydrich was posthumously honored for his role in planning the Final Solution. When the mass murder of over 2 million Polish Jews commenced in late 1942 at the death camps of Treblinka, Sobibor, and Belzec, it was code named "Operation Reinhard." Doubtless, the man Himmler was fond of calling his "Genghis Khan" would have been pleased to have his work acknowledged in such a manner. After all, among the SS knights of the Third Reich, no one had worked so hard to realize Hitler's dream of a "Jew free" Europe as Reinhard Heydrich.

What is particularly chilling about Heydrich and his other colleagues in the Nazi heroic pantheon was the fact that these individuals were regarded by Hitler and Himmler as little more than precursors of a German super humanity that would be even more "violent, domineering, undismayed, and cruel" than the founding generation of the Third Reich. Indeed, in secret conversations with his henchmen during World War II, Hitler waxed eloquent about a postwar German empire in Russia cleansed of Jews, Gypsies, and Bolsheviks and served by a semi-literate population of Slav slaves whose cultures and cities had been completely obliterated. The Nazi overlords of this eastern imperium were to be a eugenically engineered race of Aryan super heroes, many of them born and bred in a postwar SS kingdom of Burgundy, carved out of France, Switzerland and the Low Countries, and governed by Himmler. Physically strong, intellectually advanced, emotionally hard, ruthless, amoral, and driven by an unquenchable thirst for power, these SS warrior princes would govern the greater Germanic Reich, maintain order in the East, and carry Hitler's racial jihad to all four corners of the Earth, and, in time, to the stars.[40]

Ludicrous as all of this may sound, the fact remains that a very real attempt was made from 1933–1945 to usher in a Nazi heroic age. Billed as an effort to save civilization and the "idea of the personality" that had made it possible, National Socialism was actually a return to an uncivilized stage in Western history where lawlessness and disorder were rife, most folk were either the slaves or dependents of whatever ape commanded the most spears, and heroes were little more than bandit warriors. Indeed, it was a complete repudiation of every ideal, every principle of civilized and heroic behavior that had held sway in the West for almost two millennia. Unfortunately, it would take a second world war, millions of deaths and the addition of the word "genocide" to the vocabulary of the West, to drive home how truly dangerous and misguided this vitalist notion of heroism really was.

CULTS, COMBINES, AND RED STARS:
HEROISM IN BOLSHEVIK RUSSIA

Vladimir Il'ich

I know —
It is not the hero
Who precipitates the flow of revolution.
The story of heroes —
is the nonsense of the intelligentsia!
But who can restrain himself
and not sing
of the glory of Ilich?...
Kindling the lands with fire
everywhere,
where people are imprisoned,
like a bomb
the name
explodes:
Lenin!
Lenin!
Lenin!...
I glorify in Lenin....[41]

The poem *Vladimir Il'ich* was penned by Vladimir Mayakovsky on the occasion of Lenin's birthday in 1920, and it is quoted here because it lays out quite succinctly the problematic nature — the dialectic if you will — of hero worship in the early Soviet state. Unlike Nazi Germany where inequality was celebrated and all progress in human affairs was attributed to the actions of personalities, Bolshevik Russia was the offspring of a Marxist ideology dedicated to egalitarianism, collectivism and the proposition that historical development proceeded from struggles between socio-economic classes rather than individuals. Mayakovsky captured this distinction nicely when he notes in the opening lines of his poem that heroes were not only irrelevant to "the flow of revolution," but also the embodiment, the "nonsense," of the individual-centered bourgeois societies and cultures Bolshevism was intent on destroying. Nevertheless, as noted earlier, heroes and ideas of heroic action were an integral part of the Russian revolutionary tradition, and Lenin's vanguard Bolshevik Party was itself a tacit acknowledgement that even the laws of history required exceptional individuals to insure their proper promulgation. This fact was also underscored in Mayakovsky's poem when he moves from his thesis — the irrelevance of heroes to the "flow of revolution" — to his antithetical climax, the admission that Lenin *is* the revolution personified and therefore worthy of unabashed hero worship.

The contradiction raised in Mayakovsky's poem between a Marxist ideology that was largely indifferent, indeed even hostile, to the hero and a Bolshevik state and society hungry for heroic figures and deeds was not easily resolvable. Determining what it meant to be a hero in early Soviet Russia and then identifying individuals worthy of the rewards, reverence, and emulation that accompanied heroic status were questions also tied to larger debates about Bolshevik Party authority, the relationship of the individual to the collective, status and privilege in an equalitarian society, and the proper format and subject matter of revolutionary literature and art. Further complicating matters was the fact that the regime's response to these issues varied according to the vicissitudes of the Soviet Union during the 20s and 30s, and these changes also affected considerations of who and what should be honored in a Bolshevik heroic pantheon.

Both prior to the Russian revolution and throughout his dictatorship, Lenin's pronouncements on heroes and hero worship were very much in keeping with orthodox Marxism. The hero, Lenin argued, was merely an extension of the liberal bourgeois glorification of personalities and individuals that Marxist ideology and the Bolshevik revolution had discredited. Classes were the agencies of change in history, not individuals or heroes, and it was the working class in particular that was the agent of revolution in Russia and abroad. Insofar as one could speak of heroism in a Marxist framework, Lenin believed it was necessary to think of it as a collective phenomenon. And within the context of the new Soviet state this meant there could be only one hero worthy of reverence and emulation, the Russian proletariat.

To be sure, Lenin and his party acknowledged that individuals could render valuable assistance to the working class in fulfilling its historical mission. The whole justification for a vanguard party and a dictatorship of the proletariat was, after all, based on the idea that Russia's workers and peasants needed the help of conscious, trained, and fully committed cadres of communist specialists. The party also praised individuals for exceptional work done on behalf of the proletariat; extolled the contributions of dead comrades to the revolution; and held up certain historical personages — Spartacus, Marat, Danton, Marx, and Engels — as revolutionary icons. Nor would any Bolshevik have denied the crucial role played by a Lenin or a Trotsky in fomenting the October Revolution, pulling Russia out of World War I, and beating back the White insurgency. These exceptions to the side, however, early Bolshevism remained committed to the idea that all loyal workers, peasants, and party members were heroic figures, and any activity by these people aimed at realizing a communist society constituted an act of heroism.

Despite the party's ideological aversion to heroes, the first six years of the Russian revolution saw the rise of a Bolshevik heroic type and a communist hero cult. Both of these developments were tied to a demographic shift that occurred in Bolshevik Party membership during the 1918–1921 Russian Civil War, which pitted Bolshevik "Reds" against anti–Bolshevik "Whites." Lenin's party entered this conflict without much in the way of a functioning government, army, or economy and in desperate need of political operatives, policemen, skilled workers, army officers, and countless other kinds of specialists. To address these deficiencies, the Bolshevik regime opened its ranks to a younger generation of poorly educated and intellectually unsophisticated youth, mostly from working class and peasant backgrounds.

Suffice it to say, this new cohort of Bolsheviks shared little in common with their besuited and bookish party elders. Shaped in a brutal war where they were given carte blanche to nationalize industry, seize private property, requisition food supplies, and commit any act of terror deemed necessary for victory, they favored simple, direct and unreflective action, preferred military tunics and leather trench coats to civilian garb, and toted Mausers on their hips. In addition to their martial inclinations, these Red warriors were also unreceptive to the party leadership's line on heroes. For them the Russian Civil War was the stuff of an epic heroic struggle in which they had played the role of Bolshevik *bogatyri*. As such, they not only believed in acknowledging and celebrating individuals who had given their full measure in defense of Soviet Russia, but also in cultivating a cadre of heroic commissars who, like themselves, would be unsophisticated, resourceful, and hard folk willing to take whatever measures — no matter how brutal and coercive — to accomplish the ends of the party and the revolution it served.[42]

These Red knights also had a model of Soviet heroism in the person of Lenin, a man they quite literally worshipped both in life and death. Like Hitler after him, much of Lenin's heroic aura emanated from the trajectory of his life. Though he possessed a formidable intellect and great drive, most of his adulthood was spent in exile among quarrelsome and ineffectual Marxists arguing the particulars of revolutionary theories and platforms that were of little concern to anyone save professional revolutionaries and the various police agents keeping an eye on them. Following the deposition of the Tsar in 1917, however, it was Lenin who was the architect, builder, and unquestioned head of the new Soviet state. From the decision to overthrow the provisional government to Brest-Litovsk, War Communism, and the New Economic Program, there was not a major initiative from 1917 to 1923 that did not bear Lenin's imprint on it. Indeed, whatever the Marxist line regarding the irrelevance of personalities in the unfolding of history, Lenin was unquestionably a significant historical player whose ideas and actions had reshaped the intellectual and political landscape of his country.

In addition to his standing as the father of the Soviet state, Lenin's lifestyle and manner drew favorable analogies with Russia's religious, aristocratic, and revolutionary heroic traditions. Like the saints of Orthodox Christianity, Lenin lived simply, was abstemious in his habits, and worked long hours on behalf of his flock. As a ruler, his:

> Style was homely. He was accessible, simple, attentive, and concerned. In short, he seemed like the simple "just tsar" of the peasants' naïve monarchism. The poor came mostly with complaints, petitions, and sometimes gifts of food (which he donated to orphanages and daycare centers). Peasants occasionally bowed low upon entering his office. Lenin was careful to show respect to the poor and uneducated, something he did not always do for his comrades and government officials.[43]

Just tsars were also expected to be hard and fierce towards their enemies, and Lenin too was merciless in his treatment of those who opposed his regime. During his rule, the dreaded Bolshevik secret police, the *Cheka*, came into being, and it was at his behest that it executed and imprisoned many thousands of real and imagined enemies of the state. And while Lenin tolerated a degree of dissent in his own party, and encouraged free and open discussion among his colleagues, once he made up his mind regarding a particular policy and pushed it through his Politburo, he tolerated no "factionalism" in the ranks.

Finally, by dint of his age, temperament, and literary bent, Lenin was also associated in the public mind with the Russian revolutionary heroes of the nineteenth century. Born in 1870, Lenin became involved in anti–Tsarist activities at the age of 17 in the aftermath of his eldest brother's execution in 1887 for conspiring to assassinate Tsar Alexander III. Like his brother and the other Russian terrorists of this period, Lenin had "no thoughts but thoughts of revolution"[44] and was willing to sacrifice everything — family, friendships, comfort, health, even his life — in order to realize a radical transformation of the world. He was also unwilling to cooperate or compromise with liberals, progressives, or other kinds of democrats, believing instead in irreconcilable class struggle. And like Chernyshevsky and the other nineteenth century revolutionaries of the pen, Lenin articulated this revolutionary zeal in a veritable torrent of letters, essays, analytical tracts, major works of Marxist theory, speeches, newspaper articles, party platforms, and much more. Indeed, long before his death, Lenin's colleagues and countrymen could discern in him all the various strands of the Russian heroic tradition — just tsar, selfless saint, fearless knight, and committed revolutionary.

Following his demise in 1924, Lenin actually became the object — in every sense of the word — of a full-fledged Bolshevik hero cult. Despite his many pronouncements against flattery and the glorification of the individual, as well as the objections of his wife, family, and closest colleagues, the Bolshevik Party decided to preserve Lenin's body and enshrine it in the equivalent of a Red temple. In a manner that could not help but evoke comparisons with Egyptian pharaohs, pre-classical Greek heroes, and Christian saints, Lenin's embalmed remains were placed on display in a glass topped sarcophagus that was enclosed in a pyramid shaped granite mausoleum next to the Kremlin in Moscow's Red Square. Until the collapse of the Soviet Union in 1991, Russia's leaders and the Communist Party faithful paid homage to Lenin by rallying at this structure every year to celebrate the revolution's major holidays, victories, and heroes. In addition to this temple-like tomb, Lenin was further honored with hagiographic biographies, iconographic posters, paeans of praise, a library to house his works, shrines in apartment buildings and factories, and a host of cities, towns, villages, roads, and avenues bearing his name.[45]

The principal promoters of this Lenin hero cult — Stalin, the Bolshevik Party's "god builders," and Bolshevism's young civil war *bogatyri*— supported the near deification of their recently departed leader for a number of reasons. For Stalin and his allies in the Politburo and the party-at-large, the creation of a cult around the popular figure of Lenin was an opportunity to mobilize support behind the regime he had created. God builders, on the other hand, saw the idolization of Bolshevism's founder as an important step in the transformation of Marxism into a secular religion. And the party's militant young "war communists" viewed Lenin's cult as no more than a formal acknowledgement of the respect, love, and reverence they already felt for the man who had created Soviet Russia and led it to victory against its enemies. Whatever their rationale in supporting the worship of Lenin, all of these different individuals and factions were agreed that he was the perfect paradigm of the Soviet hero and "new man" of the future., i.e., a tireless revolutionary leader who was simple and modest in lifestyle; direct in manner; completely dedicated to the acquisition of power; and utterly ruthless in exercising it on behalf of the working class and its vanguard party. As we will see, Stalin was particularly adept at associating himself with this Leninist model of heroic behavior.

Prior to the consolidation of Stalin's personal dictatorship, however, there were still a great many Bolsheviks, particularly among the party's utopian radicals, who shared Lenin's disdain for heroes. For these individuals, communism was a collectivist mass enterprise in which all participants were treated equally, resources were allocated according to need, and no one person was elevated above the others. By both definition and historical experience, a hero was an *individual*— usually male and often aristocratic — who was regarded as separate from and superior to the masses; accorded deferential treatment by his community;

and awarded honors, privileges and material possessions unavailable to most folk. Heroes were also only able to engage in the activities for which they were honored because they enjoyed a degree of wealth, privilege, and leisure denied the laboring classes; and their heroic actions, more often than not, defended and upheld a status quo that was usually unequal and oppressive.

This anti–hero sentiment was most pronounced in the various party debates that swirled around literary questions during the early twenties and the time of the First Five-Year Plan (1928–1932). The Bolshevik Party militant of this period, particularly those associated with the Russian Association of Proletarian Writers (RAPP), regarded novels and stories with their often anti–social, selfish, and anarchic heroic protagonists to be products of liberal bourgeois culture. Consequently, they castigated the works of early Soviet writers, such as Fyodor Gladkov (*Cement*, 1925), which featured heroes who, while supportive of socialism and Soviet industrial reconstruction, were also willful individuals often critical of the Bolshevik party and its state planning organs. In the place of these hero centered works, RAPP and its allies in the party advocated a proletarian literature that celebrated what Maxim Gorky referred to as "little men" who "shared in the great achievements of the age; and for this reason their deeds were also 'great.'"[46]

What emerged from this "little men" literary movement were "deheroized" short stories and novels that were, in the words of Soviet literary historian Katerina Clark, "a profusion of subplots in search of a central plot, or, worse still, the absence of any plot at all."[47] In works such as *Energy* (written by a chastened Gladkov in 1932), *Hydrocentral* (Marietta Shaginian, 1930–31), and *Virgin Soil Upturned* (M. Sholokhov, 1932), readers were treated — subjected actually — to boring almost unreadable accounts of factory construction and collective farming (sometimes referred to as boy meets tractor tales). The focus in these stories, and others written in the same vein, was largely on technology and the intricacies of Bolshevik Party industrial and agricultural policies. Insofar as human beings entered into these accounts, it was always in the context of a collective group differentiated only by the role each person played in the creation of a Soviet enterprise.

Suffice it to say, this deheroized writing was not popular with either the public-at-large or most Russian authors. Even Gorky came to reject it because it was lacking in "the techniques of literary mastery" and silent about the deeds "of the human hero, who gives birth to the collective heroism of the class."[48] Consequently, in the years following the First Five-Year Plan, officially sponsored Soviet literature dropped the "little man" genre in favor of stories in which heroes loomed large. Indeed, the novels of the 1930s were autobiographical in style and featured plotlines that were essentially a refashioning of traditional *bogatyr* folk literature. In them, young, daring, willful, energetic, and dedicated Bolshevik soldiers, engineers, explorers, and aviators recounted how they successfully tackled seemingly insurmountable obstacles under the guidance of the party and its ruling prince, Joseph Stalin.[49]

This embrace of the heroic in Soviet literature also reflected a shift in Bolshevik thinking about heroes and their glorification that was directly tied to the consolidation of Stalin's dictatorship in the 1930s. Lenin's successor may have emulated his predecessor's style, i.e., simple clothes, a modest manner, and direct unadorned speech, but he had very little patience with his egalitarianism. For Stalin, the Marxist dictum that goods and services should be distributed according to the principle "from each according to ability, to each according to work" was an acknowledgement that people were not equal and that certain kinds of activity could and in fact should be privileged. Stalin believed the work of party leaders, specialists, shock workers, scientists, and explorers required a high level of ability, was critical to the survival of Soviet Russia, and deserved to be acknowledged with special privileges and distinctions. Most of the Red cadres that had entered the Bolshevik Party during and after the Civil War years, and were managing the industrialization of the nation, agreed with him. Like their boss, these individuals also saw their work as dictators of the proletariat and managers of Soviet industry as essential, deserving of greater wages, and worthy of special acknowledgement. Consequently, when Stalin denounced "vulgar egalitarianism" in his famous "Six Conditions" speech of June 23, 1931, he did so with the full support of his party.

Having dispensed with the idea that a socialist society was a place where everyone was equal, Stalin's regime was free to create its own cult of heroes. On April 17, 1934, it did just that by creating an Order of the Hero of the Soviet Union. In a Decree on Heroes issued the following day in *Izvestia*, as well as in subsequent articles published in *Pravda* and other official journals over the course of the next two years, the Bolshevik Party argued that an official cult of Soviet heroes was necessary both to single out and honor certain kinds of socially beneficial characteristics and actions, as well as to provide a counter heroic ideal to that of bourgeois and Nazi society. These tracts stressed that the men and women selected for inclusion in the Soviet heroic pantheon were above all merely "firsts among equals," i.e., they were of the masses but their feats of extraordinary strength, skill, cogitation, discipline, and daring had singled them out as models for their fellows to follow and where possible emulate. Like Lenin and Stalin, these heroic folk were also expected to be modest, selfless, organized, disciplined, enthusiastic, courageous, and unwilling to brook any obstacle to the achievement of their goals. And unlike the selfish adventurers of liberal society, eager for gold and glory, or the bestial god-like führers of Nazi Germany, Soviet heroes were characterized as men and women from humble beginnings who were dedicated to the service of the working class and the Bolshevik dictatorship charged with safeguarding its interests.[50]

The highest tier of this new Soviet heroic pantheon was occupied by Lenin and his "beloved" successor Stalin. While Lenin remained a potent heroic icon, his hero cult was largely eclipsed by the one that sprang up around Stalin during the years of his dictatorship. Unlike Lenin, Stalin openly cultivated an image of himself as a kind of Red Tsar in the mould of Peter the Great or Ivan the Terrible; and he often referred to his lieutenants and others elevated by him to heroic stature as his faithful *bogatyri*. Something of a thug, Stalin was harsh, brutal, contemptuous of human life, and absolutely ruthless in his dealings with enemies real or imagined. At his command countless millions died during the collectivization of the country's agriculture, as well as in the purges of the party in the late 1930s. Not surprisingly, the folk he favored for membership in the USSR's cult of heroes were people like himself—ambitious, daring, disciplined, organized, cruel, and hard like the steel after which he was named.

These characteristics were quite common among the individuals who occupied the second tier of the Soviet heroic pantheon, i.e., the party magnates of Stalin's inner leadership circle. Among these individuals, perhaps the one who best exemplified what it meant to be a heroic leader of the Stalinist era was Lazar Kaganovich. The semi-literate son of a Ukrainian Jewish cobbler, "Iron Lazar" had risen in the Bolshevik Party by dint of hard work, good organizational skills, toughness, and unswerving loyalty to Stalin. As head of the Soviet Union's Commissariat of Transportation and Moscow party boss, Kaganovich earned the nickname "The Locomotive" for his forceful, ruthless, and willful management style. He had a violent temper, frequently carried around a hammer, which he was fond of using on subordinates, and enjoyed a reputation for getting things done. Among his achievements were the brutal suppression of peasant uprisings in the Caucasus and Siberia during the collectivization of Soviet agriculture; the wholesale destruction of Moscow historical landmarks and neighborhoods during the construction of the capital's subway system; and the exploitation of hundreds of thousands of slave laborers in the construction of Russian heavy industry. Indeed, Kaganovich's reputation as a "Bolshevik's Bolshevik" was such that he enjoyed a hero cult approaching Stalin's own.[51]

Among the heroes of the Stalinist period who were not leaders of the Bolshevik Party and state, the ones most highly regarded by both the Soviet leadership and the public-at-large were the country's aviators and Arctic explorers. As John McGannon has noted in his work on Soviet polar exploration from 1932–39, these figures not only exhibited all of the heroic virtues celebrated by Stalin's regime — daring, courage, willfulness, organization, discipline, technical proficiency, and toughness — but they performed extraordinary feats of flight and polar exploration, which advanced science, furthered economic development, and fostered national pride.[52] They also enjoyed a special symbiotic relationship with Stalin, who rewarded their slavish sycophancy — it was customary for heroic pilots and scientists to routinely credit all of their achievements to the example and guidance of the country's glorious leader — with honors, material rewards, hagiographic media coverage, and elevation into the highest ranks of the communist cult of heroes.

Indeed, by the end of the 1930s, quite a few star aviators had been dubbed "Stalin's Falcons" and inducted into the Soviet heroic pantheon.[53] Of these, the one who most epitomized the ideal of the communist hero pilot was Valery Pavlovich Chkalov, the Bolshevik Charles Lindbergh. A brilliant, daring aviator whose flying was characterized by reckless stunts and a complete disregard for his personal safety, Chkalov flew almost the entire width of the USSR without stopping, setting a world record for long distance aviation. He also piloted a non–stop 63 hour flight from Moscow to Vancouver, Washington via the North Pole, for which he was given a hero's welcome in Washington, D.C., New York and Moscow. While he was spontaneous, impetuous, and often rebellious, Chkalov was also a dutiful son of the party declaring that Stalin was the father of all aviators, the man:

> Who teaches us and rears us. We are as dear to his heart as his own children. We Soviet pilots all feel his loving, attentive, fatherly eyes upon us. He is our father.[54]

When Chkalov was killed in a fatal airplane crash in 1938, his affection and loyalty to Stalin was rewarded with a state funeral that enshrined him as one of the greatest heroes of the Soviet state. His body was placed on view in Moscow's Hall of Columns in the Trade Union House — the site of Stalin's laying in state in 1953 — and thousands came to pay their last respects. Afterwards, the party leadership — Stalin, Molotov, Andreev, Voroshilov,

Kaganovich, and Beria—served as Chkalov's pallbearers, interring his remains in the Bolshevik equivalent of Westminster Abbey, the Kremlin Wall.[55]

Another key figure in this period of Soviet Arctic heroism was Otto Shmidt, a noted mathematician, astronomer, geophysicist, and polar explorer who was the head of *Glavsevmorput*, the Commissariat charged with control of all Soviet territory east of the Urals and north of the 62nd parallel, including Russian holdings and interests in and around the Arctic Ocean. A bearded giant of a man who actually looked like a *bogatyr* warrior, Shmidt ran his "Commissariat of Ice" with all the requisite toughness of a Stalinist manager, carving out an empire that encompassed fisheries, gold mines, timber, furs, and not a few concentration camps. He was also an avid, daring and impetuous adventurer who led expeditions into the Arctic. One of these, the *Sibiriakov* voyage of 1932, successfully completed the first single-season crossing of the Northwest Passage. Another, the *Cheliuskin* expedition of 1933–34, almost ended in disaster when its steamship was crushed by icepacks in early February 1934 and sank. Under Shmidt's leadership, however, the 111 members of the crew escaped the sinking ship to an iceberg where they set up camp and managed to survive until their rescue by air in April.

To honor Shmidt and his brave Cheliuskinites, the Bolshevik Party choreographed a hero's welcome that was reminiscent of those accorded by the Greeks to their crown game champions. By train and air, this heroic band and its intrepid leader slowly progressed across Russia to Moscow, receiving the accolades of various cities and towns along the way. In the capital, they were greeted by throngs of admirers and treated to a ticker tape parade down Gorky Street to Red Square where they were greeted in the Kremlin by Stalin, his magnates and other heroes of the Soviet Union. Special honors and benefits were accorded to these individuals—in Shmidt's case admission into the Order of Soviet Heroes—exhibitions and museums featured accounts of their heroism, and their exploits became the stuff of novels, films, and monuments. This heroic jubilee played so well with both the public-at-large and the foreign press that it became the model for all future celebrations of Soviet heroes and their deeds.

Finally, no account of the Stalinist heroic pantheon would be complete without mention of those individuals who were heroized for their labor, i.e., the Stakhanovites. Named after Aleksei Stakhanov, a Donbass coal miner who harvested 102 tons of coal in a single shift in August 1935, rather than the normal quota of 7, Stakhanovism was a movement of norm busters, or as they were more commonly called, "shock workers." Haling from heavy industry and agriculture, these individual men and women challenged production norms and strove to demonstrate that there were "no fortresses Bolsheviks cannot storm." Like the other heroic figures of this time, Stakhanovites attributed their successful "storming" of the heights to the inspiration of Stalin, and he returned the favor by naming them a new Soviet type that was not only strong, daring, resourceful, and tough, but also clean, orderly, thoughtful, and eager for self-improvement. As with its Arctic heroes, the party also decorated these proletarian *Übermenschen* in public ceremonies, paid them hefty cash bonuses, gave them the pick of new apartments, and celebrated their lives and deeds in novels, poems, and films.[56]

Unlike Chkalov, Shmidt, and the Cheliuskinites, however, these worker heroes of Soviet industry and agriculture were largely loathed by their peers. Stakhanovite storming often damaged valuable machinery and wreaked havoc on the efforts of state planners and engineers to rationalize Soviet production. And norm busting also led to the raising of production quotas for every Soviet worker and farmer, a development which only served to worsen what was already an oppressive and marginal existence for most of Russia's populace during the 1930s. Indeed, Stalin's "new types" were so hated that many of them died in mysterious "accidents" and several were actually lynched by their comrades.

This rejection of the Stakhanovites raises the question of just how effective this Stalinist cult of heroes was in mobilizing support for the Bolshevik Party and state, providing Russian society-at-large with a model of "communist" heroic behavior, and cultivating a leadership cadre of efficient, organized, and tough Red *bogatyri*. Addressing this question is difficult — if not impossible — given the fact that survival in Stalin's Russia often meant towing the party line, making public demonstrations of loyalty to Stalin and his factotums, and kowtowing to one's boss. Consequently, it is hard to know what the Soviet public actually thought about their country's official hero cult, as well as whether or not it actually affected anyone's behavior. Did Soviet citizens, for example, flock to Lenin's tomb and cheer on their leadership at rallies in Red Square because they revered these figures, or were they acting out of fear that failure to do so might get them arrested and sent to a camp? Concurrently, was the public's adoration of Chkalov, Shmidt and others like them also a statement of support for the Bolshevik regime, or just an expression of national pride and a thank you for giving folks a break from the tedium of life in the USSR? And finally, were young communists actually striving to become heroic "new men and women," or were they just opportunists saying and doing whatever they felt was necessary in order to get promoted and rewarded?

As with so much else in Soviet history, the response of party members and the public-at-large to Stalin's hero cults was probably shaded by elements of both genuine ideological fervor as well as fear and considerations of self–interest. In an impoverished war torn country largely comprised of peasants raised to revere saints, just tsars, and heroic warriors, it is difficult to imagine that there was not a strong yearning for heroes capable of restoring order, providing security, and pointing the nation in a new direction. Consequently, deifying Lenin, transforming his successor into a Red Tsar, and associating Stalin's magnates with the *bogatyri* probably played well with the Soviet population and helped rally support to the regime.

It is also fair to say that the heroization of record-breaking aviators and intrepid polar explorers was a very savvy piece of Bolshevik public relations work. Aviation and Arctic exploration were associated with the age old dream of human flight, the discovery of virgin lands, economic development, and national defense. Patronizing these activities and honoring their participants allowed Stalin and his associates to share in their glory and bask in the national pride aroused by their successes. And heroizing these individuals also had the added advantage of distracting a weary and impoverished citizenry from the oppressive dreariness of daily life in the USSR.

Whatever its efficacy in mobilizing support for the Bolshevik regime, Stalin's cult of heroes did legitimize hero worship in the Soviet Union and establish the criteria that determined who would be worthy of it. Following the establishment of the Order of the Soviet Hero in 1934, the idea that certain individuals were superior to others and therefore deserving of special honors and privileges became a mainstay of Bolshevik political orthodoxy. And while the Soviet heroic pantheon was officially open to anyone in any line of work, it remained a very exclusive club that admitted only extraordinarily talented people who were perfectly aligned with the party and had shown themselves to be daring, willful, efficient, organized, loyal, self–critical, and hard as steel.

It is impossible to ascertain the degree to which this Communist heroic ideal actually influenced the behavior of people in the Soviet Union. This said, however, there is some fragmentary evidence that a desire to be one of the heroic "new men or women" of the USSR was an important factor in the lives of many of the so-called *vydvizhentsy*, the Communist workers who were promoted to administrative posts during the 20s and 30s to fill the Bolshevik Party's need for skilled and reliable Red cadres in industry, agriculture, and administration. In a fascinating history of diaries and diary writing during the Stalinist period, *Revolution on My Mind*, historian Joachen Hellbeck introduces us to one of these aspiring Soviet *novi homines*, an ambitious mining engineer by the name of Leonid Potemkin.

Born into a peasant family of modest means in 1914, Potemkin left home in 1931 to take part in the heavy industrialization campaigns going on in eastern Russia at this time. He was accepted for study at the Ural Mining Institute in Sverdlovsk in 1933, graduated with honors in 1939, and soon thereafter was made the head of the Balkhash copper works following the purge of its leading personnel during the *Yezhovchina* (the Great Purge of 1937–38). When Germany invaded the USSR in 1941, Potemkin joined the Communist Party and spent the war years on various exploratory missions in the Caucasus. After the war, he rose rapidly in the ranks of the party and state; laying the foundations of a major industrial city in the northern Pechenga region of the Soviet Union; becoming a party secretary of the Ministry of Non-Ferrous Metallurgy in 1955; rising to party secretary of Moscow's Lenin District in 1956; and finally being appointed deputy minister of geology of the Russian Republic in 1965.[57]

Potemkin's life and career trajectory was a typical one for the *vydvizhentsy*. What distinguishes him from his cohort, however, is the fact that he left extensive diaries in which he reflected on his life, dreams, ambitions, and activities. In these writings, he made it quite clear that he very much wanted to be a heroic "new man" of the Soviet Union and towards that end he worked to develop such personality traits as unwavering Marxist convictions, iron willpower, inner concentration, decisiveness, simplicity of manner, and a willingness to act. The methods that he used to achieve this reconstruction of himself included constant study, applying techniques of labor rationalization to his work and rest cycles, daily gymnastics, exercising bodily self–control, and acquiring cultural refinement (among other things, he was the organizer of a class on ballroom dancing among his classmates in 1934). Potemkin was also an avid reader of the writings of various authors deeply influenced by Nietzschean thought, e.g., Maxim Gorky, Anatoly Lunacharsky, Nikolai Ostrovsky, Jack London, and Upton Sinclair, and like these writers he too subscribed to the view that existence was a state of struggle and that society must bend its energies towards the creation of a race of supermen that would go beyond man as he currently existed. He also believed Bolshevism offered the only way of achieving this end and was consequently in complete sympathy with the violence the Stalinist regime unleashed against those it deemed enemies of the revolution.[58]

Some 150,000 *vydvizhentsy* workers and Communists were nurtured in the same heroic culture as Leonid Potemkin during the late 20s and 30s, and these individuals were the core of the Stalinist elite after the Great Purge of 1937–8. As Sheila Fitzpatrick notes, they:

> Were young men (and a much smaller number of women) with a sense of purpose and, in the Calvinist meaning of the term, election. They were the chosen builders of socialism, sons of the working class whom the Revolution had rewarded and trusted with great responsibilities....Their personal commitment was not so much to the fighting party of the Civil War as to the industrializing party which, under Comrade Stalin's leadership, had broken with Russia's historic backwardness and accomplished its first Five-Year Plan.[59]

Among this Soviet elect were numbered all of the post–Stalin leaders of the USSR prior to the ascension of Gorbachev in 1985, i.e., Nikita Khrushchev, Leonid Brezhnev, Aleksei Kosygin, Yuri Andropov, and Konstantin Chernenko. All of these individuals regarded themselves as heroes of the Soviet Union (indeed, Brezhnev awarded himself the Order of the Soviet Hero four times, more than any other holder of the honor in Soviet history), and they behaved in a fashion suitable to individuals who were counted members of the Communist heroic pantheon. Though not in the same league as a Lenin or Stalin, they were nonetheless extraordinarily adept politicians who were efficient, organized, and absolutely ruthless in the exercise of power. For three decades, they steadfastly defended the house their hero — Comrade Stalin — had built; transforming the Soviet Union into a superpower, silencing all dissent at home; and brutally crushing the many risings against their rule in the "fraternal socialist republics" of eastern Europe. Unfortunately for these men, nearly a century of war, mass murder, and tyranny had dispelled the glamour of heroic vitalism and its "new men" on both the right and left. Indeed, by the time the USSR collapsed in 1991, the Communist hero cults of these men and their predecessors had become little more than the stuff of empty "necro-rituals."

There Will Be Blood: Heroic Vitalism and Its Offspring

As this chapter was being written, the P. T. Anderson film *There Will Be Blood* opened in theaters across the United States. Loosely based on Upton Sinclair's muckraking novel, *Oil!*, an exposé of the U.S. petroleum industry during the first decades of the 20th century, it relates the story of a self–made oilman by the name of Daniel Plainview. The film follows Plainview's life in the hard scrabble oil fields of Texas and Southern California at the turn-of-the-nineteenth century, a Hobbesian realm of unceasing and merciless struggles with nature and other men. As Plainview's story unfolds, we discover that he is well-suited to this world because he is both a competitive man wishing "no one else to succeed," and a loner who, as his name suggests, views existence plainly through eyes unblinkered by family ties, romantic sentiment, morality, or religion. Anderson's protagonist is also smart, tough and completely ruthless, and over the course of the movie we watch him war with and win out against the earth, corporate oil, con artists, ignorant resentful farmers, and a Christian "false prophet." These victories are not without cost, however, and at the end of the film we find Plainview an isolated half mad murderer covered in blood gnawing on a piece of meat like some great beast of prey.

Mention is made of this film because it could easily serve as a celluloid parable of the heroic vitalist ideology examined in the preceding pages. The incessant and cruel struggles for survival and mastery that run throughout *There Will Be Blood* correspond perfectly with the vitalist view of existence as a godless, nasty, and often brutish war of "every man against every man." The character traits of Anderson's protagonist — his "will to power;" refusal to live by any rules or morals save his own; strong instincts; hardness; misanthropy; and willingness to take any steps necessary to achieve his ends — are exactly those the vitalists celebrated in the heroic figures they worshipped. The ruthless empire building that is Plainview's *raison d'être* is also in keeping with Carlyle and Nietzsche's idea that heroes are history's "robbers and conquerors," inventors, men of industry, and destroyers of iniquity. And the tragic fate of Plainview at the end of the film could easily serve as a kind of vitalist coda in which hero worshippers are reminded that where one finds heroic greatness, there too will one find isolation, madness, and blood.

Whether or not P. T. Anderson set out to produce a movie about a turn-of-the-century American *Übermensch* is beyond the ken of this author. More likely, the striking parallels between his film and the tenets of heroic vitalism are due to the fact that his movie's storyline is based on the novel of an early twentieth century American writer who was both an active socialist and an aficionado of Nietzschean ideas. Like Nietzsche, Upton Sinclair viewed the liberal capitalist societies of the West as jungles in which the masses were preyed upon by rapacious beasts of prey (aka "robber barons") and Christian fakirs. He was also critical of bourgeois democracy, believed in the necessity of revolution, was enamored with heroes (particularly of the left variety), and dreamed of a society dedicated to the unleashing of every individual's heroic potential. Indeed, Sinclair could easily be counted among the hero worshippers examined in this chapter.

That fact is important to remember because aside from helping to clarify the vitalist trajectories in Anderson's movie, Sinclair also serves to remind us of the prominent role litterateurs played in the history of heroic vitalism. Carlyle, Nietzsche, Langbehn, Shaw, London, and the others we have grouped together in this cult of hero worship, were not formal philosophers, economists, or full-time politicos (though some of them, including Sinclair, periodically engaged in serious political activity). Instead, these individuals were very much belletrists with wide ranging interests that they gave expression to in novels, plays, poems, aphorisms, and essays. And like a great many other writers in the West's republic of letters, it should also be noted that these hero worshipping litterateurs tended to be lonely misanthropes with large egos, who were difficult to get along with, often mentally unstable, and usually at odds with their societies.

Mention is made of the literary bent and disagreeable natures of these vitalist scriveners because they tended to see the problems of their times as essentially a classical tale of conflict between a group of extraordinary protagonists — much like themselves — and an antagonistic assortment of monstrous collectivities bent on destroying the entire idea of the individual personality. Among the villains in this story were all of those things in urban industrial society heroic vitalists hated — the masses, political parties and movements, organized religions, capitalist cartels, and various "inferior" races, most notably the Jews. While the principal antagonists in this drama varied depending on the particular prejudices of the vitalist-in-question, the hero of the piece was always the same; a Homeric superman unconstrained by morality, indifferent to suffering, hard and cruel towards his enemies, and intent only on the acquisition of power and glory. As in a fairy-tale, this heroic figure — often identified as a latter-day knight — was expected to appear in a time of need, clean house, set matters aright, and ride off into the sunset. Also like a folktale, the "happily ever after" part of the story was seldom addressed.

This vitalist plotline was simple, seemingly apparent — the industrial West was full of lonely crowds, warring mass movements, and capitalist combines that appeared directly contrary to any notion of individuality — and offered a solution that resonated well with populations inculcated from birth with myths, legends, romances, and histories celebrating the deeds of extraordinary individuals appearing in dark times and leading their peoples to salvation. Of course, what makes for the stuff of a ripping good yarn is not necessarily an appropriate heuristic for industrial societies grappling with widespread poverty and misery, class conflict, and new technologies and markets. Individuals, no matter how talented and brilliant, could not address these challenges by themselves (or even in the company of similarly gifted "wonder kids"), and no amount of "willfulness" could resolve all of the problems set in motion by the industrial and political revolutions of the 18th and 19th centuries. Indeed, tackling the various woes of the West's emerging mass societies would require the very kinds of social collaboration, rational planning, laws, bureaucracy, and selflessness vitalist heroes were pledged to destroy.

All of this became readily apparent when self–styled heroic leaders assumed power in various European countries in the decades following the First World War. Acquiring state control required a Mussolini, Hitler, Lenin, or Stalin to build and maintain mass political movements in which individuals — heroic or otherwise — were organized, regimented, and exploited to realize the aims of bosses ostensibly acting at the behest of providence, destiny or history. Addressing the ills of unemployment, poverty, and ignorance necessitated increased industrialization, urbanization, and capital development rather than a return to the medieval past or some anarcho-syndicalist communal future. And in the absence of Judeo-Christian morality, rule by law, parliamentary oversight, and rational bureaucratic procedures, the direction of these totalitarian "command" states fell to heroic cadres that were little more than collections of sycophantic, sadistic, savage, and supremely selfish secret policemen.

One thing the vitalist ideology of hero worship did get right, however, was the prediction that there would be blood — lots of it — accompanying any effort to usher in a new heroic age. Spurred on by leaders and ideologies that believed the end of history was in sight, SS black angels and Communist "new men" raped, pillaged, and murdered with abandon, confident they were preparing fields and sowing seeds guaranteed to cultivate a higher more elevated humanity. Instead, the dragon's teeth these individuals sowed helped secure the triumph of the enlightened, liberal and capitalist mass societies they despised; and besmirched forever the idea of the hero they so fervently worshipped. The future would belong to the "anti–hero" and it is to this iteration of the Western heroic ideal that we will now turn.

10

Rogues, Reprobates, Outcasts, and Oddballs
The Anti-Hero

"Human grandeur," said Pangloss, "is very dangerous, if we believe the testimonies of almost all philosophers; for we find Eglon, King of Moab, was assassinated by Aod; Absalom was hanged by the hair of his head, and run through with three darts; King Nadab, son of Jeroboam, was slain by Baaza; King Ela by Zimri; Okosias by Jehu; Athaliah by Jehoiada; the Kings Jehooiakim, Jeconiah, and Zedekiah, were led into captivity: I need not tell you what was the fate of Croesus, Astyages, Darius, Dionysius of Syracuse, Pyrrhus, Perseus, Hannibal, Jugurtha, Ariovistus, Caesar, Pompey, Nero, Otho, Vitellius, Domitian, Richard II of England, Edward II, Henry VI, Richard III, Mary Stuart, Charles I, the three Henrys of France, and the Emperor Henry IV.
"Neither need you tell me," said Candide, "that we must take care of our garden."

— Voltaire: *Candide*

There's no question of heroism in all this. It's a matter of common decency.... Heroism and sanctity don't really appeal to me.... What interests me is being a man.

— Albert Camus: *The Plague*

Where have you gone, Joe DiMaggio?
A nation turns its lonely eyes to you (Woo woo woo).
What's that you say, Mrs. Robinson?
"Joltin' Joe has left and gone away" (Hey hey hey, hey hey hey).

— Simon and Garfunkel: *Mrs. Robinson*

The idea for this book began in 2004 as a freshman history seminar on the idea of heroism from Homer to the present. Beginning with the first meeting of this class — and in every subsequent iteration of the course — I have asked my students to identify someone they regard as a hero and to explain the reasons behind their choice. Over the years, I have repeatedly been struck by the propensity of those enrolled in my seminar to name as their personal heroes either family members (usually mothers, grandparents, and older siblings) or imaginary comic book characters. In the case of those who selected relatives, a combination of admirable traits — industriousness, dedication, loyalty — and a willingness to lend a sympathetic ear and/or a helping hand were most often cited as grounds for elevating a family member to heroic status. Those who opted for comic book characters on the other hand, tended to single out outcasts, loners, and outlaws in the vein of Marvel Comics' X-Men and Spiderman, or DC's Batman. The reasons most often given for selecting these fictional protagonists were their "awesome" powers and resources, their unblinkered, realistic view of existence, and their willingness to try "to do the right thing" despite doubts about the efficacy of their actions.

To be sure, there have also been students — usually no more than five — who named as their heroes individuals who were neither related to them nor conceived of by the writers, artists, and inkers of comicdom's many talented bullpen gangs. Two or three of these folks will select conventional historical figures such as Gandhi or Martin Luther King. A devout Christian in the class will invariably use this exercise as an opportunity to volunteer that Jesus is their personal savior. And one, maybe two, students will insist that they neither have a hero nor need one. Surprisingly, practically no one in my seminars singles out a contemporary public figure — politician, entrepreneur, artist, entertainer, or athlete — as a heroic figure. On the rare occasion that such a person is named, it is usually Oprah.

I relate this anecdote about my seminars because my students' tendency to heroize nurturing familial figures and fictional social outcasts reflects a distinctively modern way of thinking about heroes and heroism that has gained increasing currency in the West since World War II. Indeed, over the last sixty years, pop psychology, New Age spirituality, self-improvement fads, and the popularization of the late Joseph Campbell's *The Hero of A Thousand Faces* have all worked together to enshrine the notion that every human being who embarks on life's journey and meets its challenges is heroic. Concurrently, a great many postwar novels, plays, films, mysteries, science fiction space operas, and superhero comic books have heroized protagonists who are self-conflicted loners — in some cases out-in-out losers — alienated from family and society, unlucky at love, and struggling to survive in a world that often compels them to make amoral or even immoral choices.

This idea of the hero as either an "everyman" or a disaffected outsider represents a radical reformulation of what it has meant to be heroic. While the Western heroic pantheon has admitted into its membership a more representative cross-section of humanity over the last three millennia, and redefined heroism to encompass more diverse kinds of human activity — warfare, martyrdom, athletic prowess, great charity, intellectual and artistic exploration, revolutionary struggle, and even mass murder — the criteria for membership have remained largely the same. Simply put heroes:

- Are not ordinary;
- Do things that most people either cannot or will not do;
- Dedicate their lives to some abstract ideal — glory, god, excellence, beauty, the end of history;
- Defend the status quo or create a new one;
- Are accorded in life special honors, privileges, and wealth by their peers and inferiors; and
- Enjoy a measure of immortality after death through cults, monuments, stories, poems, and songs.

While it is certainly true that the ordinary people, who raise families, work hard, pay their taxes, and help out their neighbors are admirable, and the various non-conformists, drifters, grifters, and outlaws celebrated in post-war literature and film often force us to question our assumptions and illusions about life, by the criteria outlined above, these folks are certainly not heroes. Rather, they are representatives of a countervailing current in the history of heroism that views the traditional hero as responsible for much of the human misery in the world, and embraces the idea that mundane inglorious acts like tending your garden, keeping your head down, and trying to stay alive are those that should be celebrated and commemorated. Instead of the often flawed and problematic heroic figures who have sailed uncharted seas, murdered, maimed, and pillaged foreign peoples, and boasted and bragged their way into history from Homer to the present, the proponents of "anti-heroism" posit an unheroic hero who is:

- Decidedly, even proudly, ordinary in lifestyle, habits, and ambitions;
- Focused on survival and the banal details of day-to-day life;
- Wary of and skeptical about lofty ideals and ethereal abstractions;
- Critical of the status quo, though disinclined to rebel openly against it;
- Largely invisible in life; and
- Unremarked upon in death save by immediate family, friends, and colleagues.

This anti-heroic impulse emerges in the modern era of Western history and is a direct response to the near constant tumult, warfare, economic dislocation, and ideological fanaticism that has accompanied the religious reformations, nation building, and scientific, industrial and political revolutions of this period. For the overwhelming majority of people living during this time, survival, often against daunting odds, has been the central focus of existence, and those figures lauded as heroic by church and state — empire building monarchs, warriors, religious firebrands, national liberators, and titans of industry — are the very individuals whose actions have made life a terribly difficult affair. As the rubric applied to them suggests, anti-heroes are a reaction against the oppression, cruelty, and inequity of the modern world and the "great men" who have made it possible. And these figures have been increasingly embraced by populations weary of "interesting times," hungry for normalcy, and disillusioned with extraordinary deeds and discoveries that only seem to bring us closer to Armageddon.

As with the various heroic types examined in this work, these anti-heroes are a varied lot. During the religious wars and the rise of the European state system in the 16th, 17th and 18th centuries, the anti-hero often took the guise of the rogue in picaresque literature or the sly and cunning trickster celebrated in popular folklore. Gifted with good luck, and adept at deceit and petty theft, these figures expose the foibles and hypocrisies of their betters, carve out a comfortable niche for themselves in society, keep their heads down, and end life with a full belly and no regrets. The rise of the various "isms" of the 19th century, and the totalitarian regimes, two world wars, "cold" conflicts, concentration camps, and mass murder programs of the 20th, bring to the fore an anti-hero who is first and foremost a survivor. Usually the targets of ideologies intent on consigning them to oblivion solely because of their ethnicity, race, or class, these individuals take whatever steps are necessary to just stay alive and, when and where possible, maintain some modicum of human dignity. Finally, in the success and celebrity driven mass societies of the late 20th and early 21st centuries, the anti-hero is increasingly either a nonconformist "rebel without a cause," or an everyday "slacker" at odds with conventional society and intent on living life completely on his or her own terms. An assorted collection of oddballs and outcasts, these folks are the bohemians, beatniks, hipsters, and hopheads who view existence as meaningless — even absurd — and seek personal, mundane reasons to go on living rather than the abstractions and grandiose projects of history's more traditional heroic figures.

The following pages attempt to arrive at an understanding of this modern tradition of anti-heroism through a close analysis of its principal "unheroic" types, i.e., the knave of early modern picaresque literature and peasant folklore, the survivor of the 20th century's gulags and death camps, and the disaffected non-conformist of the post–World War II era. Specifically, this chapter focuses on the historical conditions out of which these varied anti-heroes emerged with an eye aimed at identifying both their common characteristics and the reasons for the widespread following they have enjoyed in the West over the last four centuries. It concludes with some remarks as to what this anti-heroism may portend for the future of the Western heroic ideal.

Howling with the Wolves: Rogues and Reprobates

As the preceding chapters make clear, heroes are often guilty of unethical and even criminal conduct. Homer's Odysseus delights in dissimulation, trickery and lies, and he is also guilty of rape, theft, and murder during the two decades he is away from Ithaca. King David, the champion of Israel and the beloved of Yahweh, does a stint as a bandit, works as a hired hand for his people's Philistine enemies, and thinks nothing of murdering men whose women he covets. Richard the Lionheart and his fellow knights pledge themselves to defend the church, widows, orphans, and the weak, and then proceed to pillage, sexually abuse, and slaughter defenseless men, women and children in Christian and non–Christian communities alike. Intrepid explorers like Christopher Columbus and Hernando Cortes sail off into *terra incognita*, discover unknown peoples, and enslave them. Brilliant scientists — Fritz Haber, Edward Teller, Andrei Sakharov — do groundbreaking work in the physical sciences and then help the military establishments of their countries turn their discoveries into weapons of mass destruction. And heroic revolutionaries from Robespierre to Stalin rob banks, murder political opponents, commit acts of terror, and eliminate whole populations.

The chroniclers and apologists of these heroes justify such moral and legal transgressions in various ways. Homer essentially presents the rapacious bloodthirsty banditry of his protagonists as conduct befitting semi-divine warriors seeking undying glory in a warlike age of iron. The authors of the Hebrew Testament make it quite clear that though the heroes of Israel enjoy the favor of their god, they are still terribly flawed human beings liable to lapses in moral judgment (for which Jehovah in his infinite mercy is willing to forgive them). Troubadours, heralds, and the Catholic hierarchy excuse the injuries Christian knights inflict on the innocent as the residual, albeit regrettable, casualties of "just" wars and holy crusades. Governments and their trading companies honor rather than punish the depredations of their explorers, especially when the new lands they discover offer the prospect of gold and glory. And visionary scientists, artists, and political leaders are often exempted from moral conventions, especially if their discoveries, insights and actions lead to a deeper understanding of the world, moving works of art, and more just societies.

Whatever the nature of the wrongdoing or the apologias for it, heroes are neither remembered nor honored because of their misdeeds. This is not the case, however, with the anti-heroic picaro, or "rogue," who makes his first appearance in *Lazarillo de Tormes*, a Spanish novel published anonymously in 1554. In this story, the title character, a Salamanca town crier named Lazaro, relates his struggle to survive in an impoverished country where the starving many are forced to serve a selfish and hypocritical elite of aristocrats and churchmen. Leading an itinerant existence, Lazaro serves a number of different masters — beggar, priest, squire, friar, pardoner, chaplain, and bailiff — whom he robs with varying degrees of success. Along the way, he exposes the foibles, follies, mummeries, and cruelties of his betters, enters into a marriage of convenience with the mistress of a churchman, and ends his life with a small house, a regular measure of grain, meat on the high holydays, some occasional fine loaves of bread, and the priest's hand-me-down socks.

Not surprisingly, *Lazarillo de Tormes* was not well received by either the Spanish crown or the Catholic Inquisition, both of which banned the book in the areas under their control. Despite these bans, however, the novel was translated into French, English, Dutch, German, and Italian editions, became something of an early modern best seller, and inspired a host of imitators. Among the more famous knockoffs of the book were *Simplicius Simplicissimus* by H. J. C. von Grimmelshausen (1669), a story about a freebooting German philanderer, thief and killer during the Thirty Years War; Alain-René Lesage's *Gil Blas* (1715), a tale of a low born French lackey and brigand who ultimately finds favor with his king and ends life in a castle; Daniel Defoe's *Moll Flanders* (1722), a novel relating the life of an orphaned, illegitimate woman who seeks security by trading sexual favors and engaging in petty theft; Tobias Smollett's *The Adventures of Roderick Random* (1748), an account of an impoverished nobleman compelled to live the life of a vagabond, seaman, and imposter; and Henry Fielding's *The History of Tom Jones* (1749), a recounting of the misadventures of a lusty young man who spends most of his life on the road in the company of various reprobates.

While these picaresque novels differ in some details and points of emphasis, they share a number of common characteristics. Key among these are protagonists who are largely destitute and, more often than not, commoners. Even in those stories where the picaroon can claim noble parentage on at least one side of the sheets, blue blood is no guarantee of financial security. Bereft of pedigree and property, these individuals inhabit a cold, unsympathetic, cruel world where they are compelled to become itinerant laborers, servants, thieves, whores, gamblers, soldiers of fortune, and imposters in order to survive. And these varied life experiences reveal to them that churchmen are often false, public officials are usually corrupt, bourgeois businessmen are greedy hypocrites, aristocrats are fools, kings are largely unconscious of their subjects' sufferings, and God is seemingly indifferent to the needs of those created in his own image and likeness. Rather than take up arms against such a patently imperfect and unjust state of affairs, however, picaros accept society as it is, reject the notion that heaven can be realized on earth, take advantage of the opportunities that come their way, and usually end their lives reasonably well fed, clothed, and housed.[1]

One also finds these kinds of picaresque protagonists and plotlines in the popular folklore of the early modern period. In the original unexpurgated versions of the Mother Goose rhymes, Grimm's *Kinder und Hausmärchen*, and other collections of peasant folk stories, audiences are treated to tales of low born tricksters — Tom Thumb, Puss 'n Boots, Petit Jean, and, in some versions, Little Red Riding Hood (sans the hood) — struggling to make their way in a world where the overwhelming majority of people are poor, hungry, over-worked, and subject to the depredations of wild animals, thieves, and freebooters. Lacking families, friends, and finances, these characters use lies, cunning ruses, theft, and sometimes murder to best the nasty neighbors, wicked step-parents, cruel tyrants, and bloodthirsty monsters that try to exploit and/or kill them during the course of their lives. As with their picaresque brethren, these fairy tale scoundrels are also singularly unconcerned with chang-ing the world that oppresses them, opting instead to finagle their way into a warm bed under a dry roof with a full larder.[2]

The miscreants celebrated in these early modern folktales and novels are a decidedly different lot from the more conventional heroes of Western myth, history, and religious hagiography. Whereas most of the heroic figures we have examined up to this point com-mand considerable resources, are gifted with extraordinary abilities, and serve some abstract ideal, these fictional rogues are low born, impoverished, bereft of any singular talent or skill save cunning, and have no purpose in life except to survive by "hook or crook." Indeed, the sole accomplishment of these figures is that in a cruel world ruled by vicious predators they have learned to "howl with the wolves,"[3] and in the process of doing so secured a "piece of the action" for themselves.

Despite the fact that the protagonists of these picaresque novels and fairy tales are essen-tially common criminals, they were much loved during the early modern period. Under-standing why this was so requires us to consider briefly what life was like for the people who followed the misadventures of these rascals during the centuries between the Protes-tant Reformation and the French Revolution. By all accounts, for most of these folks, this era was not the best of times to be alive, particularly if you were low born and impecu-nious. Hunger was a constant of daily existence and starvation a very real possibility. Life expectancy was short, and death from malnutrition, illness and plague not uncommon. Infanticide was also widely practiced, child labor was the rule, and children from one mar-riage often found themselves exploited, abused, and turned out by the husband or wife of a different union. Young men were often forced to leave their homes and seek their fortune on the open road, an experience that frequently led them to a life of imposture and brig-andry followed by deportation, galley slavery, or a quick death on the gallows. Women could either eke out a living as prostitutes or give themselves over to the backbreaking labor and endless childbearing of an arranged and usually loveless marriage. And religious tur-moil and dynastic warfare were a seemingly permanent part of the European landscape, bringing in their wake confessional riots, anti-semitic pogroms, witch hunts, mass killings, seizures of crops and livestock, forced conscription, famine, and disease.[4]

Given these conditions, it is not surprising that people during the early modern period were fond of the picaroons and tricksters of fiction and folklore. Like their audiences, these rascals too suffered from chronic hunger, harsh childhoods, itinerancy, sexual exploitation, and war. Their desperate struggle to survive and find a sinecure requiring little or no work was also the *raison d'être* of most of the folks following their stories. And the mendacity, deceit, pretense, and varying degrees of petty criminality these characters engage in to stay alive and secure a comfortable living for themselves, were also actions frequently employed by impoverished people at this time to defend themselves against the predations of neighbors, nobles, and various other kinds of secular and ecclesiastical nabobs.

Aside from these experiential affinities, early modern audiences were also drawn to the narratives of these fictional scoundrels because they were useful survival guides. As historian Robert Darnton notes in his own work on peasant folklore, the experiences of the rogues in these stories:

> Erect warning signs around the seeking of fortune: "Danger!" "Road out!" "Go slow!" "Stop!" ... [And] they demonstrate that laudable as it may be to share your bread with beggars, you cannot trust everyone you meet along the road. Some strangers may turn into princes and good fairies; but others may be wolves and witches, and there is no sure way to tell them apart.[5]

Nor do these picaroons merely warn their audiences about the pitfalls awaiting them in life. They also offer their counterparts in the real world strategies of cunning and tricksterism to cope with enemies who are bigger, stronger, richer, and more powerful.

By comparison, the stories of more conventional heroes offered little that was familiar, edifying, or particularly helpful to a majority of people living at this time. While righteous knights in shining armor, just kings, and miracle working saints remained much loved and highly popular figures, they were neither commonplace nor easy to emulate. Indeed, the only people with the time, wherewithal, or inclination to actually follow in the footsteps of these heroic types were the very churchmen, absolute monarchs, and professional warriors whose policies of religious purification and imperial aggrandizement were responsible for so much of the widespread misery of the early modern era.

Confronted with a reality in which heroes were either the stuff of fantasies or a bunch of murderous megalomaniacs, common folk in the first centuries of the modern period embraced figures of fiction who were anti-heroic everymen like themselves. These characters were fixated on survival rather than glory or God. They lacked all resources save their wits. And they were not above committing immoral acts and capital crimes to fill their bellies and defend themselves against the depredations of their social superiors. They were, in short, heroic types perfectly suited to an age where most people saw themselves as underdogs in a game of life where hypocrisy was rampant and virtuous behavior was no guarantee of success.

The political and economic upheavals that ushered in the modern period did little to dispel the allure of these fictional anti-heroes. On the contrary, the French Revolution, the dramatic breakthroughs in science and industry during the 18th and 19th centuries, and the rise of the various "isms" that followed in the wake of these events, brought untold misery to countless millions of people around the globe. And, as in the early modern era, many novelists highlighted the various ills of this time by recounting the stories of picaresque-like protagonists with whom readers could easily identify. William Makepeace Thackeray's Becky Sharp, Mark Twain's Tom Sawyer and Huck Finn, Rudyard Kipling's Kim, Thomas Berger's Jack Crabb, and George MacDonald Fraser's Harry Flashman, are but a few of the literary scoundrels and drifters whose misdeeds and misadventures were used by their creators to expose the moral hypocrisy of society's middle and upper classes, the sufferings of the poor, the horrors of slavery, and the monumental ineptitude and callous indifference to human life of so many of the age's "great men."

Nor were all of these unheroic knaves imaginary. Westerners in the modern era have also shown an inordinate fondness for actual outlaws whose sole motivation for wrongdoing was greed and whose only claim to fame was success in satisfying their avarice. Included in this wing of the anti-heroic pantheon are such notable criminals as 18th century highwayman John "Sixteen String Jack" Rand; William Pierce, the mastermind of the great gold heist of 1855; Depression era bank robbers Bonny and Clyde; and forger, trickster and imposter Frank Abignale, Jr. Despite the fact that these individuals acted out of selfishness, and never shared their ill-gotten gains with anyone save themselves, they have all been admired as latter-day Robin Hoods by a public that continues to feel itself victimized by big money and big government.

Perhaps nothing illustrates this bandit worship better than the affection many residents of rural Washington State continue to feel towards air highwayman D. B. Cooper. In November 1971, Cooper successfully hijacked a Boeing 727 jet, ransomed it for $200,000, and parachuted over Clark County, Washington never to be seen again. As a journalist reporting on this story noted:

> The guy pulled a daring stunt, hurt no one and took the government for a couple of hundred thousand dollars. [Quipped a local resident of the area into which Cooper parachuted:] "Around here, we got a name for someone like that. Hero. And you're invited to the next party."[6]

In the end, it is this sense of familiarity, this idea that one could socialize, or "party" with these reprobates — real or fictitious — that makes them such popular and enduring figures in the history of Western heroism. Their struggle to survive and get ahead in a world dominated by wealthy and powerful elites is an experience with which most can identify. Similarly, their roguery rings true to any person who has ever felt it necessary to feign ignorance, pretend competence, be less than forthcoming about taxes, or refrain from telling the whole truth. Most importantly, their success in using their native intelligence to best their betters and secure a room of their own affirms the idea that there is indeed something remarkable, something heroic about the ongoing efforts of ordinary folk to just stay alive. In the pages that follow, we will see just how extraordinary that struggle can actually be.

Ordinary People in Extreme Situations: The Survivor

Scoundrels may not fit the mould of the conventional hero, but they do exhibit characteristics that make them logical candidates for inclusion in the heroic pantheon of the West. Though everymen, the path they opt to follow in life is not one widely chosen by their peers; and while journeying down this less traveled road, they often display a native intelligence and a gift for dishonesty and dissimulation worthy of an Odysseus. Concurrently, while they are principally focused on survival and fearful of death, these individuals are also capable of bold actions that often land them in jail or bring them perilously close to the gibbet. And like many of the other heroes examined up to this point, their stories of misrule and misadventure remain popular staples of the Western canon (albeit often in a considerably sanitized format).

Such parallels are completely absent in the case of the anti-heroes treated in this section. For the survivors of the 20th century's gulags, ghettos and death camps there was only one path to follow and it was usually traveled in cattle cars or on forced marches. At the end of this journey were houses of pain and death that offered their inmates few opportunities for cleverness, dissembling or acts of boldness. And the stories of those fortunate enough to escape from these hell holes were of such a horrific nature that few wanted to hear them, and most, including their narrators, just wanted to forget that such experiences had been possible.

Who were these survivors and how was it that they found themselves in such extreme situations? For the most part, they were individuals who were unfortunate enough to be counted among the imaginary demons and dragons of the heroic vitalists treated in the preceding chapter. In the case of the Nazis, they haled from the peoples Hitler and his SS regarded as racial enemies — primarily Jews, but also considerable numbers of Poles, Russians, Sinti Roma, and German homosexuals. On the Soviet end of the vitalist spectrum, they were among the political opponents, old Bolsheviks, dissident intellectuals, Ukrainians, Balts, Chechens, Tatars, Volga Germans, and Eastern Europeans who Stalin and his Red *bogatyri* labeled counterrevolutionaries and class enemies.

Whether they were bugbears of the Nazis or the Communists, these folks were for the most part ordinary men, women and children from every walk of life who were guiltless of any crime save belonging to a group regarded as an "other" inimical to Hitler's thousand year Reich or Stalin's classless paradise. As such, they were demonized and dehumanized in party pronouncements, press releases, and popular propaganda; stripped of legal rights, property and occupational mobility; concentrated and imprisoned in jails, transit camps and ghettoes; and finally transported to a special archipelago of forced labor and extermination centers where they were either worked to death or simply murdered outright.

Once caught up in this mechanism of murder, these individuals found themselves quite literally transformed into everymen. Distinctions based on nationality, class, occupation, education, and religious confession were whittled away in the process by which people were first transformed into enemies of the state, and then herded like cattle into the various camps where they were expected to suffer and die. Arrival in these places of incarceration was accompanied by additional assaults on individual identity, which included the confiscation of personal property, separation from family members, the replacement of one's name with a number, the issuance of standard prison garb, and the assignment to mass barracks and work details where one's background and skills level were often irrelevant. Malnutrition, chronic illness, lack of hygiene, filth, and infestation by various vermin further eroded differences between inmates and reduced all to the status of what one survivor described as "putrefying corpses moving on two legs."[7]

As in the world of the early modern rogue, the principal, indeed the only concern of these hapless souls, was to survive. Unlike the picaroon, however, the survival options that were open to the inhabitants of this "gulag archipelago" were extremely limited. Barbed wire and armed guards prevented one from escaping to the open road, dissimulation was impossible, and inmates exercised little, if any, control over the work they were assigned to do.

Heroics were also of little use to the individuals struggling to survive in these places of incarceration and death. No matter how brave or bold an inmate might be, any effort at open resistance or rebellion was immediately met with overwhelming force and, if the would-be hero was lucky, a swift demise. Concurrently, a willingness to embrace death rather than succumb to the demands of one's captors — a longstanding hallmark of the West's heroic warriors, martyrs, and saints — was essentially pointless in an environment where the captive was expected to die anyway.

To be sure, there were more than a few old-style heroes among the many people who found themselves ensnared in the Nazi and Soviet apparatus of terror. Mordechai Anielewicz, a young Polish Zionist, set up an underground newspaper and a Jewish Combat Organization (the *Zydowska Organizacja Bojowa,* or ZOB for short) in the Warsaw Ghetto. When the Germans began transporting the Ghetto's population to the Treblinka death camp, Anielewicz led his ZOB in a four month long uprising (January 18–May 16, 1943) that momentarily stopped the murder operation and pinned down some 2000 German troops. Maxmilian Kolbe, a Franciscan priest imprisoned in Auschwitz for aiding Jews and the Polish underground, volunteered his life in place of a condemned inmate with a family, was starved and injected with phenol, and later declared a martyr and saint by John Paul II. In 1936, hundreds of Trotskyites, Anarchists and other political opponents of Stalin staged a hunger strike in the Soviet concentration camp at Vorkuta that lasted 132 days. And in the Russian logging camp of Ust-Usa, a former Gulag inmate, Mark Retyunin, planned, organized, and executed a mass breakout of 100 inmates in January 1942.[8]

Admirable as these actions were, however, they were essentially suicidal acts that changed nothing, and in many cases only made what was already an intolerable situation even worse. Anielewicz's rebellion, for example, resulted in the leveling of the Warsaw Ghetto by SS and German soldiers armed with tanks and flame throwers. While this offensive cost the Germans sixteen dead and eighty-five wounded, thousands of Jews were burned alive, asphyxiated by smoke inhalation, or buried in the debris. The 56,000 ghetto inhabitants who survived the Nazi assault were subsequently shipped to various labor camps and death centers in Poland. Concurrently, while Father Kolbe's self-sacrifice was certainly noble and actually did save the life of another human being, it did nothing to hinder the mass murder operations of Auschwitz. As for the abovementioned Soviet rebels, the hunger strikers of '36 were liquidated in the *Yezhovchina* of 1937, and their counterparts in Ust-Usa were all tracked down and executed within days of their breakout in 1942. Indeed, the rising at Ust-Usa sparked a series of investigations into counter-revolutionary activities in the Soviet Gulag, investigations that resulted in thousands more prisoners being tortured and killed.

In the end, most of the people who survived the German and Soviet concentration camps were unheroic individuals who desperately wanted to stay alive and were fortunate enough to find a way to keep reasonably healthy, eat more, and avoid killing labor. Richard Glazar, a Czech Jew who survived Treblinka, was a case in point. Upon arriving at this death camp in October 1942, Glazar was lucky enough to be selected for the "special work" of gathering together the discarded clothing of gassed Jews and preparing it, and other personal items deemed of value to the German war effort, for shipment to the Reich. As Glazar noted in his post-war memoir, "to be chosen to live even for an extra day was nothing but luck, one chance in a thousand."[9]

In addition to his good fortune, Glazar also possessed a number of other qualities that helped him stay alive in Treblinka. Key among these:

Was an intangible quality, not peculiar to educated or sophisticated individuals. Anyone might have it. It is perhaps best described as an over-riding thirst — perhaps, too, a talent for life, and a faith in life.[10]

For Glazar, what this talent for life entailed was remaining inconspicuous; becoming numb to the horrors of camp existence; mimicking SS behavior when necessary; staying as clean as possible; finding work — kitchen, laundry, infirmary, or automobile duty — that did not destroy body and spirit; and forming networks of mutual aid with other prisoners. Of these survival strategies, Glazar was particularly emphatic about the importance of cultivating relationships with one's fellow inmates. Indeed, whether these associations were based on criminal activity, ethnicity, political affiliations, family ties, or chance encounters in barracks and/or labor details, they were absolutely essential to staying alive in the camps. For it was these connections that afforded an inmate some measure of protection from other prisoners, as well as access to extra food, additional clothing, a dryer berth, medicine, and easier work assignments. As Glazar noted:

> There were people who survived who were loners. They will tell you now they survived because they relied on no one but themselves. But the truth is probably — and they may either not know it, or not be willing to admit it to themselves or others — that they survived because they were carried by someone, someone who cared for them as much, or almost as much as for themselves.[11]

One other thing that kept survivors like Glazar alive was an ability to keep their minds focused on something other than the daily horrors of camp life. Intellectuals, such as Alexander Solzhenitsyn and Primo Levi, composed poetry in their heads and recited it from memory. Musicians and actors were sometimes able to "play for time," performing in camp orchestras and theatres. Inmates without such artistic gifts often became fixated on doing their assigned work as perfectly as possible. Many focused on remembering the particulars of their captivity against the day when they might be able to bear witness against their tormentors. Perhaps nothing captures this latter exercise of the mind better than the following lines from *Requiem*, Anna Akhmatova's poetic monument to the sufferings of all those caught up in Stalin's terror during the 1930s:

> In the terrible years of the Yezhov terror I spent seventeen months
> waiting in line outside the prison in Leningrad. One day somebody in the
> crowd identified me. Standing behind me was a woman, with lips blue
> from the cold, who had, of course, never heard me called by name before.
> Now she started out of the torpor common to us all and asked me in a
> Whisper (everyone whispered there):
> "Can you describe this?"
> And I said: "I can."
> Then something like a smile passed fleetingly over what had once been
> her face....

Avoiding death at all costs; keeping one's head down; taking only carefully calculated risks; caring for others when and where such assistance was possible; maintaining some sense of self-dignity; and keeping one's mind alive and active — these were the kinds of actions that made it possible for individuals to survive the extreme conditions of the concentration camps. As writer and critic Tzvetan Todorov notes in his work on concentration camp morality, such conduct was far removed from what most people would regard as heroic because it served no abstract ideal or cause, entailed few acts of derring-do, was completely inglorious, and offered posterity a collection of gritty life stories so full of horror and moral ambiguity that few could handle hearing them.[12] Despite the unheroic nature of this behavior, however,

> The survivor is the figure who emerges from all those who fought for life in the concentration camps, and the most significant fact about their struggle is that it depended on fixed activities: on forms of social bonding and interchange, on collective resistance, on keeping dignity and moral sense active.[13]

Such behavior not only puts the lie to the notion that human beings are by nature little more than savage beasts locked in an amoral struggle for survival, but it also suggests that heroism can encompass something other than the remarkable deeds of larger-than-life individuals. Indeed, in the extreme circumstances of the camps, the ability of ordinary people to stay alive with some modicum of dignity, empathy, and intelligence can only be counted an extraordinary act. And, as the many memorials to the numberless victims of these places remind us, that achievement is worthy of our respect, reverence, and remembrance.

Oddballs and Outcasts: Anti-Heroes Existential and Everyday

In the years following the end of the Second World War, anti-heroes figure prominently in Western fiction and film. Prominent writers, such as Albert Camus, J. D. Salinger, Carson McCullers, Joan Didion, Ken Kesey, and Jack Kerouac, people the pages of their novels with drifters, dropouts, and drug addicts. Playwrights Tennessee Williams, Henry Miller, Samuel Beckett, David Mamet, and Sam Shephard pen plays in which deranged divas, itinerant hoboes, blue collar workers, and white collar salesmen take center stage. And on the big screen, audiences are treated to films in which James Dean, Marlon Brando, Jane Fonda, Jack Nicholson, and Robert De Niro play juvenile delinquents, gang members, prostitutes, gumshoes, and maladjusted taxicab drivers.

These postwar protagonists are much like the picaroons of the early modern era. They too are either common folk or out-and-out lumpenproletariat. They also lack resources, direction, ambition, and talent; are alienated from their societies; and often engage in behavior that is either criminal or of questionable legality. Rebellious by nature, they espouse no causes, offer no remedies for the ills of the world, and constitute little if any threat to the status quo. In short, in the "real world," these individuals would be largely unnoticed in life and unremarked upon in death.

Unlike their picaresque and survivor counterparts, however, this particular crop of anti-heroes does not behave as they do out of a need to stay alive. Their bellies do not rumble with hunger, wars are not fought in their backyards, and no abstract ideology has singled them out for exploitation and extinction. Rather, these protagonists act in a disaffected and anti-social manner because they feel themselves to be trapped in an existence that lacks meaning and moral purpose, and in a civilization that values little save wealth, consumption and power.

The character of Sal Paradise in Jack Kerouac's "Beat" classic *On the Road* is a case in point. Starting from the premise that "nobody knows what's going to happen to anybody besides the forlorn rags of growing old,"[14] Kerouac's protagonist dedicates his life to living fully in the moment, free of personal and professional commitments, and unfettered by social conventions or prejudices. Towards that end, he attaches himself to the "son of a wino" and ex-car thief, a "holy con-man with the shining mind" named Dean Moriarty, and begins a series of spontaneous road trips across America and Mexico in search of authentic experiences. Along the way, he befriends an eclectic band of bohemian writers and artists, tries his hand at various odd jobs, discovers jazz, becomes chemically educated (does drugs), and associates with all manner of humanity — migrant laborers, African American musicians, and Mexican whores. Though he concludes his journeys weary of the road and convinced that life is essentially without meaning, Sal's last thoughts are of Dean Moriarty, the holy hobo who eschews normalcy in favor of a life lived solely on his own terms.

The anomie of Kerouac's characters, as well as their rejection of the "straight" world in favor of an unconventional life filled with experience, was emblematic of the disillusionment and discontent of Western intellectuals and artists during the Cold War era. Confronted by a world where the mass murder of millions had elicited no response from heaven, and mutual assured destruction was the cornerstone of Western statecraft, it was difficult for these individuals to accept the notion of a divinely ordered moral universe governed by sweet reason. Concurrently, the idea of blithely ignoring these realities and continuing to live a life boundered by the values, practices and institutions that made them possible seemed patently absurd.

Unlike their *fin-de-siècle* counterparts, however, post–World War II intellectuals were not much enamored with programs of change or all purpose panaceas that included convention shattering supermen, utopian schemes of social engineering, or purgative bloodbaths. Hitler and Stalin had clearly demonstrated the dangers inherent in giving self-styled *Übermenschen* absolute authority over powerful nation states. Auschwitz served as a constant reminder of where the dream of improving "the average human type" might lead. And in a world filled with nuclear weaponry, any talk of cleansing cataclysms sounded ridiculous if not suicidal.

Further, the West's postwar societies were not particularly well suited to any of the classical hero types. Constitutional governments acted as a check on charismatic leaders; guaranteed rights of religion, speech, press and assembly made martyrdom unnecessary; welfare states filled many of the charitable functions once exercised by saintly men and women; mechanized warfare was incompatible with the kinds of single combat practiced by an Achilles or a Lancelot; and the quest for glory and adventure had little relevance in a consumer culture where most people were fixated on acquiring the latest commodities and personal services. In the face of these realities, it was difficult for intellectuals to conceive of traditional heroes as anything more than romantic anachronisms.

Instead, Cold War writers, artists and filmmakers opted to focus on the anti-heroes mentioned at the beginning of this section. Though maladjusted, these plebeian protagonists were nonetheless ordinary people living in small towns and suburbs, working in factories, offices and service jobs, raising families, struggling with relationships; and trying to do good and avoid evil. To the degree that they were disaffected with their societies, this disaffection did not take the form of grandiose inhumane schemes of social engineering. Rather, it was manifested in actions aimed at carving out an identity and style of living consistent with their own sense of who they were and what they needed to do in order to get through life.

In peopling their pages, stages, and screenplays with alienated every-men and- women, mid-twentieth century intellectuals were decisively breaking with the hero worship of their vitalist predecessors and affirming their commitment to a more democratic, humane society. They were also translating into fiction an existentialist take on the world that was widespread in the decades immediately following the Second World War. Not unlike the heroic vitalism of the previous century, this existentialism rejected the idea that human life was informed, boundered, or governed by anything — gods, morals, or essences — outside of the historical moment into which a person was born. Unlike vitalism, this school of thought also ruled out the notion that human beings were compelled to engage in a struggle for domination and power by dint of physical and biological drives over which they exercised little if any control. Instead, existentialists argued that human behavior was a socio-cultural construct that was fluid, flexible and subject to change depending on the needs and inclinations of different civilizations and their individual members.

Within this existential framework, a hero was any individual who embraced the moment within which they were born, accepted their finitude, and decided to exercise their autonomy, i.e., their right to choose a life of their own without reference to traditions, values, or any kind of physical determinism. Considerations of class, ability, intellect, or ideology were irrelevant to this decision. And every life choice, be it leading a revolution or tending to one's garden, was of equal validity.[15]

While this existential heroism is decidedly more equalitarian and benign than its vitalist counterpart, it still allowed for a considerable degree of amoral and anti-social behavior. In fact, postwar literature, drama, and film abound with examples of existential protagonists who are either self-indulgent or sociopathic. In *On the Road*, Kerouac's main characters, Dean Moriarty and Sal Paradise, blithely use and then abandon various friends, wives, and lovers in their quest for authentic experiences. In his play *Caligula*, Albert Camus' Roman protagonist decides that life is meaningless and proceeds to commit random acts of murder and violence to demonstrate there are no a priori moral constraints on the exercise of power. And in *Taxi Driver*, Martin Scorsese's mentally disturbed cabbie, Travis Bickle, takes it upon himself to cleanse New York City of its human scum by going on a killing spree in a Manhattan brothel. Indeed, in an existential world, as long as the individual accepts full responsibility for his or her actions, a hero can be either a saintly nun or a death camp commandant.

This problem of moral relativity to the side, these existential oddballs and outcasts were well suited to the "baby boomers" that came of age during the Cold War era. At odds with their elders on everything from hair styles and clothing to civil liberties and national security, this generational cohort challenged authority at every turn and demanded for each of its members the right to complete self-determination. As might be expected with such a fractious generation, their heroes were folks who disdained normalcy, distrusted establishments, questioned age-old shibboleths, embraced alternative ways of thinking and living, and sought self-fulfillment. Consequently, all the various "rebels without a cause" that graced the novels, plays and film screens of the 1950s found their way into the boomer heroic pantheon; as well as an equally motley crew of countercultural bikers, raucous rock stars, angry folk singers, and just about any character played by Jack Nicholson.

Before taking our leave of these atomic age anti-heroes, it should be noted that there were folks during the Cold War era who were not much enamored with any kind of hero, anti- or otherwise. These individuals regarded all heroic types, whether they were knights on horseback or brooding motorcycle riding hoodlums, to be essentially the same, i.e., abnormal, self-indulgent egoists alienated from the world and prone to actions likely to get their non-heroic counterparts hurt or killed. Rather than revering and emulating these characters, their postwar critics recommended institutionalizing them instead, and heroizing in their place the ordinary men and women of the world who work hard, pay taxes, and raise families.

One of the best known proponents of these "everyday heroes" is the American underground comic book writer Harvey Pekar. A file clerk for 40 years in the Veterans Administration Hospital of his native Cleveland, Pekar is an ill-groomed, overweight, misanthropic slob. He lives in a shabby, squalid apartment where he spends most of his time reading and listening to jazz records. Over the course of his life, he has cultivated a small circle of nerdy friends from among his co-workers; gone through two divorces; settled down with a third wife who is often depressed; survived lymphoma; and adopted a foster daughter, Danielle.

In 1962, Pekar met and befriended underground comic artist, Robert Crumb, also a Cleveland native. In conversations with Crumb, he raised the idea of writing a comic book that focused not on fantasy, sci-fi, and superheroes, but on the details of his everyday life. Pekar actually self-produced and distributed this autobiographical comic book series from 1976 to 1993, and was fortunate enough to get Crumb and a number of other artists to illustrate his stories (by his own admission, Pekar is unable to draw a straight line). Entitled *American Splendor*, this comic book saga recounted in a realistic, unsentimental fashion Pekar's life "adventures," i.e., surviving Cleveland winters; dealing with fellow employees at the Veterans Administration; hanging out with a self-styled nerd named Toby Radloff; living with a depressed wife; fighting cancer; and raising a child.

In recounting stories about his daily life rather than thrillers about superhuman beings, Pekar was driven by a desire:

> To write literature that pushes people into their lives rather than helping people escape from them. Most comic books are vehicles for escapism, which I think is unfortunate. I think that the so-called average person often exhibits a great deal of heroism in getting through an ordinary day, and yet the reading public takes this heroism for granted. They'd rather read about Superman than themselves.[16]

By focusing on the trials and tribulations of his own existence, Pekar attempts to show his readers the ways in which they themselves are all supermen and women writ small. Indeed, as his stories demonstrate, it requires considerable courage, fortitude, patience, and intelligence to deal with the slings and arrows of everyday life. Enduring a boring job; making ends meet on wages inadequate to the cost of living; staying healthy; caring for parents and friends; trying to keep a relationship together; and working to insure a decent life for one's children; these are all daunting challenges that common folk confront and overcome — often in the face of long odds — on a daily basis. More to the point, these everyday heroes face these existential trials without recourse to doting divinities, special powers, great resources, intellectual sophistry, criminal scams, or delinquent behavior.

Pekar's heroization of his own life, as well as that of his "unhip, unhandsome, depressed and depressing"[17] friends, family, and co-workers, was followed in the late 1990s and early years of the new millennium with a slew of darkly humorous stories and films — *Ghost World, The Big Lebowski, The Good Girl, Rushmore, Clerks, Sideways,* and, appropriately enough, *American Splendor* — that celebrated the flawed lives of under- and unemployed losers. Produced by unconventional writer-directors like Mike White, the Coen brothers, Wes Anderson, Alexander Payne, Terry Zwigoff, Todd Solondz, and Robert Pulcini, these movies featured:

> The latest incarnation of the antihero [who] like Pekar, [is] neither tough nor sexual he's an everyday schlump who rejects conventional ideas of romance, success and even basic grooming. Unhappy, depressed, confused, he slouches through life, in places like Omaha or Cleveland, sometimes mocking traditionalists.[18]

Ironically, even though these characters are regarded as "the latest incarnation of the antihero," they are really a mockery of that tradition. Unlike their historical counterparts, the protagonists of these films suffer little physical discomfort and are not locked in any kind of struggle for survival. Though mildly disaffected with modern existence, their lifestyles are neither rebellious nor countercultural. And insofar as these folks have any point to their lives, it is largely about filling time and finding love — aims, it should be noted, that are not always achieved. After three millennia, it would appear that the West has arrived at a moment in time where even slackers can be heroes.

Homer must be rolling in his grave.

Quo Vadis *or Where Does the Hero Go from Here?*

Despite the fact that we appear to be living in a world where everyone can lay claim to a hero's laurels, it is unlikely that the death knell of the traditional hero will be sounded anytime soon. As Harvey Pekar notes:

> There are some people who aren't going to take a lot of comfort from what I write. It depresses them to read about themselves; when you shove their faces into their lives it burns them out. They don't want to deal with it, they say, "Hey man, I have to live through this stuff. When I go home I want to watch something on the tube with romance and excitement and stuff like that. I don't wanna be reading about the kind of life I have to live."
>
> Of course some comic book fans don't know what to make of American Splendor. They think a normal comic book should be about super beings who can fly, that a comic dealing with everyday people doing everyday things is weird. Ordinary is weird to them. Wow, that's really ironic.[19]

Ironic it may be, but in a world of troubles where terrorists fly hijacked jets into skyscrapers, global warming cooks the planet, and most folks are a paycheck away from the street, people long for somebody to ride in on a white horse and save the day. The phenomenal success of *Star Wars,* super-hero comic books and movies, Peter Jackson's film version of *Lord of the Rings,* and the entire Harry Potter series, all attest to the continuing hunger on the part of the modern public for heroic figures that have extraordinary abilities, which they are willing to use for the common good.

What is striking, however, about these contemporary manifestations of the demigods and knights errant of the past, is how anti-heroic they often are. Han Solo is a picaroon who inadvertently becomes a hero; Marvel's mutated web spinners, telepaths, and daredevils feel alienated from society, have decidedly mixed feelings about their powers, and often yearn for normalcy; hobbits are everyday folk indifferent to glory and to those who seek it; and whatever his abilities, Harry Potter is ultimately a teenager subject to the same hormonal urges, temper tantrums, and manic-depressive behavior as any muggle his age. Like the century in which they have come to the fore, these characters and others like them are insecure, anguished, cynical, and unsure of how best to address the challenges of their time. Despite their extraordinary abilities, they are no less *human* than the rest of us.

This focus on the humanity of these characters is one of the legacies of the anti-heroic tradition in the history of Western heroism. If swashbucklers and super heroes now contend with the trials and tribulations of daily life, it is because picaroons, camp survivors, and depressed losers have demonstrated the heroism involved in navigating an everyday existence that is often as treacherous as any sea sailed by Odysseus. Concurrently, if a George Lucas or a J. K. Rowling makes a point of underscoring their protagonists all too human flaws and foibles, it is because the anti-hero has reminded them and us that villainy follows close behind the hero who foregoes his humanity.

Aside from the ways in which it has humanized our current crop of big screen warriors and wizards, the anti-heroic tradition has also dramatically expanded the Western understanding of what it means to be a hero. While "heroic" will continue to be a rubric applied to the titans among us, anti-heroes have also made it possible to apply this term to ordinary people who care for others, struggle for freedom and dignity, and strive for authentic experience. Indeed, in a world where the stuff of traditional heroism — single combat, martyrdom, discovering unknown lands, revolutionary iconoclasm — is in short supply, and super heroes do not exist, it is comforting to know that the modest deeds of common citizens to foster community, good government, and opportunities for cultural enrichment are now deemed worthy of heroization. As the late Joseph Campbell was fond of reminding us, in the end, the hero does indeed wear a thousand faces.

Epilogue

I thought of that old joke: This guy goes to a psychiatrist and says, "Doc, my brother's crazy, he thinks he's a chicken." And the doctor says, "Well why don't you turn him in?" and the guy says, "I would, but I need the eggs." Well, I guess that's pretty much now how I feel about relationships. They're totally irrational and crazy and absurd, but I guess we keep going through it because most of us need the eggs.

— Woody Allen: *Annie Hall*

As mentioned in the preceding chapter, this work originated in a seminar on the Western idea of the hero that I have taught at UCLA since 2004. While teaching this class, I became interested in how and why a rubric originally reserved for a race of demigods became a ubiquitous expression for just about anyone with a claim to distinction in some area of human endeavor, be it war, sports, child rearing, acting, or just being an exceptional loser. To answer this question, I focused on some of the types most closely associated with heroes and heroism over the last three millennia — warriors, martyrs, saints, athletes, scientists, artists, anti-heroes — with an eye aimed at discerning why these figures were and continue to be revered and emulated by so many people in Europe and the Americas. While trying to isolate the "right stuff" that earned many of these folks a hero's laurels, I also addressed the historical conditions surrounding and informing these heroic typologies; the ways in which they were different and alike; and how they were exploited by various individuals and groups bent on influencing and shaping political, social and ethical behavior.

Much of what I have found in the study of these types confirms certain longstanding preconceptions about what it means to be a hero. Perhaps the best example of this is that whatever their occupation these figures are counted "heroic" because, like Hesiod's *hemitheoi*, their lives and actions single them out as "extra" ordinary human beings. Samson does not slay just one Philistine with the jawbone of an ass, but *scores* of them. Martyrs for a faith or cause don't just die, they die well, usually after enduring exceptional privation and pain. Award winning athletes, Olympic or otherwise, can wrestle rampaging bulls to the ground, hurl objects at incredible speeds, and literally defy gravity while running, jumping, or pole vaulting through the air. Nobel Prize winning scientists understand and manipulate natural mysteries that were once the sole property of gods; and their counterparts in the arts compel us to see seemingly ordinary things in completely new ways. Even a chronically stoned slacker like the Big Lebowski bowls better than the rest of us.

For most of Western history, these exceptional individuals have also been primarily male, martial and aristocratic. From the Bronze Age through the early modern period, to be a hero was first and foremost to be a man of respectable lineage with great skill in combat. Indeed, this idea of the hero as a warrior with a good pedigree has informed and shaped all the heroic typologies examined in this narrative. Plato, as well as his Jewish and Christian imitators, transformed the subjects of their martyrologies — male and female alike — into noble fighting men worthy of the honors normally reserved for Olympic champions and fallen soldiers. Heroic sportsmen were usually aristocrats whose athletic pastimes counted as a form of training for a military career. Saintly men and women were seldom commoners, and no matter how sedentary and pacific their lifestyles, they were regarded in life and death as *milites* of the risen Christ. Scientists often sported patents of nobility and were always eager to identify themselves as latter day Argonauts extending the power and glory of their royal patrons with scientific instruments that also had military applications. And most of the unconventional artists and rebels treated in these pages haled from good families that afforded them the wherewithal to "struggle" mightily against an oppressive and philistine status quo.

In addition to the expectation that heroes are well born, combative, and gifted with exceptional abilities, all of these figures contend with publics that expect some form of service in return for being counted worthy of the heroic rubric and its perquisites. Odysseus, no less than Aeneas and Arthur, is expected to defend his community from foreign enemies, keep local bandits at bay, and bring back booty from his military adventures abroad. Athletic champions win honor not just for themselves, but for their communities and patrons. Martyrs and saints affirm the beliefs of their respective confessions and secure the blessings of the gods or secular movements they serve. Scientists discover and invent things that allow humanity to manipulate the natural world to its advantage. Even the self-absorbed romantic rebels of the 19th and 20th centuries create memorable literature, painting, and music; and many actually help advance the causes of various oppressed peoples.

Because these figures are associated with exceptional breeding, ability, valor, and public service, and are also exemplars of virtue and right conduct for the communities that honor them, heroes have also been of particular interest to individuals and groups that are eager to shape human behavior and advance various agendas. Indeed, the preceding pages are filled with examples of such efforts that have markedly changed both the heroic ideals of the West and the contours of its civilization. Alexander the Great's appropriation of Homer's heroes, for example, inspires and justifies his drive to the east, and provides a model for the Roman "heroic imperialism" that establishes a shared Greco-Roman culture throughout much of Europe, Africa, and the Near East. The Aeneas of Virgil, coupled with the power machinations of his imperial patron, enshrine the idea of the military champion as first and foremost the pious servant of his people; a notion that is the cornerstone of modern military service. First century Hellenized Jews and their gentile counterparts in the early Christian movement transform the anti-hero Jesus of Nazareth into a nobly born warrior, and in so doing make him an acceptable redeemer for a declining empire and the Germanic kingdoms that succeed it. Catholic prelates create a heroic pantheon of their own and fill it with knights and saints whose example continues to inspire present-day philanthropists and Jedi-wannabes. And the attempts of various 20th century messianic mass movements to effect a latter-day heroic age unleash instead a "blood-dimmed tide" that extinguishes the lives of countless millions.

Important as the heroic ideal has been to the civilizing process of the West, however, it would be a mistake to argue, as did the vitalists of the 19th and 20th centuries, that heroes are the engines of historical development. There were a great many factors other than extraordinary individuals that contributed to the development of Christianity, modern science, liberal democracy, the isms of the 19th century, industrialization, and mass society. Indeed, most of the shifts in thinking over the last three millennia about what constitutes an exceptional person worthy of respect and emulation have occurred in tandem with these major developments in Western history. For example, whatever the sleight-of-hand that turned Jesus into a glorious warrior, his movement and the religion it spawned could not help but heroize any Christian — rich/poor, high or low born, man/woman — who lived their lives in a suitably Christ-like manner. Similarly, liberal enlightenment society's love affair with individual freedom and science made it highly amenable to heroizing scientists, explorers, romantic artists, and dissidents of every stripe. And the gross inequities, injustices, wars, and crimes against humanity that have been the hallmarks of the modern period have made it possible for all manner of rogues, reprobates, survivors, and oddballs to claim if not heroic, at least anti-heroic status.

Perhaps what is most striking about the historical development of this idea is that it comes to the fore in a time when life for most people is short, brutish and nasty, and human nature is viewed as something to be transcended. The hero of these times was someone who actually tried and, for at least a moment in time, did slough off the limitations of their humanity through some set of actions that set him apart from what Nietzsche disdainfully described as the common "herd." While this person still died like the rest of us, he did so with the guarantee that his transcendent moments would be celebrated in deathless songs.

Three thousand years later, in a West where living is considerably more comfortable, our humanity is something we embrace, and everyone feels entitled to at least fifteen minutes of fame, we celebrate the idea of the hero as anyone who is both unordinary in some fashion and yet very much a part of that great herd within which we all live and work. To a large degree, this is the logical outcome of those developments alluded to above that have brought to the fore a Western civilization committed to the idea that every life has worth, possibilities, and a chance at self-development. While such a formulation affords to all the right to aspire to heights once reserved only for a few, it also allows every act of self-realization, be it scaling Everest or losing weight, to be construed as heroic.

This liberalization of the heroic ideal requires us to consider whether or not a rubric once reserved only for gods, champions, and the doers of daring deeds has any future in an increasingly democratic equalitarian West. As noted in the final chapters of this history, many of the figures addressed in these pages are by modern standards little more than arrogant selfish egoists. Many of them would also be found guilty of capital crimes and incarcerated in maximum security prisons. And when a Harvey Pekar can plausibly argue that any person can lay claim to a hero's status simply because they get up in the morning and go to work, one could argue that the term is essentially meaningless.

These considerations aside, it is also evident that the idea of the hero is not yet ready to be consigned to the rubbish heap of history. The search for champions in all walks of life continues, and the yearning for extraordinary folk who speak to "the better angels of our nature" and strive to achieve the impossible manifests itself in the movies we watch, the books—fiction and non-fiction—that we read, the action figures our children collect, and the reality TV shows—*American Idol, Survivors, Project Runway*—that we watch on a weekly basis. Indeed, from the time of the Greeks to the present, when we seek out the meaning of excellence, virtue, and, yes, even villainy, it is to our heroes that we turn for guidance and enlightenment.

Perhaps nothing captures the significant role heroes continue to play in our societies better than the following passage from the blockbuster movie *Spiderman II*. Speaking about a local neighbor kid's admiration for the intrepid web slinger, Spidey's Aunt May notes that there are:

> Too few characters out there, flying around like that saving old girls like me. And Lord knows, kids like Henry need a hero.... Everybody loves a hero. People line up for them.... And years later, they'll tell how they stood in the rain for hours just to get a glimpse of the one who taught them to hold on a second longer. I believe there's a hero in all of us ... that keeps us honest ... gives us strength ... makes us noble ... and finally allows us to die with pride, even though sometimes we have to be steady and give up the thing we want the most—even our dreams. Spider-Man did that for Henry and he wonders where he's gone. He needs him.

As do we all.

Chapter Notes

Introduction

1. This sentence is an obvious play on Jared Diamond's excellent work *Guns, Germs, and Steel: The Fate of Human Societies* (New York: W. W. Norton Company, 1999).

2. This notion of the civilizing process is taken from Norbert Elias' *The History of Manners: The Civilizing Process: Volume I* (New York: Pantheon Books, 1978), 3–4.

Part One

1. Jennifer Larson, *Greek Heroine Cults* (Madison: University of Wisconsin Press, 1995), 5.

Chapter 1

1. On the origins and uses of the word *heros*, see the superb monograph *Pindar and the Cult of the Heroes* by Bruno Currie (Oxford: Oxford University Press, 2005), specifically pages 62–67.

2. See Lewis Richard Farnell, *Greek Hero Cults and Ideas of Immortality* (Oxford: Oxford University Press, 1921), 15–16 regarding the theory that the word hero may have been derived from a term for a chthonian goddess. The expression "powerful dead" is used in the entry dealing with **hero-cults** in the *Oxford Classical Dictionary*, Simon Hornblower and Anthony Spawforth, eds. (Oxford: Oxford University Press, Revised third edition published 2003), 693–4.

3. C. Kerényi, *The Heroes of the Greeks* (New York: Thames and Hudson, 1981), 14.

4. In Plato's *Apology* (London: Penguin Books, 1969), 75, Socrates notes "If on arrival in the other world, beyond the reach of our so-called justice, one will find there the true judges who are said to preside in those courts, Minos and Rhadamanthys and Aeacus and Triptolemus and all those other half-divinities who were upright in their early life, would that be an unrewarding journey?" All four of the named individuals in this passage were regarded as heroes and their designation as dispensers of justice in the underworld further underscores the idea that the term hero originally referred to the powerful dead. Minos, Rhadamanthys and Aeacus were mortal sons of Zeus and became judges in the underworld as a reward for their earthly justice and piety, and Triptole-mus, son of the king of Attica, taught farming and the mysteries of Demeter to humanity and was made a god after death for his good deeds.

5. In the case of heroes such as Heracles and Dionysus, however, cult sanctuaries and ritual practices were every bit as impressive as those of the other Olympian deities.

6. See the aforementioned works by Farnell and Kerényi for more details on heroic-cult practice in Greece. The entry on hero-cults in the *Oxford Classical Dictionary* is also quite good and underscores the difficulties attendant on any effort aimed at generalizing the rituals that were practiced in Greek hero-cults.

7. Anthony Snodgrass in his *Archaic Greece: The Age of Experiment* (London: J.M. Dent & Sons Ltd., 1980) argues that the ostensible achievements of the legendary figures of the Heroic Age — city building, metallurgy, writing, martial prowess, agricultural innovation, and good kingship — served as an inspiration for the many developments in the archaic period that would lead to the glories of the 5th century. See in particular pages 37–38, 68–69, 76–77,80, 115–16.

8. See Currie's "Introduction," in his *Pindar and the Cult of Heroes* on this tendency, as well as his chapter dealing with the "Heroization of the War Dead."

9. *Oxford Classical Dictionary*, Simon Hornblower and Anthony Spawforth, eds. (Oxford: Oxford University Press, Revised third edition published 2003), 693–4.

Chapter 2

1. Peter Levi, *A History of Greek Literature* (New York: Viking Press, 1985), 42.

2. Much of the information in this chapter on Archaic Greek society, economics, politics, and values is taken from Anthony Snodgrass, *Archaic Greece: The Age of Experiment* (London: J.M. Dent & Sons Ltd., 1980) and M.I. Finley, *The World of Odysseus* (New York: New York Review of Books, 1982).

3. Finley, 81–108.

4. Homer, *The Odyssey*, Book IX, 39–43.

5. Finley, 142.

6. Homer, *The Odyssey*, Book XI, 579–80.

7. Indeed, M.I. Finley, Bernard Knox, and others have all made convincing arguments that the Homeric epics can actually be used as lenses through which we can discern actual historical conditions during the Greek Dark Ages.

8. Homer, *The Iliad*, Book VI, 168–73.

9. As Daniel Mendelsohn notes in his splendid review of Wolfgang Petersen's *Troy*, "Those who have read the *Iliad* closely know that a standard modifier for battle is, in fact, "bringing-glory-to-men." "A Little Iliad," *New York Review of Books*, June 24, 2004, 48.

10. Menelaus' claim to the kingship of Sparta rested on his marriage to Helen, whose father, Tyndareos, was the former ruler of that kingdom. Doubtless the gold that she took with her to Troy (*Iliad*, Book III, 110), was an important source of revenue for both Menelaus and his brother Agamemnon, the high king of Mycene.

11. Finley, 143–44. The quoted remarks in this passage are from E.R. Dodds, *The Greeks and the Irrational* (University of California Press, 1951), 29.

12. Homer, *The Odyssey*, Book XI, 414–420.

13. Finley, 21. Sir Cecil Maurice Bowra's *The Greek Experience* (London: Weidenfeld & Nicolson, 1957), especially Chapter 2, "The Heroic Outlook," also addresses this conflict between the Greek heroic ethos, Judeo-Christian morality, and the needs of society.

14. Plutarch, *Twelve Lives* (Cleveland: Fine Editions Press, 1950), 232.

15. For a superb analysis of the ways in which Alexander fit his life into a "Homeric pattern," see Leo Braudy's chapter "The Longing of Alexander" in his *The Frenzy of Renown: Fame and Its History* (Oxford: Oxford University Press, 1986).

16. The particulars of Alexander's life can be found in any number of histories. The present account owes much to the excellent overview of the Macedonian conqueror's life that is provided in Daniel Mendelsohn's critique "Alexander, the Movie!" in *New York Review of Books*, January 13, 2005, 43–46.

17. Braudy, *The Frenzy of Renown*, 32.

18. On the Augustan political and military settlement, see M. Cary, *A History of Rome: Down to the Reign of Constantine* (New York: MacMillan St. Martin's Press, 1967), 473–482, 505–511, 515–516.

19. Virgil, *The Aeneid*, Book II, 1074.

20. Ibid., Book I, 742–46.

21. Ibid., Book XII, 252–50

22. The literature on Virgil and the *Aeneid* is vast and this author does not pretend to any authority in this area. There were three works, however, that I found particularly useful and insightful in writing about Virgil's heroic epic. These were: Richard Jenkyns, *Virgil's Experience: Nature and History: Times, Names and Places* (Oxford: Oxford University Press, 1998), specifically Chapter 15 in that book "A Roman Experience: Virgil, Augustus, and the Future;" Paul Zanker, *The Power of Images in the Age of Augustus* (Ann Arbor: The University of Michigan Press, 1990); and Jasper Griffin's article on "Virgil" in John Boardman, Jasper Griffin, Oswyn Murray, eds., *The Oxford History of the Classical World* (Oxford: Oxford University Press, 1986).

Chapter 3

1. Whatever the vagaries of public opinion, the acceptability of the cause for which someone lays down their life has always been central to whether or not that individual is regarded as heroic. At the beginning of the 21st century, most would agree the cause for which Stephen Biko and Martin Luther King laid down their lives — the struggle against racism and apartheid — sanctified their sacrifice and conferred on them heroic status. By contrast, while National Socialism and white supremacy once commanded considerable followings in the 20th century, few in the present would regard either Hermann Goering or Timothy McVeigh as heroes despite their purported sacrifice to those causes.

2. A bibliographical survey of the literature on Socrates prepared by the French scholar V. de Megalhaes-Vilhena in 1952 came to more than eight-hundred pages. Since that time, the scholarly work on Socrates has continued to grow and shows no signs of abatement. T.C. Brickhouse and N.D. Smith's work, *Socrates on Trial* (Oxford: Oxford University Press, 1989), provides an updated and somewhat comprehensive bibliography of the modern literature on Socrates (pages 272–316). Of this secondary literature, the following works of modern scholarship have been particularly useful in the preparation of this section: Gregory Vlastos, *Socrates, Ironist and Moral Philosopher* (Ithaca, New York: Cornell University Press, 1991); A.E. Taylor, *Socrates* (London: P. Davies, Ltd., 1932); I.F. Stone, *The Trial of Socrates* (Boston: Little, Brown and Company, 1988); Lacey Baldwin Smith's chapter "Socrates: The Genesis of Martyrdom" in his *Fools, Martyrs, and Traitors: The Story of Martyrdom in the Western World* (New York: Alfred A. Knopf, 1997); and C.C.W. Taylor, *Socrates* (Oxford: Oxford University Press, 1998).

3. For those interested in investigating the Socratic sources, the following works by Mario Montuori are particularly useful: *Socrates, Man and Myth: The Two Socratic Apologies of Xenophon* (London, 1957); *Socrates: Physiology of a Myth* (Amsterdam: J. C. Gieben, 1981); and *Socrates: An Approach* (Amsterdam: J. C. Gieben, 1988). The Socratic works themselves are available in many excellent English translations. Standard scholarly practice is to use the Loeb Classical Library editions of Plato, Xenophon, and Aristophanes' works, which provide the reader with the original Greek and a facing English translation. Citations in this section are from Loeb's editions of Plato, *Euthyphro, Apology, Crito, Phaedo, Phaedrus* translated by Harold North Fowler (London and New York, 1923); Xenophon, *Memorabilia* and *Oeconomicus* translated by E.C. Marchant (London and New York, 1923), as well as his *Symposium* and *Apology* translated by O.J. Todd (London and New York, 1922); and Aristophanes' *Clouds* translated by B.B. Rogers (London, 1924). Diogenes Laertius' "Socrates" can be read in *Diogenes Laertius: Lives of Eminent Philosophers*, trans. R.H. Hicks (Cambridge: Harvard University Press, 1991). For the lesser known ancient sources alluded to above, the reader is directed to *Socrates: A Source Book* (London: MacMillan, 1970) by John Ferguson. This work makes available in English not only the various fragmentary references to Socrates in Greek and Latin literature, but also the *Apology of Socrates* by Libanius.

4. Plato, *Crito* 50D; Xenophon, *Oeconomicus* 2.3; Plutarch, *Life of Aristides* 1.9; and Libanius, *Apology of Socrates* 3.7.

5. Though he is often portrayed as impoverished, it

is more likely that Socrates' lifestyle was a voluntary one that reflected his predilection for a life lived in pursuit of truth rather than personal wealth. Though some have conjectured that the supposed bad temper of his wife, Xanthippe, was due to Socrates' poverty and refusal to work, there is nothing in the contemporary sources of his life to indicate this or that Socrates was unable to support his family.

6. Xenophon, *Symposium* 5.5–7; Plato, *Symposium* 215B, 216D; Aristophanes, *Clouds* 362. With regard to Socrates' purported baldness, C.C.W. Taylor notes in his *Socrates* (Oxford: Oxford University Press, 1998), 8, that we have two marginal notes in manuscripts of *Clouds* written in late antiquity, which say that he was bald. He also notes that there is no contemporary authority for this assertion.

7. While A.E. Taylor's *Socrates* (Boston: Beacon Press, 1951) is old, it is still one of the best scholarly efforts at piecing together the life of Socrates and I have followed his lead in this section. For what Taylor has to say about Socrates' early and midlife, see pp. 37–93.

8. Plato, *Apology* 28E; *Charmides* 153A; *Symposium* 219E, 221A-B; *Laches* 181A.

9. These trances are mentioned in Plato's *Symposium* 174D and 220 C-D. See Plato's *Apology* for Socrates' description of his "mission," specifically 30 A-E and 31 A-C.

10. See in particular Plato's *Gorgias* for Socrates' harsh judgment of Athens' greatest statesmen and of course the *Apology* 21 A-E, 22 A-E, and 23 A-B for his account of the ways in which Socrates exposed the ignorance of Athens' leading citizens.

11. Irving F. Stone's *Trial of Socrates* lays out the particulars of these events (pp. 140–156) and discusses in some detail the role they played in the decision to bring Socrates to trial.

12. Plato, *Euthyphro* 2B.

13. Xenophon, *Apology* 6–7.

14. Plato, *Apology* 28D.

15. I.F. Stone covers this lack of interest in Socrates, as well as the absence of any revulsion for his death, in his *Trial of Socrates*. See in particular pages 174–180.

16. Aristotle, *Rhetoric* 1.5.9. See also 1.9.38 for his criteria of what virtues were regarded as worthy of praise, which are directly applicable to our discussion of heroic status in the fifth century.

17. Stone, *The Trial of Socrates*, 4.

18. Anthony Meredith's piece on philosophy in the Roman Empire in *The Oxford History of the Classical World* edited by John Boardman, Jasper Griffin, and Oswyn Murray (Oxford: Oxford University Press, 1986), 698–717 goes into some detail on the influence of Plato among the intellectuals of the late Roman Republic and the first 250 years of the Principate.

19. An examination of the comments in Ferguson's *Source Book* makes it quite clear that Socrates was highly regarded by the Greco–Roman elites in the centuries following his death. Typical of this commentary are the following remarks by Cicero, Marcus Aurelius and Julian: Cicero, 8.1.4, page 191 "On the evidence of all men of learning and the general judgment of Greece he [Socrates] was far and away the leading man in good sense, keen judgement, charm, subtlety, eloquence,

range, and wealth of argument in any field he chose." Marcus Aurelius, 8.5.2, page 203 "It is not enough that Socrates died more impressively, disputed more shrewdly with the sophists, showed more toughness in spending the whole night in the freezing cold, when ordered to arrest Leon of Salamis thought it more gallant to say No, 'held his head high as he walked the streets.'" Julian, 8.13.7, page 208 "I assert that Sophroniscus' son accomplished greater achievements than Alexander. I attribute to him Plato's wisdom, Xenophon's military prowess, Antisthenes' toughness, the philosophies of Eretria and Megara, Cebes, Simmias, Phaedo, thousands of others, not to mention the colonies from the same source — the Lyceum, Stoa and Academy.... All who today owe their salvation to philosophy owe their salvation to Socrates."

20. See in particular the remarks of Seneca (8.2.7 and 8.2.13) and Valerius Maximus (9.4.3 and 9.4.4) in Ferguson's *Source Book*.

21. Quoted in Ferguson, *Socrates: A Source Book*, Justin Martyr 12.1.3, page 305. See also the comments by Tertullian (12.4.7), Origen (12.6.1 and 12.6.6), Jerome (12.15.4), Augustine 12.16.5) and Isidore (12.20.1).

22. Smith, *Fools, Martyrs, Traitors*, 23.

23. Cicero, *For Rabirio* 5.16.

24. See Jerome H. Neyrey's *Honor and Shame in the Gospel of Matthew* (Louisville: Westminster John Knox Press, 1998), 70–89 and 139–162 for an excellent treatment of ancient epideitic rhetoric. With one exception, the criteria I have listed for a noble death are taken from his account. It is also noteworthy that Quintilian actually commented on the noble nature of Socrates' death in his work on Oratory: "Everyone knows that nothing would have contributed more to Socrates' acquittal than if he had used familiar forensic defense advocacy, conciliated the minds of the jury by speaking with humility and been at pains to rebuke the actual charge. But it would not have been like him. *So he made his defense like a man who was going to reckon his sentence a supreme honor* [my italics]. The wisest man in the world preferred to lose his future rather than his past. His own generation failed to understand him. He kept himself for the verdict of posterity. He gave up the short period of old age remaining to him for an *immortality of fame* [my italics]." Quoted in Ferguson, Quintilian 9.12.9, page 244.

25. For an excellent analysis of the early Israelite constitution and faith see John Bright, *A History of Israel* (Philadelphia: Westminster Press, Third Edition, 1981).

26. For more on heroic figures in Judaism, see John J. Collins and George W.E. Nickelsburg, Eds. *Ideal Figures in Ancient Judaism: Profiles and Paradigms* (Chico: Scholars Press, 1980) and Menachem Mor, Ed. *Crisis & Reaction: The Hero in Jewish History* (Omaha: Creighton University Press, 1995).

27. On the circumstances surrounding the self–deaths of Saul, Samson and other individuals in the Hebrew Testament, see Arthur J. Droge and James D. Tabor, *A Noble Death: Suicide and Martyrdom Among Christians and Jews in Antiquity* (San Francisco: Harper Collins, 1992), 54–55.

28. The term Apocrypha refers to the fifteen books or parts of books (including Maccabees) from the pre–Christian period that Catholics accept as canonical literature but that most Protestants and Jews do not. As

the Anchor Bible notes, however, this question of canon-
icity is less important than the fact that these non-canon-
ical books are accepted by both Christians and Jews alike
as extremely valuable historical documents that are central to our understanding of the history of Israel and Judaism during the period between the end of the Old Testament period and the beginning of the Christian era.
With regard to the Books of the Maccabees referred to
here, the First Book is our most important historical
source for the forty-one year period of the Maccabean revolt. Scholars believe that this book was probably penned
during the second half of the second century BCE by a
Jewish inhabitant of Palestine familiar with the events
recounted in it. The Second Book of Maccabees, which
covers the period from 176 BCE to shortly before the
death of Judas Maccabeus, is believed to be a summary of
a longer history of the Maccabean revolt by one Jason of
Cyrene, who is believed to have been an eyewitness to
many of the events related in his historical work. The
Fourth Book mentioned here is not part of the standard
Apocrypha and was probably written either late in the
first century BCE or early in the first century CE. The content of this book is largely philosophical and it makes use
of the events of the Maccabean revolt, particularly the
ordeals of the martyrs, to underscore the need to cultivate
pious reason over passion. For more on the Books of Maccabees and other sources related to this period see Moshe
Pearlman, *The Maccabees* (New York: Macmillan Publishing Co., Inc., 1973) 265. References to the Books of
Maccabees in this chapter are to *I Maccabees*, trans.
Jonathan Goldstein, *The Anchor Bible*, vol. 41 (New York:
Doubleday, 1976); *II Maccabees*, trans. Jonathan Goldstein, *The Anchor Bible*, vol. 41A (New York: Doubleday,
1983); and *The Third and Fourth Books of Maccabees*, ed.
and trans. Moses Hadas (New York: Harper, 1953).

29. This highly condensed version of the history of the
Jews under the Seleucid Empire is primarily derived from
two sources, the aforementioned *The Maccabees* by
Moshe Pearlman, pages 13–57 and Bright's *History of Israel*, pages 412–427. Anyone interested in a more in-
depth analysis of the events related here should definitely
look at the much more exhaustive treatment of this period that is to be found in these two excellent histories.
Antiochus' various atrocities are detailed in Maccabees I:
20–64 and II 6: 1–12.

30. Maccabees IV 5: 4.

31. Ibid., 5: 29–33.

32. Ibid., 6: 6.

33. Ibid., 6: 9–10.

34. Ibid., 6: 18–21.

35. Ibid., 6: 25–26.

36. Maccabees II VIII: 31.

37. The mother is not named in the Books of Maccabees. However, she was given the name 'Hannah' in a
10th century CE narrative history of the Maccabean martyrdom, *The Book of Josippon*, that was based on the Second Book of Maccabees for its account of the deaths of
Eleazar, the mother and her sons.

38. Maccabees IV 8: 12–14.

39. Ibid., 9: 1–7.

40. Ibid., 17: 17.

41. See in particular Hades on this in his translation
of *The Third and Fourth Books of Maccabees*, page 119.

42. See Goldstein on this in his translation of Maccabees I, page 34.

43. Maccabees IV 17: 9.

44. Ibid., 17: 13–16.

45. Goldstein addresses the parallels between the two
cases in some detail in his translation of Maccabees II. See
in particular his notes on page 285 of that work.

46. Maccabees II VIII: 31

47. It is primarily in Maccabees IV that one finds this
idea that the deaths of these martyrs will bring about
atonement for the sins of Israel.

48. Maccabees IV 18: 3

49. Ibid.

50. Ibid., 282.

51. Hades, *The Third and Fourth Books of Maccabees*,
125–27,

52. From Augustine's, *City of God*, 18.36 quoted in
Hades, *The Third and Fourth Books of Maccabees*, 125.

53. Tertullian, *Apologeticus* 50.2

54. Gregory J. Riley's *One Jesus, Many Christs: How
Jesus Inspired Not One True Christianity, But Many* (San
Francisco: Harper Collins Publishers, 1997) is particularly
good at demonstrating the parallels between Jesus' story
and that of the ideal hero of antiquity. See in particular
Chapter 4 *The Story of Jesus*, pages 61–95. In his work
Honor and Shame in the Gospel of Matthew (cited earlier
in this chapter), Jerome H. Neyrey argues convincingly
that the evangelist responsible for Matthew's Gospel followed the formal rules of classical epideictic rhetoric (the
rhetoric of praise and blame) to create a narrative that
demonstrated the extraordinary, heroic nature of Jesus.

55. Neyrey, *Honor and Shame*, Chapter 7 *An En-
comium for Jesus A Noble Death* exhaustively analyzes the
rhetorical strategies that Matthew employs to demonstrate that Jesus' death was that of a hero worthy of the
highest possible praise.

56. Ibid., 211.

57. This quote, as well as the details of the martyrdom
of St. Pionius is taken from H. Musurillo, *The Acts of
the Christian Martyrs* (Oxford: Clarendon Press, 1972),
137–167. This quote is found on page 159.

58. Ibid., 165.

59. Ibid.

60. Ibid.

61. This brief biography of Rufinus is taken from
Robin Lane Fox's *Pagans and Christians* (San Francisco:
Harper and Row, Publishers, 1986), 460–467.

62. Ibid., 473.

63. Ibid., 419.

64. On the language used to describe the early Christian martyrs, see Riley, *One Jesus, Many Christs*, 157–178.

65. Quoted in Fox, *Pagans and Christians*, 448.

66. For more on this issue, see W.H.C. Frend's *Martyrdom and Persecution in the Early Church: A Study of a
Conflict from the Maccabees to Donatus* (Oxford: Oxford
University Press, 1965). This book remains the definitive
account on the subject of martyrdom in the first centuries of the Common Era.

67. On these "voluntary martyrdoms" see Fox, *Pagans and Christians*, 441–42 and Smith, *Fools, Martyrs,
Traitors*, 95–6.

68. Tertullian, quoted in Smith, *Fools, Martyrs, Traitors*, 93.

69. Quoted in Smith, *Fools, Martyrs, Traitors*, page 93.

70. Of course, as we will see, Christians will often find themselves at odds over what constitutes a just cause and these internecine conflicts will give rise to a great many martyrs.

Chapter 4

1. This chapter's two epigraphical quotations are from separate translations of Pindar's *Odes*. Pythian 8. 95–7 is taken from *The Odes and Selected Fragments* translated by G.S. Conway and Richard Stoneman (London: Everyman's Library, Orion Publishing Group, 1997), and Nemean 6. 1–7 is a translation by the historian David C. Young reprinted from his *A Brief History of the Olympic Games* (Oxford: Blackwell Publishing, 2004), 73. All other translations of Pindar's *Odes* in this chapter are from the two volume Loeb edition edited and translated by William H. Race (Cambridge, Massachusetts: Harvard University Press, 1997).

2. The "professionalism" of the athletes who competed in the circuit games of ancient Greece has been a much contested issue in the history of ancient sports. The best analysis of this issue (and the one to which I subscribe) is David C. Young, *The Olympic Myth of Greek Amateur Athletics* (Chicago: Ares Press, 1984).

3. As with the issue of professionalism, the distinctiveness of Greek athletics is a subject of much debate. A good summary of this discussion can be found in Mark Golden, *Sport and Society in Ancient Greece* (Cambridge: Cambridge University Press, 1998), 28–33. For opposing views, see M. Bernal, *Black Athena: The Afroasiatic Roots of Classical Civilization* (New Brunswick: Rutgers University Press, 1987); M.R. Lefkowitz and G.M. Rogers, Eds. *Black Athena Revisited* (Chapel Hill: University of North Carolina Press, 1996); H.D. Evjen, "Competitive athletics in ancient Greece: the search for origins and influences," *Opuscula Atheniensia* (*Oath*) 16.5:51–6 (1996); and "The origins and functions of formal athletic competition in the ancient world," in W. Coulson and H. Kyrielesi, Eds. *Proceedings of an International Symposium on the Olympic Games (5–9 September 1988).* (Athens: Deutsches Archäologisches Institut Athen, 1992). Information on Roman attitudes towards Greek athletics can be found in H.A. Harris, *Sport in Greece and Rome* (Ithaca: Cornell University Press, 1972), 44–74.

4. Golden, *Sport and Society in Ancient Greece*, 23.

5. Golden addresses this theory in some depth, pages 23–28. One of the more current iterations of Greek athletics as "war minus the shooting" is to be found in Nigel Spivey, *The Ancient Olympics* (Oxford: Oxford University Press, 2004), 1–29.

6. Homer, *Iliad*, 667–71.

7. Quoted in Golden, 28.

8. Ibid.

9. On the idea of an innate Greek competitive character, see Volume 4 of Jakob Burckhardt's, *Griechische Kulturgeschichte* (Stuttgart and Berlin, 1902), 87–122; 214–19; and E. N. Gardner, *Athletics of the Ancient World* (Oxford: Oxford University Press, 1930). See also

Michael Poliakoff, *Combat Sports in the Ancient World* (New Haven Connecticut: Yale University Press, 1997), 104–11; and Thomas F. Scanlon, *Eros and Greek Athletics* (Oxford: Oxford University Press, 2002), 9–10. In his *Sport and Society in Ancient Greece*, 30–45, Golden argues, I think convincingly, that competitiveness among the Greeks might also have constituted a "discourse of difference" that they used to define what it meant to be Greek and to further differentiate themselves from one another.

10. It should be noted that local contests were often open to Greeks from other communities, and seasoned athletes could and did compete in these events for the sake of winning their prizes. The presence of these outsiders and professionals was probably welcomed because local youths could learn from their example and experience.

11. The dates I have listed here for the establishment of the different circuit games are those given by Mark Golden in his *Sport in the Ancient World from A–Z* (New York: Routledge, 2004). Golden's book also addresses some of the other foundation myths associated with the *periodos* games that I have neglected to mention.

12. Golden, *Sport and Society in Ancient Greece*, 11

13. On the social distinctions between *periodos* contestants, see Golden's discussion of class difference in *Sport and Society in Ancient Greece*, pages 141–145. Information regarding the various aristocratic and non–aristocratic champions in the games is found in Young, *A Brief History of the Olympic Games*, 95–97,

14. Joe Maguire, "Towards a Sociological Theory of Sport and the Emotions: A Process-Sociological Perspective," page 104 in Eric Dunning and Chris Rojek, Eds. *Sport and Leisure in the Civilizing Process: Critique and Counter-Critique* (Toronto and Buffalo: University of Toronto Press, 1992)

15. For a detailed description of the various honors bestowed on an athletic champion see Bruno Currie's *Pindar and the Cult of the Heroes* (Oxford: Oxford University Press, 2005), 139–152.

16. On Milo's remarkable career, see Golden, *Sport in the Ancient World from A–Z*, 103 and Stephen G. Miller, *Ancient Greek Athletics* (New Haven and London: Yale University Press, 2004), 160.

17. Quoted in Miller, *Ancient Greek Athletics*, 163–4.

18. In addition to Miller, Golden's *Sport in the Ancient World from A–Z* also provided information on the career of Theogenes, 163.

19. Golden, *Sport in the Ancient World from A–Z*, 103

20. One rather odd case of oracular intervention that secured an athlete a hero cult is that of Kleomedes of Astypalaia. Stripped of his boxing crown at Olympia because foul play on his part had resulted in the death of his opponent, Kleomedes returned home mad with grief, entered a local school, pulled down the roof, and killed sixty children. Kleomedes' countrymen chased him into a temple of Athena where he hid in a chest. Breaking the chest open, the Astypalaians found no trace of the offending athlete and, upon inquiring of his whereabouts at Delphi, were told by the oracle that "Kleomedes of Astypalaia is the last of the heroes. Honor with sacrifices him who is no longer mortal." Ever obedient to the will of their gods, the Astypalaians complied. This odd ac-

count is found in Miller, *Ancient Greek Athletics*, page 162. On page 161 of the same work, Miller also relates the story of an athlete Polydamas, who was honored with a hero cult because his statue at Olympia was reputed to have healing powers.

21. Currie, *Pindar and the Cult of the Heroes*, 139–152.
22. Pindar, *Pythian* 8. 96
23. Pindar, *Nemean* 6. 5
24. Pindar, *Pythian* 3. 111–115.
25. Young, *A Brief History of the Olympic Games*, 68.
26. Miller, *Ancient Greek Athletics*, 235.
27. Ibid., 227–230.

Chapter 5

1. I am referring here to two clerics in particular, i.e., Adalbero, Bishop of Laon who wrote "Here below, some pray, others fight, still others work;" and Gerard of Cambrai who noted that "from the beginning, mankind has been divided into three parts, among men of prayer, farmers, and men of war."

2. Much of this section's discussion about the transformation of the medieval knight from a common retainer to the embodiment of aristocracy is based on the following works: Marc Bloch, *Feudal Society*, L.A. Manyon, trans. (Chicago: University of Chicago Press, 1961); Georges Duby, *The Chivalrous Society*, Cynthia Postan, trans. (Berkeley and Los Angeles: University of California Press, 1977) and *Three Orders: Feudal Society Imagined* (Chicago: University of Chicago Press, 1980); and Joseph R. Strayer, "The Two Levels of Feudalism," in Robert S. Hoyt, ed., *Life and Thought in the Early Middle Ages* (Minneapolis: University of Minneapolis Press, 1967).

3. Maurice Keen, *Chivalry* (New Haven: Yale University Press, 1984), 23–25.

4. Ibid., 25–27.

5. Strayer, "The Two Levels of Feudalism," and Duby, "The origins of knighthood," in *The Chivalrous Society*, 158–161.

6. Duby, "The origins of knighthood," 161–170; and "Laity and the peace of God," also in *The Chivalrous Society*, 122–133.

7. Keen, *Chivalry*, 30–34.

8. A good succinct summary of chivalry's many usages can be found in James Ross Sweeney's entry on *Chivalry* in the *Dictionary of the Middle Ages*, Joseph R. Strayer, Editor in Chief (New York: Charles Scribner's Sons, 1986), 301. See also Keen, *Chivalry*, 2 and Richard W. Kaeuper, *Chivalry and Violence in Medieval Europe* (Oxford: Oxford University Press, 1999), 4.

9. On William the Marshall, see the following Paul Meyer, ed., *L'Histoire de Guillaume le Maréchal*, 3 vols. (Paris: Librairie Renouard, H. Laurens, successeur, 1891–1901); David Crouch, *William Marshal, Court, Career and Chivalry in the Angevin Empire, 1147–1219* (London and New York: Longman, 1990); Sidney Painter, *William Marshal: Knight-Errant, Baron and Regent of England* (Baltimore: John Hopkins Press, 1933); and Keen, *Chivalry*, 20–21, 89.

10. Quoted in Kaeuper, *Chivalry and Violence*, 80.
11. Ibid., 76.

12. Ibid., 135.

13. There is an extensive literature on the Crusades and the Crusader states. Among the works consulted for the all too cursory treatment afforded them in this chapter are: Thomas F. Madden, *The New Concise History of the Crusades* (Lanham, Maryland: Rowman and Littlefield Publishers, Inc., 2005); Jonathan Riley-Smith, *The Oxford Illustrated History of the Crusades* (Oxford: Oxford University Press, 2001); and Steven Runciman, *A History of the Crusades*, 3 Volumes (The Folio Society, 1994).

14. On the Knights Templar, see Malcolm Barber, *The New Knighthood: A History of the Order of the Temple* (Cambridge: Cambridge University Press, 1994); Marie Louise Buist-Thiele, "The Influence of St. Bernard of Clairvaux on the Formation of the Order of the Knights Templar," in Michael Gervers, ed., *The Second Crusade and the Cistercians* (New York: St. Martin's Press, 1992); Norman Housley, Editor, *Knighthoods of Christ : Essays on the History of the Crusades and the Knights Templar, Presented to Malcolm Barber* (Aldershot, England; Burlington, VT: Ashgate, 2007); Stephen Howarth, *The Knights Templar* (London: Collins Press, 1982); Sean Martin, *The Knights Templar: The History and Myths of the Legendary Military Order* (New York: Thunder's Mouth Press, 2004);

15. On these two orders of knighthood, see Malcolm Barber and Helen Nicholson, Editors, *The Military Orders*, 2 Volumes (Aldershot, Hampshire: Valorium, 1994 and Brookfield, VT: Ashgate, 1998); Alan Forey, *Military Orders and Crusades* (Aldershot, Hampshire: Valorium and Brookfield, VT: Ashgate, 1994); Helen Nicholson, *Templars, Hospitallers, and Teutonic Knights: Images of the Military Orders, 1128–1291* (Leister, New York: Leister University Press, 1993); William Urban, *The Baltic Crusade* (Chicago: Lithuanian Research and Studies Center, 1994) and *The Prussian Crusade* (Lanham, MD: University of America, 1980).

16. Keen, *Chivalry*, 49–50,

17. This summary of the *Ordene* is taken from Keen's much more detailed description of the work in his *Chivalry*, 7.

18. On this whole issue of royal chivalry, the reader is directed to Richard Kaeuper's treatment of the links between kings and their knights in *Part III. The Link With Royauté* of his *Chivalry and Violence*. See also his comments on Robin Hood in this section, pages 113–114.

19. Ibid., 110.

20. On the ways in which knighthood read chivalric literature, see Elspeth M. Kennedy, "The Knight as Reader of Arthurian Romance," in *Culture and the King: The Social Implications of the Arthurian Legend, Essays in Honor of Valerie M. Lagorio*, Ed. Martin B. Schichtman and James P. Carley (Albany: State University of New York Press, 1994).

21. Charny's biographical information is taken from Richard W. Kaeuper's introduction to *A Knight's Own Book of Chivalry*, Geoffroi de Charny, Trans. Elspeth Kennedy (Philadelphia: University of Pennsylvania Press, 2005).

22. Ibid., 13–14.
23. Ibid., 48.
24. Ibid., 51.

25. Ibid., 56.
26. Ibid., 56–7.
27. Ibid., 55.
28. Ibid.
29. Ibid., 67.
30. Ibid., 97.
31. Ibid.
32. Ibid., 49.
33. Ibid.
34. Ibid., 95.
35. Ibid.
36. Ibid., 99.
37. Ibid., 34.

Chapter 6

1. On the development of early sainthood, see André Vauchez, *Sainthood in the Later Middle Ages* (Cambridge: Cambridge University Press, 1997), 13–21.
2. As noted in Chapter III, Gregory J. Riley's *One Jesus, Many Christs: How Jesus Inspired Not One True Christianity, But Many* (San Francisco: Harper Collins Publishers, 1997) is particularly good at demonstrating the ways in which the early Church fathers used pagan heroic tropes to promote the new faith.
3. Ronald N. Swanson, *Religion and Devotion in Europe, 1215–1515* (Cambridge: Cambridge University Press, 1995), 154.
4. Ibid., 158–163. See also Patrick Geary's essay "Humiliation of the saints" in *Saints and Their Cults: Studies in Religious Sociology, Folklore, and History* edited by Stephen Wilson (Cambridge: Cambridge University Press, 1983), 123–140.
5. Wilson, *Saints and Their Cults*, 1–4.
6. Vauchez, *Sainthood*, 139.
7. Ibid., 148–156. Vauchez actually lists a number of men and women who fall into this category of "popular sainthood" on pages 148–151.
8. For more on Saint Guinefort see Stephen de Bourbon, *Anecdotes historiques*, ed. A. Lecoy de la Marche (Paris: Librairie Renouard, H. Loones, successeur, 1877); and Jean Claude Schmitt, *The holy greyhound : Guinefort, healer of children since the thirteenth century* translated by Martin Thom (Cambridge ; New York : Cambridge University Press; Paris: Editions de la maison des sciences de l'homme, 1983.)
9. Quoted in Vauchez, *Sainthood*, 25.
10. Ibid., 28.
11. Ibid., 51–56.
12. Ibid., 61.
13. Ibid., 279. See 279–283 for Vauchez's analysis of saintly social origins at this time.
14. Ibid., 270–279. With regard to the absence of saints from the Low Countries, Vauchez acknowledges that there does not appear to be as of yet any plausible explanation for this phenomenon.
15. Ibid., 257–270. On the politics of sainthood at this period, also see Michael Goodich "The politics of canonization in the thirteenth century: lay and Mendicant saints," in Wilson, *Saints and their Cults*, 169–187.
16. A very good overview of this 12th century Catholic reformation can be found in F. Donald Logan,

A History of the Church in the Middle Ages (London and New York: Routledge, 2002), 131–225.
17. Matthew 20: 7–10.
18. Aside from his many hagiographies, there are a number of excellent biographies of St. Francis of Assisi. The ones consulted for this brief account of his life are Adrian House, *Francis of Assisi: A Revolutionary Life* (London: Chatto and Windus, 2000); Michael Robson, *St. Francis: The Legend and the Life* (London: Geoffrey Chapman, 1999); and Aviad M. Kleinberg, *Prophets in Their Own Country: Living Saints and the Making of Sainthood in the Later Middle Ages* (Chicago and London: The University of Chicago Press, 1992), 126–148. For translations of St. Francis' writings, see *Francis of Assisi, Early Documents* (3 volumes), edited by R.J. Armstrong, J.A.W. Hellermann and W.J. Short (New York: New York City Press, 1999–2001). Logan's *A History of the Church in the Middle Ages*, has an excellent summary treatment of the mendicant orders on pages 213–223. And for a more complete history of the Franciscan movement, see John Moorman, *A History of the Franciscan Order: From Its Origins to the Year 1517* (Chicago: Franciscan Herald Press, 1988).
19. Edmund Gardner, "St. Catherine of Siena" in *The Catholic Encyclopedia* (New York: Robert Appleton Company, 1908). Retrieved from New Advent: *http://www.newadvent.org/cathen03447a.htm.*
20. It should be noted that Karen Scott's analysis of the relationship between Catherine of Siena and Raymond of Capua is much more nuanced than the extremely cursory mention made of it here. For her complete argument, see Karen Scott, "Mystical Death, Bodily Death: Catherine of Siena and Raymond of Capua on the Mystic's Encounter with God" in *Gendered Voices: Medieval Saints and Their Interpreters* edited by Catherine M. Mooney (Philadelphia: University of Pennsylvania Press, 1999.)
21. For more on Catherine of Siena, see Raymond of Capua's *The Life of Catherine of Siena*, trans. Conleth Kearns (Wilmington, Del.: Glazer, 1980); *The Letters of Catherine of Siena*, trans. Suzanne Noffke, O.P. (Binghamton, N.Y.: Center for Medieval and Early Renaissance Studies, 1988); *I Catherine: Selected Writings of Catherine of Siena*, trans. Kenelm Foster and Mary John Ronayne (London: Collins, 1980). There is also a recent bibliography of works by and about Catherine in English included in Suzanne Noffke, O.P., *Catherine of Siena: Vision Through a Distant Eye* (Collegeville, Minn.: Liturgical Press, 1996).
22. Thomas Heffernan, *Sacred Biography: Saints and Their Biographers in the Middle Ages* (New York: Oxford University Press, 1988), 63.

Chapter 7

1. Brian Greene, "Questions, Not Answers, Make Science the Ultimate Adventure," *Wired Magazine*, April 20, 2009.
2. Those interested in a more in-depth account of Galileo's life and work are directed to the following biographies, M. Sharratt, *Galileo: Decisive Innovator* (Oxford: Oxford University Press, 1994) and S. Drake,

Galileo: Pioneer Scientist (Toronto: University of Toronto Press, 1990).

3. On Galileo's scientific work and methods, see S. Drake, Translator, *Discoveries and Opinions of Galileo* (Garden City, New York: Doubleday, 1957).

4. Galileo Galilei: Letter to the Grand Duchess Christina of Tuscany, 1615, *Internet Modern History Sourcebook*, http://www.fordham.edu/halsall/mod/galileo-tuscany.html.

5. Two excellent works covering the various political factors that informed Galileo's career and his troubled relationship with the Catholic Church are Mario Bagioli, *Galileo, Courtier: The Practice of Science in the Culture of Absolutism* (Chicago: University of Chicago Press, 1993) and Margaret C. Jacob, *Scientific Culture and the Making of the Industrial West* (Oxford: Oxford University Press, 1997), 18–28.

6. *Papal Addresses to the Pontifical Academy of Sciences 1917–2002 and to the Pontifical Academy of Social Sciences 1994–2002* (Vatican City: Ex Aedibvs Academics in Civitate Vaticana, 2003), 83.

7. Mary Wollstonecraft Shelley, *Frankenstein* (New York: Barnes and Noble Classics, 2003), 42.

8. Those interested in a fuller treatment of Newton's life and discoveries, or for that matter any of the individual scientists treated in the following pages, should consult Charles C. Gillispie, ed., *Dictionary of Scientific Biography*, 16 vols. (New York: Scribner, 1970). R. S. Westfall's *The Life of Isaac Newton* (New York: Cambridge University Press, 1993) is also a well-regarded biography on this scientist and his contributions to physics and astronomy. For the social and political context within which Newton worked, see the aforementioned Jacob, *Scientific Culture*, 51–96.

9. For the exact wording of Descartes' method, see his *Discourse on Method and The Meditations* (London: Penguin Books, 1968), 41.

10. For an interesting treatment of Descartes' skepticism and its place in European intellectual history, see Richard H. Popkin, *The History of Scepticism from Erasmus to Descartes* (Assen, Netherlands: Van Gorcum, 1964). See also Jacob, *Scientific Culture*, 34–50 for an interesting discussion on the social and cultural significance of Cartesianism.

11. Aside from Gillispie, a good introduction to Descartes' life and philosophical work is A. Kenny, *Descartes* (New York: Random House, 1968).

12. On the importance of Francis Bacon in the early development of science see Paolo Rossi, *Francis Bacon: From Magic to Science* (Chicago: University of Chicago Press, 1968); B. Farrington, *The Philosophy of Francis Bacon* (Liverpool: Liverpool University Press, 1964); and Charles Webster, *The Great Instauratian: Science, Medicine and Reform, 1626–1660* (London: Duckworth, 1975).

13. Francis Bacon, *New Atlantis* (Montana: Kessinger Publishing Company), 321.

14. Ibid., 330.

15. Ibid., 331.

16. See J. R. Jacob's "Restoration, Reformation and the Origins of the Royal Society," in *History of Science*, vol. 13 (1975), 155–176, for more information on the influence of Bacon in the founding of the Royal Society.

17. Vincenzo Ferrone, "The Man of Science," in *Enlightenment Portraits*, Michel Vovelle, ed. (Chicago and London: The University of Chicago Press, 1992), 208.

18. Mary Terrall, "Heroic Narratives of Quest and Discovery," in *Configurations* 6.2 (1998), 223–242.

19. Ibid., 229.

20. Ibid., 230.

21. Ferrone, "The Man of Science," 206.

22. Ibid.

23. Terrall, "Heroic Narratives," 239.

24. The information on Lagrange's life, work and many honors is gleaned largely from Gillispie's entry on him in his *Dictionary of Scientific Biography*. Ferrone has some interesting things to say about Lagrange as "the ideal type" of the Enlightenment savant in his essay on "The Man of Science," 208–09. Readers are also directed to E. T. Bell's chapter on Lagrange in his *Men of Mathematics* (New York: Simon and Schuster, 1953), as well as to what Carl B. Boyer has to say about him in his *A History of Mathematics*, revised by Uta C. Merzbach (New York: John Wiley & Sons, 1991).

25. From Kurt R. Biermann's entry on Humboldt in Gillispie, ed., *Dictionary of Scientific Biography*, 550–51.

26. Ibid., 551.

27. Not surprisingly, there is an exhaustive literature on Alexander von Humboldt. Readers wishing for more than the cursory treatment accorded to him here should take a look at Biermann's bibliography at the end of his article in Gillispie, ed., *Dictionary of Scientific Biography*, 553–555. The definitive biography of Humboldt remains Hanno Beck's 2 volume (in German) *Alexander von Humboldt* (Wiesbaden: F. Steiner, 1959–61). A good English biography is L. Kellner, *Alexander von Humboldt* (London, New York: Oxford University Press, 1963). I would also recommend these more recent accounts of Humboldt: Aaron Sachs, *The Humboldt Current: Nineteenth Century Exploration and the Roots of American Environmentalism* (New York: Viking Press, 2006); Daniel Kehlmann's 2005 fictional account of Humboldt's life, *Die Vermessung der Welt*, translated into English by Carol Brown Janeway as *Measuring the World: A Novel* (New York: Pantheon, 2006); and David G. McCullough's essay on Humboldt's South American expedition, "Journey to the Top of the World," in his *Brave Companions: Portraits in History* (New York: Prentice Hall Press, 1992).

28. The idea of scientific revolutions as "paradigm shifts" is the subject of Thomas Kuhn's groundbreaking study, *The Structure of Scientific Revolutions* (Chicago: University of Chicago Press, 1970).

29. On the close relationship that existed between Romantic writers and scientists see Richard Holmes, *The Age of Wonder: How the Romantic Generation Discovered the Beauty and Terror of Science* (New York: Pantheon Books, 2008). See also Freeman Dyson's review of this book "When Science & Poetry Were Friends" in *The New York Review of Books*, 13 August 2009, 15–18. And of course Sinclair Lewis' *Arrowsmith* remains perhaps the best fictional account of the religious fervor science excited among its devotees at the turn-of-the 19th century.

30. R. R. Palmer and Joel Colton, *A History of the Modern World* (New York: Alfred A. Knopf, 1978), 905.

31. Probably the best account of the relationship between the mass press and the traveling scientists of this

time is Beau Riffenburgh, *The Myth of the Explorer: The Press, Sensationalism, and Geographical Discovery* (London: Belhaven Press, 1993).

32. Quoted in Riffenburgh, *The Myth of the Explorer,* 167.

33. Seth Shulman, *Owning the Future* (Boston: Houghton Mifflin, 1999), 158–60. Probably the best account about Edison's "invention factory" at Menlo Park is William S. Pretzer, ed. *Working at Inventing: Thomas A. Edison and the Menlo Park Experience* (Dearborn, Michigan: Henry Ford Museum & Greenfield Village, 1989).

34. The standard biography of Edison is Matthew Josephson, *Edison* (New York: McGraw Hill, 1959). Neil Baldwin's *Edison: Inventing the Century* (Chicago: University of Chicago Press, 2001) is also quite good and very readable.

35. Sir David Brewster, *Memoirs of the life, writings, and discoveries of Sir Isaac Newton* (Edinburgh: T. Constable & Co., 1856), Volume 2, Chapter 27.

Chapter 8

1. Jerry Hopkins and Daniel Sugerman, *No One Here Gets Out Alive* (New York: Warner Books, 1980), vii-viii.

2. John P. McKay, Bennett D. Hill, John Buckler, *A History of Western Society* (Boston: Houghton Mifflin, 1987), 741.

3. Terry Castle, "Mad, Bad and Dangerous to Know," *The New York Times.* 13 April, 1997: 11–10.

4. I owe the observation that romanticism is characterized by a love of the "unclassifiable" to R. R. Palmer and Joel Colton's *A History of the Modern World* (New York: Alfred A. Knopf, 1978), 428.

5. The expression "fixities and definities" was coined by J. L. Talmon in his *Romanticism and Revolt: Europe 1815–1848* (New York: Norton, 1979), 136.

6. Richard Friedenthal, *Goethe: His Life and Times* (London and New York: Weidenfeld and Nicolson, 1963), 128.

7. William Wordsworth, *The Prelude* (Harmondsworth, 1971), 109. For a more in-depth look at Wordsworth and this period in English Romanticism, see J. Wordsworth, *William Wordsworth and the Age of English Romanticism* (New Brunswick, N.J.: Rutgers University Press, 1987).

8. Eric Hobsbawm, *The Age of Revolution 1789–1848* (New York: Vintage Books, 1996), 255.

9. The reader interested in the history of romanticism and its premier artists is directed to the following works: M. Cranston, *The Romantic Movement* (Oxford: Oxford University Press, 1994); H. Honour, *Romanticism* (New York: Harper and Row, 1979); Roy Porter and Mikul Teich, eds. *Romanticism in National Context* (New York: Cambridge University Press, 1988); Nicholas V. Riasanovsky, *The Emergence of Romanticism* (New York: Oxford University Press, 1992); and H. G. Schenk, *The Mind of the European Romantics* (Garden City, N.Y.: Doubleday, 1969).

10. For those interested in what 19th century commentators had to say about dandies see: Charles Baudelaire, "Le peintre de la vie moderne," Volume II, and "Mon Coeur mis à nu," Volume I, in his *Oeuvres completes,* ed. Claude Pichois (Paris: Pléiade, 1976); Barbey d'Aurevilly, "Du dandysme et de George Brummell," in his *Oeuvres romanesques completes,* ed. Jacques Petit, Volume II (Paris: Pléiade, 1966); Honoré de Balzac, *La comédie humaine,* Volume XII (Paris: Pléiade, 1981), 247. Secondary works addressing this subject that are also excellent are Leo Braudy, *The Frenzy of Renown: Fame and Its History* (New York and Oxford: Oxford University Press, 1986); Ellen Moers, *The Dandy: Brummell to Beerbohm* (Lincoln: University of Nebraska Press, 1978); and Hiltrud Gnüg, "The Dandy and the Don Juan Type," in Gerhart Hoffmeister, ed. *European Romanticism: Literary Cross-Currents, Modes, and Models* (Detroit: Wayne State University Press, 1990).

11. Braudy, *The Frenzy of Renown,* 404.

12. William Jesse, *The Life of Beau Brummell by Captain Jesse,* 2 Volumes (London: Saunders and Otley, 1844), I, 22.

13. For a detailed listing of Brummell's standing in popular culture see pages 2 and 3 of the Wikipedia entry on him at http://en.wikipedia.org/wiki/Beau_Brummell.

14. Ibid., 3

15. A. Alvarez, *The Savage God: A Study of Suicide* (New York: Random House, 1972), 201.

16. For Chatterton's Wikipedia entry go to *http://en. wikipedia.org/wiki/Thomas_Chatterton.* Alvarez also has some insightful things to say about this poet in his *Savage God,* 187–206. And John Cranstoun Nevill's biography *Thomas Chatterton* (London and Toronto: Muller, 1948) is quite good as well.

17. Remark of Emile Bouvier quoted in Alvarez, *The Savage God,* 228.

18. Quoted in Alvarez, *The Savage God,* 228.

19. Ibid., 229.

20. Ibid.

21. From André Breton's *First Surrealist Manifesto,* 1924, a copy of which can be found in Patrick Waldberg, *Surrealism* (New York: McGraw-Hill, 1971), pp. 66–75.

22. There is an extensive literature on Byron. For a listing of the many works on the poet up to 1973 see Oscar Jose Santucho's *George Gordon, Lord Byron: A Comprehensive Bibliography of Secondary Materials in English, 1807–1973* (Metuchen, N.J.: Scarecrow Press, 1977). The following books are also highly recommended: Benita Eisler, *Byron: Child of Passion, Fool of Fame* (New York: Vintage Books, 2000); Leslie A. Marchand, *Byron: A Portrait* (New York: Knopf, 1970); Peter L. Thorslev, *The Byronic Hero: Types and Prototypes* (Minneapolis: University of Minnesota Press, 1962); Edward John Trelawny's *Recollections of the Last Days of Shelley and Byron* (Boston: Ticknor and Fields, 1859).

Chapter 9

1. The term "heroic vitalism" was penned by critic and playwright Eric Bentley in his *The Cult of the Superman: A Study of the Idea of Heroism in Carlyle and Nietzsche, with Notes on Other Hero-Worshippers of Modern Times* (Gloucester, Mass.: Peter Smith, 1969)

2. Robert C. Tucker, Editor, *The Marx-Engels Reader* (New York/London: W.W. Norton Co., 1978), 476.

3. Ibid., 160.

4. For those who are interested in a more detailed analysis of the life and work of Thomas Carlyle, the following biographies are highly recommended: James Anthony Froude, *Thomas Carlyle: A History of the First Forty Years of His Life, 1795–1835; A History of His Life in London, 1834–1881.* 4 vols. London, 1882, 1884 (this particular work was penned by an intimate of Carlyle who was authorized by him to write his biography after his death); Fred Kaplan, *Thomas Carlyle: A Biography* (Cambridge: Cambridge University Press, 1983); Simon Heffer, *Moral Desperado: A Life of Thomas Carlyle* (London: Weidenfeld and Nicolson, 1995); and John Morrow, *Thomas Carlyle* (London: Humbledon Continuum, 2006). The following collections of essays on Carlyle's work and influence are also quite informative: John Clubbe, Editor, *Carlyle and His Contemporaries: Essays in Honor of Charles Richard Sanders* (Durham: Duke University Press, 1976); K. J. Fielding and Rodger Tarr, Editors, *Carlyle Past and Present* (London: Vision, 1976); Charles Richard Sanders, *Carlyle's Friendships and Other Studies* (Durham: Duke University Press, 1977); and Jules Paul Siegel, Editor, *Thomas Carlyle: The Critical Heritage* (London: Routledge and K. Paul, 1971).

5. Bentley, 54.

6. Appropriately enough, the medal was presented to him by his hero Bismarck.

7. The biographical information on Nietzsche in this chapter is largely drawn from Walter Kaufmann's *Nietzsche: Philosopher, Psychologist, Antichrist* (Princeton: Princeton University Press, 1968). Though this is an old biography and there have been a number of other more recent Nietzsche biographies, I still find Kaufmann the preeminent authority in all matters pertaining to Nietzsche.

8. It is interesting to note that not only did Carlyle and Nietzsche experience a crisis of faith in their first years in college, but in both cases this crisis was occasioned by exposure to books that were popular at the time. In Carlyle's case the text that turned him away from the ministry was Gibbon's *The Decline and Fall of the Roman Empire*, and with Nietzsche the book that is reputed to have occasioned his break with Christianity was David Strauss' *Life of Jesus*.

9. Quoted in *The Portable Nietzsche*, Walter Kaufmann, Editor (New York: Penguin Books, USA, 1968), 7–8.

10. Including Carlyle, who he dismissed as a noisy romantic seeking to fill the void left by his loss of faith.

11. Kaufmann, op. cit., 97.

12. Ibid.

13. Thomas R. Hinton, *Nietzsche in German Politics and Society 1890–1918* (Manchester: Dover N.H.: Manchester University Press, 1983).

14. The best historical work in English dealing with *völkish* ideology from the 19th century through the Third Reich is George L. Mosse's *The Crisis of German Ideology: Intellectual Origins of the Third Reich* (New York: Schocken Books, 1981). See pages 150–52 of this work for Mosse's discussion regarding the adherents of this movement, and Part I which deals with its ideological foundations in German history.

15. For a fuller discussion of the idea of a conservative revolution and its principal proponents in Germany, see Fritz Stern, *The Politics of Cultural Despair: A Study in the Rise of Germanic Ideology* (Berkeley: University of California Press, 1961).

16. Ibid., 62–3.

17. See Bernice Glatzer Rosenthal regarding the parallels between Orthodox Christianity and Nietzschean thought in her superb treatment of Nietzsche's influence on Russian revolutionary thinking and action *New Myth, New World: From Nietzsche to Stalinism* (University Park, Pennsylvania: Pennsylvania State University Press, 2002). See in particular pages 16–20 in that work.

18. For more on naïve monarchism in Russia, see Daniel Field, *Rebels in the Name of the Tsar* (Boston: Houghton Mifflin, 1976).

19. To read some of the *bogatyri* tales, see *An Anthology of Russian Folk Epics* translated with an introduction and commentary by James Bailey and Tatyana Ivanova (Armonk, N.Y.: M.E. Sharpe, Inc., 1998). On Stalin's use of these tales, see Frank Miller *Folklore for Stalin* (Armonk, N.Y.: M.E. Sharpe, Inc., 1990) and Felix J. Oinas "Folklore and Politics in the Soviet Union." *Slavic Review* 32 (1973): 45–58.

20. On the Russian literary intelligentsia of the nineteenth century, see E. H. Carr's *The Romantic Exiles: A Nineteenth Century Portrait Gallery* (Boston: Beacon Press, 1961) and Richard Pipes, ed. *The Russian Intelligentsia* (New York: Columbia University Press, 1961). With regard to the various Russian terrorist movements of this time, see Nicholas Berdyaev, *The Origin of Russian Communism* (London: Bles, 1937); Abbot Gleason, *Young Russia: the Genesis of Russian Radicalism in the 1860s* (Chicago: University of Chicago Press, 1985); and Daniel Brower, *Training The Nihilists: Education and Radicalism in Tsarist Russia* (Ithaca: Cornell University Press, 1975).

21. Again, the most exhaustive work in English dealing with the influence of Nietzsche's ideas on the Russian left is Rosenthal's *New Myth, New World: From Nietzsche to Stalinism*. See in particular her section on Nietzschean Marxists, pages 68–93, where she addresses among other things, Bolshevik god building.

22. This and the following excerpts from Adolf Hitler, *Mein Kampf*, trans. Ralph Manheim (Boston: Houghton Mifflin, 1943, 1971) are found on pp. 442–51.

23. Ibid.

24. Ibid.

25. The idea of "working towards the Fuehrer" is the motif and organizing principle of Ian Kershaw's superb two-volume biography *Hitler: 1889–1936 Hubris* and *Hitler: 1936–1945 Nemesis* (New York: W. W. Norton, 2000). Kershaw uses this expression, articulated by a minor Nazi functionary in 1934, as a way to explain both the nature of Hitler's extraordinary power and the ongoing radicalization of his regime. I find this notion equally applicable to the National Socialist effort to define a Nazi ideal of heroism.

26. For those interested in Hitler's life and career, the most current and, in this author's humble opinion, best biography of the German Führer is Ian Kershaw's two-volume *Hitler: 1889–1936 Hubris* and *Hitler: 1936–1945*

Nemesis. Kershaw's work is exhaustive, addresses past and contemporary interpretations of the Nazi dictatorship and its leader, and focuses considerable attention on forces external to Hitler's personality that shaped his policies and those of his regime. Older biographies that still merit attention are Alan Bullock, *Hitler: A Study in Tyranny* (New York: Harper and Row, 1964); Joachim Fest, *Hitler* (New York: Harcourt Brace Jovanovich, 1974); and William Carr, *Hitler: A Study in Personality and Politics* (New York: Harper and Row, 1964).

27. Those interested in reading a more exhaustive treatment of these figures and the uses to which they were put by the Nazi regime should see Jay W. Baird *To Die for Germany: Heroes in the Nazi Pantheon* (Bloomington and Indianapolis: Indiana University Press, 1990).

28. For an excellent description of the mind and personality of Heinrich Himmler see Joachim C. Fest, *The Face of the Third Reich* (Munich: R. Piper & Co. Verlag, 1963), 111. For a more complete biography of Hitler's SS chief, see Richard Brietman, *The Architect of Genocide: Heinrich Himmler and the Final Solution* (Hanover: University Press of New England, 1992).

29. John Toland, *Adolf Hitler* (New York: Doubleday & Company, Inc., 1976), 111.

30. Felix Kersten, *The Kersten Memoirs 1940–1945* (New York: Macmillan Company, 1957), 115–116.

31. Toland, 1047.

32. For a thorough description of Himmler's effort to establish the SS as a kind of quasi-religious knightly order see Heinz Höhne, *The Order of the Death's Head. The History of the SS* (New York: Ballantine Books, 1967), 163–181.

33. Information on the social composition of the SS can be found in Höhne, pp. 152–156.

34. Quoted in Höhne, 433.

35. James J. Weingartner, "Law and Justice in the Nazi SS-The Case of Konrad Morgen," *Central European History*, 6 (1983), 282.

36. Fest, 118–119.

37. Quoted in Höhne, 183.

38. Both Fest and Höhne argue that Heydrich's actions were driven by considerations of power rather than ideology. Given the close interrelationship between power and ideology in Hitler's Germany, this distinction seems really quite meaningless.

39. Details of Heydrich's funeral are found in Baird, 215–216. Hitler's remarks are quoted on 216.

40. On Hitler's plans for the colonization of Russia see *Hitler's Secret Conversations, 1941–1942* (New York: Octagon Books, 1976), 28–30, 56–57, 343–45. Translated by Norman Cameron and R. H. Stevens. Details regarding Himmler's dream of an SS Burgundian state are found in Kersten, 184–86. There are also a number of "counterfactual" histories that elaborate what these Nazi fantasies might have meant to the world in the event of a German victory or stalemate during World War II. Among the best of these are: Philip K. Dick, *The Man in the High Castle* (New York: Berkeley Medallion Books, 1962); Norman Spinrad, *The Iron Dream* (New York: Avon Books, 1972); Robert Harris, *Fatherland* (New York: Random House, 1992); and Gregory Benford & Martin Harry Greenberg, Editors, *Hitler Victorious: Eleven Stories of the German Victory in World War II* (New York: Berkeley Books, 1987).

41. V. V. Mayakovsky, "Vladimir Il'ich" quoted in Nina Tumarkin, *Lenin Lives! The Lenin Cult in Soviet Russia* (Cambridge, Massachusetts, and London, England: Harvard University Press, 1983), 100.

42. On "War Communism" and its impact on the Bolshevik Party, see the following: Sheila Fitzpatrick, "The Civil War as a Formative Experience," in Abbot Gleason, Peter Kenez, and Richard Stites, eds., *Bolshevik Culture: Experiment and Order in the Russian Revolution* (Bloomington and Indianapolis: Indiana University Press, 1985), 57–76; Robert C. Tucker, "Stalinism as Revolution from Above," in Tucker, ed., *Stalinism: Essays in Historical Interpretation* (New York: Norton Press, 1977), 77–104; and Geoffrey Hosking, *The First Socialist Society: A History of the Soviet Union from Within* (Cambridge: Harvard University Press, 1985), 57–92.

43. Tumarkin, 54–55.

44. Lenin's one-time friend Pavel Axelrod (one-time because he ultimately sided with the Menshevik wing of Russian social democracy) remarked that Lenin "for twenty-four hours of the day is taken up with the revolution, has no thoughts but the revolution, and even in his sleep dreams of nothing but revolution." Quoted in R. R. Palmer and Joel Colton, *A History of the Modern World* (New York: Alfred A. Knopf, 1978), 696.

45. For a more detailed account of the development of this Lenin cult see Tumarkin, particularly Chapter 6 "The Body and the Shrine" and 7 "Lenin's Life After Death."

46. Quoted in Katerina Clark, "Little Heroes and Great Deeds: Literature Responds to the First Five Year Plan," in Sheila Fitzpatrick, ed., *Cultural Revolution in Russia 1928–1931* (Bloomington: Indiana University Press, 1984), 191.

47. Clark, "Little Heroes," 202.

48. Ibid., 204–205.

49. The progress of Soviet literature from little men to Bolshevik *bogatyri* is a fascinating subject ably addressed by Katrina Clark in her *The Soviet Novel: History as Ritual* (Chicago and London: University of Chicago Press, 1985). See in particular her remarks in this book about Socialist Realism in the period of high Stalinism, pages 136–155.

50. On the discussion in various party organs about the hero question, see Rosenthal, 390–391.

51. An excellent treatment of Stalin's leadership circle is Simon Sebag Montefiore's *Stalin: The Court of the Red Tsar* (New York: Vintage Books, 2005). Kaganovich's career and character are treated extensively in this work.

52. John McGannon, *Red Arctic: Polar Exploration and the Myth of the North in the Soviet Union, 1932–1939* (New York, Oxford: Oxford University Press, 1998).

53. In fact, the initial impetus behind the creation of an Order of the Soviet Hero was to honor seven pilots — Anatoly Liapidevsky, Sigizmund Levanevsky, Vasili Molokov, Mayrikiv Slepnev, Nikolai Kamanin, Ivan Doronin, and Mikhail Vodopianov — who participated in the successful aerial search and rescue of the crew of the steamship *Cheliuskin*, which sank in Arctic waters on February 13, 1934 during its voyage across the Northwest Passage.

54. McGannon, op. cit., 107. See also pages 98–103 for McGannon's insightful discussion of Chkalov as an

example of Katarina Clark's theory of the Soviet hero under Stalinism as "the dialectical synthesis of spontaneity and consciousness."

55. Ibid., 107–08.

56. There are two excellent books in English that deal exhaustively with the Stakhanovite heroes of labor in industry and agriculture, Lewis H. Siegelbaum, *Stakhanovism and the Politics of Productivity in the USSR, 1935–1941* (Cambridge: Cambridge University Press, 1988) and Mary Buckley, *Mobilizing Soviet Peasants: Heroines and Heroes of Stalin's Fields* (Lanham: Rowman & Littlefield Publishers, Inc., 2006).

57. All of this biographical information is taken from Joachen Hellbeck, *Revolution on My Mind: Writing a Diary Under Stalin* (Cambridge, Massachusetts: Harvard University Press, 2006), 238–239.

58. For more on Potemkin, see Chapter 7 in Hellbeck, pages 223–284

59. Sheila Fitzpatrick *The Russian Revolution 1917–1932* (Oxford: Oxford University Press, 1982), 134.

Chapter 10

1. There is a considerable literature on the picaresque novel. Some works that have been helpful to me in the writing of this chapter are: *The Oxford Companion to English Literature, Fifth Edition*, Edited by Margaret Drabble (Oxford: Oxford University Press, 1985); Ulrick Wicks, *Picaresque Narrative, Picaresque Fictions: A Theory and Research Guide* (Hadley, New York: Greenwood Press, 1989); Frederick Monteser, *The Picaresque Element in Western Literature* (University, Alabama: University of Alabama Press, 1975); Robert Alter, *Rogue's Progress: Studies in the Picaresque Novel* (Cambridge: Harvard University Press, 1964); Frank Wadleigh Chandler, *The Literature of Roguery* (New York: Burt Franklin, 1958)

2. See Robert Darnton's essay "Peasants Tell Tales" in his *The Great Cat Massacre: And Other Episodes in French Cultural History* (New York: Random House, 1985) for an enlightening and entertaining exposition on how peasants used folktales during the early modern period and what these stories also tell us about conditions during that time.

3. Ibid., 55.

4. For those interested in the social history of the early modern period, particularly that of the common people, the following works are highly recommended: Fernand Braudel, *The Mediterranean and the Mediterranean World in the Age of Philip II* (New York: Harper and Row, 1976) and *The Structures of Everyday Life: Limits of the Possible* (New York: Harper and Row, 1979); Emmanuel Le Roy Ladurie, *The Peasants of Languedoc* (Urbana: University of Illinois Press, 1974); and Natalie Zemon Davis, *The Return of Martin Guerre* (Cambridge: Harvard University Press, 1985). For a more detailed look at the political and military struggles that characterized these centuries see: Trevor Aston, Editor, *Crisis in Europe, 1550–1660: Essays from Past and Present* (New York: Basic Books, 1965); J. R. Hale, *War and Society in Renaissance Europe, 1450–1620* (Leicester: Leicester University Press, 1985); R. N. Hatton, *Europe in the Age of*

Louis XIV (New York: Norton, 1979); Geoffrey Parker, *The Thirty Years' War* (London, New York: Routledge, 1997). On the belief in witchcraft at this time and its consequences, see Brian P. Levack, *The Witch-Hunt in Early Modern Europe* (Harlow, England; New York: Pearson Longman, 2006).

5. Darnton, *The Great Cat Massacre*, 53.

6. Tomas Alex Tizon, "Hijacker's trail may be warming," *Los Angeles Times*, 30 March 2008, sec. A15.

7. Quoted in *The Survivor: An Anatomy of Life in the Death Camps* by Terence Des Pres (Oxford: Oxford University Press, 1976), 62. There is a vast literature regarding the experiences of people caught up in the Holocaust and the Soviet Gulag. A few of the most important firsthand accounts of the Holocaust include: Raul Hilberg, Stanislaw Staron, and Josef Kermisz, eds. *The Warsaw Diary of Adam Czerniakow: Prelude to Doom* (New York: Schocken, 1979); Chaim Kaplan, *A Scroll of Agony* (New York: Collier Books, 1973); Gerda Klein, *All But My Life* (New York: Hill & Wang, 1957); Janusz Korczak, *Ghetto Diary* (New York: Holocaust Library, 1978); Primo Levi, *Survival in Auschwitz* (New York: Collier Books, 1969); Emmanuel Ringelblum, *Notes from the Warsaw Ghetto* (New York: Schocken Books, 1974); Gertrude Schneider, *Journey into Terror* (Westport, Conn.: Praeger, 2001); Rudolf Vrba and Alan Bestic, *I Cannot Forgive* (London: Sidgwick & Jackson, 1963); and Elie Wiesel, *Night* (New York: Hill & Wang, 1960). Among the translated memoirs and works of literature addressing the Gulag, the following are recommended: Joseph Brodsky, *Less Than One* (New York: Farrar Straus Giroux, 1986); Margarete Buber-Neumann, *Under Two Dictators* (London: Pimlico, 2008); Evgeniya Ginzburg, *Into the Whirlwind* (London: Collins/Harvill, 1967); Gustav Herling, *A World Apart* (London: Heinemann, 1951); Lev Kopalev, *To Be Preserved Forever* (Philadelphia, Lippincott, 1977); Nadezhda Mandelstam, *Hope Against Hope* (New York: Atheneum, 1970); Alexander Solzhenitsyn, *One Day in the Life of Ivan Denisovich* (New York: Praeger, 1963) and *The Gulag Archipelago*, 3 Volumes (New York: Harper and Row, 1974–78); Kazimierz Zarod, *Inside Stalin's Gulag* (Sussex: Book Guild, 1990).

8. On Mordechai Anielewicz and the Warsaw Ghetto Uprising see Yisrael Gutman, *The Jews of Warsaw, 1939–1943: Ghetto, Underground, Revolt* (Bloomington: Indiana University Press, 1983) and Yuri Suhl, ed. *They Fought Back* (New York: Crown, 1967). On Father Kolbe, there are a number of laudatory biographies, among them Maria Winowska, *The Death Camp Proved Him Real: The Life of Father Maximilian Kolbe, Franciscan* (Kenosha, Wisconsin: Prow, 1971) and Diana Dewar's *The Saint of Auschwitz: The Story of Maximilian Kolbe* (London: Darton, Longman & Todd, 1982). Information on hunger strikers in the Soviet Gulag and the Ust-Usa rising can be found in Anne Applebaum's *Gulag: A History* (New York: Doubleday, 2003), 402–408.

9. From a reprint of *Into That Darkness* by Gitta Sereny (New York: Vintage, 1974) in *The Holocaust: Problems and Perspectives of Interpretation*, Donald L. Niewyk, ed (Lexington, Massachusetts: D.C. Heath and Company, 1992), 77.

10. Ibid., 76–77.

11. Ibid., 77.

12. Tzvetan Todorov, *Facing the Extreme: Moral Life in the Concentration Camps* (New York: Metropolitan Books, 1996).

13. Des Pres, *The Survivor*, vii.

14. Jack Kerouac, *On the Road* (New York: Penguin Books, 1976), 310.

15. A good intro to Existentialism for the general reader is Walter Kaufmann, *Existentialism from Dostoevsky to Sartre* (New York: Meridian, 1956). With regard to existential heroes, see the essay in Kaufmann's book by Jean Paul Sartre, "Existentialism is a Humanism," 287–311.

16. From *The New Comics* "Interview with Harvey Pekar" by Gary Groth (New York: Berkeley Publishing Group, 1998), 215.

17. Lynn Smith, "Losers on the rise," *Los Angeles Times*, August 17, 2003, Sunday Calendar, Section E.1.

18. Ibid.

19. Groth, "Interview with Harvey Pekar," 216.

Bibliography

Alter, Robert. *Rogue's Progress: Studies in the Picaresque Novel*. Cambridge: Harvard University Press, 1964.

Alvarez, A. *The Savage God: A Study of Suicide*. New York: Random House, 1972.

Applebaum, Anne. *Gulag: A History*. New York: Doubleday, 2003.

Aristotle. *On Rhetoric*. Translated by George A. Kennedy. New York: Oxford University Press, 2007.

Aristophanes. *Clouds*. Translated by B.B. Rogers. London: W. Heinemann; New York, G.P. Putnam Sons, 1924.

Armstrong, R.J., and W. J. Short, eds. *Francis of Assisi, Early Documents* (3 volumes). New York: New City Press, 1999–2001.

Aston, Trevor, ed. *Crisis in Europe, 1550–1660: Essays from Past and Present*. New York: Basic Books, 1965.

Bacon, Francis. *The New Atlantis*. Whitefish, MT: Kessinger, 2004.

Bagioli, Mario. *Galileo, Courtier: The Practice of Science in the Culture of Absolutism*. Chicago: University of Chicago Press, 1993.

Bailey, James, and Tatyana Ivanova, eds. and trans. *An Anthology of Russian Folk Epics*. Armonk, N.Y.: M.E. Sharpe, Inc., 1998.

Baird, Jay W. *To Die for Germany: Heroes in the Nazi Pantheon*. Bloomington and Indianapolis: Indiana University Press, 1990.

Baldwin, Neil. *Edison: Inventing the Century*. Chicago: University of Chicago Press, 2001.

Balzac, Honoré de. *La comédie humaine*. Paris: Pléiade, 1981.

Barber, Malcolm. *The New Knighthood: A History of the Order of the Temple*. Cambridge: Cambridge University Press, 1994.

_____ and Helen Nicholson, eds. *The Military Orders*. Aldershot, Hampshire: Valorium, 1994 and Brookfield, VT: Ashgate, 1998.

Baudelaire, Charles. *Oeuvres complètes*. Paris: Pléiade, 1976.

Beck, Hanno. *Alexander von Humboldt*. Wiesbaden: F. Steiner, 1959–61.

Bell, E.T. *Men of Mathematics*. New York: Simon and Schuster, 1953.

Benford, Gregory, and Martin Harry Greenberg, eds.

Hitler Victorious: Eleven Stories of the German Victory in World War II. New York: Berkeley Books, 1987.

Bentley, Eric. *The Cult of the Superman: A Study of the Idea of Heroism in Carlyle and Nietzsche, with Notes on Other Hero-Worshippers of Modern Times*. Gloucester, Mass.: Peter Smith, 1969.

Berdyaev, Nicholas. *The Origin of Russian Communism*. London: Bles, 1937.

Bernal, M. *Black Athena: The Afroasiatic Roots of Classical Civilization*. New Brunswick: Rutgers University Press, 1987.

Bloch, Marc. *Feudal Society*. Translated by L.A. Manyon. Chicago: University of Chicago Press, 1961.

Bourbon, Stephen de. *Anecdotes historiques*. Edited by A. Lecoy de la Marche. Paris: Librairie Renouard, H. Loones, successeur, 1877.

Bowra, Cecil Maurice. *The Greek Experience*. London: Weidenfeld & Nicolson, 1957.

Boyer, Carl B. *A History of Mathematics*. New York: John Wiley & Sons, 1991.

Braudel, Fernand. *The Mediterranean and the Mediterranean World in the Age of Philip II*. New York: Harper and Row, 1976.

_____. *The Structures of Everyday Life: Limits of the Possible*. New York: Harper and Row, 1979.

Braudy, Leo. *The Frenzy of Renown: Fame and Its History*. Oxford: Oxford University Press, 1986.

Brietman, Richard. *The Architect of Genocide: Heinrich Himmler and the Final Solution*. Hanover: University Press of New England, 1992.

Brewster, David. *Memoirs of the Life, Writings, and Discoveries of Sir Isaac Newton*. Edinburgh: T. Constable & Co., 1856.

Brickhouse, T.C., and N.D. Smith. *Socrates on Trial*. Oxford: Oxford University Press, 1989.

Bright, John. *A History of Israel*. 3rd ed. Philadelphia: Westminster Press, 1981.

Brodsky, Joseph. *Less Than One*. New York: Farrar Straus Giroux, 1986.

Brower, Daniel. *Training The Nihilists: Education and Radicalism in Tsarist Russia*. Ithaca: Cornell University Press, 1975.

Buber-Neumann, Margarete. *Under Two Dictators*. London: Pimlico, 2008.

Buckley, Mary. *Mobilizing Soviet Peasants: Heroines and Heroes of Stalin's Fields*. Lanham: Rowman & Littlefield, 2006.

Buist-Thiele, Marie Louise. "The Influence of St. Bernard of Clairvaux on the Formation of the Order of the Knights Templar." In *The Second Crusade and the Cistercians*, edited by Michael Gervers. New York: St. Martin's Press, 1992.

Bullock, Alan. *Hitler: A Study in Tyranny*. New York: Harper and Row, 1964.

Burckhardt, Jakob. *Griechische Kulturgeschichte*. Stuttgart and Berlin, 1902.

Carr, E. H. *The Romantic Exiles: A Nineteenth Century Portrait Gallery*. Boston: Beacon Press, 1961.

Carr, William. *Hitler: A Study in Personality and Politics*. New York: Harper and Row, 1964.

Cary, M. *A History of Rome: Down to the Reign of Constantine* (New York: Macmillan St. Martin's Press, 1967.

Castle, Terry. "Mad, Bad and Dangerous to Know." *The New York Times*. 13 April, 1997, pp. 11–10.

Catherine of Siena. *The Letters of Catherine of Siena*. Translated by Suzanne Noffke, O.P. Binghamton, N.Y.: Center for Medieval and Early Renaissance Studies, 1988.

_____. *I Catherine: Selected Writings of Catherine of Siena*. Translated by Kenelm Foster and Mary John Ronayne. London: Collins, 1980.

Chandler, Frank Wadleigh. *The Literature of Roguery*. New York: Burt Franklin, 1958.

Charny, Geoffroi de. *A Knight's Own Book of Chivalry*. Translated by Elspeth Kennedy. Philadelphia: University of Pennsylvania Press, 2005.

Clark, Katrina. *The Soviet Novel: History as Ritual*. Chicago and London: University of Chicago Press, 1985.

Clubbe, John, ed. *Carlyle and His Contemporaries: Essays in Honor of Charles Richard Sanders*. Durham: Duke University Press, 1976.

Collins, John J., and George W.E. Nickelsburg, eds. *Ideal Figures in Ancient Judaism: Profiles and Paradigms*. Chico: Scholars Press, 1980.

Cranston, M. *The Romantic Movement*. Oxford: Oxford University Press, 1994.

Crouch, David. *William Marshal, Court, Career and Chivalry in the Angevin Empire, 1147–1219*. London and New York: Longman, 1990.

Currie, Bruno. *Pindar and the Cult of the Heroes*. Oxford: Oxford University Press, 2005.

Darton, Robert. *The Great Cat Massacre: And Other Episodes in French Cultural History*. New York: Random House, 1985.

D'Aurevilly, Barbey. *Oeuvres romanesques complètes*. Paris: Pléiade, 1966.

Davis, Natalie Zemon. *The Return of Martin Guerre*. Cambridge: Harvard University Press, 1985.

Des Pres, Terence. *The Survivor: An Anatomy of Life in the Death Camps*. Oxford: Oxford University Press, 1976.

Descartes, René. *Discourse on Method and The Meditations*. London: Penguin Books, 1968.

Dewar, Diana. *The Saint of Auschwitz: The Story of Maximilian Kolbe*. London: Darton, Longman & Todd, 1982.

Diamond, Jared. *Guns, Germs, and Steel: The Fate of Human Societies*. New York: W. W. Norton Company, 1999.

Dick, Philip K. *The Man in the High Castle*. New York: Berkeley Medallion Books, 1962.

Dodds, E.R. *The Greeks and the Irrational*. Berkeley and Los Angeles: University of California Press, 1951.

Drabble, Margaret, ed. *The Oxford Companion to English Literature*. 5th ed. Oxford: Oxford University Press, 1985.

Drake, S. *Discoveries and Opinions of Galileo*. Garden City, New York: Doubleday, 1957.

_____. *Galileo: Pioneer Scientist*. Toronto: University of Toronto Press, 1990.

Droge, Arthur J., and James D. Tabor. *A Noble Death: Suicide and Martyrdom Among Christians and Jews in Antiquity*. San Francisco: Harper Collins, 1992.

Duby, Georges. *The Chivalrous Society*. Trans. Cynthia Postan. Berkeley and Los Angeles: University of California Press, 1977.

_____. *Three Orders: Feudal Society Imagined*. Chicago: University of Chicago Press, 1980.

Dyson, Freeman. "When Science & Poetry Were Friends." *The New York Review of Books*. 13 August 2009, pp. 15–18.

Eisler, Benita. *Byron: Child of Passion, Fool of Fame*. New York: Vintage Books, 2000.

Elias, Norbert. *The History of Manners: The Civilizing Process: Volume I*. New York: Pantheon Books, 1978.

Evjen, H.D. "Competitive Athletics in Ancient Greece: The Search for Origins and Influences," *Opuscula Atheniensia (Oath)* 16.5. pp. 51–6, 1996.

_____. "The Origins and Functions of Formal Athletic Competition in the Ancient World." In the *Proceedings of an International Symposium on the Olympic Games (5–9 September 1988)*, edited by W. Coulson and H. Kyrielesi. Athens: Deutsches Archäologisches Institut Athen, 1992.

Farnell, Lewis Richard. *Greek Hero Cults and Ideas of Immortality*. Oxford: Oxford University Press, 1921.

Farrington, B. *The Philosophy of Francis Bacon*. Liverpool: Liverpool University Press, 1964.

Fest, Joachim. *The Face of the Third Reich*. Munich: R. Piper & Co. Verlag, 1963.

_____. *Hitler*. New York: Harcourt Brace Jovanovich, 1974.

Field, Daniel. *Rebels in the Name of the Tsar*. Boston: Houghton Mifflin, 1976.

Fielding, K. J., and Rodger Tarr, eds. *Carlyle Past and Present*. London: Vision, 1976.

Ferguson, John. *Socrates: A Source Book*. London: MacMillan, 1970.

Ferrone, Vincenzo. "The Man of Science." In *Enlightenment Portraits*, edited by Michel Vovelle. Chicago and London: University of Chicago Press, 1992.

Finley, M.I. *The World of Odysseus*. New York: New York Review of Books, 1982.

Fitzpatrick, Sheila, ed. *Cultural Revolution in Russia 1928–1931*. Bloomington: Indiana University Press, 1984.

_____. *The Russian Revolution 1917–1932*. Oxford: Oxford University Press, 1982.

Forey, Alan. *Military Orders and Crusades*. Aldershot, Hampshire: Valorium; Brookfield, VT: Ashgate, 1994.

Fox, Robin Lane. *Pagans and Christians*. San Francisco: Harper and Row, 1986.

Frend, W.H.C. *Martyrdom and Persecution in the Early Church: A Study of a Conflict from the Maccabees to Donatus*. Oxford: Oxford University Press, 1965.

Friedenthal, Richard. *Goethe: His Life and Times*. London and New York: Weidenfeld and Nicolson, 1963.

Froude, James Anthony. *Thomas Carlyle: A History of the First Forty Years of His Life, 1795- 1835; A History of His Life in London, 1834–1881*. London, 1882, 1884.

Gardner, E.N. *Athletics of the Ancient World*. Oxford: Oxford University Press, 1930.

Gillispie, Charles C., ed. *Dictionary of Scientific Biography*. New York: Scribner, 1970.

Ginzburg, Evgeniya. *Into the Whirlwind*. London: Collins/Harvill, 1967.

Gleason, Abbot. *Young Russia: the Genesis of Russian Radicalism in the 1860s*. Chicago: University of Chicago Press, 1985.

_____, Peter Kenez, and Richard Stites, eds. *Bolshevik Culture: Experiment and Order in the Russian Revolution*. Bloomington and Indianapolis: Indiana University Press, 1985.

Golden, Mark. *Sport and Society in Ancient Greece*. Cambridge: Cambridge University Press, 1998.

_____. *Sport in the Ancient World from A-Z*. New York: Routledge, 2004.

Goldstein, Jonathan. *I Maccabees*. New York: Doubleday, 1976.

_____. *II Maccabees*. New York: Doubleday, 1976.

Gnüg, Hiltrud. "The Dandy and the Don Juan Type." In *European Romanticism: Literary Cross-Currents, Modes, and Models*, edited by Gerhart Hoffmeister. Detroit: Wayne State University Press, 1990.

Greene, Brian. "Questions, Not Answers, Make Science the Ultimate Adventure." *Wired Magazine*, 20 April, 2009.

Griffin, Jasper. "Virgil," *The Oxford History of the Classical World*. Edited by John Boardman, Jasper Griffin, Oswyn Murray. Oxford: Oxford University Press, 1986.

Groth, Gary. *The New Comics*. New York: Berkeley, 1998.

Gutman, Yisrael. *The Jews of Warsaw, 1939–1943: Ghetto, Underground, Revolt*. Bloomington: Indiana University Press, 1983.

Hades, Moses, ed. and trans. *The Third and Fourth Books of Maccabees*. New York: Harper, 1953.

Hale, J. R. *War and Society in Renaissance Europe, 1450–1620*. Leicester: Leicester University Press, 1985.

Harris, H.A. *Sport in Greece and Rome*. Ithaca: Cornell University Press, 1972.

Harris, Robert. *Fatherland*. New York: Random House, 1992.

Hatton, R. N. *Europe in the Age of Louis XIV*. New York: Norton, 1979.

Heffer, Simon. *Moral Desperado: A Life of Thomas Carlyle*. London: Weidenfeld and Nicolson, 1995.

Heffernan, Thomas. *Sacred Biography: Saints and Their Biographers in the Middle Ages*. New York: Oxford University Press, 1988.

Hellbeck, Joachen. *Revolution on My Mind: Writing a Diary Under Stalin*. Cambridge, Mass.: Harvard University Press, 2006.

Herling, Gustav. *A World Apart*. London: Heinemann, 1951.

Hilberg, Raul, Stanislaw Staron, and Josef Kermisz, eds. *The Warsaw Diary of Adam Czerniakow: Prelude to Doom*. New York: Schocken, 1979.

Hinton, Thomas R. *Nietzsche in German Politics and Society 1890–1918*. Manchester, UK: Manchester University Press, 1983.

Hitler, Adolf. *Hitler's Secret Conversations, 1941–1942*. Translated by Norman Cameron and R. H. Stevens. New York: Octagon Books, 1976.

_____. *Mein Kampf*. Translated by Ralph Manheim. Boston: Houghton Mifflin, 1943, 1971.

Hobsbawm, Eric. *The Age of Revolution 1789–1848*. New York: Vintage Books, 1996.

Höhne, Heinz. *The Order of the Death's Head. The History of the SS*. New York: Ballantine Books, 1967.

Holmes, Richard. *The Age of Wonder: How the Romantic Generaton Discovered the Beauty and Terror of Science*. New York : Pantheon Books, 2008.

Homer. *The Iliad and The Odyssey*. Translated by Robert Fitzgerald. New York: Farrar, Straus and Giroux, 1998.

_____. *The Iliad and The Odyssey*. Translated by Robert Feagles. London: Penguin Books, 1990.

Honour, H. *Romanticism*. New York: Harper and Row, 1979.

Hopkins, Jerry, and Daniel Sugerman. *No One Here Gets Out Alive*. New York: Warner Books, 1980.

Hornblower, Simon, and Anthony Spawforth, eds. *The Oxford Classical Dictionary*. Oxford: Oxford University Press, 2003.

Hosking, Geoffrey. *The First Socialist Society: A History of the Soviet Union from Within*. Cambridge: Harvard University Press, 1985.

House, Adrian. *Francis of Assisi: A Revolutionary Life.* London: Chatto and Windus, 2000.

Housley, Norman, ed. *Knighthoods of Christ: Essays on the History of the Crusades and the Knights Templar, Presented to Malcolm Barber.* Aldershot, Hampshire: Ashgate; Burlington, VT: Ashgate, 2007.

Howarth, Stephen. *The Knights Templar.* London: Collins Press, 1982.

Jacob, J. R. "Restoration, Reformation and the Origins of the Royal Society." *History of Science* 13 (1975): 155–176

Jacob, Margaret C. *Scientific Culture and the Making of the Industrial West.* Oxford: Oxford University Press, 1997.

Jenkyns, Richard. *Virgil's Experience: Nature and History: Times, Names and Places.* Oxford: Oxford University Press, 1998.

Jesse, William. *The Life of Beau Brummell by Captain Jesse.* London: Saunders and Otley, 1844.

Josephson, Matthew. *Edison.* New York: McGraw-Hill, 1959.

Kaeuper, Richard W. *Chivalry and Violence in Medieval Europe.* Oxford: Oxford University Press, 1999.

Kaplan, Chaim. *A Scroll of Agony.* New York: Collier Books, 1973.

Kaplan, Fred. *Thomas Carlyle: A Biography.* Cambridge: Cambridge University Press, 1983.

Kaufmann, Walter. *Existentialism from Dostoevsky to Sartre.* New York: Meridian, 1956.

_____. *Nietzsche: Philosopher, Psychologist, Antichrist.* Princeton: Princeton University Press, 1968.

_____. *The Portable Nietzsche.* New York: Penguin Books, 1968.

Keen, Maurice. *Chivalry.* New Haven: Yale University Press, 1984.

Kehlmann, Daniel. *Measuring the World: A Novel.* New York: Pantheon, 2006.

Kellner, L. *Alexander von Humboldt.* London, New York: Oxford University Press, 1963.

Kennedy, Elspeth M. "The Knight as Reader of Arthurian Romance." In *Culture and the King: The Social Implications of the Arthurian Legend, Essays in Honor of Valerie M. Lagorio*, edited by Martin B. Schichtman and James P. Carley. Albany: State University of New York Press, 1994.

Kenny, A. *Descartes.* New York: Random House, 1968.

Kerényi, C. *The Heroes of the Greeks.* New York: Thames and Hudson, 1981.

Kerouac, Jack. *On the Road.* New York: Penguin Books, 1976.

Kershaw, Ian. *Hitler: 1889–1936 Hubris.* New York: W. W. Norton, 2000.

_____. *Hitler: 1936–1945 Nemesis.* New York: W. W. Norton, 2000.

Klein, Gerda. *All But My Life.* New York: Hill & Wang, 1957.

Kleinberg, Aviad M. *Prophets in Their Own Country: Living Saints and the Making of Sainthood in the Later Middle Ages.* Chicago and London: University of Chicago Press, 1992.

Kopalev, Lev. *To Be Preserved Forever.* Philadelphia, Lippincott, 1977.

Korczak, Janusz. *Ghetto Diary.* New York: Holocaust Library, 1978.

Kuhn, Thomas. *The Structure of Scientific Revolutions.* Chicago: University of Chicago Press, 1970.

Ladurie, Emmanuel Le Roy. *The Peasants of Languedoc.* Urbana: University of Illinois Press, 1974.

Laertes, Diogenes. "Socrates." *Diogenes Laertius: Lives of Eminent Philosophers.* Translated by R. H. Hicks. Cambridge: Harvard University Press, 1991.

Larson, Jennifer. *Greek Heroine Cults.* Madison: University of Wisconsin Press, 1995.

Lefkowitz, M.R. and G.M. Rogers, eds. *Black Athena Revisited.* Chapel Hill: University of North Carolina Press, 1996.

Levack, Brian P. *The Witch-Hunt in Early Modern Europe.* Harlow, England; New York: Pearson Longman, 2006.

Levi, Peter. *A History of Greek Literature.* New York: Viking Press, 1985.

Levi, Primo. *Survival in Auschwitz.* New York: Collier Books, 1969.

Lewis, Sinclair. *Arrowsmith.* New York: New American Library, 2008.

Logan, F. Donald. *A History of the Church in the Middle Ages.* London and New York: Routledge, 2002.

Madden, Thomas F. *The New Concise History of the Crusades.* Lanham, Maryland: Rowman and Littlefield, 2005.

Maguire, Joe. "Towards a Sociological Theory of Sport and the Emotions: A Process- Sociological Perspective." In *Sport and Leisure in the Civilizing Process: Critique and Counter-Critique*, edited by Eric Dunning and Chris Rojek. Toronto and Buffalo: University of Toronto Press, 1992.

Mandelstam, Nadezhda. *Hope Against Hope.* New York: Atheneum, 1970.

Marchand, Leslie A. *Byron: A Portrait.* New York: Knopf, 1970.

Martin, Sean. *The Knights Templar: The History and Myths of the Legendary Military Order.* New York: Thunder's Mouth Press, 2004.

McCullough, David G. *Brave Companions: Portraits in History.* New York: Prentice Hall Press, 1992.

McGannon, John. *Red Arctic: Polar Exploration and the Myth of the North in the Soviet Union, 1932–1939.* New York, Oxford: Oxford University Press, 1998.

McKay, John P., Bennett D. Hill, and John Buckler. *A History of Western Society.* Boston: Houghton Mifflin, 1987.

Mendelsohn, Daniel. "Alexander, the Movie!" *New York Review of Books.* 13 January 2005, pp. 43–46.

_____. "A Little Iliad." *New York Review of Books.* 24 June 2004, pp. 46–49.

Meyer, Paul, Ed. *L'Histoire de Guillaume le Maréchal.*

Paris: Librairie Renouard, H. Laurens, successeur, 1891–1901.

Miller, Frank. *Folklore for Stalin.* Armonk, N.Y.: M.E. Sharpe, Inc., 1990.

Miller, Stephen G. *Ancient Greek Athletics.* New Haven and London: Yale University Press, 2004.

Moers, Ellen. *The Dandy: Brummell to Beerbohm.* Lincoln: University of Nebraska Press, 1978.

Montefiore, Simon Sebag. *Stalin: The Court of the Red Tsar.* New York: Vintage Books, 2005.

Monteser, Frederick. *The Picaresque Element in Western Literature.* University, Alabama: University of Alabama Press, 1975.

Montuori, Mario. *Socrates: An Approach.* Amsterdam, J. C. Gieben, 1988.

_____. *Socrates, Man and Myth: the Two Socratic Apologies of Xenophon.* London, 1957.

_____. *Socrates: Physiology of a Myth.* Amsterdam, J. C. Gieben, 1981.

Moorman, John. *A History of the Franciscan Order: From its Origins to the Year 1517.* Chicago: Franciscan Herald Press, 1988.

Mor, Menachem, ed. *Crisis and Reaction: The Hero in Jewish History.* Omaha: Creighton University Press, 1995.

Morrow, John. *Thomas Carlyle.* London: Humbledon Continuum, 2006.

Mosse, George L. *The Crisis of German Ideology: Intellectual Origins of the Third Reich.* New York: Schocken Books, 1981.

Musurillo, H. *The Acts of the Christian Martyrs.* Oxford: Clarendon Press, 1972.

Nevill, John Cranstoun. *Thomas Chatterton.* London and Toronto: Muller, 1948.

Neyrey, Jerome H. *Honor and Shame in the Gospel of Matthew.* Louisville: Westminster John Knox Press, 1998.

Nicholson, Helen. *Templars, Hospitallers, and Teutonic Knights: Images of the Military Orders, 1128–1291.* Leister, New York: Leister University Press, 1993.

Niewyk, Donald L., ed. *The Holocaust: Problems and Perspectives of Interpretation.* Lexington, Massachusetts: D.C. Heath and Company, 1992.

Noffke, Suzanne, O.P. *Catherine of Siena: Vision Through a Distant Eye.* Collegeville, Minn.: Liturgical Press, 1996.

Oinas, Felix J. "Folklore and Politics in the Soviet Union." *Slavic Review* 32 (1973): 45–58.

Painter, Sidney. *William Marshal: Knight-Errant, Baron and Regent of England.* Baltimore: John Hopkins Press, 1933.

Palmer, R. R., and Joel Colton. *A History of the Modern World.* New York: Alfred A. Knopf, 1978.

Papal Addresses to the Pontifical Academy of Sciences 1917–2002 and to the Pontifical Academy of Social Sciences 1994–2002. Vatican City: Ex Aedibus Academicis in Civitate Vaticana, 2003.

Parker, Geoffrey. *The Thirty Years' War.* London, New York: Routledge, 1997.

Pearlman, Moshe. *The Maccabees.* New York: Macmillan Publishing Co., Inc., 1973.

Pindar. *Odes.* Translated by William H. Race. Cambridge: Harvard University Press, 1997.

_____. *The Odes and Selected Fragments of Pindar.* Translated by G. S. Conway and Richard Stoneman. London: Everyman's Library, Orion Publishing Group, 1997.

Pipes, Richard, ed. *The Russian Intelligentsia.* New York: Columbia University Press, 1961.

Plato. *Euthyphro, Apology, Crito, Paedo, Phaedrus.* Translated by Harold North Fowler. London and New York: Loeb Classical Library, 1923.

Plutarch. *Twelve Lives.* Cleveland: Fine Editions Press, 1950.

Poliakoff, Michael. *Combat Sports in the Ancient World.* New Haven Connecticut: Yale University Press, 1997.

Popkin, Richard H. *The History of Scepticism from Erasmus to Descartes.* Assen, Netherlands: Van Gorcum, 1964.

Porter, Roy, and Mikul Teich, eds. *Romanticism in National* Context. New York: Cambridge University Press, 1988.

Pretzer, William S. ed. *Working at Inventing: Thomas A. Edison and the Menlo Park Experience.* Dearborn, Michigan: Henry Ford Museum & Greenfield Village, 1989.

Raymond of Capua. *The Life of Catherine of Siena.* Translated by Conleth Kearns. Wilmington, Del.: Glazer, 1980.

Riasanovsky, Nicholas V. *The Emergence of Romanticism.* New York: Oxford University Press, 1992.

Riffenburgh, Beau. *The Myth of the Explorer: The Press, Sensationalism, and Geographical Discovery.* London: Belhaven Press, 1993.

Riley, Gregory J. *One Jesus, Many Christs: How Jesus Inspired Not One True Christianity, But Many.* San Francisco: Harper Collins Publishers, 1997.

Riley-Smith, Jonathan. *The Oxford Illustrated History of the Crusades.* Oxford: Oxford University Press, 2001.

Ringelblum, Emmanuel. *Notes from the Warsaw Ghetto.* New York: Schocken Books, 1974.

Robson, Michael. *St. Francis: The Legend and the Life.* London: Geoffrey Chapman, 1999.

Rosenthal, Bernice Glatzer. *New Myth, New World: From Nietzsche to Stalinism.* University Park, Pennsylvania: Pennsylvania State University Press, 2002.

Rossi, Paulo. *Francis Bacon: From Magic to Science.* Chicago: University of Chicago Press, 1968.

Runciman, Steven. *A History of the Crusades.* The Folio Society, 1994.

Sachs, Aaron. *The Humboldt Current: Nineteenth Century Exploration and the Roots of American Environmentalism.* New York: Viking Press, 2006.

Sanders, Charles Richard. *Carlyle's Friendships and Other Studies*. Durham: Duke University Press, 1977.

Santucho, Oscar Jose. *George Gordon, Lord Byron: A Comprehensive Bibliography of Secondary Materials in English, 1807–1973*. Metuchen, N.J.: Scarecrow Press, 1977.

Scanlon, Thomas F. *Eros and Greek Athletics*. Oxford: Oxford University Press, 2002.

Schenk, H. G. *The Mind of the European Romantics*. Garden City, N.Y.: Doubleday, 1969.

Schmitt, Jean Claude. *The holy greyhound : Guinefort, healer of children since the thirteenth century*. Translated by Martin Thom. Cambridge; New York : Cambridge University Press ; Paris : Editions de la maison des sciences de l'homme, 1983.

Schneider, Gertrude. *Journey into Terror*. Westport, Conn.: Praeger, 2001.

Scott, Karen. "Mystical Death, Bodily Death: Catherine of Siena and Raymond of Capua on the Mystic's Encounter with God." In *Gendered Voices: Medieval Saints and Their Interpreters*, edited by Catherine M. Mooney. Philadelphia: University of Pennsylvania Press, 1999.

Sharratt, M. *Galileo: Decisive Innovator*. Oxford: Oxford University Press, 1994.

Shelley, Mary Wollstonecraft. *Frankenstein*. New York: Barnes and Noble Classics, 2003.

Shulman, Seth. *Owning the Future*. Boston: Houghton Mifflin, 1999.

Siegel, Jules Paul, ed. *Thomas Carlyle: The Critical Heritage*. London: Routledge and K. Paul, 1971.

Siegelbaum, Lewis H. *Stakhanovism and the Politics of Productivity in the USSR, 1935–1941*. Cambridge: Cambridge University Press, 1988.

Smith, Lacey Baldwin. *Fools, Martyrs, and Traitors: The Story of Martyrdom in the Western World*. New York: Alfred A. Knopf, 1997.

Smith, Lynn. "Losers on the rise." *Los Angeles Times*. August 17, 2003, Sunday Calendar, Section E.1.

Snodgrass, Anthony. *Archaic Greece: The Age of Experiment*. London: J.M. Dent & Sons, Ltd., 1980.

Solzhenitsyn, Alexander. *The Gulag Archipelago*, 3 Volumes. New York: Harper and Row, 1974–78.

_____. *One Day in the Life of Ivan Denisovich*. New York: Praeger, 1963.

Spinrad, Norman. *The Iron Dream*. New York: Avon Books, 1972.

Spivey, Nigel. *The Ancient Olympics*. Oxford: Oxford University Press, 2004.

Stern, Fritz. *The Politics of Cultural Despair: A Study in the Rise of Germanic Ideology*. Berkeley: University of California Press, 1961.

Stone, I.F. *The Trial of Socrates*. Boston: Little, Brown and Company, 1988.

Strayer, Joseph R. ed. *Dictionary of the Middle Ages*. New York: Charles Scribner's Sons, 1986.

_____. "The Two Levels of Feudalism." In *Life and Thought in the Early Middle Ages*, edited by Robert

S. Hoyt. Minneapolis: University of Minneapolis Press, 1967.

Suhl, Yuri, ed. *They Fought Back*. New York: Crown, 1967.

Swanson, Ronald N. *Religion and Devotion in Europe, 1215–1515*. Cambridge: Cambridge University Press, 1995.

Talmon, J. L. *Romanticism and Revolt: Europe 1815–1848*. New York: Norton, 1979.

Taylor, A.E. *Socrates*. London: P. Davies, Ltd., 1932.

Taylor, C.C.W. *Socrates*. Oxford: Oxford University Press, 1998.

Terrall, Mary. "Heroic Narratives of Quest and Discovery." *Configurations* 6.2 (1998): 223- 242.

Thorslev, Peter L. *The Byronic Hero: Types and Prototypes*. Minneapolis: University of Minnesota Press, 1962.

Tizon, Tomas Alex. "Hijacker's trail may be warming." *Los Angeles Times*. 30 March 2008, sec. A15

Todorov, Tzvetan. *Facing the Extreme: Moral Life in the Concentration Camps*. New York: Metropolitan Books, 1996.

Toland, John. *Adolf Hitler*. New York: Doubleday, 1976.

Trelawny, Edward John. *Recollections of the Last Days of Shelley and Byron*. Boston: Ticknor and Fields, 1859.

Tucker, Robert C., ed. *The Marx-Engels Reader*. New York/London: W.W. Norton Co., 1978.

_____, ed. *Stalinism: Essays in Historical Interpretation*. New York: Norton Press, 1977.

Tumarkin, Nina. *Lenin Lives! The Lenin Cult in Soviet Russia*. Cambridge, Massachusetts, and London, England: Harvard University Press, 1983.

Urban, William. *The Baltic Crusade*. Chicago: Lithuanian Research and Studies Center, 1994.

_____. *The Prussian Crusade*. Lanham, MD: University of America, 1980.

Vauchez, André. *Sainthood in the Later Middle Ages*. Cambridge: Cambridge University Press, 1997.

Virgil. *The Aeneid*. Translated by Allen Mandelbaum. Berkeley and Los Angeles: University of California Press, 1982.

Vlastos, Gregory. *Socrates, Ironist and Moral Philosopher*. Ithaca, New York: Cornell University Press, 1991.

Vrba, Rudolf and Alan Bestic. *I Cannot Forgive*. London: Sidgwick & Jackson, 1963.

Waldberg, Patrick. *Surrealism*. New York: McGraw-Hill, 1971.

Webster, Charles. *The Great Instauratian: Science, Medicine and Reform, 1626–1660*. London: Duckworth, 1975.

Weingartner, James J. "Law and Justice in the Nazi SS — The Case of Konrad Morgen." *Central European History*, 6 (1983): 276–294.

Westfall, R. S. *The Life of Isaac Newton*. New York: Cambridge University Press, 1993.

Wicks, Ulrick. *Picaresque Narrative, Picaresque Fic-*

tions: *A Theory and Research Guide*. Hadley, New York: Greenwood Press, 1989.

Wiesel, Elie. *Night*. New York: Hill & Wang, 1960.

Wilson, Stephen, ed. *Saints and Their Cults: Studies in Religious Sociology, Folklore, and History*. Cambridge: Cambridge University Press, 1983.

Winowska, Maria. *The Death Camp Proved Him Real: The Life of Father Maximilian Kolbe, Franciscan*. Kenosha, Wisconsin: Prow, 1971.

Wordsworth, Jonathan, Jaye, Michael C., and Robert Woof. *William Wordsworth and the Age of English Romanticism*. New Brunswick, N.J.: Rutgers University Press, 1987.

Wordsworth, William. *The Prelude*. Harmondsworth, 1971.

Xenophon. *Memorabilia, Oeconomicus*. Translated by E.C. Marchant. London and New York: Loeb Classical Library, 1923).

_____. *Symposium, Apology*. Translated by O.J. Todd. London and New York: Loeb Classical Library, 1922.

Young, David C. *A Brief History of the Olympic Games*. Oxford: Blackwell, 2004.

_____. *The Olympic Myth of Greek Amateur Athletics*. Chicago: Ares Press, 1984.

Zanker, Paul. *The Power of Images in the Age of Augustus*. Ann Arbor: University of Michigan Press, 1990.

Zarod, Kazimierz. *Inside Stalin's Gulag*. Sussex: Book Guild, 1990.

Index